MAINTAIN THE RIGHT

also by Ronald Atkin
Revolution! Mexico 1910-20

RONALD ATKIN

Maintain The Right

*The Early History of the North West
Mounted Police, 1873–1900*

The John Day Company / An Intext Publisher

New York

The John Day Company, 257 Park Avenue South,
New York, N.Y. 10010

Library of Congress Cataloging in Publication Data

Atkin, Ronald, 1931–
   Maintain the right.

   1. Canada. Royal Canadian Mounted Police—History.
I. Title.
HV8157.A8   363.2′0971   72-10116
ISBN 0-381-98230-0

Printed in Great Britain

CONTENTS

5

CONTENTS

PART FOUR: Lawrence William Herchmer

LIST OF ILLUSTRATIONS

7

Sketch Maps

The author and publishers acknowledge their gratitude for permission to reproduce photographs to the following:

The Royal Canadian Mounted Police (Plates 1, 3, 4, 5, 7, 8, 9, 11, 12, 13, 14, 15, 19, 20, 22, 23, 24, 25, 26, 27, 28, 29, 31, 32, 33, endpapers and title-page crest); The Public Archives of Canada, Ottawa (Plates 2, 18, 21); Glenbow–Alberta Institute, Calgary (Plates 5, 6, 10, 16, 17); Mrs E. McCoy (Plate 34); The Provincial Museum and Archives of Alberta (Plate 30).

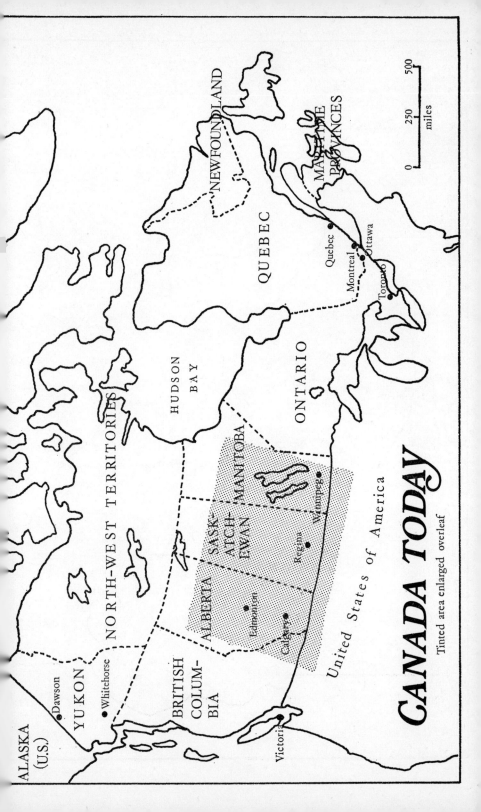

ALASKA (U.S.)

YUKON
• Dawson
• Whitehorse

NORTH-WEST TERRITORIES

BRITISH COLUMBIA

• Victoria

ALBERTA
• Edmonton
• Calgary

SASKATCHEWAN
• Regina

MANITOBA
• Winnipeg

HUDSON BAY

ONTARIO

QUEBEC

• Quebec
• Montreal
• Ottawa
• Toronto

NEWFOUNDLAND

MARITIME PROVINCES

United States of America

CANADA TODAY

Tinted area enlarged overleaf

0   250   500
miles

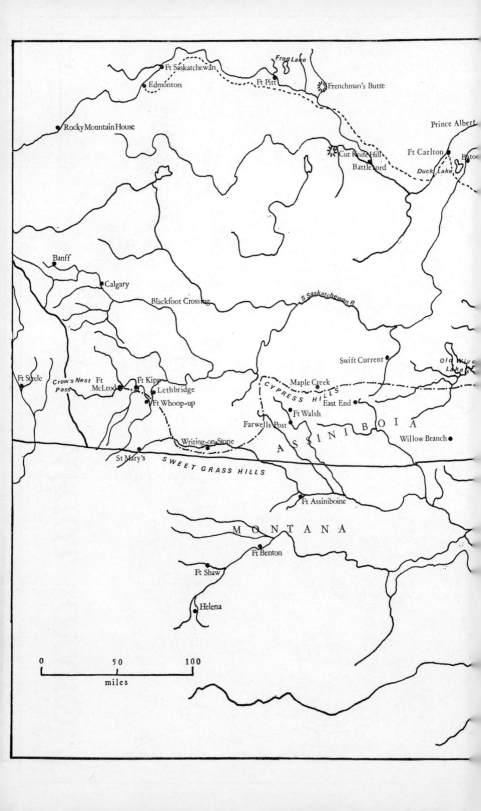

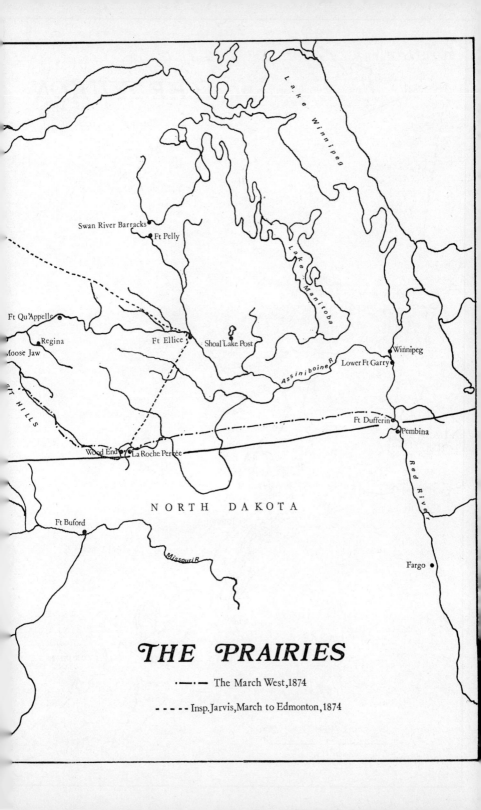

Lake Winnipeg

Swan River Barracks
Ft Pelly

Lake Manitoba

Ft Qu'Appelle

Regina

Moose Jaw

Ft Ellice

Shoal Lake Post

Assiniboine R

Lower Ft Garry

Winnipeg

Ft Dufferin
Pembina

T HILLS

Wood End
La Roche Percée

Red River

NORTH   DAKOTA

Ft Buford

Missouri R

Fargo

THE PRAIRIES

— · — The March West, 1874

- - - - - Insp. Jarvis, March to Edmonton, 1874

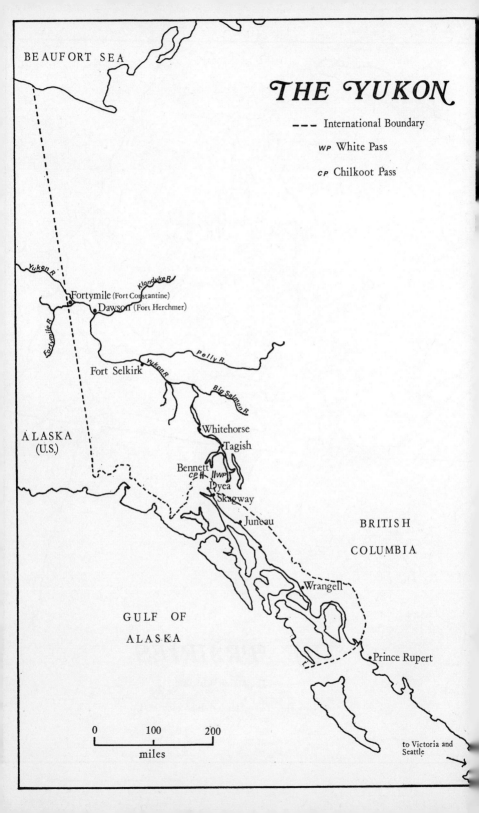

BEAUFORT SEA

THE YUKON

- - - International Boundary

WP White Pass

CP Chilkoot Pass

Yukon R.

Klondyke R.

Fortymile (Fort Constantine)
Dawson (Fort Herchmer)

Fortymile R.

Pelly R.

Fort Selkirk
Yukon R.

Big Salmon R.

ALASKA
(U.S.)

Whitehorse
Tagish

Bennett
CP ∥ ∥WP
Dyea
Skagway

Juneau

BRITISH

COLUMBIA

Wrangell

GULF OF

ALASKA

Prince Rupert

0   100   200
└──────┴──────┘
miles

to Victoria and
Seattle

The Police have protected us as the feathers
of the bird protect it from the frosts of winter

Crowfoot, Chief of the Blackfoot tribe
20 October 1877

PREFACE

IN August 1973 the Royal Canadian Mounted Police, the world's most romantic – and most extravagantly romanticised – police force, celebrates its centenary. All the world knows (or thinks it knows) a Mountie – a handsome man in scarlet tunic singing of his love for Rose Marie; a six-foot bachelor in Boy Scout hat taming savage Indians, tussling with villainous half-breeds, fighting wolf packs bare handed, and winning the Canadian West singlehanded.

Twenty-five years ago the Mounted Police's own magazine, *RCMP Quarterly*, pointed out with a touch of resigned weariness, 'The public's reading about the Mounted Police is almost wholly fiction, and rather cheap fiction at that', and there is still much validity in the magazine's comment that, 'If the Force were a myth like Sherlock Holmes the inaccuracies and misconceptions instilled in continents of readers would not matter, but the Force, at first useful, then important, and now of national stature, cannot afford to be misunderstood any more than Parliament or the Supreme Court.'

The Mounties have been embarrassed and irritated for many years by the myths which have obscured their arduous, eventful and inspiring history. They didn't always 'get their man' by any means, though in the days when swift transportation across the empty plains and through the Yukon's wastes was non-existent their record of arrests was certainly impressive.

This book is an attempt to present the unvarnished story of the first quarter-century of the North West Mounted Police (as they were then known) from their foundation in 1873 until the end of the nineteenth century, when settlement of the lonely lands they had patrolled and more sophisticated methods of transportation vastly changed their duties. The account is composed mainly from the reports, diaries and memoirs of the men who lived through those harsh and historic years and portrays them for what they were – flesh and blood rather than cardboard cut-outs. As one early Mountie put it, 'we were as God made us – and oftentimes even worse'. Inevitably, the early Mounted Police force had its share of drunks, deadbeats, cheap adventurers and malingerers, which made its tremendous accomplishments all the more praiseworthy.

One Canadian politician of the day said, 'No more wildly impossible undertaking was ever staged than the establishment of Canadian authority and Canadian law throughout the western prairies by a handful of Mounted Police'. The story seems even more astonishing when compared to the costly and bloody subjugation of the American Indian and the settlement of the central and western United States. The vital difference is that the Mounted Police, hurriedly formed to combat the corruption of the Plains Indians by whiskey traders, arrived *in advance* of settlement, unlike the American army which was called in to protect people already disputing ownership of land with the natives of the country.

In achieving a peaceful settlement of the Canadian West, a pathetically small band of scarlet-coated police overcame the handicaps of extreme weather, hunger, low morale, disorganisation, maladministration, short-sighted government policies and searing public criticism.

This is the story of those men.

PART ONE

George Arthur French

'Is there any Englishman who will blame us
for making Empires?'

— Roger Pocock (ex-N W M P) 'The Riders of the Plains',
Chamber's Journal, Vol. 75, 1898

Chapter 1

THE GREAT LONE LAND

THE Prime Minister of Canada, Sir John Macdonald, had specifically requested 'as little gold lace, fuss and feathers as possible' in planning his new peace-keeping force, the North West Mounted Police. Sensitive to American opinion about guns and uniforms near the recently surveyed frontier along the 49th Parallel, the Canadian government wanted it to be essentially a civil and only incidentally a military organisation 'for the rough and ready – particularly ready – enforcement of law and justice'.

But, at least on 8 July 1874, the Mounted Police's commanding officer, George Arthur French, a combative Irishman and loyal British Army soldier who had served in the Maori War, ensured that – even if gold lace and feathers were lacking – there was plenty of fuss in the tiny Manitoba settlement of Dufferin as his 300 Mounted Police, glittering, scrubbed and polished, prepared to ride west, carrying law and order into the emptiness of Canada's prairies. Certainly Dufferin, a collection of half-breeds' shacks and whiskey saloons, dominated by a Hudson's Bay Company store and a government warehouse, had never staged an occasion like it.

George French was a soldier of the Queen, and his men, if not soldiers, were also unmistakably servants of Victoria. They were decked out in scarlet tunics, white gauntlets and pith helmets, whose brass chinstraps dazzled in the bright sun. Swords, buttons and boots glistened briefly before being blanketed by the choking dust of the yellow prairie. As French himself put it in all modesty, 'the column of route presented a very fine appearance'. With a keen sense of occasion he had mounted his six troops of fifty men on horses of different colours. In A Division they rode splendid dark bays, the men of B Division had been allocated dark browns, C were on bright chestnuts, D had greys, E were on black horses and F light bays.

Behind the brave parade, towing ribbons of dust, trundled the ammunition and supply carts (drawn by oxen and driven by half-breeds all too evidently fresh from the saloons), a herd of cattle for slaughter and mowing machines to cut fodder for the animals *en route*. Even when closed up for the start the column stretched a mile and a half. 'To a stranger it would have appeared an astonishing cavalcade,' French admitted. 'But that little force had a double duty to perform; to fight if necessary but in any case to establish posts in the far west.'

With a rousing cheer they were off. As one of the policemen noted in his diary, 'It was a splendid sight, destined to last but a short time'.

To understand the size of the task facing them one has only to look at a map of Canada. It is a country which was stitched together by political necessity and expediency rather than geographical boundaries. Even today much of the land along that most arbitrary of borders, the 49th Parallel, is sparsely inhabited. In 1874, when the police marched west, the prairie was empty of humans, apart from bands of nomadic Indians, a handful of fur traders and Hudson's Bay Company employees, groups of their half-breed descendants of intermarriage with Indian women, and the occasional dedicated missionary.

As a self-governing country Canada was only seven years old and its population was well under four million. In 1867 three of the colonies of British North America – the Atlantic coast communities of Nova Scotia and New Brunswick and the Province of Canada, which consisted of present-day Quebec and Ontario – joined in confederation as the Dominion of Canada. Four years later the colony of British Columbia, which occupied the land between the Rocky Mountains and the Pacific Ocean, entered the

Confederation. But between Toronto, the westernmost city of sizeable population in the eastern provinces of Canada, and British Columbia's capital, Victoria, lay almost 3000 miles of lakes, forest wilderness, prairies and mountains.

The only settlement of any importance was around the valley of the Red River, 1300 miles west of Toronto. Its centre was the primitive but fast-developing village of Winnipeg. Dufferin, the Mounted Police's departure point, was sixty miles south of Winnipeg just on the Canadian side of the 49th Parallel. West of Winnipeg and Dufferin stretched 900 miles of prairie, ending abruptly at the Rocky Mountains, the spine of the North American continent. On these plains, whose monotony was relieved by occasional hills, ravines and rivers, the extremes of climate were fierce. Summers were short and hot – though only four months on average were frost-free, temperatures sometimes rose above 100° F. Winters were long and so cold that mercury had been known to freeze in thermometers and the temperature dropped lower than 50° F. below zero. Rainfall was uncertain and prairie fires ravaged the country.

'The Great Lone Land' it was called by William Francis Butler, the British Army captain who journeyed nearly 3000 miles through it in the winter of 1870–1. 'There is no other portion of the globe where loneliness can be said to live so thoroughly' he wrote. The region was so little known that early maps of North America had shown the prairies as a vast inland sea, and one British publication dismissed the area as a place of 'hailstones, hostile Indians, frost, rocks and bogs'.

The main Indian tribes of the Canadian prairies were the Crees, their hereditary enemies of the Blackfoot Confederacy (a form of loose military alliance which consisted of the Blackfoot, Peigan, Blood and Sarcee nations) and the Assiniboines, a branch of the Sioux. The Crees were divided into Wood (or Swampy) and Plains tribes. The Wood Crees, a relatively mild and peaceful people, inhabited the forest and lake areas on the northern fringes of the prairie, while the Plains Crees, fiercer and more warlike, hunted buffalo along the mainly treeless stretches of country between the North and South Saskatchewan rivers.

Most feared and respected of the Canadian Plains Indians were the Blackfoot,* whose name is popularly supposed to derive from the stains left on their feet and moccasins when they crossed tracts of burned prairie. Intelligent, good hunters and fierce fighters, the Blackfoot nation occupied 50,000 square miles along the foothills of the Rocky Mountains in the southern section of what is now the province of Alberta. Anthony Henday, who had been exiled from England in 1748 for smuggling and had travelled west to join the Hudson's Bay Company, spent three days with a band of Blackfoot in 1754 and found them 'a clean people and more sprightly than other natives', though he was not quite so taken with their habit of using dried horse-dung as tobacco, a concoction which they preferred to Henday's authentic brand.

Though the Indian monopoly of the plains and northern forests was not disturbed until the eighteenth century, the first European presence in the area came, in the late 1660s, as a result of the explorations of two French fur-traders, the brothers-in-law Pierre Radisson and Medard Groseilliers, to the fringes of the bay discovered by the English navigator Henry Hudson and named after him. When their bid for French backing was rejected, Radisson and Groseilliers travelled to England and interested a group of noblemen and merchants in outfitting a trading expedition which they led to Hudson Bay. Pausing only long enough to claim the territory for England and load their ship, the *Nonsuch*, with furs bartered from the Indians, the party sailed back to England in triumph. In 1670 the jubilant supporters of the venture, recognising the potential profitability of the fur trade, formed – under Royal Charter from Charles II – 'The Company of Adventurers of England Trading into Hudson Bay', a title which was swiftly abbreviated to The Hudson's Bay Company.

* Although many eighteenth- and nineteenth-century writers referred to them as Blackfeet, the correct plural is Blackfoot.

The Company was awarded the trading monopoly and full title to a vast area whose limits were never officially defined but which measured more than two million square miles, and stretched west to the Rockies, south into what is now the United States and east to the Atlantic coast of Labrador. This territory it named Rupert's Land after King Charles's cousin, the cavalier Prince Rupert, who was one of the Company's stockholders, and over the next 200 years the Hudson's Bay Company built a string of trading posts, beating off all rival fur-traders.

The Company did not attempt to encourage the settlement of the Canadian West, partly from a sincere belief that the country was too bleak for colonisation but mainly from an unwillingness to see its comfortable fur-trade with the Indians disrupted. However, early in the 1800s, Thomas Douglas, the fifth Earl of Selkirk, obtained from the Company a grant of 116,000 square miles in the Red River valley for the token payment of ten shillings. In this area – four times the size of Scotland and which he named Assiniboia – Selkirk began to settle the dispossessed victims of the infamous Highland Clearances. Despite a series of disastrous setbacks the colony survived, though it did not actually flourish for many years.

The country's staggering potential remained unrealised, even when an official mission of scientists and geologists, backed by the Royal Geographical Society and led by a cheerful Irish militia captain, John Palliser, and an Edinburgh geologist, Dr James Hector, spent three years criss-crossing Rupert's Land in the 1860s. Indeed, Palliser considered most of the prairie arid and unfit for cultivation and reported, 'The knowledge of the country on the whole would never lead me to advocate a line of communication across the continent to the Pacific, exclusively through British territory. The time has now forever gone by for effecting such an object.' Twenty-five years later the Canadian Pacific Railway would span the continent.

Palliser was preceded and followed by small groups of Europeans who were drawn to the area by a masochistic urge to suffer the extreme discomforts of the wilds and possessed of a single-minded addiction to the slaughter of any wild life they could lay their gunsights on. Most of them faithfully chronicled their adventures and disasters, and the publication of their diaries and travel jottings helped a little to lift the mantle of ignorance about the Canadian West.

The high-minded young Earl of Southesk, laden with several volumes of Shakespeare, shot his way across Rupert's Land and back again in 1859–60, attempting to strengthen his body and purify his mind by exercise, harsh outdoor life and a variety of unattractive ordeals. His trip consisted of 'long wearisome riding, indifferent monotonous eating, no sport to speak of, a hard bed upon the ground, no companion of my own class', but he admitted, 'Nevertheless, I am happier than I have been for years.'

Steadfastly, Southesk ate moose and bear steaks, and munched his way through skunk and beaver tail ('like pork fat sandwiched between layers of Finnan haddock'). And just as steadfastly, in fair weather and foul, the Earl read his Shakespeare: 'Sat up late reading *Much Ado About Nothing*. The wolves howled, the night was very cold.' And again, when reading *Othello* at his tent doorway: 'Seated so close to an enormous fire of logs that my cloth leggings were scorched . . . the wind struck so cold on the side of my face that tears kept dropping from eyes and nose upon the book before me, and each drop instantaneously froze where it fell.'

Even Southesk's bizarre diet could not compare to the concoction of two cheerfully incompetent Englishmen, Viscount Milton and his physician-companion Dr Walter Butler Cheadle, who spent a winter of semi-starvation in a lonely prairie hut in 1863. They roused themselves enough to prepare a Christmas pudding ('as big as my head' noted Cheadle) made of suet and filled with raisins, buckshot, tobacco and soap, which Cheadle termed 'delicious beyond all anticipation'. They not only survived this but also blundered safely through the Rockies to the Pacific coast, adding another page to the world's knowledge of the prairies, if little to the art of gastronomy.

Immediately after Confederation, Sir John Macdonald, the Dominion of Canada's first Prime Minister, applied a skilful mixture of persistence and patience to interest the Pacific coast colony of British Columbia in joining. His main bait was the offer to build a railway from the Atlantic to the Pacific. But the Hudson's Bay Company's ownership of the continent's empty centre posed a problem which was aggravated by the frequently expressed wish of many Americans to see a United States stretching from the North Pole to Panama. (In 1866 a Bill was even introduced into the House of Representatives in Washington which proposed the offer of ten million dollars to the Hudson's Bay Company in return for its charter.) But Sir John Macdonald, stubborn and tenacious, was alert to the threat, if reluctant to saddle his infant Dominion with the crippling expense of opening up and developing the prairies. 'I would be quite willing, personally, to leave the whole country a wilderness for the next half-century,' he said, 'but I fear that if Englishmen do not go there Yankees will'.

When the British and Canadian governments began their protracted negotiations with the Hudson's Bay Company in 1868 to take over Rupert's Land, Macdonald also prepared the groundwork for a force of soldier-policemen to bring law to the land and provide settled conditions for the expected flood of immigrants. After a year of hard bargaining the Company agreed to the transfer, in exchange for £300,000 and generous grants of land around its forts and posts in the territory. At a stroke Canada had become a territorial – if impecunious – giant: in order to close one of history's most momentous real-estate deals Canada had to borrow money from Britain to pay the Company.

The transfer of power was set for 1 December 1869 and William McDougall, Sir John Macdonald's Minister of Public Works, was appointed the territory's first Lieutenant-Governor. When his party set off in October for the Red River colony in Assiniboia, among the tasks with which McDougall was charged by Macdonald was the formation of a force of mounted policemen for the new territories.

McDougall had been sent west to his new job while the land still belonged to the Hudson's Bay Company in order to probe the feelings of the population of the Red River area. The Prime Minister reminded McDougall that he was 'approaching a foreign country, under the government of the Hudson's Bay Company. ... You cannot force your way in.' And he admitted privately that he anticipated McDougall 'will have a good deal of trouble, and it will require considerable management to keep those wild people quiet ...'.

Sir John's fears were well founded. The Red River settlers and half-breeds were hoping for some form of representational government when Rupert's Land became part of Canada, and many of them regarded the appointment of the moody and individualistic McDougall without reference to them as the first step towards their subjugation by eastern Canada. They were also exasperated by the government's sending of surveyors and road-builders to measure their lands. There were angry meetings and demands for action, and when McDougall and his party arrived at the American frontier village of Pembina after taking the easier overland route from eastern Canada through the United States they were handed a curt note in French informing them that they could not enter Assiniboia without special permission of an organisation called the National Half-Breed Committee of Red River. The note was signed by a twenty-five-year-old French-Canadian half-breed named Louis Riel. So, even before the country belonged to her, Canada had an insurrection on her hands.

The fact of Canadian Confederation had taken two years to make its full impact on the Red River colony. Only then did the *métis* (as the French-speaking half-breeds were called) realise the threat hanging over their carefree life of buffalo hunting, fur trapping and sporadic farming. The *métis*, who made up about half the Red River settlement's polyglot population of 12,000, understandably began to have fears about a loss of influence and a threat to land titles, language, religion and culture in the face of a possible influx of settlers from the east. Both they and their English-speaking neighbours were also palpably uninformed about the high-level negotiations which had so profoundly affected their lives. Not even the local Hudson's Bay governing body, the Council of Assiniboia, had been told what was happening.

While other sections of the community, even the English and Scottish half-breeds, remained warily neutral, the *métis* dissidents gathered around Riel, who had been born in the Red River settlement of St Boniface and educated in Montreal. His background, eloquence and ability to speak good English made him a natural choice as leader. But he had serious defects, too. He was young, inexperienced, quick-tempered and unwilling to accept criticism. Nor was his dress sense quite that expected of the politician he obviously imagined himself to be. The statesmanlike black frock coat and trousers, silk cravat and starched collar which he affected for meetings were rather undermined by his habit of wearing moccasins. And his erratic manner was typified by his signing one letter 'Your humble, poor, fair and confident public servant'.

After turning back McDougall and his party at Pembina, Riel and the National Half-Breed Committee occupied without resistance the Hudson's Bay post of Fort Garry, the strategic centre of the Red River settlement about a mile from the village of Winnipeg. From the fort they issued a List of Rights demanding continued freedom of language, religion and 'customs and usages.' Riel was declared president of a provisional government and, as American annexationists rubbed their hands in anticipation, a flag was designed and run up in place of the Union Jack. The new standard showed a fleur-de-lis and shamrock on a white background, the shamrock being in honour of the Irish-American Fenian supporters of the insurrection.

The Canadian government, meanwhile, refused to accept the official transfer of the territory or to pay Hudson's Bay the £300,000 compensation until peace was restored; and McDougall, the governor with no country to govern, sat meanwhile in Pembina issuing profound proclamations and vainly appealing to the

Canadian and English elements in Red River to rise and support him. Eventually, just before Christmas, he gave up, went back to the new capital of Ottawa, 'very chop-fallen and sulky' according to Macdonald, and resigned from the job he had never begun. But there *was* opposition within the Red River community to Riel and his home-grown regime. Several outspoken critics were imprisoned and soon Riel committed what was probably the crucial mistake of his life when he ordered the execution of one of these men, an Ontario Orangeman named Thomas Scott, who had threatened to assassinate Riel if he got the chance. The execution kindled the racial and religious passions – which were never far under the surface in Canada – and caused a storm of protest, particularly in the predominantly Protestant province of Ontario, where posters appeared in the streets demanding 'Shall French Rebels Rule Our Dominion?' and 'Men of Ontario, Shall Scott's Blood Cry in Vain for Vengeance?' In the heavily Catholic province of Quebec there was instinctive sympathy for Riel and the *métis*.

Despite Ontario protests, Riel's provisional government was invited to send a group of negotiators to Ottawa, where they demanded the admission of Assiniboia into the Canadian Confederation as a member province. Sir John Macdonald, a practised hand at reconciling Canada's diverse interests and aware of the need to placate the Quebec faction in his Conservative government, drafted the required legislation. The comparatively tiny segment of 11,000 square miles was accepted into Confederation and nearly one and a half million acres of land was set aside for the *métis* farmers. At the same time Sir John managed to lean the other way and stifle Ontario indignation by arranging to send a joint expeditionary force of the British Army and Canadian Militia to Red River, ostensibly to oversee the peaceful transfer of the Hudson's Bay lands to Canada. Despite Macdonald's increasing alcoholism towards the final, demanding stages of negotiation (Sir Stafford Northcote, the new Governor of the Hudson's Bay Company, wrote to the British Prime Minister Benjamin Disraeli,

'His habit is to retire to bed, to exclude everybody, and to drink bottle after bottle of port . . . he is conscious of his inability to do any important business and he does none') the Canadian Prime Minister was able to cable the Colonial Office in London 'A province named Manitoba erected' just before being stricken with gallstone trouble. The bill became law in July 1870 and the Red River settlement, renamed Manitoba, emerged as Canada's first western province.

But the half-breeds' jubilation soon turned sour. The 1200-strong military expedition, led by Colonel Garnet Wolseley, was despatched to restore order at Red River and, although it was stressed that they were not a punitive force, Louis Riel wisely fled into the United States just before the eager troops, spoiling for a fight after a long and exhausting slog through the wild forests and swamps of northern Ontario, approached Fort Garry. The disappointed members of the soldiery, who had quietly vowed to avenge the execution of Thomas Scott, persecuted some of Riel's *métis* followers and, despite the Ottawa assurances of land entitlement and the issue of a scrip authorising the half-breeds to select their property in the new province, there were several cases of rough justice. Some *métis* returned from a prairie hunt to find their land in the possession of Ontarian newcomers, who had even renamed a local river the Boyne. Many half-breed farmers, unable to eradicate their suspicion of paper promises – and in some cases unable to read them – sold their scrip to arriving settlers from the east and retreated into the prairie lands in a pathetic and doomed attempt to preserve their old way of life, joining the half-breed communities which already existed around the fur-trading posts.

Sir John Macdonald had devoted considerable time during the spring of 1870 to furthering his scheme for a mounted police force for the West, and in April an Order-in-Council revealed his planning. The force was to be 200 strong and details were given of the uniforms and arms to be supplied. Recruiting was actually begun. But Riel's flight and the clashes in Manitoba between half-breeds and troops ensured the retention of soldiers in the area for some time and so the idea of a police force was shelved, though not forgotten.

In his absence in exile, Riel was elected by acclamation a Member of Parliament for his community, but he never took his seat and four years later was expelled from the House. The *métis* problem was temporarily dampened down, but far from solved. Fifteen years later the same Louis Riel would lead his people into an infinitely more tragic uprising.

Chapter 2

THE PRAIRIE BUCCANEERS

THOUGH law had come to the south-east segment of Canada's vast new acquisition, the withdrawal of Hudson's Bay Company rule and the shelving of Macdonald's plans for a police force left the remainder of the area (which became known as the North West Territories) without government or authority of any kind. American traders and whiskey peddlers had already begun to make inroads into the Company's fur business with the Indians in the decade before Canada assumed control of Rupert's Land. Now in 1870, with the country a no-man's-land, their spread was totally unopposed. The people most affected were the Indian tribes, already beginning to disintegrate because of their contacts with a more complex civilisation.

The encroachment of white men and their ways first revolutionised, then wrecked, Indian society. Horses won in battle from American tribes to the south made the Plains Indians more mobile, and guns obtained in trade at Hudson's Bay posts and from liquor peddlers increased their hunting capacity and deadliness in war. It was, however, another western import, smallpox, which decimated and demoralised them in the nineteenth century and had effectively broken their power by the time the whiskey traders moved on to the scene, though it was left to the vendors of the vile home-made liquor to reduce the Indian nations to ultimate degradation and poverty.

Smallpox had made earlier appearances in the West, notably in the 1830s, but the epidemic of 1869-70 swept away about a third of Canada's Plains Indians. The disease was carried north through the United States up the Missouri river to the head of navigation at Fort Benton in Montana, from where it spread to the southern tribes of Blackfoot. The Crees were warned by missionaries and traders to avoid contact with the Blackfoot but the advice was ignored as soon as the raiding season opened in the spring of 1870. When one war-party of Crees came across an abandoned Blackfoot camp containing the swollen and decomposing bodies of smallpox victims, the jubilant warriors carried away clothing and easily taken scalps. And with them they took smallpox.

The Indians dreaded the disease more than any other, not only because of its virulence but because the disfigurement which accompanied it destroyed their sense of dignity. The few missionaries in the country worked desperately to help (one Methodist minister, George McDougall, lost two of his own daughters during the epidemic) but the Indians were irreversibly ravaged. In their agony they blamed all white men for their plight and tried to return the disease to its donors. Tearing the scabs from their bodies, they rubbed their open sores on door handles and gates and left rotting corpses to the windward of trading posts, hoping to poison the very air.

They died in heaps; more than a hundred perished around the stockade of Fort Pitt alone. Captain Butler described the plight of the Crees in the summer of 1870: 'By streams and lakes, in willow copses and upon bare hillsides, often shelterless from the fierce rays of the summer sun . . . the poor, plague-stricken wretches lay down to die.' The Sarcees, who numbered several thousand before the epidemic, were reduced to a few hundred.

It was also from the Montana settlement of Fort Benton (dubbed the 'sagebrush Sodom' by one historian) that another pestilence spread – the whiskey trade. Formerly a stronghold of the American Fur Company, one of Hudson's Bay's liveliest rivals, Benton towards the end of the 1860s was a treeless, dusty shanty town which rejoiced in the self-awarded title of Chicago of the Plains. Its situation at the head of navigation of the Missouri river and its mile-long levee where sternwheel steamboats unloaded goods of all kinds, made it the hub of the freighting business on the north-western prairies and a jumping-off point for adventurers and frontiersmen. It played host to a floating population of assorted characters: hunters, miners, cowboys, soldiers, Indians, trappers, prostitutes and men of god mingled on its boardwalks. In summer Benton's rubbish-strewn streets threw up a choking dust; when it rained the thoroughfares were mud-clogged and nauseating. A blanket of dust and the pervading stink of thousands of pack animals and cattle hung over the town. As if that were not enough, Benton suffered the extremes of prairie temperatures – fiercely hot summers, crushingly cold winters and the occasional spring flood thrown in for good measure.

One missionary, the Rev. John McLean, travelling on his honeymoon trip to take up a post with the Blood Indians, passed through Fort Benton and found it 'a revelation! Early in the morning the main street was literally covered with playing cards swept from the gambling saloons after the night's debauch, where a new pack was used in every game as a precaution against marking them.' A prominent Benton citizen observed sadly that 'religion and education are at a low ebb', and after visiting the town the English writer Montague Davenport felt that 'the American eagle should be portrayed with a six-shooter in his claw; he is incomplete without'. There was certainly a widespread disregard of the law: one Benton sheriff even had his horse stolen.

The Montana whiskey peddlers were first forced north over the American border in the 1860s when the United States government began, firmly if belatedly, to enforce a law enacted thirty years before forbidding the sale of intoxicants to Indians. Groups of traders decided to protect their lucrative business by moving into Canada and establishing bases from which they could smuggle liquor back into the United States. But they quickly discovered that the thirst of the Canadian Indians was equally rewarding, particularly as the influence of the Hudson's Bay Company declined. They and the other fur trading companies had supplied liquor to the Indians for years, but had carefully rationed the supplies, not wanting to strangle their source of furs by corrupting the red men. But the whiskey traders, the buccaneers of the prairies, were out for quick profits. The Indians like their liquor to burn (hence the name 'firewater') and the whiskey runners were glad to oblige with the foulest of concoctions – raw alcohol, heavily watered and spiced with lip-searing additives such as tabasco, vitriol, red peppers and Jamaica ginger, and coloured with tobacco juice, molasses or ink.

A series of trading posts, at first flimsy and ramshackle but soon by necessity sturdily built and graced with the name 'fort' sprang out of the Canadian prairie, all aptly named – Whoop-Up, Slideout, Standoff, Robbers' Roost and Whiskey Gap. Whoop-Up, about sixty miles north of the American border and approached by a road from Fort Benton known as the Whoop-Up Trail, was the most important of these colourful little forts. Originally it was a series of log huts linked by a picket fence, built in 1869 by two western adventurers from Fort Benton, John J. Healy and Alfred B. Hamilton. It was soon burned down by drunken Indians. The partners learned their lesson. It took two years to construct the next Whoop-Up at a cost of $20,000: a fourteen-foot stockade topped by sharpened stakes to discourage Indian trespassers, two bastions containing ancient brass cannons and loopholed for rifles, and roofs covered with earth to protect the buildings from fire arrows. Doors, windows and even chimneys were barred with iron to keep out drunken Indians.

When they had traded their buffalo robes and furs, the drink-crazed Indians exchanged their horses, food and even their women for more liquor. And when all their means of barter had been exhausted the Indians turned on each other, knifing and shooting and murdering, freezing to death in winter and getting themselves shot by the whites when trying to steal more liquor.

The traders, many of them bitter veterans of the American Civil War, placed cheap valuation on life. One of the men at Whoop-Up wrote to a friend in Fort Benton, 'My partner Will

Geary got to putting on airs and I shot him and he is dead. The potatoes is looking well. Yours truly, Snookum Jim.'

The Methodist minister John McDougall, a vigorous prairie parson from whose cart fluttered a tiny Union Jack and whose father George McDougall had founded a western mission in 1864, was one of the first to alert the Canadian government to the Indians' peril. He wrote, 'It is very humiliating to a British subject to witness the wholesale poisoning of a nation that ought to have protection.' With some reason, he came to the conclusion that 'the red man was in a fair way towards extinction', a fact which must have also perturbed McDougall since when he wasn't preaching to the Indians he was trading with them.

When Adams G. Archibald became Lieutenant-Governor of Manitoba and the North West Territories in the summer of 1870 he was understandably anxious to find out what was happening in the vast lands under his jurisdiction. So he commissioned Captain William Francis Butler, who had come west with Garnet Wolseley's Red River expedition that summer, to travel to the Rockies and report on the condition of the Indian tribes and the amount of lawlessness existing. Butler's journey, accomplished mostly in the harshest conditions of the prairie winter, lasted 119 days and he covered nearly 3000 miles.

He returned with the stark opinion that 'the region is without law, order or security for life or property; robbery and murder for years have gone unpunished; Indian massacres are unchecked even in the close vicinity of the Hudson's Bay Company posts, and all civil and legal institutions are entirely unknown'.

Butler warned of the Indians' deep grievances: the disappearance of the vast buffalo herds, which was blamed on the white man, followed by the periods of starvation and privation; the activities of the whiskey traders and the policy of Indian extermination being carried out on the other side of the border by American soldiers.

To stifle the lawlessness he advocated an armed force of 100 to

150 men, 'one third to be mounted', and stationed at specially established government posts rather than Hudson's Bay forts where they could be 'mistaken by the ignorant people of the country for the hired defenders of the Hudson's Bay Company'.

Nearly eighteen months after Butler's return another observer was sent, this time by the Canadian government. Colonel Patrick Robertson-Ross, Adjutant-General of the Militia, left Fort Garry on 10 August 1872. Like Butler, he threaded his way west via the string of Hudson's Bay posts, covering 1200 miles in a month. His report, presented personally to Sir John Macdonald in December, made grim reading. During the previous year eighty-eight Blackfoot Indians had been murdered in drunken brawls; a *métis*, Charles Gaudin, had killed his wife at Fort Edmonton just before Robertson-Ross's arrival and was unpunished, despite a reputation for wanton brutality – he had previously mutilated an elderly Indian woman by severing the sinews of her arms. 'Beyond the Province of Manitoba westward to the Rocky Mountains there is no kind of government at present whatever, and no security for life or property beyond what people can do for themselves.'

Robertson-Ross reported that whiskey had been sold openly to the Indians by American smugglers at Edmonton during the summer 'and on these traders being remonstrated with by the gentlemen in charge of the Hudson's Bay post, they coolly replied that . . . as there was no force there to prevent them they would do just as they pleased'.

He recommended that no time should be lost in sending a regiment of mounted riflemen to the west, 550 strong, and stationed in groups of fifty at the Hudson's Bay forts, with a larger body to be based at a Customs house and fort to be built near the American border to counter the whiskey running. Because the Indians were generally scattered, poorly armed and badly mounted, a fifty-strong group would be a formidable power on the prairies, Robertson-Ross felt. But he stressed, 'It is wiser policy and better economy to have one hundred soldiers too many than one man too few . . . the only thing the Indians really respect, and will bow to, is actual power.' He also urged that any mounted force sent among the Indians should wear scarlet as 'animosity is rarely, if ever, felt towards disciplined soldiers wearing Her Majesty's uniform in any portion of the British Empire'.

The reports of Butler and Robertson-Ross helped to publicise the need for law enforcement in the North West Territories but they did not, as some writers have maintained, lead directly to the foundation of the Mounted Police. The credit for this belongs to Sir John Macdonald, who has rightly been called 'The Father of the Force'. But Sir John was a most deliberate man (he earned the political nickname of 'Old Tomorrow') who had repeatedly put off the police's formation because of the heavy cost and the disappointing lack of settlers for the new country.

But when Robertson-Ross's report was published in March 1873, shortly after the Hudson's Bay Company had made a formal request that their trading posts be provided with protection, Macdonald capitalised on the public concern by introducing an enabling bill asking the Canadian House of Commons for 'a moderate grant of money to organise a mounted police force, somewhat similar to the Irish Mounted Constabulary. They would have the advantage of military discipline, would be armed in a simple but efficient way . . . and by being police would be a civil force.' The bill passed unopposed on 23 May and attracted practically no attention. Though Macdonald now had the legislation he needed, he was still in no hurry. He planned to organise the force the following year, 1874.

However, in August 1873 alarming reports reached Ottawa of the massacre in May of a band of Canadian Indians by some Montana trappers in the Cypress Hills, which straddle what is now the Saskatchewan–Alberta border just north of the United States frontier. Although low (4500 feet) by North American standards the hills rear sharply above the treeless plains around them and are the highest in Canada between the Atlantic Ocean and the Rockies. They received their name when early French explorers mistakenly identified the local jackpines as cypress trees. The area of some 1000 square miles was a haven for animals, a welcome break for half-breeds and Indians from the interminable plains – and since it lay almost at the junction of Cree and Blackfoot territories and the northern extremity of the hunting lands of American Indians it became a no-man's-land.

In early May 1873 the trappers were returning from a winter hunt in Canada to their Montana base at Fort Benton. When they got to the Teton river, only five miles from Benton, they were unwise enough to relax their normal vigil, and they paid for it when their horses were stolen by Indians during the night. After appealing vainly to the U.S. Army to help them recover their property, they bought supplies and new horses and set out on the trail of the thieves. The group of ten, which included some Canadians, consisted of ex-soldiers, Indian fighters and half-breeds, all of them hardened plainsmen. They trailed their stolen horses north to the Cypress Hills but lost the track and camped for the night near a trading post run by a whiskey dealer, Abe Farwell.

From Farwell, they learned that an Assiniboine camp of some forty lodges (or tepees) under Chief Little Soldier was nearby. These Indians had stolen, but quickly returned, a horse belonging to a friend of Farwell's named George Hammond, 'an unsavoury loafer' who was staying at the trading post. Next morning, a Sunday, the Montana group sat drinking at Farwell's place; in their camp the Indians were doing the same. Soon after noon Hammond discovered that his horse had been stolen a second time. In a fury, he grabbed his rifle and started for the Indian camp-ground, followed by the others.

The Indians, many of them drunk, were alarmed at the approach of armed white men and scattered to their tepees for their own guns. Firing broke out, the trappers took cover in a shallow gully and pumped bullets from their rapid-firing rifles into the Indian tents. Little Soldier's braves, armed only with muzzle loaders, charged suicidally three times, heaping their dead in front of the

38

gully, but they managed to kill only one man, a Canadian named Ed Grace who was riding to join the fight. When the Assiniboines eventually fled they left more than thirty dead, including Little Soldier.

News of the massacre did not break until 11 June, when the Montana newspaper the *Helena Herald* headlined approvingly 'Whites on the War Path', 'Forty Lodges Wiped Out by Sixteen "Kit Carsons"'. As the story spread eastwards it gained mightily in horrific detail. To the American press it was another case of undaunted frontiersmen gallantly overcoming the odds against a mob of howling savages; Canadians read in their newspapers of innocent Indians being callously mown down by drunken American border ruffians. Whatever the truth in the accounts of the killings there is no doubt that the Cypress Hills massacre was the final, deciding factor in the formation of the North West Mounted Police.

Chapter 3

A HARSH CRADLE

SIR John Macdonald decided to delay no longer. On 30 August 1873 the Order-in-Council was passed and the force officially came into being. Although it had been agreed that it should total 300, made up of six divisions of fifty, it was decided that for the time being 150 (or one man for each 2000 square miles of the vast territory they proposed to police) would be sufficient.

There was no argument about the colour of their uniform. Colonel Robertson-Ross's recommendation about scarlet coats was adopted. Red coats, to Indian minds, were known to be synonymous with friendship and fair dealing, and the legend had grown among the Indians that the red coat was dyed with the blood of the Great White Queen's enemies. Unfortunately, the rest of the proposed uniform also symbolised British tradition rather than practical thinking about the country and its climate. Canada's politicians planned to send their policemen west togged up like the soldiers who had galloped into the Russian guns at Balaclava, or had put down the Indian Mutiny. Cloaks were to be dark blue or grey, lined with scarlet ('English cavalry style'), there were white pith helmets and flat, round 'pill-box' forage caps, long brown boots and white buckskin gauntlets. In Britain, at any rate, there was hearty approval of the police's choice of colour. *The Times* noted that scarlet had been selected 'in order that no misconception may exist in the minds of either Yankee ruffians or Indian warriors as to the nationality of the force, and it is indeed a glorious livery to fight in if fighting has to be done'.

Recruits were required to be of 'sound constitution, able to ride, active and able-bodied, of good character and between the ages of 18 and 40 years, and able to read and write either the English or French language'. After the affair of Louis Riel and his *métis* followers, Macdonald had quietly ditched his plan to recruit a section of the police force from among the West's half-breed population.

Enrolment began early in September, while Macdonald cast about for a Commissioner for the police. In addition to his Prime Ministerial duties Sir John was, as Minister of Justice, responsible for the force, though most of the organisational work fell to the Deputy Minister (his brother-in-law Hewitt Bernard). But other officers were quickly appointed and given charge of the recruiting and medical checks: in the Atlantic provinces of New Brunswick and Nova Scotia Inspector Charles F. Young, formerly of Her Majesty's 50th Foot and soon to earn the dubious distinction of being the first officer dismissed from the Mounted Police, was assisted by a French-Canadian sub-inspector, Ephraim A. Brisebois, who had fought in Italy as a Papal Zouave; in Quebec the processing of recruits was in the hands of Inspector William Winder; and in Ontario the job was handled by Inspector James Morrow Walsh, who was to become one of the Mounted Police's most famous officers, 'an upstanding young man, somewhat pompous and proud, but a born leader' according to a policeman who served with him.

The intention was to drill the police in the east of Canada that winter and send them west in the spring. But Alexander Morris, who had succeeded Adams G. Archibald as Lieutenant-Governor of the North West Territories, nagged away at the Canadian government from Manitoba with a stream of telegrams, culminating with the demand on 20 September: 'What have you done as to Police Force? Their absence may lead to grave disaster.'

Although far from convinced that the situation in the West was as bad as Morris painted it, Macdonald conceded that 'the massacre of the Indians by the Americans has greatly excited the red men' and he wrote to the Governor-General, the Earl of

Dufferin, 'It would not be well for us to take the responsibility of slighting Morris's repeated and urgent entreaties. If anything went wrong the blame would lie at our door. I shall hurry the men off at once.' Macdonald was wise to take no chances. The previous year the United States had spent more money fighting Indians than Canada's entire budget. Canada simply could not afford a Wild West.

There was desperately little time to recruit, organise and equip the party of 150 and get them to Manitoba before the onset of winter made travel extremely difficult. Of the applicants engaged, forty-six gave their previous occupation as clerks, thirty-nine were tradesmen of various sorts, nine were soldiers, nine farmers, four telegraph operators, two sailors and only two had formerly been policemen. The rest were a mixture of professors, planters, gardeners, students, bartenders, lumberjacks, surveyors and drifting adventure-seekers. One of these, an Englishman named James T. Fullerton, recalled 'My friends who wanted me in the cricket club tried to dissuade me from joining, but the great adventure was too big an attraction to miss.'

The haste with which they had all been signed up became embarrassingly apparent when, at a medical re-examination three months later, it was discovered that two of the vigilant new law-keepers were blind in one eye, five were suffering from serious heart ailments, one had tuberculosis, another syphilis and one man had actually been recruited with a fracture of the leg.

Gradually the group began to assemble at Collingwood, seventy miles north of Toronto on the shore of Lake Huron, for the lake and land journey of nearly 1000 miles to the Hudson's Bay post of Lower Fort Garry, twenty miles north of Winnipeg, where they were to be quartered for the winter. More officers were appointed: James Farquharson Macleod, born on the Isle of Skye thirty-seven years previously and a former militia-major who had already been to the Red River area with the Garnet Wolseley expedition in 1870; William Dummer Jarvis, a Canadian who had served in

South Africa with the British Army; Jacob E. Carvell, who had fought for the South in the American Civil War, and Edmund Dalrymple Clark, Sir John Macdonald's nephew, who became paymaster and quartermaster.

The route lay by lake steamer from Collingwood 500 miles through Lake Huron and Lake Superior to Port Arthur (now Thunder Bay) and then a 450-mile slog to the Red River by what was known as the Dawson Route, named after an optimistic surveyor who had said that a road could be built through, around and over the forests, lakes, rivers and swamps of this forbidding country. The first group of forty men and an officer left Collingwood on 4 October aboard the steamer *Cumberland*; another party of two officers and sixty-two men set off on the *Chicora* six days later and the third contingent of three officers and fifty-three men embarked soon afterwards in the *Frances Smith*.

The first two groups had luck with the weather – a smooth lake trip and a swift, if arduous, land and water journey before they reached the Red River on 22 and 26 October respectively. The third contingent was less fortunate. Their crossing of Lake Superior was the roughest for years, and according to the cricket-loving James Fullerton every member of the police detachment was sick except the Scots officer James Macleod and himself.

Their march west from Port Arthur was accomplished in cold weather and occasional blizzards. They reached the Hudson's Bay post of Fort Frances at Rainy Lake 'like half-drowned rats' and were held up three days waiting for a boat to take them across the Lake of the Woods. When they eventually got to its western shore a driving snowstorm froze their packed tents so hard that they could not be unfolded. The men's boots were also frozen and unwearable, so feet were bundled up in underclothes and shirts for the ninety-mile final section to Lower Fort Garry. Fortunately, after a few miles they were met by some sleighs sent to collect them. The transportation must have come as a great relief to men who were struggling through deep snow in summer uniforms and with no boots. The recruits' wretched condition was matched by the food they were served, spoiled pork and musty hardtack, though Fullerton recalled

> We did have one good feed. The officers had several boxes of beef for their personal use. One dark night we reached a portage and in unloading the canoe by some 'accident' those boxes were broken. Bivouac fires that night gave off a delightful aroma of roasting beefsteaks. . . . Another very serious mishap came about that no one could understand. The officers had a 20-gallon keg of fine whiskey, presumably for use as medicine. Somehow that whiskey turned to water in the keg.

Though the third contingent arrived safely at their destination on 1 November after crossing an icebound Red River, they learned that their winter uniforms had been frozen in along the route and would not reach them until the following spring. An assortment of warm clothing was provided by Lieutenant-Colonel W. Osborne Smith, commanding the militia forces in Manitoba, who had been given temporary charge of the police until a Commissioner was appointed.

In fact, Sir John Macdonald had found the commanding officer he wanted shortly after the police had left Ontario for the West; on 18 October he appointed Lieutenant-Colonel George Arthur French the first Commissioner of the Mounted Police. French, born in Roscommon, Ireland, was thirty-two years old, a tall, vigorous Royal Artillery officer who had been lent to the Canadian government for a ten-year period and was at the time head of the School of Gunnery in Kingston, Ontario. A strict, but not humourless, disciplinarian, George French was intolerant of incompetence, particularly in politicians.

The appointment was one of Macdonald's last. On 5 November his Conservative government was defeated over a scandal about the misuse of funds for the proposed new railway to the Pacific coast. Macdonald resigned the next day and the Liberal, Alexander Mackenzie, became the new leader of Canada. Antoine Dorion was appointed Minister of Justice but Macdonald's brother-in-law Hewitt Bernard clung on to his job as Deputy

Minister, ensuring that there would be little disruption in the running of the Mounted Police. Unlike his bibulous predecessor, the new Prime Minister was an enthusiastic advocate of prohibition and responded much more promptly to complaints about the corrupting effect of the whiskey traders upon the western Indians.

While they waited for their new Commissioner to join them, the police made themselves as comfortable as possible in their temporary home on Hudson's Bay property. Lower Fort Garry (also known as the Stone Fort) had been built in 1831 on higher ground and twenty miles down the Red River from the original Fort Garry, which had several times been severely damaged by floods. The men were barracked in the Company's store buildings, while the officers occupied the attic of the Hudson's Bay officers' quarters. Altogether, Lower Fort Garry made a suitably harsh cradle for a force which was never to be coddled.

On 3 November the three divisions, A, B and C, paraded before their temporary commander, Lieutenant-Colonel Osborne Smith, who read to them the enlistment oath before they officially signed on for three years. If the hastily cast recruiting-net had swept in a few invalids, incompetents and bad elements, it had also found some outstanding young men. The first to sign was Arthur H. Griesbach, the son of an Anglican clergyman who had once been domestic chaplain to the Earl of Westmorland. Griesbach, whose family was of German stock, was the third of ten children, and though his two elder brothers had died in service he followed them into the British Army, being commissioned at eighteen in a Yorkshire militia regiment. He had served with the Cape Mounted Rifles in South Africa before moving to Canada. Like several other recruits, he had already been west with the 1870 Garnet Wolseley expedition, as captain and quartermaster. Griesbach's title of Regimental Number One was some small compensation for the vague promise someone had made to him when he joined the police that he would be made 'chief constable'. However, Griesbach was immediately appointed staff constable

45

(equivalent to sergeant in the police ranking list of sub-constable, constable and staff constable), was commissioned two years later and did not retire until 1903, after completing thirty years' service.

Percy R. Neale was second to sign and he was followed by Samuel Benfield Steele, the prototype of Hollywood's idea of a Mountie. Steele was twenty-two, tall, fair-haired and so slim-waisted when he joined that he wore a sash under his tunic to give him a less girlish appearance. Steele (who would go on to become a knight and a major-general in the Canadian Army after a distinguished career with the Mounted Police) came from a military family. A Canadian by birth, he was the fourth son of Captain Elmes Steele of the Royal Navy, who had served during the Nelson era. Other members of the Steele family had fought at Waterloo and Trafalgar and with Wolfe at Quebec. Steele had been a militiaman since he was fifteen and, like Griesbach, went to Red River with Wolseley in 1870 before becoming an artilleryman.

There was an immense amount of organisational work for the new force; local horses to be purchased, clothing, food and better accommodation to be provided. Colonel Osborne Smith was delighted to hear that Commissioner French was on his way to Lower Fort Garry ('I shall not be at all sorry to be relieved of the police work') and he wrote to Antoine Dorion, the Minister of Justice, 'I think from what little I know of him you have got a good man in French, not afraid of work and fond of his profession.' French arrived nine days before Christmas, having travelled to Manitoba by the easier overland route through the United States. What he saw appalled him. Hardly any of his Mounted Police could ride, the horses were young and unbroken and the wretched assortment of uniforms being worn must have been a severe jolt to a man schooled in British Army orderliness. He reported to Ottawa 'The officers are, practically speaking, without any uniforms . . . the men have to undergo great hardship for the want of suitable clothing.'

In temperatures which dropped to −30° F. and lower the recruits stumbled painfully through foot drill and riding practice in the open from dawn till dark. The unbroken western broncos repeatedly pitched their unskilled riders violently onto the frozen ground. When the men complained of saddle sores, French ordered an extra issue of salt for them to rub on their wounds; eventually, according to one policemen, 'We became so tough I could sit on a prickly pear.' There was much grumbling about the bruising and chilling routine. An anonymous letter published in the Toronto *Globe* had this to say about life at Lower Fort Garry:

> I'd as soon be in a penitentiary as in this corps. Our clothes are too large for us and they are made of very inferior cloth . . . thus far we have been treated more like brutes than men. We have to run like fury in an inclosure with horses that have never had a bridle on them before, some of them just taken off the prairies and lassooed before they could be captured. I'd give six months' salary to be home once more. We rise at 6 a.m. and go to bed at 9.30 p.m. We get dry bread and bad coffee for breakfast, boiled meat and worse potatoes for dinner and real bad tea and dry bread for supper – such grub!

Another constable described the rations: 'Mornings we get bread and water and a kind of tea, the rest of the day about the same.'

But the majority made the best of the grim conditions. Parties and dances were organised, and when it wasn't too cold to hold a rifle there were shooting competitions. According to James Fullerton

> Skating was our chief amusement. As the thermometer never went above 40 below all that January, and most of December too, we had miles of wonderful ice. The cold did not seem to bother us while skating but we used to relieve sentries every 15 minutes and there was a kettle of hot tea for the fellows who came in. I don't know why walking a beat was any colder than skating, unless the girls made us forget the cold.

The zealous Sam Steele spent as much time as possible with the older settlers around the Stone Fort, who could tell him something about the country stretching away to the Rockies. 'I took notes of all the information I received and was pretty well acquainted with the customs of the Indians, hunters and traders before I left Fort Garry.' Commissioner French, too, was busy trying to find out more about the West, the Indians, and the opposition they could expect from the whiskey traders. French reported to Ottawa that he was expecting 'hot work next summer' after being told by the Lieutenant-Governor, Alexander Morris, that the whiskey men had set up five forts, one of them containing a hundred desperadoes and mounting several guns which they had boldly stolen from an American army supply train.

This information, plus the knowledge that the Blackfoot alone could muster 2000 warriors, convinced French that his force needed to be doubled in size to 300, 'the lowest possible number consistent with any degree of safety'. He asked permission to recruit and equip another 150 men at once and to supply them with the best available arms and horses. 'If the outlaws and desperadoes in the forts deserve the character given them we shall doubtless have to use our guns and may possibly have some hard fighting. The result, however, can scarcely be doubtful.' When Hewitt Bernard was slow to answer his requests, French fired off an impatient note which hardly endeared him to the Ottawa politicians: 'I am well aware of the objection to reading Weekly Reports, but I really must ask that mine receive attention and *immediate* consideration.'

With some justification, French complained that many of his policemen were unfitted for the job, and thought that about two dozen would have to be dismissed on medical grounds and as many again for misconduct. He described his command as 'an unleavened mass'. Early in February the Commissioner left Lower Fort Garry for Ottawa via the United States to press his case. To his surprise he found the government fully aware of the need to strengthen the force and get it to the West as quickly as possible. The Governor-General, Lord Dufferin, had written to Sir Edward Thornton, the British Ambassador in Washington:

It is the intention of my Government about the month of June to send off an expedition consisting of three hundred mounted riflemen fully equipped, accompanied by a mountain gun or two, into the North West for the purpose of capturing a band of desperadoes who have established themselves in our territory. ... The expedition will be commanded by Col. French, an artillery officer, and though nominally policemen the men will be dressed in scarlet uniform and possess all the characteristics of a military force.

French at once organised the recruiting of three more divisions, determined that the selection mistakes perpetrated the previous autumn should not be repeated. He had little need to worry. By the spring of 1874 the Mounted Police and their expedition to the West had been written up into a romantic and idealistic mission by the Press, and the recruiting campaign met with an overwhelming response. The experience of William Parker was typical. Parker, the son of a Kentish vicar, was working on a farm in the Ontario town of London when he saw an advertisement calling for a dozen recruits from the area and adding that Commissioner French would be in the town personally on 4 April to receive applications. Carrying a reference from a local church dignitary, Bishop Helmuth ('he gave me a bully character'), Parker hung around the breakfast-room of French's hotel, managed to get a word with the Commissioner and extracted a promise that he would be taken on. But later that day when he arrived for an interview he found the place besieged by 'about 200 strapping men from Stratford. They were mostly six feet tall and I thought there was no chance for me.' But French kept his promise and Parker became a policeman.

Adventure was not the only attraction, however. A French mathematics teacher, Jean d'Artigue, was travelling by train from Montreal to Toronto to join the force when he met a man 'whose dress would indicate the clergyman, long black coat, waistcoat buttoned up to the chin, straight collar and broad-brimmed hat'. He told d'Artigue that he too planned to become a policeman because he had heard that their aim was to put an end to the liquor traffic in the West. And he told the astonished Frenchman, 'I am an apostle of temperance, sir. My whole life is consecrated to that cause.'

Whatever the reason for joining, it certainly could not be put down to a love of money. Constables were paid a dollar a day, sub-constables only seventy-five cents. Inspectors earned $1400 a year, sub-inspectors $1000; and the Commissioner's salary was $2600. Still the applications flooded in until French urgently asked the government to provide him with an 'adjutant, secretary, orderly officer or anything else you like to call him. I am getting bushels of letters and telegrams and cannot answer or keep track of them. . . . From the time I arise in the morning until I go to bed at night I am working away.'

The Commissioner's brother, John French, was one of several militia officers who joined the police as sub-inspectors. Dr John Kittson enrolled as surgeon, and an Irish gentleman named Cecil Denny (later to become the sixth baronet of Tralee Castle) accepted a commission. Sergeant-Major Joseph Francis, a much-decorated veteran of the Crimean War, added badly needed experience, while at the other end of the scale an ambitious fifteen-year-old named Fred Bagley successfully persuaded his father, who had served with Colonel French in the British Army, to intervene on his behalf. Bagley was passed medically fit with the qualifying remark 'Very youthful but may develop'.

The recruits for the three new divisions were assembled at a barracks called the New Fort in Toronto to undergo a crash course in drill, riding and target practice. The comforts were hardly an improvement on Lower Fort Garry. Jean d'Artigue was shown into a large room containing only a table and told this would be the sleeping-quarters. Riding practice, too, proved a shock at first:

> Most of us had overrated our proficiency in horsemanship. Many laughable falls ensued, even the officers were as bad as ourselves at riding. Most did not understand the simplest field manœuvres and their inefficiency was made manifest before we left Toronto. Their efforts almost invariably proved failures and produced indescribable confusion. Fortunately we had some of the sergeants from the regular army among us who would come forward, put the officers in their proper places and restore us to order.

But at least one of the recruits was thoroughly enjoying it all and looking forward to the expedition. William Parker wrote home to his family in Kent

> I still like the life very much. I rather expect we shall have pretty good times . . . we shall camp out in tents on the prairies all summer. There is most splendid shooting up there and I am taking my gun up with me, and from what I hear there is magnificent fishing, so we ought to live well. . . . We are going to take a lot of cricketing things with us so that we can still keep up the old game. The officers have bought two good footballs and we play some fiery old games of an evening.

French worked feverishly, ordering arms and clothing, arranging to purchase or requisition transportation and pack animals and the mountains of supplies needed. It was decided to combine the two arms of the force at the Manitoba settlement of Dufferin near the American border directly south of Winnipeg for the march to the Rocky Mountains. On 7 June just over 100 men of A, B and C divisions who had survived the winter's medical and disciplinary tests marched south from Lower Fort Garry on the short journey. On the previous day, nearly two weeks behind the schedule that French had drawn up, sixteen officers, 201 men, 244 horses and one journalist, Henri Julien of *Canadian Illustrated News*, left Toronto in two special trains. The party had received American permission to travel through the northern United States by rail, as long as they wore civilian clothes and their guns, ammunition and swords were packed out of sight.

Thousands of people turned up at the station to see them off and a band pumped out a selection of patriotic tunes. It was a raucous, sentimental, ludicrous occasion. Some of the recruits, apprehensive of Indian scalping parties, had shaved their heads and as they leaned from the carriage windows they drew shouts of 'jailbirds' from children. As young Fred Bagley's mother kissed him goodbye she pressed a diary and a watch into his hands and told him 'Be a good boy, say your prayers regularly and come back soon.' Jean d'Artigue overheard one old man tell his policeman son 'Remember your life belongs to the country. I would rather hear of your death than your dishonour.'

The expedition's destination was Fargo, North Dakota, 1300 miles to the west and the nearest point they could reach by rail to Dufferin, a further 160 miles away. As the trains rolled through Ontario people hung out of the windows of their homes waving handkerchiefs 'especially ladies, bless their sympathising hearts'. At the border point of Sarnia nine wagons containing equipment were added to the train, and two wagonloads of extra horses were collected in Detroit.

The men were allowed a dollar a day subsistence *en route*, and William Parker recalled that 'by telegraphing ahead we received splendid meals with handsome girls to wait on us, which we most appreciated'. In Chicago, which was reached early on the evening of 7 June in pouring rain, the horses were unloaded in the stock-yards for exercising. Their next major stopping-point was St Paul, Minnesota, where they stayed overnight, again in heavy rain, and bought up the town's supply of waterproofs and overcoats. The local newspaper complimented the Canadians on 'behaving like gentlemen' during their stopover, and added 'It is undeniable that they are as a whole a much more intellectual and respectable appearing body of men than the private soldiers of the United States Army'. (Americans thought little of their soldiers in those days: one Montana resident wrote to the *New York Herald*, 'There are only two creatures who look upon a soldier here without scorn and contempt, and they are little children and dogs.')

Some of the St Paul citizens, and the gratified merchants, who had sold the police a year's supply of oats, flour and bacon, attempted to warn them of the dangers they faced, recounting tales of army forts attacked and garrisons massacred along the northern frontier. The replies were suitably stoical. Even d'Artigue, the Frenchman, told them 'they must not forget that a Canadian fighting under the British flag considers himself equal to three or four Yankees'.

Finally, on the morning of 12 June, the trains rolled into Fargo, the end of the railway journey. They were shunted into sidings and the unloading and assembling of equipment began. It quickly became obvious that the task was going to be a monumental one. The manufacturers had bundled everything into the freight cars with no preliminary sorting. So everything had to be taken out and laid on the ground before the vast jigsaw assembly job could begin. By that evening several acres were strewn with pieces of equipment. The spectacle drew most of the population of Fargo to watch, and owners of hotels and shops were particularly pleased at the chaos, predicting that the Canadians would be in town for at least a week. French thought otherwise: 'They had little idea of what can be done with properly organised reliefs of men.' At four the next morning the Commissioner had his first squad at work. They were relieved by fresh teams at eight. And at noon and four the squads were rotated again. By five that afternoon D Division, with harness, saddles, wagons and stores assembled, drove out of Fargo to a camp site six miles away, and two hours later E Division followed, cheered on their way by the fascinated and impressed citizenry of Fargo.

Had they followed the police into camp, the spectators would have been even more fascinated. It was the first night under canvas and most of the recruits knew nothing about camp life. D'Artigue thought it 'the greatest tumult I ever witnessed ... constables were shouting for night sentries, cooks were calling for wood and water, while just by them was flowing a river whose banks were covered with fuel. Everything, in fact, was confusion that evening.' The meal, when it did appear, consisted of a large cup of tea, with bacon and biscuits. To make things worse the campers were plagued by mosquitoes so fierce and numerous that Henri Julien of the *Canadian Illustrated News* reported to his paper they could 'tear a net to pieces or put out a fire'.

By the following afternoon the third and last group, F Division, had cleared and loaded the remaining equipment and joined their comrades outside Fargo. Next day being Sunday, French rested his force before striking north along the Red River on 15 June.

The 160-mile journey to Dufferin took only five days, despite searing heat which rapidly tired, disabled – and in two cases killed – the horses, purchased in eastern Canada with an eye for their fine appearance rather than the ability to pull wagons over a lumpy prairie. Most of them objected to wearing harness, others refused to draw their loads and some stampeded, overturning the wagons. 'The circus was on every morning during the march,' reported Sub-Inspector James Walker.

The fierce pace brought many grumbles and d'Artigue recalled that French's capacity as commander of the expedition was already being questioned. He confessed later in the book he wrote about his police service, 'The reasons French had for ordering such marches are still a mystery to me.' In fact, French's reasons were fairly sound ones. First, he feared attack by war parties of American Indians known to be in the area and, second, he was increasingly worried by the knowledge that his command was already well behind the schedule he had planned for its march west. All spring he had been insisting that the police would have to get away from Dufferin by mid-June at the latest if they were to reach the Rockies before winter closed in on them.

The hectic pace did not bother William Parker, who was thoroughly enjoying the march. He wrote home to England, 'The country here is very pretty. On one side is the Red River and all along its banks the trees grow. On the other is the boundless prairie, which looks like one beautiful green field.'

After passing through the American frontier settlement of Pembina (which, Parker noted, 'chiefly consists of taverns') the force crossed the border on the evening of 19 June, and French admitted, 'I must say I felt a great load of responsibility taken off my shoulders at again being on Canadian soil.' Divisions A, B and C under James F. Macleod (who had been appointed Assistant Commissioner, or second-in-command, of the Mounted Police at the beginning of June) had arrived four days earlier from Lower Fort Garry.

Dufferin, named after Canada's Governor-General, was the head-quarters of the Canadian section of the Boundary Survey Commission which had by the summer of 1874 almost completed the monumental task of mapping and marking from the Lake of the Woods in Ontario to the Rocky Mountains along the 49th Parallel, the border line which had been agreed between the United States and British North America at the Convention of London as long ago at 1818. However, until the transfer of the Hudson's Bay lands and the unsettling Red River rebellion, there had been little need on the part of the Canadians to draw a firm boundary line. Both the American and British parties of boundary surveyors had encountered and overcome the most extraordinary handicaps, hazards and hardships as they inched their way west across the plains. Methodically provisioned and prepared (the joint British and Canadian party some fifty strong, mostly Royal Engineers, had even taken along a library of nearly a thousand books) they had established a series of depots along the border, and had graded and bridged the route.

The police set up camp on the north side of the Boundary Commission's reserve at Dufferin. The horses were turned loose in a large field fenced on three sides but closed off at the eastern end only by a line of wagons, tents and a rope. This carelessness proved costly on their second night in camp when a terrific thunderstorm broke over Dufferin. A high wind, drenching rain and huge hailstones flattened many tents and, according to French, 'there was one incessant sheet of lightning from 10 p.m. to 6 a.m.' D'Artigue, too, commented on the 'dazzling and continuous glare of lightning which seemed like one sheet of fire above our heads, crashes of thunder which appeared to shake the earth to its very centre, and a hurricane which, in spite of our utmost efforts, blew down our tents'.

About midnight a thunderbolt fell among the horses; the terrified animals broke their halters, trampled the six-man picket guard underfoot, overturned supply wagons and knocked down most of the tents which were still standing as they stampeded for the open prairie. As his sodden tent collapsed around him Fred Bagley, the boy bugler, groped around in vain for his boots before running out in bare feet to sound 'Assembly'. Some policemen, unaware of the reason for the alarm, thought they were under attack by the Sioux. Sam Steele wrote of the stampede

> I shall never forget that night. I had full view of the stampede, being not more than 50 yards from the horses as they rushed . . . scrambling and rolling over one another in one huge mass. This and the unceasing flashes of lighting, the rolling of the thunder, the loud shouts of the troopers as they vainly attempted to stop the horses . . . gave to it a weird and romantic complexion.

As soon as some of the horses had been captured and saddled, pursuit parties went after the rest. Fred Bagley was with one group under Inspector James Walsh and helped to round up eighty horses; they got back to Dufferin after spending twenty-four hours without food or rest. The young bugler was fast asleep in the saddle and had to be lifted off his horse and put to bed. Sub-Inspector James Walker tracked another bunch by lightning flashes until daylight, and he eventually caught up with them sixty miles away near Grand Forks, North Dakota. By the time he got back the following night Walker had ridden five different horses, had been soaked and dried out three times and had covered 120 miles.

Astonishingly, all but one of the horses were recovered and, equally surprisingly, no one was killed, though Sub-Constable Bill Latimer's scalp was lacerated from ear to ear when one animal hurdled him, striking his skull with its hooves. An Irish constable, E. H. Maunsell, had a similarly remarkable escape: 'How often I was toppled over I could not tell . . . I found that the sole of one of my boots was almost off, one sleeve of my shirt was gone and I felt queer all over.' He collapsed and was on the sick list for a week.

The need to rest the exhausted and terrified horses forced French to postpone further the departure from Dufferin. He was beset by other problems, too. The strength of the three divisions which had wintered at Lower Fort Garry had been much reduced by discharge and desertion, and had to be made up from the Toronto detachment. Fortunately, French had foreseen this and brought out extra recruits. He also admitted that while at Dufferin 'the men were hard worked and their meals were anything but comfortable'. Bad cooking made conditions worse, and French described the bread produced by the novice cooks as 'nothing more than dough with a crust on it'. Twice he called general parades and told his force frankly that things would become even more difficult on their march – that they could expect to be wet and cold, sometimes without food and often without water – and invited any doubters to fall out and take their discharge immediately. Some did, 'and one feels they acted properly in the matter' said French. Some took the easier way out, deserting across the American border. By the time the force left Dufferin thirty-one men were absent without leave.

But most of the Mounted Police managed to stay cheerful and loyal. One wonders what the whiskey traders and tough frontiersmen around Whoop-Up and Fort Benton would have made of the letter written from Dufferin by that energetic correspondent William Parker to his mother at the vicarage near Ashford: 'All around here where we are encamped the wild roses grow very thick. I shall put some in this letter.' Or of the comment of another Englishman, Richard Burton Deane, on the day he went to join the police: 'The prairie was carpeted with wild roses, and for a time I tried to avoid stepping on them, but they were so plentiful that the avoidance of them became irksome and I hardened my heart and walked on.'

French travelled several times to Winnipeg for discussions with Lieutenant-Governor Alexander Morris and other authorities about his expedition's route to the West, and the planned campaign against the whiskey runners. The idea was to march to Fort Whoop-Up, destroy or scatter the traders and establish a post in that area; another segment of the police would be sent further north to be stationed at the Hudson's Bay fort at Edmonton, while the balance would return eastwards – hopefully in late October – to their proposed headquarters at Fort Ellice, almost 200 miles west of Winnipeg.

French was understandably anxious to follow the border route blazed by the Boundary Commission, since it was the shortest line to the west; it had been surveyed and grass and water marked out for every day's march for the first 400 miles and the road was graded and bridged where necessary. But, still anxious about American overreaction to the movement of uniformed men along the 49th Parallel, the Canadian government ordered the police to keep away from the frontier. French's later comment to Ottawa that 'the change of direction proved very unfortunate' was a terse sentence of controlled anger from a man who usually fought the bureaucrats with a good deal more energy than tact.

There was further trouble over the 330 revolvers ordered from England. When they finally arrived in the first week of July it was discovered that they had been roughly and carelessly packed. Many were bent and some were broken, trigger guards had snapped off, screws were missing and chambers would not revolve. It was a last-minute headache that the harassed French could have done without.

Departure from Dufferin was set for 6 July but was again postponed when news arrived that a Sioux war party had attacked the American border settlement of St Joe and murdered several people. The police were hastily paraded and rode to the area, at the request of the American Army, to cut off any escape by the Indians into Canada. But they saw no Indians and returned to Dufferin dusty and disappointed.

At last, on the night of 7 July, French was satisfied that his expedition was ready. All that could be done had been done, even to the sending of a message to the Methodist missionary John McDougall in the foothills of the Rockies asking him to spread the word about the impending arrival of the police and requesting that the Indians greet the white men 'with a friendly eye'. French wrote to his superiors in Ottawa, ridiculing what proved to be an uncannily accurate forecast made by 'Fort Garry croakers' that he would lose forty per cent of his horses and not get back to Manitoba until Christmas; in London *The Times*, in a flurry of misinformed optimism, told its readers that the expedition faced a journey of some 800 miles 'and we may safely calculate it will not reach the scene of action in under a month'.

The Irish aristocrat Cecil Denny probably summed up the attitude of the group at Dufferin when he wrote later

It is curious to remember what a vague idea we really had of the journey before us. I doubt if any expedition of such importance ever before undertook a journey across vast plains without competent guides, believing that at the end of it they would have to subdue lawless bands of desperadoes, with such complete faith in themselves and such utter ignorance of what they were undertaking.

Chapter 4

THE MARCH WEST

THE story of the Mounted Police's march west from Dufferin has suffered embarrassing exaggerations and has invariably been hailed as an epic. It was certainly an epic of endurance and determination; but it was also epic in its lack of organisation, in the poor way in which it was conducted and in its incredibly close brush with disaster. Avoidable blunders and inexperience caused unnecessary hardship to men and horses, and long before the end survival had overtaken success as the main aim of the expedition. Though it came close to breaking the Mounted Police, the trek to the Rocky Mountains was in fact the making of them. They passed their first great test with flying, if tattered, colours.

Problems piled in on French until the moment of departure from Dufferin on the afternoon of 8 July 1874. Fifteen men had deserted the night before and Inspector Charles F. Young was summarily dismissed for arguing with the Commissioner. Command of Young's B Division was then given to Sub-Inspector Ephraim Brisebois. Many of the *métis* wagon drivers were drunk or suffering from hangovers, some of the horses chosen to tow the guns and mowing machines baulked, some of the oxen ran away, several men were thrown painfully from their mounts.

Eventually, by 3.30 p.m., all was ready. A total of 275 officers and men rode out westwards. Another forty-three were left behind at Lower Fort Garry and Dufferin or sent to the proposed new headquarters at Fort Ellice. Alongside French was the Assistant Commissioner, James F. Macleod. Care of the men and horses was in the hands of Dr John Kittson, his assistant Richard B.

Nevitt (who remained at Dufferin for a short time but caught up with the expedition after a few days) and the veterinary surgeon John L. Poett. Inspector William D. Jarvis led A Division, the hastily promoted Brisebois was in charge of B; C was led by Inspector William Winder, D by Inspector James Walsh, E by the American, Inspector Jacob E. Carvell, and F (for the first day only) by Inspector Theodore Richer.

The police took with them 310 horses, 142 draught oxen, 93 cattle for slaughter, 114 Red River carts with twenty *métis* drivers, 73 wagons, 2 nine-pounder muzzle-loading field guns, 2 brass mortars, several mowing machines for hay-cutting, portable forges and field kitchens. The column was as noisy as it was impressive, mainly because of the Red River carts. This *métis* invention was made entirely of wood and was durable, adaptable, flexible and easy to repair. Its two high wheels made it difficult to overturn and it could carry up to 1000 lb of goods on its box-like platform. It was ideally suited to prairie conditions, the most efficient method of transport on the plains until the arrival of the railway in the 1880s. The axle was merely a roughly squared tree-trunk bound with buffalo hide – grease could not be used since it would have collected dust and eventually frozen the hubs to the axles – and the noise made as hubs rubbed on axles was an ear-stabbing screech, 'as if a thousand fingernails were drawn across a thousand panes of glass' according to one writer. One policeman called the cart 'a wondrous, rheumatic vehicle'.

French ordered what was known as a 'Hudson's Bay start' that day; the force travelled only two miles before making camp, a measure designed to check that everything was working satisfactorily, all goods were correctly loaded and nothing had been forgotten. The Commissioner sent back to Dufferin two wagon loads of 'luxury articles' such as syrup, which he thought could be dispensed with, and two loads of oats were sent to replace them.

Next morning there was more trouble for the harassed Commissioner. Several officers were unhappy about his use of quality bloodstock as cart horses, and when a team bolted after being harnessed to a mowing machine a row broke out between French and Inspector Theodore Richer. It ended with Richer shouting at his commander, 'If you don't put me under arrest you are no gentleman'. French offered to retain Richer if he apologised, but he refused. According to d'Artigue, the arrest of Richer was a surprise 'as this officer was known to be well backed by men of high standing in the government'. Richer returned to Dufferin muttering that he would make things hot for French back in Ottawa, and Sub-Inspector Leif Crozier, a twenty-eight-year-old Newry Irishman, was given command of Richer's F Division.

Because of straying oxen and stampeding horses, the next day's march did not start until the afternoon; by the time they had battled six miles through clouds of dust borne on a strong wind, three broken-down wagons had been abandoned and one horse had died. To complete the frustration, no water could be found ahead, so the column had to turn back two miles. Initially the route lay roughly along the line of march blazed by the Boundary Commission near the American frontier. On the night of 10 July another dozen men took advantage of the proximity of the United States to desert, turning their backs on the struggling column and their hot, dusty, thirsty colleagues.

On Sunday 12 July, the anniversary of the Battle of the Boyne, a start was made at 5 a.m. The French-Canadian sub-inspector, Sévère Gagnon, who sported a full beard almost to his waist and managed to balance his forage cap over his right ear without benefit of a chinstrap, noted drily in his diary: 'Orangemen Day. They are easily noticed, for they are all displaying yellow flowers on their hats or on the heads of their horses.' The column travelled only three hours before camping for the day at the foot of the Pembina Hills near good water. Gagnon commented that it was 'a day of rest, i.e. we worked as hard as usual but we did not travel; we did our washing, cleaned our kit, got our horses shod, greased our wagons etc. etc.'

Now, in hillier country, the going became tougher and the column was scattered over miles of country. The Irish constable

E. H. Maunsell, who was relegated to the job of cattle drover as punishment for falling asleep on guard, criticised French for his ignorance of the travelling capacity of cattle in thinking that they could keep up with mounted men. The supply wagons, too, began to fall behind and there was often no food for the exhausted men at the end of the day. The diary of Constable James Finlayson of B Division for 14 July read: 'Camped on the open plain near a swamp. No water, No wood. No supper. The [supply wagons] did not get in till after midnight, therefore no provisions.' Two days later his diary told of 'one flapjack per man for breakfast, lucky to get that. Supper the same as I had for dinner. Namely nothing! Hunger and thirst is two of the worst complaints among the boys.'

The cattle drover, Maunsell, was once without food for thirty-six hours until his herd managed to catch up with a camp of half-breed drivers some four miles behind the main column. Sub-Inspector Cecil Denny (who quickly became known as Texas Jack among the men) was in charge of the rear guard on 18 July and complained

What a day I had of it. Some twenty sick horses and fifteen or twenty horse and ox teams had to be gotten along. I had to camp out the night without shelter or food and in a pouring rain, which came pretty hard on all of us.

One young constable, Pierre Lucas, became so terrified when his exhausted horse lagged far behind the column that he shot it, made his way into camp on foot and breathlessly explained that he had been forced to abandon the animal when he was attacked by a Sioux war party. The Commissioner commented, 'I do not believe his statement', but he took no action.

Progress was painfully slow, fifteen or twenty miles being considered good going. Hordes of mosquitoes left the flanks of the animals and faces of the men streaked with blood. To keep them at bay, the police dangled nets over their helmets and down to their shoulders. In the anxiety to find water, the tents were often

63

pitched near swamps, inviting even heavier mosquito bombardment. The Montreal artist-journalist Henri Julien described the attacks as

> Simply dreadful. Your eyes, your nose, your ears are invaded. If you open your mouth to curse at them they troop into it. They insinuate themselves under your clothes, down your shirt collar, up your sleeve cuffs, between the buttons of your shirt bosom. ... You can brush them off your coat sleeves in layers. ... Often in the evening when our tents were pitched and we went down to the nearest brook or rivulet to water our horses, hoping that this was to be our last work before turning in for a sweet night's rest, the mosquitoes would rise in columns out of the spongy soil under our feet and begin a regular battle against us. Our horses would rear, pitch and kick. We would be covered with scratches and blood. Our only refuge was to run our horses to their pickets, then hasten to throw ourselves on the ground and cover ourselves up in blankets.

To plunge the sufferers into deeper misery a swarm of grasshoppers descended on the camp one day, devouring everything and even stripping the paint from the wagons. They were also drenched by occasional thunderstorms, and once showered with hailstones the size of walnuts.

But the heaviest setback was the blow to their dignity when French ordered them to take turns driving the ox teams. According to the young bugler Fred Bagley, 'This was the most severe jolt Romance had been dealt since we left Toronto', although the duty did have its benefits, since the carts often contained bulk supplies of food and 'it was sometimes possible for us cart drivers by careful selection to get enough food for a substantial meal'. D'Artigue considered it 'more than discouraging' to see uniformed police driving oxen with sticks and wondered, 'What military commander who respects his men would have placed them on the same footing as those who work for mercenary motives?' D'Artigue was one of the unfortunates placed in charge of an ox team and, like the others, he fell miles behind the main column. One night he got into camp just before midnight and as he wearily approached

1. Commissioner James
Macleod

2. Sir John A. Macdonald

3. Superintendent James
Walsh

4. Commissioner George
French

5. The march west in 1874 as portrayed by Henri Julien for
The Canadian Illustrated News:
(*above*) the force in sight of the Sweetgrass Hills
(*below*) entertainment under canvas

a sentry called out, 'Who goes there?' 'A famished man,' replied d'Artigue. The sentry allowed him to pass without further explanation.

However, d'Artigue, known as The Professor among his comrades because of his previous occupation, was swift to adjust himself to the food shortage, catching frogs in the swamps with a whip and sharing the feast with some initially dubious friends. One of them, Maunsell, said, 'I soon lost my prejudice against the French for eating frogs.'

Despite all the discomforts, French was still able to report in his official diary that there was great rivalry between the divisions to see who could get away from camp first in the morning. Eventually, on 24 July, sixteen days and 270 miles from Dufferin, the expedition staggered to its first main objective, an outcrop of wind-eroded rocks on the banks of the Souris River known as La Roche Percée, venerated by generations of Indians and covered in animal carvings. 'The very place for a picnic' according to Sub-Inspector Gagnon. Here French set up a rest camp for his bedraggled column. D'Artigue reported

> What a change since our departure from Dufferin.... On our arrival at Roche Percée the column resembled a routed army corps. For a distance of several miles the road was strewn with broken carts and horses and oxen overcome with hunger and fatigue. Was it in this manner that the Canadian government had intended the Mounted Police to be managed and directed? Certainly not. Could Colonel French have done better than he did? Certainly yes.

Cecil Denny considered that 'prospects for a successful termination to the journey began to look none too rosy', and French shared his opinion. So he decided to split the column, taking with the main body only what was necessary and sending what became known as 'the barnyard contingent' of cattle, weak horses and surplus wagons under Inspector Jarvis of A Division directly to Edmonton, 900 miles to the north-west. Jarvis had to give up most of his best horses and men in exchange for the weakest and most

65

inexperienced constables and a motley collection of sick horses, cattle, ox-carts and wagons.

On Sunday 26 July at Roche Percée the first church service was held since departure from Dufferin. French took the Church of England party, and the senior Catholic, Presbyterian and Methodist officers were in charge of their denominations. 'Some held their meeting on the hills, others in the valley,' wrote d'Artigue. 'It was a grand sight to see 300 men standing in the wilderness several hundred miles from civilisation giving thanks in different manners and offering prayers to their Creator.' Gagnon merely noted that the Catholics sang the *Ave Maria Stellis* 'rather badly', while French confessed he was 'much pleased to hear many of the men singing hymns in the afternoon and evening; unfortunately the language of a great many is by no means Scriptural'.

At Roche Percée Asst Surgeon Nevitt caught up with the force, bringing letters and news from Dufferin. He told French that reports had appeared in American newspapers of the police column's extermination by Indians, and that prayers had been said in churches throughout eastern Canada for their safety.

Both horses and men benefited greatly from the four-day rest by the Souris River, and there were songs and music to enliven the evenings around the camp fires. Sub-Constable Bill Latimer, fully recovered from the ghastly scalp-wound sustained in the stampede at Dufferin, led the tunes on a fife, accompanied by Constable Frank Parks on a drum improvised from a tin dish and tent pegs. The favourite songs were 'Home, Sweet Home' and 'God Save the Queen' which was paraphrased by a cheerful Irishman, Constable Frank Norman

> Confound their politics
> Frustrate their knavish tricks
> Get us out of this damned fix
> God save all here.

On 29 July French's five divisions moved off again, leaving behind

Jarvis and his decimated A Division. Sam Steele, who stayed with Jarvis to participate in the epic march to Edmonton, admitted 'We were a disconsolate lot when we saw the force depart.'

Now French turned north-west, away from the Boundary Commission's marked trail. Though the country was rougher the weather, mercifully, was cooler; indeed, frost was beginning to settle on the tents at night. Still they were plagued by mosquitoes at every water hole, and by the eternal dust and wind. Henri Julien noted, 'Our skin felt as if on fire from the combined effects of hot winds, dust and mosquito bites. . . . The men looked hideous with their smutty faces. There is no use washing while on the march, which I am afraid was a great relief to many, who were not too fond of the water in any case.' When they got to the Dirt Hills the men had to help the horses to tow the cumbersome (and, as it was to transpire, worthless) nine-pounder guns up the inclines. Julien said of these guns, 'They were always in the way, retarded our march, took up the time of several men and the service of several good horses. . . . But I suppose they looked military and had therefore to be dragged along with us, as much for show as anything else.'

As they plodded on across the sun-beaten plains, the expedition began to run short of wood, water and food. By some extraordinary oversight water bottles had not been included in the equipment, and the drinking of alkaline water from the stagnant sloughs caused widespread dysentery; twenty-two reported sick on 2 August. Bugler Bagley's lips became so swollen and blistered that he was unable to produce a note. French wrote to his superiors in Ottawa

> If you saw the delight with which we hail the sight of a wet swamp you would be astonished, and if the relatives of some of the Ottawa boys saw their hopefuls standing in a swamp till enough water ran down over the soles of their boots to get a drink, they might not turn up their noses so much at Ottawa's turbid stream.

Sugar had disappeared, bread was strictly rationed and there was little fat or grease to be had. When one man found a tin of machine oil left behind by boundary surveyors he sprinkled a few drops on his food at every meal and refused to share it.

There was a flurry of excitement on 12 August when scouts reported a small Sioux camp ahead at a place called Old Wives Lake, and a formal 'pow-wow' was arranged for the following morning. The police were eagerly looking forward to their first sight of the noble red man. The disappointment was immense. The Indians were a dejected and verminous bunch, with dangling, matted hair and wrapped in filthy blankets. 'Sooty Sons of the Plains' they were dubbed by Dr Kittson, and Constable E. H. Maunsell said, 'No imagination could manufacture a Hiawatha or Minnehaha of such material.' Henri Julien described the arrival in the police camp of the group, about thirty men, women and children:

> They came marching in line, their wives behind, chanting something in a dirge-like monotonous tone, almost drowned in the clarion tones of our trumpets belching forth glad sounds of welcome. They were conducted to a kind of pavilion made by putting two large square tents into one. We at first met them with closed lips as we did not know what to say. The usual How-do-you-do would have sounded ridiculous and the Happy-to-see-you would have been a lie on our lips, as they were a most wretched lot. However, we soon got into the 'How' of our red brothers.

The police elbowed each other outside the doorway of the tent, trying to get a glimpse of what was going on inside, where the traditional smoking of a pipe was followed by a conference and the distribution of gifts. French, trying to impress the Sioux, succeeded only in amusing them when he told them that the Great White Mother whom he served 'had red children, white children and black children'.

Julien described the Indian men as 'dirty and ugly, low browed, dull eyed and brutish in appearance'. Nor did he think much of their womenfolk, who 'did not possess a single feminine grace.

The man must be hard up indeed who takes such for wife. And still, like their sisters the world over, these women put on airs. They cast sheep's eyes at you, and squint to see whether you are admiring them.'

However, the Indians managed to leave a lasting impression on their hosts in the form of fleas and lice. 'Within a week every man, from the Colonel down, was infested,' wrote Maunsell. There was much suffering and cursing until the force was paraded naked and each policeman rubbed down with juniper oil. They also learned from their half-breed drivers how to remove the lice from their clothing by placing them on ant hills. Commented Maunsell, 'It was amusing when we stopped for dinner to see the men running over the prairie seeking ant hills'.

French camped several days near Old Wives Lake after he had heard that there was a surplus supply of oats available at the Boundary Commission depot at Wood Mountain, forty miles south of them. Assistant Commissioner Macleod took a convoy of wagons to the depot and brought back 15,000 lb of oats, as well as the promise of delivery of another 20,000 lb to the 'Cripple Camp' which French had decided to set up in the area, where there was good grass, water and food. Here he left behind fourteen wagons, twenty-eight of the poorest horses, seven sick men and some footsore cattle, as well as provisions for the section of his force which would be returning to the area on its way back to headquarters in the autumn. Then as quickly as possible ('I grudged the loss of a day, even an hour') French pushed his expedition west again. Free of the encumbrance of most of the cattle and the worst of the horses, the column briefly made brisk time and on 24 August they sighted the Cypress Hills, scene of the massacre of Little Soldier's Assiniboines the previous year. Here they found plentiful signs of buffalo, but no actual animals. However, some of their marksmen managed to kill several antelope and deer and the marchers enjoyed their first fresh meat since leaving Dufferin, 600 miles to the east. There were other luxuries. 'Here we got better water and gorged ourselves on berries,' said

Maunsell. The police were also warned to watch out for possible Indian raiding parties and French ordered them to travel at all times in their scarlet tunics for easy identification and to wear ammunition belts.

As they left the Cypress Hills behind, heading for what they thought was the last lap towards Fort Whoop-Up, food soon began to run short again and travelling was made doubly miserable because the weather had at last broken and many of the horses were too exhausted to be ridden. Constable James Finlayson noted in his diary, 'Raining again this morning. Mud sticks to our feet so that we are scarcely able to lift them,' and the following day: 'The last ration of bacon served out today.' But relief was near at hand – meat on the hoof. On 2 September, amid great excitement, the first buffalo were sighted. Cecil Denny described it:

> Most of us joined in the hunt; guns popped in every direction. I remember seeing one man riding alongside an old bull, in his excitement beating him with the butt of his empty gun until someone came to his assistance and brought down the game.

Five buffalo were killed, one of them by Colonel French which, when dressed, produced 953 lb of meat. Each policeman was issued with 2 lb but the anticipated feast was a disappointment; when fried, the meat – from tough old bulls – defied their teeth. But the police were now into the last stronghold of the buffalo. Denny wrote 'Many times we killed them from the saddle without going out of the line of march'. The police soon became adept at searching out young, fat cows which provided the best meat.

Maunsell commented on their new diet: 'For some weeks our only food was buffalo. I cannot congratulate our cooks on the scientific manner in which they prepared it. They would just cut it into chunks and boil it. . . . Straight boiled meat soon palled on the palate. We were all attacked with diarrhoea, which greatly weakened us.'

Though the buffalo herds produced badly needed food they

70

also swept away every blade of vegetation and trampled the water holes into muddy morasses. Into this foul mixture of urine and mud the police dipped their cans, boiled the evil-smelling liquid, added tea and attempted to drink it. As Maunsell pointed out, 'When one is without water for perhaps twenty-four hours one will drink almost anything.' Denny wrote later, 'The farther west we travelled the more plentiful became the buffalo. There were places where, as far as the eye could reach, untold thousands were in sight, the country black with them.'

The first known white man to see the buffalo was the Spanish *conquistador* Francisco Vásquez Coronado, who rode into what is now Texas from Mexico in 1541. Along a valley floor in front of him and stretching to the horizon was an unbroken mass of animals. It was estimated that at one time sixty million of them roamed the North American continent, but even this figure seems conservative. The Indians had been hunting them for hundreds of years, often with horrifyingly wasteful methods, such as stampeding huge herds into ravines or driving hundreds into corrals and slaughtering them all, young or old, useful or useless. But they had made little impression on the buffalo population until the white man came west with his more sophisticated methods of extermination. In the eastern United States buffalo tongues became prized as delicacies and buffalo robes were sought as coats. American politicians and generals encouraged the indiscriminate slaughter, since it would speed the end of the Indian, too. The herds began to shrink.

After travelling the prairies in 1860 the Earl of Southesk wrote about 'immense herds stringing across the whole face of the country' and he compared the noise they made to the booming of a distant ocean. This description was echoed by Captain John Palliser: 'We were now more than two miles from the buffalo, who were not in sight. They were in such numbers that their peculiar grunts sounded like the roar of distant rapids in a large river, and causing a vibration also something like a trembling in the ground.' But Southesk, whose path across the plains was strewn with skulls and other buffalo remains, noted, 'They are now rapidly disappearing everywhere; what will be the fate of the Indians when this, their chief support, fails it is painful to imagine. Large as were the herds I saw, they were nothing to what I have heard or read of.' Yet as late as 1873 one party of hunters travelling south from the Cypress Hills and covering up to thirty miles a day took a week to ride through one grazing herd.

By now the weather was turning decidedly chilly, horses were dying daily, food and tempers were short. French suspected that the half-breed hired to guide them to Fort Whoop-Up was deliberately sending them the wrong way (though he was merely following an erroneous map given to him by the police). French grumbled, 'He is the greatest liar I have ever met.'

A series of extracts from the diary of Constable James Finlayson shows the perilous position of the expedition:

> 9 September: Last night it was very cold and eight horses died. We called the place Dead Horse Camp.
> 10 September: B Troop refused to leave camp until they had had breakfast. . . . The reason was very good, namely we had no dinner or supper yesterday. The weather getting very cold, I have put on drawers.
> 11 September: We are lost on the prairie. No one knows where we are . . . horses and oxen dying fast, provisions getting scarce, things looks very dark.

And French's diary for 10 September noted

> I had a blanket taken from every officer and man last night so that each horse was covered and protected from the cold rain and wind. I began to feel very much alarmed for the safety of the Force. If a few hours' cold rain kills off a number of horses what would be the effect of a 24-hour snowstorm?

That same day the creaking column reached the junction of the Bow and South Saskatchewan rivers, where Colonel Robertson-Ross's report had wrongly placed the site of Fort Whoop-Up (in fact it was seventy-five miles away, at the junction of the Bow and St. Mary's rivers). The police halted, lost and bewildered, though they were in fact only a few miles from the heavily travelled Whoop-Up trail running from Fort Benton into Canada. Three dilapidated, roofless log huts were the only sign of man's presence in the area where they had expected to find a fort bristling with cannons and heavily armed desperadoes; the luxuriant pasturage they had been told to expect was non-existent, too. The ground was parched and poor; there was not a tree in sight. They were 800 miles from Dufferin, the weather was steadily deteriorating and French urgently needed to find a camping area with grass, wood and water where horses and men could rest. He sent out two scouting parties along the Bow and South Saskatchewan rivers but they returned with the gloomy news that the country they had explored was even more desolate. So it was decided to head eighty miles south to an area known as the Sweet Grass Hills, near the American border.

Painfully the column readied itself for another march. In the first thirty-six hours nine horses died, paralysed by cold and hunger. Maunsell wrote, 'This march had all the appearance of a retreat. . . . It was well for us that the Indians did not prove hostile. None of us would have returned.' They took five days to reach the Sweet Grass Hills, whose peaks were already dusted with the first snow of the season. Bugler Fred Bagley was one of the few to complete the march in style. He had taken off his boots to massage his blistered and bleeding feet and could not get them back on. So Inspector James Walker, whom Bagley described as 'a handsome giant of a man' carried the youngster the rest of the way on his back.

The weary contingent settled down gratefully in more comfortable surroundings, but they were almost as pathetic a bunch as their horses. According to the veterinary surgeon John Poett, the condition of the horses when they got to Sweet Grass camp 'was a sight that will not soon be forgotten'. As for the men, according to Bagley 'A glance around the camp would reveal very little to remind us of the brilliant parade of the Force at Dufferin a few months ago. The sentry in front of the Commissioner's quarters had gunny sacking wrapped around his feet, his rags of clothing fluttering in the breeze.' Bagley felt the police looked like the popular image of the outlaws they were supposed to be chasing, and described the condition of his comrades as 'forlorn and wretched'. When Constable James Finlayson decided to wash his uniform he had to shiver in his underclothes and shirt until it was dry. His diary complained: 'If the people of Canada were to see us now, with bare feet, not one half-clothed, picking up fragments left by the American troops and hunting buffalo for meat, I wonder what they would say of Colonel French.'

Colonel French had no time to wonder. He decided to strike out at once for the American town of Fort Benton to pick up badly needed supplies and equally urgently required news. With a small party and empty wagons, French and Macleod reached Benton, eighty miles away, in three days although for much of the time they were travelling through another vast buffalo-herd, estimated at 80,000 animals. French's first task was to contact Ottawa by telegraph, to learn that in his absence *en route* the site of the police's winter headquarters had been changed from Fort Ellice to the more distant Swan River, near Fort Pelly and more than 250 miles north-west of Winnipeg, where barracks were under construction.

French decided to split the column once more, leaving the 150 men of B, C and F divisions under Macleod (whom he described as 'a capital fellow, my right hand') to find Whoop-Up and build their own fort nearby, while he led the other divisions, D and E, all the way back to Manitoba. Fresh horses, warm clothing and wagon loads of supplies were bought on credit from the Fort Benton merchants, who also promised to help the police find Fort Whoop-Up, though some of them had active business interests in that place. Leaving Macleod in Fort Benton French hurried back into Canada with some of the winter clothing and food for his eastward-bound column. The two men were never to meet again.

Now that he was back in civilisation, or at least its approximation as represented by Fort Benton, Macleod was quickly able to plan the final push towards that seemingly unattainable goal, Fort Whoop-Up. While organising his supply lines with the leading Benton trader, I. G. Baker, Macleod sent word for the camp at Sweet Grass Hills to be moved westward along the border to await his arrival. After four days' march the police struck the well-beaten Whoop-Up trail and pitched their tents along the nearby Milk River to await Macleod. But the first man to reach them was an enterprising Fort Benton merchant, John Glenn, who loaded a wagon with sugar, flour, syrup and canned fruit, headed for the police camp and sold out in minutes to the luxury-starved men.

To guide Macleod and his force to Whoop-Up, I. G. Baker lent him the services of a short, bow-legged, monosyllabic half-breed scout named Jerry Potts. Thus was forged a bond between Potts and the Mounted Police which was to last twenty-two years. Potts's father, Andrew R. Potts, was an Edinburgh Scot who had worked as a clerk for the American Fur Company at Fort Mac-kenzie on the Missouri river; his mother was a Blood Indian, Crooked Back. When he was only a year old Potts lost his father, murdered by an Indian at Fort Mackenzie, and as he grew up he divided his time between Indian camps and white settlements. He fought with Blackfoot, Blood and Peigan war parties, and worked at the whiskey forts, where he developed an ardent and life-long addiction to liquor. (One police corporal said that Potts had 'an unquenchable thirst which a camel might have envied. He drank whiskey when he could get it. If he could not get it he would take Jamaica ginger, or essence of lemon, or Perry Davis' painkiller, or even red ink.')

Potts was hired at a salary of ninety dollars a month as guide and interpreter, but it was as a guide that he served the police so well for so many years. As for the interpreting part of his duties, the word laconic might have been invented especially for Jerry Potts. After one meeting between some Blackfoot and the police, Potts was asked to interpret the lengthy speech of a chief. He shrugged his shoulders and muttered, 'Dey damn glad you're here'. And on the march north from Fort Benton to Whoop-Up, as Macleod's group approached a hill Potts was asked, 'What's beyond that hill?' 'Nudder hill' was the reply. One policeman said of him, 'The chief difficulty about his interpretations was that after he had interpreted from the Blackfoot into the English language you weren't much further ahead, for his English was weird – particularly if he had had a few jolts of one of his favourite toddies.' But Potts was fondly looked upon by the Mounted Police and when he died in 1896 of cancer of the throat, aggravated by prolonged drinking, he was buried with full military honours and a police guard fired three volleys over his grave.

Potts's value was immediately demonstrated when Macleod rejoined B, C and F Divisions at Milk River. On the first day of the renewed march to Whoop-Up, Potts rode ahead of the column and when the others caught up with him at midday the guide had selected a stopping-place and killed and dressed a fat buffalo cow ready for the policemen's lunch. The next day Potts led them to the best springs they had drunk from since leaving Dufferin.

Eventually, on 9 October, near the Porcupine Hills and where the smaller St Mary's river swept to its junction with the Bow, Macleod and his men topped a rise and looked down on Fort Whoop-Up. The field guns and mortars, dragged from Dufferin at such terrible cost in horseflesh, were unlimbered and trained on the fort, and Macleod and Potts rode forward, dismounted and hammered on the main gate. It was opened by a tall, goatee-bearded American, Dave Akers, who disconcerted Macleod by inviting him to dinner. So, instead of the expected fight, the police sat down to eat fresh vegetables provided from a flourishing garden inside the fort. Akers explained that his partners were 'away on business'. In reality they had received ample warning of the arrival of the Mounted Police and had prudently removed themselves and their liquor elsewhere.

Macleod was so impressed by the solid construction of Whoop-Up that he tried to buy it as a ready built winter headquarters for his detachment. But Akers refused and, with the need for shelter becoming daily more urgent, Jerry Potts led the column twenty-eight miles to a fine site in a broad loop of the Old Man's (or Oldman) River. There was ample pasture for the horses, groves of cottonwood trees provided timber for building, there was water and wild game in abundance in the area, and it was centrally situated for supervision of the trading-trail that ran northwards from the United States. Here Macleod planned to erect with all possible speed the Force's first fort in the West. By unanimous wish of his officers and men, it was to be named after Macleod. Work began immediately. Twelve-foot logs placed upright in trenches three feet deep served both as the stockade and the outer walls of the buildings in the 200-foot-square fort. All the buildings faced inward; on the east side were the men's quarters and saddle room; on the west, officers' quarters and orderly room; the north side housed stables, blacksmith's shop and another saddle area, and inside the south wall were the stores, hospital, guard-room and latrines. The roofs were flat, of interwoven poles covered with several inches of earth. The floors, too, were of bare earth, and running across the officers' mess could be plainly seen the indentation of a buffalo trail. Windows and doors were hauled in from Fort Benton by contractors in 'bull trains', heavy wagons drawn by oxen.

Macleod's main concern when a heavy snowstorm blanketed them at the end of October was for the ailing horses. They were herded in the shelter of woods, wrapped in blankets and fed liberally on oats and corn. He wrote to French, 'I have made up my mind that not a single log of men's quarters shall be laid till the horses are provided for, as well as a few sick men. The men's quarters will then be proceeded with, and then the officers'.' Gradually the little fortress took shape. By the beginning of December everybody was out of tents and under a roof, though some were in cramped conditions (the officers set up home in a kitchen until their rooms were finished). By the middle of the month the work was complete and Macleod was able to write, 'All ranks are as comfortable as could be wished.'

Private enterprise quickly followed in the police's wake. The Fort Benton firm of I. G. Baker & Company, which had negotiated a year's contract to supply the police, promptly built a store alongside Fort Macleod. According to Sub-Inspector Cecil Denny it was

> pretty well filled up with all sorts of goods, such as canned fruits etc. and a good thing they made out of it with fruit at one dollar per can and everything else in proportion. As we had received no pay up to this time it was all credit, but after the long march on short rations no price was begrudged for luxuries.

While the construction work was going on, Macleod's men struck their first blow at the illegal liquor traffic. A minor Indian chief, Three Bulls, reported that he had exchanged two of his ponies for two gallons of firewater supplied by a negro named William Bond who was trading at Pine Coulee, about fifty miles north of Fort Macleod. Three Bulls guided a ten-man detachment under Inspector Crozier to the place. Two days later they were back with Bond and four other men, including Harry 'Kamoose' Taylor, a 'squaw man' and general Western character ('kamoose' being an Indian word for 'woman-stealer', a title Taylor earned when, his offer of dowry for the squaw he desired being refused, he crept into an Indian camp one night disguised as a dog and abducted her). The patrol also brought back two wagons laden with alcohol, sixteen horses, rifles and revolvers and a pile of buffalo robes. All this property was confiscated, the liquor was spilled and the traders were heavily fined – in some cases $200. Being unable to pay they were all put in custody until a Fort Benton merchant named J. D. Weatherwax arrived to pay for the release of all but the unfortunate Bond.

Soon, however, it was the turn of Weatherwax himself to be arrested. A patrol commanded by Sub-Inspector Cecil Denny and guided by an Indian informant trekked from Fort Macleod in bitter cold to an isolated trading cabin where they found Weatherwax ('We thought him well named,' wrote the Rev. John

McDougall, 'cool, calculating, polished, using the finest of English, crafty') and another man known as Diamond R. Brown. The police also uncovered a hoard of liquor and hundreds of valuable robes and furs. When Macleod fined the pair $240 each, confiscated their furs and property and ordered the liquor destroyed, Weatherwax threatened to 'make the wires to Washington hum'. Unimpressed, the Assistant Commissioner put him in the guardroom, and the Fort Benton merchant spent a week cutting wood and mucking out stables until his fine was paid.

The incident provoked an outburst in the *Fort Benton Record*, edited by John J. Healy, who had turned to journalism after his own whiskey enterprise at Whoop-Up had been terminated by the Mounted Police: 'We knew from experience that wherever the English flag floats might is right, but we had no idea that the persons and property of American citizens would be trifled with.'

After the arrests Macleod wrote off smugly to Ottawa, 'I am happy to be able to report *the complete stoppage of the whiskey trade throughout the whole of this section of the country*, and that the drunken riots, which in former years were almost of a daily occurrence, are now entirely at an end.' But within a month Macleod was having to confess that Bond, the police's first prisoner, had escaped. He made a run for it when being transferred from one building to another at the fort and though the sentry fired at him he got clean away. The constable responsible was reduced in rank; the rest of his colleagues sat in their primitive quarters huddled around stoves and wondering what Christmas and the New Year of 1875 had in store for them.

Meanwhile, nearly 300 miles to the north of Fort Macleod, Inspector William Jarvis and his 'barnyard contingent' of A Division had staggered into the Hudson's Bay Company post at Edmonton at the end of an astonishing march in which they covered 900 miles in 88 days, including rest stops. When the division was left behind at Roche Percée by the rest of French's expedition towards the end of July, both officers and men were downcast.

'They have taken all our best horses,' grumbled the French-Canadian inspector, Sévère Gagnon, noting that the animals his command had been given in exchange were 'nearly all sick, the refuse of the other troops'. And when Jarvis set off on 1 August he had only three other officers with him (Inspector Albert Shurtliff and Quartermaster Charles Nicolle – who were travelling with him only as far as Fort Ellice, 150 miles away – and Gagnon), twenty-seven other ranks, a dozen half-breed drivers and a guide to herd along fifty-seven ox carts, twenty-six wagons, nearly a hundred cows and calves, sixty-three oxen and sixty horses in varying stages of decrepitude. But there was one compensation. The route, though long, was frequently used by traders and trappers, and there were rest and supply halts available at the Hudson's Bay posts of Fort Ellice (which was still planned, at this stage, as the Force's winter headquarters), Carlton and Victoria. Though they had to cope with the vagaries of the weather as well as the travelling farmyard, most of the men shared the opinion of Jean d'Artigue about being away from French and his main column:

> Jarvis was as fond of short marches as French was of long ones, and he was right, for the proverb 'slow but sure' is always the safest to follow in long marches. Since we were detached from the main column we were living together like a family. No more of this quasi-discipline. We performed our duties not only for our country's sake but to please our commander. If Jarvis had asked us to follow him, even to the North Pole, not one of us would have refused.

At times it must have seemed as if they *were* heading for the North Pole as they plodded on day after day through strength-sapping heat, heavy rain or thunderstorms. Fort Ellice, on the Assiniboine River, was reached on 12 August and after resting the animals for a week Jarvis set out again to cover the remaining 750 miles, leaving behind Inspector Shurtliff, Quartermaster Nicolle, several of his constables and some wagons and weak animals.

The weather variations were alarming. On 24 August, Gagnon's diary recorded 'Very warm'; nine days later, 'There was ice in the pails this morning.' Though water was occasionally scarce, game was plentiful and a regular supply of ducks, geese, prairie chickens and the occasional skunk varied the monotonous diet. Once, Constable Carr brought down eleven geese with one shot. By mid-September there were regular heavy frosts and occasional snow. The horses began to fail at an alarming rate, and when they lay down to rest they became so stiff that they had to be raised with poles passed underneath their bodies and their joints had to be rubbed before they could move off. D'Artigue reported, 'By October . . . the horses were but living skeletons.' And by the time the column reached Fort Victoria on 19 October (where all the surviving cattle and most of the oxen were left behind) they were dying at the rate of one a day.

The last seventy miles from Victoria to Edmonton were the most nightmarish of all. Sam Steele described the final stage:

> Our progress was slow and the going very difficult. Our loose horses often fell, one fine animal being lifted bodily by Carr and myself at least a dozen times by means of a pole. The other horses had to be helped along in the same manner. . . . The trail was worse than any we had encountered. It was knee-deep in black mud, sloughs crossed it every few hundred yards, and the wagons had to be unloaded and dragged through them by hand. Many small ponds covered with a thin coating of ice lined the sides of the trail, and gave us much trouble while we were engaged in unloading the wagons. The poor animals, crazed with thirst and feverish because of their privations, would rush to the ponds to drink, often falling and having to be dragged out with ropes. . . . It mattered not how often they were watered, the same performance had to be gone through time after time.

For the final twelve miles horses were carried bodily along on poles and several men walked alongside their horses supporting them with one arm at the head and the other at the shoulder to keep the pathetic creatures on their legs; in this manner A

Division of the North West Mounted Police entered the gates of Fort Edmonton.

Inspector Jarvis commented on the amazing journey, 'I wonder how we ever accomplished it with weak horses, little or no pasture, and for the last 500 miles with no grain, and the latter part over roads impossible until we made them.' And he said of the horses – most of which died during the winter of their experiences on the trail – 'Had they been my own property I should have killed them, as they were mere skeletons.'

And so the second western detachment of the police settled down for what proved to be a sedentary winter in Edmonton. No one could begrudge them their rest.

The two divisions, D and E, which were to return with the Commissioner to winter at the new headquarters at Swan River, ten miles from Fort Pelly, enjoyed indian-summer weather for the early stages of their march eastwards along the Boundary Commission's route from the Sweet Grass Hills in October. With freshly purchased horses and plentiful supplies – and free of the encumbrance of cannons and cattle – they averaged twenty-five miles a day, enough to assuage even the anxious French. The men and horses left behind at Cripple Camp near Old Wives Lake in August were collected on the way home; a cheerful call was made at Qu'Appelle trading post, where Henri Julien of *Canadian Illustrated News* left the column to make his way back to Montreal. At last there was a plentiful supply of wood, causing French to note, 'The men ... could not build their camp fires big enough; whole trees were chopped down and placed on the fires, as if to make up in some measure for the deficiency in fuel for the last thousand miles we had marched.'

On 21 October the Commissioner rode ahead of his column, eager to see the fine new headquarters put up for the police by the Department of Public Works. What he saw horrified him: the barracks – still incomplete – were being erected on top of a snake-infested, treeless hill covered with massive granite boulders.

Instead of being grouped in a fort-like pattern the buildings were strung out in a line a thousand feet long, fully exposed to the north wind which was already beginning to search and bite at the flesh. A massive prairie fire, which was still raging in the area, had burned the ground to within twenty feet of the barracks and half the hay cut for the winter use of the police had been lost in the blaze.

The Canadian government's choice of this God-forsaken spot for a police headquarters (because it was on the planned westward route of the Canadian Pacific Railway, though subsequently the railway went nowhere near it) came in for scathing press criticism. The Toronto *Globe* commented, 'Why such a spot was chosen no one seems to know. If the object was to pitch upon the most barren and uncongenial spot in the whole North West, the genius who recommended the location has been admirably successful, for there is scarcely cultivable land enough in this neighbourhood to make a garden patch.' And the *Manitoba Free Press* of Winnipeg wondered, 'Why [Swan River] should be selected as headquarters for the peelers does not at once strike a person. In fact, it don't strike a person after some thought.'

Undoubtedly the worst aspect of Swan River was its remoteness, both from the Canadian capital and the far west where the police presence was most needed. Fort Macleod, which had speedier contact with Ottawa via Fort Benton's telegraph line, would have been a far more sensible choice as headquarters.

Furious that this wretched place had been picked out for him without his agreement, French decided to leave only E Division, under Inspector Jacob Carvell, at Swan River and take D Division back with him to Winnipeg. The Commissioner had decided it was time to have words with the Ottawa politicians.

On the way, French met up with, and turned back to Winnipeg, a small group under the Paymaster, Inspector Dalrymple Clark, heading for the new headquarters. Among Clark's party was Constable William Parker, who had only got as far as Roche Percée on the march west in July before being sent back to

Dufferin suffering from typhoid. French's column, according to Parker

> was a wonderful sight, straggled out two or three miles, nearly every man walking, horses like lathes, swaying and wobbling from side to side and odd team horses every once in a while falling down. The men appeared rosy and in the best of health but oh what a sight! All virtually in rags, odd ones no hats and most of them no boots.

By 7 November, D Division was back in Winnipeg, having been away from Dufferin a day under four months and having covered in that time 1800 miles. The experience of Inspector James Walker was probably typical of the whole division. On the trip he marched the soles off two pairs of boots and wore out half a dozen pairs of moccasins.

Despite the heavy wastage of horses, no policeman had lost his life on the march, though two had died of typhoid at Dufferin. French was extremely proud of his men – and paid them a sincere tribute in his official report:

> Tied down by no stringent rules or articles of war, but only by the silken cord of a civil contract, these men by their conduct gave little cause of complaint. . . . Disobedience of orders was very rare. Day after day on the march, night after night on picquet or guard, and working at high pressure during four months from daylight until dark, and too frequently after dark, with little rest, not even on the day sacred to rest, the Force ever pushed onward, delighted when occasionally a pure spring was met with; there was still no complaint when salt water or the refuse of a mud hole was the only liquid available. And I have seen this whole Force obliged to drink liquid which when passed through a filter was still the colour of ink. . . . Of such a march, under such adverse circumstances, all true Canadians may well be proud.

Privately, French confessed, 'I was not sorry when it was all over.'

Chapter 5

MONOTONY AND MUTINY

By the end of 1874 the Mounted Police command was split into six parts. Easily the biggest and most important detachment was at Fort Macleod, with its garrison of ten officers and 140 men. There were another sixty at Dufferin, thirty-eight at Swan River, twenty-two at Edmonton, fifteen at Winnipeg and six at Fort Ellice.

At the fort which bore his name, James Macleod received a succession of Blackfoot, Blood and Peigan chiefs, entertaining them and issuing reassurances about the reasons for the police's appearance in their country. Most expressed pleasure at the protection they were now being afforded, and one old tribal leader told Macleod, 'Before you came the Indian crept along, now he is not afraid to walk erect.' Macleod in his turn considered them 'a very intelligent lot of men', particularly the chief who called on him on the first day of December. He was Crowfoot, chief of the Blackfoot Confederacy, a distinguished poet, orator, politician and warrior. Crowfoot appeared at the gates of Fort Macleod carrying an eagle's wing, symbol of the highest office in his tribe; and from this first meeting the two became good friends. It was Crowfoot who gave Macleod his Indian name, Stamix Otokan (Bull's Head), partly because of his shaggy beard and also because of the buffalo head which adorned his office. Eventually the buffalo-head symbol was made part of the police crest, together with the motto *Maintiens le Droit*, Maintain the Right.

But if the Indians were happy about the redcoats' presence, some of the police themselves were not so thrilled with the raw

85

life at Fort Macleod. A natural phenomenon known as the chinook, a warm, dry wind from the Pacific Ocean which raced through the clefts in the mountain barrier of the Rockies, was capable of lifting temperatures from twenty below zero to forty above in a matter of hours and softening the rigours of the western winter in the area around Fort Macleod. But it also played havoc with the earth roofs and floors of the barracks. The roofs leaked liquid mud – and occasionally collapsed – and oil-cloth sheets had to be strung permanently over beds to protect the occupants, while the floors were unhealthily damp. According to Sub-Inspector Cecil Denny, 'These combined miseries were enough to sap the morale of any body of men.'

The dissatisfaction came to a head on the Sunday before Christmas when Macleod ordered an extra fatigue parade to strengthen security at the fort after the escape of the whiskey trader, William Bond. Many of the men refused to answer the Fall-In bugle. The complaint of Constable William Knowles was typical: since his arrival at Fort Macleod he had not had a free Sunday, and had not even found enough spare time to wash his clothes. Furthermore, he was owed $125 in back pay and in order to live had to borrow money at five-per-cent interest from traders around the fort. In his forthright fashion, the Assistant Commissioner went from barrack to barrack discussing the problems. 'They all cheered me most heartily as I left each room,' he commented later. Macleod considered Knowles and a Sub-Constable Dunbar the chief malcontents, so Knowles was reduced in rank to sub-constable, while Dunbar 'a thoughtless young fellow' got a vigorous telling-off from Macleod in front of his room mates 'in the plainest and strongest English that I am capable of'. Thanks to Macleod's prompt and humane reaction the trouble blew over, but the early years of the Mounted Police were to be plagued by these minor mutinies.

The food, too, was plain and dull – buffalo meat, pork, beans, flapjacks and tea, with potatoes an expensive rarity – but at Christmas a special effort produced a memorable meal. The menu included turkey, freighted in from Fort Benton by the Baker Company, and plum pudding. The garrison sat down to eat under a motto erected by Macleod, 'Pioneers of a Glorious Future', though the Assistant Commissioner was forced to propose the toast to absent friends in cold water. But a so-called whiskey, mainly composed of raw alcohol and Jamaica ginger, was unofficially always available and in heavy demand in the barrack rooms at five dollars a bottle. This strong addiction to liquor among the members of a force whose main purpose was the strict enforcement of prohibition was a continuing problem for French and succeeding Commissioners; drinking was regarded by the men themselves as one of their few escapes from the tedium of life in an empty, undeveloped country.

At Dufferin, too, liquor was circulating at Christmas. William Parker wrote to his mother on Boxing Day: 'The boys kept up Christmas Eve with a vengeance. We drank to absent friends and relatives so often that I am ashamed to say I got a little tender in my feet, and in consequence was very sick all Christmas Day.'

The tiny detachment at Fort Edmonton prepared an elaborate feast and ball, to which every policeman contributed a month's pay and to which every settler and trader within a radius of 100 miles was invited. There was a supper and dance (partners being almost exclusively half-breed girls) on Christmas Eve, and on Christmas Day Inspector William Jarvis presided over a table laden with buffalo tongues and steaks, venison, prairie chicken, geese, plum-puddings and mince pies. Queen Victoria's health was drunk in tea.

The year of 1875 opened on a tragic note. Two constables named Frank Baxter and Thomas Wilson, who were part of the small garrison manning the former whiskey-trading post known as Fort Kipp, halfway between Fort Macleod and Whoop-Up, had spent Christmas with their colleagues in Macleod. On New Year's Eve they set off to ride back to Kipp in crisp, clear weather but were overtaken by a blizzard. Sub-Inspector Cecil Denny was also caught in the storm while on his way from Macleod to collect a sack of mail for the police which had been delivered from Fort Benton to Whoop-Up. 'I had difficulty keeping my eyelids from freezing together,' Denny wrote afterwards. 'I only saved myself by dismounting at intervals and running beside the horse.' Denny's animal led him through the driving snow to the safety of Fort Kipp but the horses belonging to Baxter and Wilson eventually came into the fort riderless. A search party found Baxter frozen stiff; Wilson was still alive but his arms, legs and most of his body were frozen. Mercifully, he died within hours.

At least the Fort Macleod detachment had the occasional benefit of the chinook's warming influence. At the Force's headquarters, Swan River, the winter was one of unrelieved cold and misery. The average temperature in January 1875 was −21°F. The cutting wind whistled through the cracks and chinks in the unseasoned lumber of the exposed buildings; there were gaping holes in roofs; snow lay unmelted on the beds and floors of the living-quarters. On 25 January the commanding officer at Swan River, Inspector Jacob Carvell, requested a supply of reliable thermometers for the barrack rooms: 'When the men go to bed I think they should know if it is cold enough to freeze their ears if left exposed, as was the case with Sub-Constable McCrum.'

A letter from Swan River, signed 'Rocky', was published that month in the *Manitoba Free Press*: 'Life is fearfully monotonous here and nights very long. We have to devise ways and means to while away the long hours. Performances on the horizontal bar and other gymnastic antics are resorted to, to while away the time.'

Dissatisfaction erupted in another mutiny, or 'buck' as the police called them, on the night of 17 February. Three Indians had brought in a sick squaw for treatment at Swan River, and afterwards they asked Inspector Albert Shurtliff, temporarily in command in the absence of Inspector Carvell, for something to eat. The camp cook, Sub-Constable William McCarthy, was ordered by Shurtliff to feed them but he refused, saying he wasn't the Indians' cook, and instead gave them tea, bread and syrup. He was fined $10 for insubordination and when Carvell returned to barracks the cook appealed so vigorously against the fine that he was arrested for being 'extremely rude and insolent'.

An angry group of McCarthy's friends stormed the guard-room and released him, explaining that the cook had only been trying to protect their meagre food supplies. Further, they claimed, McCarthy had received an 'unlawful order' from Inspector Shurtliff and therefore was not guilty of insubordination in refusing to carry it out. 'We feel sure that had Inspector Carvell been at home our cook would never have received any such order,' they wrote in a letter of justification afterwards, apologising for their rashness in releasing a prisoner from custody.

Carvell found the whole group of twelve (who included the young bugler Fred Bagley) guilty of insubordination. The N.C.O.s concerned were reduced to the ranks and every man was fined thirty days' pay. McCarthy, the original cause of the trouble, was released without further punishment and soon afterwards received the discharge for which he had applied before the incident. His replacement, a constable named Fitzgerald, was a man of considerably livelier humour. On April Fool's Day he served up some appetising-looking buns which, when opened, contained brown paper and bacon rinds. French wrote to the Deputy Minister of Justice, Hewitt Bernard, regretting that the Police Act as constituted provided for nothing more severe than a fine for 'such a gross act of insubordination' as McCarthy's.

Food, clothing and supplies were all short at Swan River that first winter. Carvell was told that no more candles could be sent to him; instead he was provided with moulds for the men to make their own. Sub-Inspector Edmond Frechette caused considerable amusement by attending morning stables clad in pyjamas, riding-boots, spurs, cloak and helmet, while Fred Bagley's 'uniform' that winter (all purchased from Hudson's Bay stock to replace his worn-out police-issue) consisted of a rough red shirt, moleskin trousers, heavy brogue boots and a disreputable helmet, all much too big for him. 'The glory has departed,' he noted sadly in his diary. Bagley managed to supplement his wardrobe by killing a deer, skinning it and making himself a pair of trousers after an amateurish attempt to smoke the hide. 'After I donned them, expecting to create a sensation (in which I was not disappointed) a view from the front showed the right leg black and the left one white – well, Bond Street, London, is a long way from here so who cares?'

By April the Swan River garrison were reduced to eating bread and pork three times a day. The meat was nearly all fat, and a revolting mixture of shades of yellow and green; it was nicknamed Rattlesnake Pork, and the many policemen who could not stomach it were faced with an unvarying diet of bread and tea. In June a board of officers inspected the pork and condemned it as unfit for consumption; no comment was made on the fact that it had been issued at Swan River nearly every day since E Division arrived there the previous October.

Complaints about living conditions were not confined to the constables. After voicing his dissatisfaction in front of some constables, Sub-Inspector H. J. N. LeCain was sent to Dufferin in March to be dismissed by French. He and his companion were caught in a snowstorm and got lost. One of their horses died, and the pair were so hungry that they ate the rotten carcase of an ox which had been lying in the open since the previous autumn. Eventually they got to Dufferin, virtually snowblind. French noted sympathetically, 'LeCain was in such a condition that to break to him the news of his services having been dispensed with was a duty, the implementation of which you can readily imagine.'

There was also a total lack of replacement clothing at Fort Macleod and no prospect of getting any until summer. Men appeared on parade or on guard in strange garbs, half-European and half-Indian, muffled in home-made caps and trousers and wrapped in buffalo coats or blankets, sometimes with raw buffalo-skin tied around their boots to hold them together. Cecil Denny recalled, 'On parade, in our uncouth garments, we were a motley crew.'

Nor had the men been paid since they left Dufferin the previous July. Traders caused unrest by telling the police of the high wages to be made in Montana mines, and there were several desertions across the border into the United States. At last Macleod sent a messenger to Fort Benton with a telegraph message for Ottawa pleading for funds to be forwarded and adding the warning, 'Eighteen have deserted for want of pay. If paid, many more will doubtless desert.'

The Canadian government arranged for a bank in Helena, Montana, to advance Macleod $30,000, so on 15 March the Assistant Commissioner set off on the 300-mile journey to that American town with Sub-Inspector Denny, Sub-Constables David Cochrane and Charles Ryan, and the half-breed Jerry Potts to collect the money. They took with them saddle and pack horses, blankets, tea, bacon and biscuits – but no tent. Near Milk River the party was enveloped in a fierce blizzard, with no wood available for fire-making. Potts showed them how to gain make-shift shelter from the howling wind by digging a deep hole into the river bank. There they crouched for thirty-six hours, waiting for the storm to blow itself out and eating biscuits and raw bacon. A buffalo herd also swarmed into the river bottom seeking protection from the weather, forcing the party to take two-hour shifts holding their horses' halter ropes to prevent the animals becoming lost among the buffalo. Deciding that to remain there longer would mean death by freezing, Potts led the party towards a place called Rocky Coulee, twenty-five miles distant, where he said there was better shelter. Denny wrote of their experience:

A more forlorn company it would be hard to imagine as we moved off on foot, dragging the horses through the storm. We had gone some way when we missed Ryan. I rode back to search for him and found him sitting in the snow holding his horse. 'What's the matter?' I asked. 'We'll never get through, Mr Denny. You go on, I can't make it any further.' I learned that he had endeavoured to march but was unable to do so, his buffalo skin breeches had frozen stiff and he was unable to bend his knees. I lifted him, helped to place him in the saddle and we rejoined the party.

When the storm abated they were challenged by an American Army patrol who mistook them for whiskey smugglers. Once they realised their mistake, the Americans led the group to Fort Shaw, where Denny had to be left behind to recover from snow blindness and a frostbitten foot, while the others pushed on to Helena, a rough frontier-town which had sprung into being after the discovery of gold nearby. Here Macleod collected the police pay and made preliminary arrangements for an extradition hearing against the men who were accused of the Cypress Hills massacre. In Helena he was also approached by some of his command who had deserted from Fort Macleod. Disillusioned with mining life they begged Macleod to take them back into the Force; under the authority of a telegram from the Deputy Minister of Justice, Hewitt Bernard, saying 'Encourage good men to return to duty' Macleod re-engaged seven of them and they suffered no punishment beyond loss of pay during the period of their desertion.

French, who had again not been consulted, was furious when he heard the news, and soon afterwards the Police Act was amended to provide punishment for deserters of up to six months' hard labour instead of suspension, dismissal or a fine. All that winter French had fought a running – and losing – battle with the Ottawa politicians. It had erupted when French refused to accept Swan River as the Force's headquarters and returned instead to Winnipeg and Dufferin. A telegram from Hewitt Bernard on 12 January 1875 demanded 'an explanation for your complete disregard of orders'. This stung French into an angry and injudicious reply:

It may possibly have been too much to expect but certainly after coming off such a long and arduous march . . . I did expect some thanks, both for myself and the officers under my command. . . . I had hoped that as the Department [of Justice] became fully alive to the state of affairs at Swan River my action would have been endorsed. In this, as yet, I have not only been disappointed but in an official letter dated 26 January my action is referred to as 'the absence of compliance with orders'.

French demanded that his name be cleared or that an investigation be made into his conduct as Commissioner. He was deeply hurt by the government's rebukes and wrote to Hewitt Bernard, 'I have slaved night, noon and morning in the public interest and I feel I have deserved a little more consideration.' However, a government memorandum described French's scathing criticisms of Swan River as 'most unfortunate', particularly since Sir John Macdonald's Conservative opposition was making much of them, and Antoine Dorion, the Minister of Justice, wrote, 'The actions of Colonel French from first to last appear to be in defiance of the wishes of the government.' The row even attracted the attention of the Prime Minister, Alexander Mackenzie, who commented, 'We have had a great deal of trouble with French. His letters and general mismanagement seem . . . very bad.'

Still the Commissioner struck out, complaining to Ottawa that he was being kept 'in entire ignorance' about the government's policy towards the police, and upbraiding Macleod for not reporting to him the events in the West. He told Macleod he had first read of the deaths of the frozen constables, Baxter and Wilson, in the Manitoba newspapers, and added:

> Full particulars of the wholesale desertion which has occurred from your command are going the rounds of the barracks here while I am entirely uninformed on the matter, or was until the information was obtained from a sub-constable in the Force here.

French was finally told bluntly to return to Swan River with D Division – or else. He managed to drag his heels until late spring, but left Dufferin on 20 May, taking with him some new recruits and officers' families, including his own wife.

At Swan River the resident E Division (who had celebrated Queen Victoria's birthday on 24 May by having a snake-killing competition in the vicinity of the barracks which netted 1110 reptiles) turned out for inspection to welcome him in their best 'uniforms' – deerskin jackets and trousers, and large fox-fur caps with the tails hanging down their backs. Only the occasional remnant of a scarlet tunic indicated that these were Mounted Policemen and not a Davy Crockett brigade. French took one look, exclaimed 'Good God', wheeled his horse around and rode away.

When he had recovered from the shock, French loosed off another salvo of complaints about conditions at Swan River. There were two-inch gaps between the shrunken timbers of the hospital, which had no toilet, kitchen or washroom, so that sick men had to go outside in all weathers 'to perform the ordinary functions of nature'. In fact there was no latrine in the entire barracks; nor was there a blacksmith's, carpenter's or saddler's shop, quarters for married officers, or even a guard-room. The barrack floors were unplaned and difficult to keep clean. French requested urgent action to make Swan River habitable before another winter set in; fully aware of the anger he had already aroused in Ottawa, he wrote:

> It is with much reluctance that I have brought myself to write this letter, as I feel that I may again lay myself open to being charged with not acting heartily in concurrence with the policy of the government regarding these buildings. I prefer taking the risk of doing so, however, rather than that a still larger number of the Force . . . should have to undergo the exposure and hardship which Insp. Carvell's division suffered during the past winter.

Thomas Scott, the architect responsible for the Swan River disaster, replied that planing the unplaned floors would be 'a good punishment for soldiers' and excused the lack of officers' married quarters with the comment 'Married officers are not supposed to exist on a frontier', but he did agree that, if funds existed, workmen on the site should be instructed to plaster the draughty walls and instal latrines.

Still French plugged away gamely. Ottawa officials were told in

94

September that the Swan River stables had neither roofs nor lofts, and that there was no wood to make them. The married quarters for officers and men were only half finished and the rapid approach of winter 'in their present airy abodes' was alarming his command. In his own house the rain not only came through the roof but also through the floor of the upper storey into the ground-floor living-rooms; daylight could be seen through the ceilings and roofs in many of the buildings. Having delivered a final broadside at the local representatives of the Department of Public Works ('singularly disorganised') French asked for a 'competent and independent person' to investigate the whole mess. Then he sat back in his draughty house to await winter.

But Inspector Jacob Carvell, the former Confederate Army officer had had enough after one winter at Swan River. He went on leave to the United States that summer, and deserted. But he did it like a true Southern gentleman, posting his resignation from Boulder, Colorado. French recommended that Sub-Inspector James Walker be given command of E Division and that Staff Constable Frank Norman, a B.A. from Trinity College, Dublin, be promoted to sub-inspector. It was typical of the low regard in which French was held by the government that Hewitt Bernard wrote to Macleod asking him for his recommendations in the matter; the Assistant Commissioner nominated Sub-Inspector Jackson and Constable William Antrobus. When French heard of this divisive move he was beside himself with anger and told Bernard he would 'await with some impatience to see whether the recommendations of the Commanding Officer or the recommendations of a subordinate are acted on'. French won that one.

By the early summer of 1875 the Canadian government was ready to proceed with extradition charges against some of the men believed to have been implicated in the Cypress Hills massacre two years previously. With the help of the U.S. Army seven of them were arrested in Fort Benton, but two escaped. The others,

John H. Evans – who had led the Cypress Hills party – Tom Hardwick, Trevanion Hale, Elijah Devereaux and Charlie Harper, stood trial in Helena, Montana, on 7 July; Assistant Commissioner Macleod travelled down from Fort Macleod to attend.

The arrests and trial sparked off demonstrations in Helena; many Montanans thought it was a Hudson's Bay Company plot to stifle American competition, others were angry because they felt Canadians were trying to block what they felt was a god-given right to take the law into their own hands where Indians were concerned. At one stage of the rowdy, chauvinistic proceedings a defence lawyer bellowed that he would 'wade knee-deep in British blood' before Americans were handed over for trial in Canada. Not surprisingly, the five defendants were released. One of them, Elijah Devereaux, briefly managed to have Macleod arrested on a charge of false imprisonment, but he was freed almost immediately.

A torchlight procession through Helena celebrated the release of their heroes, and when the five got back to Fort Benton a civic welcome had been prepared and a day's holiday declared. Underneath the Stars and Stripes hung signs 'Home Once More' and 'Didn't Extradite' and a drawing of the British lion having its tail twisted by a vigorous American eagle. John Evans capitalised on his new popularity by opening the Extradition Saloon in Fort Benton.

Three more of the men involved in the Cypress Hills affair – Philander Vogle, James Hughes and G. M. Bell – were picked up in Canada and taken to Winnipeg for trial. Though they spent the winter in prison they too were acquitted the following year for lack of evidence. The outcome was perhaps distressingly predictable, but the Mounted Police had given forceful indication of the length and strength of their arm, and the *Manitoba Free Press* considered the trials 'will do more to establish the confidence of the Indians in the government than any quantity of presents, promises and pow-wows'.

If the police had needed any reminder of their worth to the

6. (*Above*) Swift Runner, the Cree cannibal, with Police guard

7. (*Left*) Jerry Potts

8. (*Right*) Blood Indians in ceremonial dress, 1874

9. The uniforms of 1874, Inspector Jack French is seated and Francis Dickens (with beard) is standing behind

Canadian West, it was spelled out by one American whiskey
trader:

> If we had only been allowed to carry on the business in our own
> way for another two years there would have been no trouble
> now as to feeding the Indians, for there would have been none
> left to feed: whiskey, pistols, strychnine and other like pro-
> cesses would have effectively cleared away these wretched
> natives.

Though they might not have changed their attitudes, many of
the liquor traders had changed their ways, settled around Fort
Macleod and tried to earn a more legitimate living. One, Tony La
Chappelle, had opened a store which sold tobacco and sweets and
also housed two billiard tables, highly popular with the police. In
addition to the trading post established the previous winter by the
I. G. Baker Company, another Fort Benton firm, T. C. Powers
& Company, opened a general store there. William Gladstone,
the man who had built Fort Whoop-Up, ran a carpenter's shop;
and among the other early businesses were a blacksmith and a
shoemaker.

With the area around Fort Macleod and Whoop-Up now rid of
whiskey peddlers and with friendly relations established with the
Indians, it was decided to spread the influence and authority of
the police by sending two of the three divisions stationed there to
build and occupy forts in other parts of the North West Territories. In May 1875, the men of B Division, under Inspector
James M. Walsh and led by Jerry Potts, trekked 160 miles east to
the Cypress Hills and, close to the site of the massacre of 1873,
this small group took only six weeks to erect a fort slightly larger
than Macleod and named in honour of their commanding officer.

Fort Walsh was built in a half-mile-wide valley, through which
ran a small river, Battle Creek. One Irish constable wrote that
their new home was 'nicely situated in a valley surrounded by
wooded hills, and at this time of the year looks nice'. The fact
that the fort was surrounded by hills might have been 'nice' but it
wasn't very sound military thinking, and the site also proved to be

an unhealthy location. In spite of this, a small community quickly arose round Fort Walsh – the inevitable trading stores of the Fort Benton merchant kings, Baker and Powers, a log billiard-hall, crude hotel, restaurant and barber shop.

In August F Division, under the twenty-five-year-old Ephraim Brisebois, left Fort Macleod and headed north to set up a third post. The site chosen was on a plateau at the traditional heart of the Blackfoot nation, the junction of the Bow and Elbow rivers. Cecil Denny was with the party when they reached the location:

> The view amazed us. Before us lay a lovely valley, flanked on the south by rolling hills. Thick woods bordered the banks of both streams, to the west towered mountains with their snowy peaks. . . . The knowledge that a fort was to be built here and that it would become our permanent residence gave us all the greatest satisfaction.

The building was again done along the lines of Forts Walsh and Macleod – pine logs set upright in trenches to form the stockade and outer walls of the buildings. But this time the construction work was contracted out to the Fort Benton firm of I. G. Baker, while the police made temporary homes in tents and dug-outs roofed over with brushwood and earth. By November, just as the weather worsened, the fort was finished and the men moved indoors, gratefully congregating around the unaccustomed luxury of stone fireplaces piled high with a plentiful supply of wood. As with the other forts, the new post immediately attracted businesses, half-breeds and Indians; one of the most popular stores was the Baker Company's shop, where cider made from raisins sold at twenty-five cents a glass.

Inspector Brisebois made persistent attempts to have the new fort named after himself, even writing 'Fort Brisebois' at the head of all outgoing correspondence and on bills and invoices. But Brisebois was unpopular with both his division and his superiors (French said of him in a confidential report, 'This officer was in command of B Division but there was so much crime and misconduct that I had to remove him. He is now in command of

F Division. He is inclined to be insubordinate and to make difficulties about trifles'), so instead the suggestion of Assistant Commissioner Macleod that it should bear the Gaelic title Calgarry (meaning 'clear, running water') was accepted. The name became corrupted to Calgary in correspondence and has stayed that way since. Poor Brisebois never overcame the shock to his dignity, and the following summer left the Force to become a registrar of land titles.

There was construction work, too, near the Hudson's Bay post at Edmonton, where Inspector William Jarvis and his company of twenty-one had passed a quiet winter. Early in the year Jarvis received instructions from Commissioner French to select a site within twenty miles of Edmonton in the spring, build a fort, fence the land and sow crops. As soon as these orders became generally known a deputation of Edmonton citizens descended on Jarvis 'with blood in their eyes' according to Sam Steele, demanding that the barracks should be built at Edmonton for their protection. Their tactless approach annoyed Jarvis, and Steele wrote of the incident, 'I have no doubt that if the settlers had let him alone he would have built the new post on the opposite side of the river. As it was, he chose a position twenty miles east, where he thought there would be a good railway crossing.' The choice of site of the barracks, at first called Sturgeon Creek Post but soon renamed Fort Saskatchewan, might have soothed Jarvis's feelings but it was a poor decision. The post was well away from the most-travelled trails and was inconvenient of access.

When Jarvis attempted to get his tiny command to erect a fort there was another 'buck' against authority. Already dissatisfied at having to buy clothing and supplies at high Hudson's Bay prices, the police refused to become builders and farmers. Jarvis solved that one by promising to pay them an extra fifteen cents a day to help with the construction, some of which he contracted out to local labour. Unfortunately, he had neglected to obtain permission for the letting of contracts, and he received a stiff letter from

French expressing 'astonishment' at his action and reminding him that if official approval was not given for the work then Jarvis himself would be responsible for the expense incurred. Fortunately for Jarvis's bank balance, the contracts made by him were later approved.

Sir John Macdonald's Conservative party and their supporting newspapers had made much capital out of the Mounted Police's early organisational troubles, and in May 1875 – in an attempt to block the flood of parliamentary criticism – Prime Minister Mackenzie sent Major-General Edward Selby Smyth, commander of the Canadian Militia, to make a tour of inspection of the police forts and to report on the 'organisation, equipment, distribution and general efficiency of the Force'. Selby Smyth covered 11,000 miles between the end of May and the middle of November and decided that 'for a newly-raised force, hastily enrolled and equipped, it is in very fair order', but he felt there was room for improvement. Because of the pressing need to build their own accommodation, he considered not enough attention had been paid to discipline, the care of horses and equipment, or even to the duties of policing the country. He was impressed by the constables ('conspicuous for willingness, endurance and, as far as I can learn, integrity of character'), not so happy about the standard of officers ('I think some of the inspectors fall short of the power, ability or attainments necessary . . .') but his report contained the firm opinion that the Mackenzie government – and indeed the Opposition led by the Force's founder, Sir John Macdonald – had wanted to hear: 'Too much value cannot be attached to the North West Mounted Police, too much attention cannot be paid to their efficiency.'

In order to enforce the law thoroughly, magistrates and courts were needed to follow up the work of the police. Late in 1875 it was decided by the Council of the North West Territories to appoint three stipendiary magistrates. Assistant Commissioner Macleod was offered one of the posts and accepted, resigning from the Force on New Year's Day 1876. His successor as second-in-command to French was Superintendent Acheson Gosford Irvine, a native of Quebec.

After the loss of the man he had described as 'my right hand', French pursued his battle against the Ottawa politicians with diminished enthusiasm. His requests now were made mainly with the comfort of the men in mind – he asked for a piano and a library for Swan River, and also recommended that a police band should be formed there: 'If this place is to be the seat of government for the North West the presence of an efficient band would be very desirable – the fact of the musicians being able to provide entertainments during the long winter is almost sufficient reason for the establishment of a band.' The band *was* organised – though the members had to buy their own instruments and pay for them to be shipped by dog sled from Winnipeg – and they made their official début at reveille on 24 May, Queen Victoria's birthday, when they gathered at the foot of the Swan River flagstaff and played 'God Save the Queen'.

Early in March 1876 French asked permission to visit Ottawa to resolve the problems besetting his command. But he was coldly informed that this was not possible 'at present'. French next offered to pay his own way to the Canadian capital, but was again flatly told that the government 'is not disposed to authorise your coming to Ottawa'. The reason was soon apparent. On 22 July 1876 an Order-in-Council was issued recommending that French be sacked. (After French had left the Force a further Order-in-Council was passed, permitting him to resign and protect his dignity).

Although many of his subordinates had shared the government's dislike of French in the early months, particularly during the march west, the Commissioner's unrelenting efforts to improve living conditions at Swan River had made him popular there. As Constable E. H. Maunsell put it, 'Colonel French was a man who would never inspire those serving under him with love, but who gained increasing respect the longer we knew him.' Just before his departure in August the officers at Swan River gave him a banquet and the entire command presented him with a gold watch which had cost $200 and Mrs French with a silver tea-service valued at $300. The government gave him nothing, not even their thanks.

However, the dismissal did not harm French's subsequent career. He returned to England, rejoined the British Army and went on to serve in Australia and India. He was promoted major-general in 1900 and when he retired two years later he was knighted. The Force's first Commissioner died in London in 1921.

PART TWO

James Farquharson Macleod

'Once I was rich, plenty of money, but the Americans stole it all in the Black Hills. I have come to remain with the White Mother's children.'

— Sitting Bull, Sioux Chief, 2 June 1877

Chapter 6

'THE GOOD INDIAN HAS NOTHING TO FEAR'

GEORGE FRENCH'S successor was James Farquharson Macleod, probably the outstanding figure in the Canadian West at that time, and until the beginning of the year the man who had been second-in-command of the Mounted Police. Along with his new post, however, Macleod retained his job as one of the North West Territories stipendiary magistrates, a crippling double burden which was to take its toll within four years.

When he accepted the Commissionership Macleod was forty. He had been born on the Isle of Skye, the third son of a British Army officer who settled in Canada. James Macleod was educated at Upper Canada College, Toronto (Canada's Eton), afterwards studied law, and was called to the Ontario Bar in 1860. But he inherited his father's military spirit; he was a Canadian militiaman by the age of twenty and ten years later had risen to major. He joined the Garnet Wolseley expedition to Red River in 1870 as brigade-major, and was mentioned in dispatches for 'exemplary conduct'. One of the first to join the Mounted Police in 1873, Macleod quickly gained a reputation for ability, charm, toughness – and a capacity for liquor.

Macleod's impressive appearance was enhanced by his full beard, parted in the centre, and a large moustache with long curling ends. According to one policeman who served under him, Macleod had a habit of twisting the ends of his moustache while hearing evidence against members of the Force brought up on disciplinary charges. 'Generally the severity or the length of the sentence could be anticipated by the number of twists the colonel had given to his facial ornament.'

Macleod's extraordinary ability with whiskey was demonstrated on one occasion when he visited the American army post at Fort Assiniboine, Montana. His reputation as a hard-drinking man had preceded him, and the officers at the fort decided to put him to the test, using relays of companions until they had finally seen off their guest. One of Macleod's colleagues wrote,

> As the evening wore on and the bottle circulated freely, man after man disappeared, either under the table or into an armchair or some other seclusion, and when Col. Macleod assisted the one solitary survivor up the stairs to his bed, the man stopped short on the first landing and said 'By God Colonel, where d'you put it?

The departed Commissioner, George French, might have managed a rueful smile had he heard that one of his successor's first duties was to move police headquarters from the bleak Swan River site to Fort Macleod. But it was Swan River's geographical position, rather than its shortcomings, which had forced the decision. The annihilation of the rash General George Armstrong Custer (known as Hard Backsides by the Indians he unremittingly pursued from the saddle) and five companies of the Seventh U.S. Cavalry at Little Big Horn, North Dakota, by a massed force of Sioux and Cheyenne on 25 June 1876, had galvanised the Canadian, as well as the American, West; Sioux messengers slipped into the camps of the Blackfoot Confederacy urging them to forget past enmities and unite in war against the white man. The Mounted Police were needed in the greatest strength their tiny command could muster to watch the American border, and also to supervise the peaceful transfer of Indian lands to Canada by treaty.

There had been treaties made with the Indians of the North West as long ago as 1817 by Lord Selkirk at Red River, but the first official negotiation, known as Treaty No. 1, was conducted at

Lower Fort Garry in 1871 with the local Crees and Ojibwas, who in exchange for the cession of the vast lands were allocated reserves (160 acres for each family of five), annuity payments and a little food. This was swiftly followed by other treaties as Canada extended its control, and by the time the Mounted Police ended their great trek in the late autumn of 1874 much of the habitable land in the vast triangle between Lake Superior, Hudson's Bay and the Rocky Mountains had been given up with great pomp, but little fuss, by the Indians. By 1876 the government was ready to go ahead with the sixth of these treaties, involving the heart of the Cree nation, some 120,000 square miles around the north and southbranches of the Saskatchewan River. Proceedings were conducted at the Hudson's Bay Company posts, Fort Carlton and Fort Pitt, in late August and early September by the Hon. Alexander Morris, in a cocked hat and uniform laden with gold braid and lace. The Cree chiefs were given uniforms (to be replaced every three years) and silver medals, horses, wagons and agricultural tools; each member of their tribe was to be awarded land, $12 annually, and – most important as it turned out when the buffalo were exterminated soon afterwards – a promise was made by the government to provide aid and rations in the event of any 'pestilence or general famine'.

Now, of all the Canadian Plains Indians, only the Blackfoot Confederacy had not signed away their land, some 50,000 square miles of the most fertile territory between the Cypress Hills and the Rockies, in what is now southern Alberta. Negotiations were opened with Chief Crowfoot in the spring of 1877 to set up the final, and perhaps most important treaty, No. 7. The place chosen by Crowfoot for the great meeting in September 1877 was a favourite Indian camping-site in a picturesque valley near a shallow section of the Bow River known as Blackfoot Crossing – or, as the Indians called it, 'The Ridge Under the Waters' – about eighty miles north of Fort Macleod and fifty miles south-east of Fort Calgary.

Chief representative of Queen Victoria at the talks was the

forty-four-year-old David Laird, a 6 ft 4 in. native of Prince Edward Island whose honest manner impressed the Indians even more than his height. They christened him 'The Man Who Talks Straight'. When it was decided in 1876 to appoint a political head specifically to look after the North West Territories, Laird – a journalist who had switched careers and had become a leading politician – was appointed the first Lieutenant-Governor of the area, backed by Commissioner Macleod and the North West's two other stipendiary magistrates, Matthew Ryan and Hugh Richardson, based first at Swan River and then, when this site was abandoned, at the new capital of the Territories, the settlement of Battleford. (After the first meeting of the council, Macleod wrote to a friend, 'There are three members, Richardson, Ryan and myself. The first two do not speak to each other and Ryan does not speak to me. I have proposed a triangular duel to settle the matter'.)

Since many Blackfoot were away hunting buffalo during the summer, it was not possible to assemble them all until September. For the great meeting Macleod took personal command of Lieutenant-Governor Laird's police escort, 108 men including the band which had been formed at Swan River and a small unit in charge of the two nine-pounder guns towed west in 1874. The talks opened formally in perfect autumn weather on 17 September. The setting, too, was perfect – a meadow about a mile wide stretching along three miles of the banks of the Bow, with excellent grazing and plenty of fuel. Cecil Denny described the scene when the police contingent reached Blackfoot Crossing:

> There must have been a thousand lodges. They were plentifully supplied with meat, having only just left a large buffalo herd downstream to the east. Their horses covered uplands to the north and south of the camp in thousands. It was a stirring and picturesque scene; great bands of grazing horses, the mounted warriors threading their way among them and as far as the eye could reach the white Indian lodges glimmering among the trees along the river bottom. By night the valley echoed to the dismal howling of the camp's curs and from sun

to sun drums boomed from the tents. Never before had such a concourse of Indians assembled on Canada's western plains.

The number of Blackfoot, Peigans, Bloods and Sarcees exceeded 4000, and as their leading chiefs passed a mounted guard of honour towards the conference tent to open the talks the police band struck up the hymn 'Hold the Fort'. Laird opened by telling the chiefs that the Great Mother 'loves all her children, white men and red men alike'. He went on

> The bad white men and the bad Indian alone she does not love, and them she punishes for their wickedness. The good Indian has nothing to fear from the Queen or her officers. You know this to be true. When bad white men brought you whiskey, robbed you and made you poor, she sent the Mounted Police to put an end to it. You know how they stopped this and punished the offenders, and how much good this has done. I have to tell you how much pleased the Queen is that you have taken the Mounted Police by the hand and helped them and obeyed her laws since their arrival.

Laird warned the Indians of the impending destruction of the buffalo and promised them government help to raise crops and cattle. Then he detailed what else the Indians would get in return for handing over all their land titles and privileges 'for as long as the sun shines and the rivers run' – continued hunting rights in the surrendered tract, generous reserves of land in the choicest parts of the territory based on a square mile for each family of five, an immediate cash payment of $12 for each Indian at Blackfoot Crossing, further annual payments of $25 for each chief, $15 for minor chiefs and $5 for every other Indian 'of whatever age', a limited amount of ammunition for hunting; clothing, medals and flags for the chiefs to commemorate the occasion, and cattle and agricultural tools when they showed a desire to abandon their nomadic life and settle on their reserves. Laird closed his speech by waving a bible in the air and telling the chiefs, 'As soon as you settle, teachers will be sent to you to instruct your children to read books like this one.'

In reply Button Chief, a Blood, praised the police: 'Before their arrival, when I laid my head down at night every sound frightened me; now I can sleep sound and am not afraid. The Great Mother sent you to this country and we hope she will be good to us for many years.' Then, on a practical note, he told Laird that his tribe were hoping for plenty of supplies, and not the meagre handouts of flour issued by the American government to their treaty Indians.

But it was obvious that most of the other chiefs were biding their time until their leader, Crowfoot, addressed the council. Crowfoot was described by one early settler as 'like a dark Duke of Wellington in feature, with something of the level-headedness and shrewdness of the Iron Warrior'. His manners, too, were apparently acceptable to whites. The same settler told how, on visits to his house, Crowfoot 'would gulp down gallons of hot tea, and then cool himself off with the fan provided by one of the ladies of the house'. Crowfoot finally spoke on 21 September, apologising for his long deliberation but pointing out that he wanted to be absolutely certain that what he was doing was for the good of his people. It was, he said, the honest attitude of the Mounted Police which had helped him to make up his mind, and went on

> If the police had not come to the country, where would we all be now? Bad men and whiskey were killing us so fast that very few of us would have been alive today. The Mounted Police have protected us as the feathers of the bird protect it from the frosts of winter. . . . I am satisfied. I will sign the treaty.

Crowfoot's speech breached the Indians' caution. Chief after chief spoke in favour of the treaty, and most of them praised the police. Typical was the comment of Red Crow, head of the Bloods: 'Three years ago, when the Police first came to the country, I met and shook hands with Stamix Otokan [James Macleod]. Since that time he has made me many promises. He kept them all – not one of them was ever broken. Everything that the police have done has been good.'

110

The following day, 22 September, Treaty No. 7 was signed. First to put his name to the agreement was Crowfoot – 'I have been the first to sign; I shall be the last to break.' He was followed by the other most important chiefs such as Old Sun, head of the northern Blackfoot, Bull's Head of the Sarcees and Red Crow. The list of Indian signatories was long and colourful, including such names as Medicine Calf, Many Spotted Horses, Running Rabbit, Eagle Rib, Sitting on an Eagle Tail, Many Swans, Morning Plume, Bear's Paw, Bull Backfat, White Antelope, Heavily Whipped, Bull Turn Round, Low Horn, Bear Shield and Calf Robe.

Underneath the signature of Laird were those of Macleod, Assistant Commissioner Irvine, Inspectors Dalrymple Clark, Winder, Denny, Shurtliff, Crozier and Antrobus – and three of their wives, Mary J. Macleod, Julia Winder and Julia Shurtliff – together with an assortment of missionaries and settlers. The ceremony was closed with a thirteen-gun salute and the police band's rendering 'God Save the Queen'. Canada had won its West without a drop of blood being spilled.

The termination of the negotiations seemed to excite, rather than calm, the younger element among the Indians. Next day, a Sunday, while most of the police and white spectators were at an open-air church-service, about 500 mounted warriors in war paint and feathered head-dresses staged a mock attack on the camp, circling the tents, yelling and firing off their rifles which, according to Laird, 'sent the bullets whistling past the spectators in such close proximity as to create most unpleasant feelings'. Cecil Denny wrote afterwards

> They were only half in fun and had fear been shown by us it is hard to tell what would have occurred. The sham battle might easily have become one of grim earnestness, but we went on quietly with the service and after a while the Indians tired themselves out and by degrees returned to their camps.

Several more days were taken up in making treaty payments to the Indians. A total of 4392 men, women and children were paid $52,954. Since there was then no bank in the Canadian West, the money had been brought up from Fort Benton, in denominations of from one dollar to $20, by the I. G. Baker Company, but as the Indians were totally ignorant of the value of paper money it was quickly decided to pay them in one-dollar bills to reduce the chance of their being cheated by the traders swarming around Blackfoot Crossing. There were still occasional cases of Indians being swindled, however. Sometimes, when they sought the assistance of the police to help them count their change after buying goods, Denny recalled, 'We found they had been given the labels off fruit jars or cans as money, being none the wiser. We then had to hunt up the culprit and deal with him.'

In the end, their money spent and their bellies full, the Indians dispersed. If the Canadian government were satisfied with the way Treaty No. 7 had gone, they were no more pleased than the canny Crowfoot. For him, the treaty had come just in time. His country was being overrun by American Sioux, the killers of Custer and hereditary enemies of the Blackfoot.

Chapter 7

'THE WARRIORS WERE SILENT AND SOLEMN'

NEXT to the Algonquins, the Sioux were the largest of North American tribes. There were more than thirty groups of the Sioux nation, whose territory stretched from the Rocky Mountains in the west to Minnesota in the east, where they were steadily being rolled back by settlers and soldiers. Despite disease, famine and the debilitating toll of wars with the white man, the Sioux in 1876 numbered about 50,000. They were the fiercest and proudest of the American Plains tribes.

Successive gold rushes in the western United States had driven great holes through the Indian lands. Wagon trails and telegraph lines pierced the hunting-grounds, military posts were built to protect those who were trespassing on the territory solemnly pledged to the Sioux by treaty in 1868. And when gold was discovered in the Black Hills of Dakota in 1874 the rush was on again; this time the Indians fought the invaders. By the spring of 1876 cavalry columns were hunting down all Cheyenne and Sioux bands who were off their reservations, the buffalo were dwindling and after a hard, bitter winter many Indians were starving. The section of the Seventh Cavalry which was annihilated with Custer formed part of a massive column under the command of Brigadier-General Alfred H. Terry, attempting to execute a pincer movement against the thousands of Sioux and Cheyenne gathered in the valley of the Little Big Horn River, some 300 miles south of Fort Walsh. The impetuous Custer, ahead of the other columns

113

and unwilling to wait for them, attacked an overwhelmingly superior number of Indians under the command of war chiefs such as Gall, Crazy Horse, Rain In The Face and Spotted Eagle, and under the overall influence of a stocky, bow-legged, pock-marked medicine man of the Hunkpapa branch of the Sioux known as Tatanka Yotanka, or Sitting Bull, who had gained his name after an injury received in a fight as a youth left him permanently lame. Because of the Custer massacre (though Sitting Bull always denied it was a massacre, since the cavalry had invaded his country in an attempt to kill *him*) he was to become the best-known Indian in North America.

Only the aftermath of the Little Big Horn, and not the details of that epic engagement, belong in this narrative, but Sitting Bull was wise enough to realise that by winning a battle he had lost much more than a war. He and his people had drawn down on themselves the wrath of the whole American Army, and he knew they were doomed if they remained in the United States. So he determined to make for Canada, the land of the Great White Mother, where he had heard that there was peace. Gradually the Sioux drifted north, and in the early winter of 1876 began to filter across the frontier. The chilling experience of a French-Canadian trader, Jean-Louis Legaré, who operated a store at Wood Mountain, near the border with Montana, was the first indication that the feared American Sioux were in Canada:

On the afternoon of 17 November the weather was cold and I was in my store with two of my men when a dozen Indians on horseback made their appearance. Little Knife was their leader. Without dismounting, they came directly to the window and started looking at us. They were completely clad in buffalo hides. They kept inspecting us that way for at least half an hour, but none of us was paying the least attention to their presence. Finally, Little Knife came in, left the door open and watched us for a long while. Thereafter, just ignoring us, he advanced quietly to the middle of the room, sat down on the floor and called his companions one after the other. They all came in and left the door open as he did.

114

As for me, I took care not to say a word nor to make a gesture, peacefully waiting for what they were going to do. The scene lasted two hours. All of a sudden, Little Knife jumped to his feet, came to us to shake hands and returned to his place. His companions did the same thing. One of them called Crow was the speaker of the band. After turning to the four cardinal points, Crow began a pacific speech. 'We have come from the American border because we could not sleep in peace there and also because we heard that the Great Woman was kind to her children.' Thereafter he explained that they were in great need; this was very obvious. They told me that if I would give them ammunition for hunting purposes, powder, caps, tobacco, they would trade for me. In order to get rid of them without offending them I gave them merchandise for the amount of $30 and they went away.

The police had been warned, through scouts and Indian contacts, of the imminent arrival of the refugee Sioux. Inspector James Walsh, who had been away from Fort Walsh on sick leave in Hot Springs, Arkansas, recovering from a severe attack of an inflammatory skin disease, was hurriedly recalled (on his return his division hung a message on the gates of the fort 'Long Life to Our Inspector'): Walsh's deputy, Inspector Leif Crozier, was ordered to patrol the border closely and the log buildings at Wood Mountain which had formerly belonged to the Boundary Commission's surveyors were converted into a small police-post. The American newspaper, the *Fort Benton Record*, was full of admiration. 'The Mounted Police don't scare worth a cent,' it reported. 'Parties of two and three men are scouting along the line looking for Sitting Bull.' (It was also this newspaper which originated the 'get their man' phrase which still makes every Mountie cringe: discussing the suppression of the whiskey traffic, the *Record* said the police 'fetched their man every time'.)

Early in December about 500 Sioux warriors, accompanied by a thousand women, 1400 children, 3500 horses and 30 captured U.S. Army mules, straggled over the border and camped at Wood Mountain – about 150 miles east of the Cypress Hills – near the village of some Santee Sioux under White Eagle who had been living peacefully in Canada for fifteen years since fleeing from American troops in the aftermath of the Minnesota Indian uprisings, and who deeply resented the intrusion of their fellow tribesmen. Walsh, a man skilled in the traditions of Indian negotiations, rode into the Indian camp four days before Christmas and was introduced by White Eagle to the newly arrived chiefs, some of whom – Black Moon, Spotted Eagle, Long Dog and Little Knife, the man who had startled the trader Legaré – had taken part in the Custer fight. Walsh explained that the Sioux would have to obey the Queen's laws while they were in her country, and extracted a promise from the chiefs that they would not return south to make war on the Americans after recuperating in Canada. When Walsh asked why the Sioux had come, he was told that they had been driven from their homes by the Americans and had come to look for the peace which their grandfathers had assured them they would find in the land of the British. Moved by their plight, Walsh arranged to supply the Indians with a limited amount of ammunition so that they could hunt. When he got back to his fort after a nine-day journey in bitter weather, Walsh sent an urgent message to Commissioner Macleod telling him of his interview with the Sioux and adding 'from what I can learn there are more Indians coming'.

There were indeed. Three months after meeting the first bunch of refugees, Walsh came across another, smaller camp under the elderly Teton Sioux leader, Four Horns. He was saddened by their condition and their pathetic eagerness to settle in Canada: 'The warriors were silent and solemn; the mothers' hearts were beating; the maidens' eyes were dim; war had made the children forget how to play.' Late in May, Sitting Bull and a large following crossed into Canada and camped about sixty miles south-east of Fort Walsh, and James Walsh paid a call on the new arrivals. When he asked if Sitting Bull would obey the laws of the Great Mother, the chief replied, 'I have buried my weapons.' Sharing Walsh's curiosity, Assistant Commissioner Irvine decided to visit the great Sioux leader. But the evening before his departure six

Sioux warriors, armed with guns and ammunition captured at Little Big Horn, arrived at Fort Walsh with a message from Sitting Bull. Three Americans had entered his camp and had been made prisoner; he wanted advice from the police about what to do next. Accompanied by Walsh and an escort, Irvine left for the Sioux camp:

> As we rode up, all the Indians emerged from their lodges and a long line of tremendously big men met us; we could not get past without shaking hands with them. . . . They all had a powerful grip and some nearly pulled me off my horse. The children were frightened at first whenever we went near them; after I had chucked one or two under the chin they got quite friendly and soon discovered we were friends. . . .
>
> I was particularly struck with Sitting Bull. He is a man of somewhat short stature but with a pleasant face, a mouth showing great determination and a fine, high forehead. When he smiled, which he often did, his face brightened up wonderfully. I should say he is a man of about forty-five years of age . . . He believes no one from [the United States] . . . and said so. His speech showed him to be a man of wonderful capability.

The Sioux immediately complained bitterly about the three American intruders in their camp. One was a Benedictine priest, Father Martin Marty, a fluent speaker of the Sioux language who had followed Sitting Bull into Canada on an injudicious mission bearing a letter from the Department of Indian Affairs in Washington and hoping to persuade him to return south, where he could be dealt with. The priest had been accompanied by two scouts. At the meeting with the Mounted Police officers, Sitting Bull turned on Father Marty and told him, 'You told me you came as the messenger of God. What you told me was not good for me. Look up, you will see God. I don't believe the Americans ever saw God, and that is the reason they don't listen to me. You know as a messenger of God that they tried to kill me. Why did you wait until half my people were killed before you came?'

The Indian then told Irvine that he had no wish to fight the Americans, but that they had attacked him and stolen his horses and land. He wanted to live in peace, and asked Irvine, 'Will the White Mother protect us if we remain here?' Irvine told him that as long as the Sioux obeyed the laws they would be safe and unmolested in Canada. 'In the Queen's land we all live like one family. You need not be alarmed. The Americans cannot cross the line after you. You and your families can sleep sound.' Even Father Marty was impressed by Irvine's comments and told Sitting Bull, 'I think you would be better on British soil.' The Sioux chief agreed: 'What would I return for, to have my horses and arms taken away? What have the Americans to give me? Once I was rich, plenty of money, but the Americans stole it all in the Black Hills. I have come to remain with the White Mother's children.'

The priest and his companions were turned loose, lucky to escape with their lives, while the police party prepared to spend the night in the Sioux camp, where spirits were high after receiving Irvine's promise of protection and fair treatment. Late that night Sitting Bull, accompanied by an interpreter, paid a surprise visit to Irvine's tent: 'He sat on my bed until an early hour in the morning telling me in subdued tones his many grievances against the Long Knives [American soldiers].' Before leaving, Sitting Bull removed his fine beaded moccasins and presented them to the Assistant Commissioner.

Though the Sioux were delighted with their reception, the tribes of the Blackfoot Confederacy – their traditional enemies – were far from happy at the intrusion. The presence of a large body of American Indians in their territory was bound to deplete the thinning buffalo-herds at an even faster rate. Crowfoot offered to lend his support if the police chose to drive the Sioux back into the United States. In fact, Irvine sought government approval to raise a force of 100 mounted Blackfoot warriors, to be fed by the government and paid twenty-five cents a day, to bolster the meagre police strength, but nothing ever came of the move.

The Blackfoot concern was shared by Commissioner Macleod

and the Canadian government. Macleod reported to the Prime Minister, Alexander Mackenzie, that the presence of the Sioux in Canada was 'a matter of very grave importance'. He recommended that an attempt be made to get them back across the American border: 'The longer it is delayed the more difficult it will be to accomplish.' Secretary of State R. W. Scott, whose department had taken over control of the Mounted Police from the Department of Justice in April 1876, put the view of his alarmed government in a telegram to Macleod: 'Important that Sitting Bull and other U.S. Indians should be induced to return to reservations.' But he stressed, 'Our action should be persuasive, not compulsory.' Scott also passed on the information that, at the urging of Ottawa, a negotiating party from the American government was on its way to confer with the refugee Sioux.

The anxious messages passing between the police forts, Ottawa, London and Washington in the summer of 1877 marked the opening of four years of drawn-out negotiations and exchanges of countless notes and legal niceties between the three governments concerned. Macleod was only too well aware that his tiny command could not hold the Indians in check over such a vast expanse of unguarded frontier. He wasn't sure how long his mice could go on attempting to dictate to cats. It was all a black comedy on an international scale, with Sitting Bull the pawn that everybody wanted to be rid of; or, in the words of the American historian Paul Sharp, 'A diplomatic scalp dance, with the nations' spokesmen outwardly expressing grave concern for the welfare of the Sioux, but inwardly praying that they would somehow vanish from the earth.' The Washington newspaper *National Republican* summed up these feelings: 'Sitting Bull is not a denizen to be desired by any country.'

But the Sioux had no intention of vanishing. A correspondent from the *Manitoba Free Press* found them 'perfectly satisfied with their new quarters'. The news quickly spread. As Irvine noted, 'in an extremely short time Canada became the home of every Sioux Indian who considered himself antagonistic to the

119

American government. In all they numbered some 700 lodges
... some 5600 souls.'

Meanwhile, the proposed American commission to visit the
exiled Sioux chiefs suffered a series of irritating delays. First
there was trouble finding politicians or soldiers willing to serve on
it, then the commission's leader, Brigadier-General Alfred H.
Terry, was taken ill (in any case, the choice of Terry was a disastrous one; he had led the campaign against the Sioux the previous summer). Next there was an embarrassing shortage of funds
to cover transportation and expenses. Finally, by the time they
got under way, fighting had broken out between the Nez Percé
Indians – who did not want to be shipped to reservations hundreds of miles from their homes – and the U.S. Army, and the
commission was stranded at Fort Shaw, Montana. It was this
final factor which killed any lingering hope of persuading the
Sioux to return to the United States, for a segment of the Nez
Percé tribe, some 200 battered survivors under White Bird,
managed to join the Sioux in Canada. They were in a wretched
condition. Nearly all the men were wounded, children were
suffering from broken arms and legs, and one woman somehow
still managed to ride a pony with a child strapped to her back
though horriby injured – she had been shot through the breast
and the bullet had passed out through the side of her head. Was
this what *they* could expect if they went back across the Medicine
Line, the Sioux wondered? It was only after patient persuasion
that James Walsh managed to get the Sioux chiefs to travel with
him to Fort Walsh to talk to the Americans.

Macleod himself was at the frontier to meet General Terry's
group, who were accompanied by three companies of cavalry, an
infantry escort for their supply train and two journalists, one of
whom, Jerome B. Stillson of the *New York Herald*, dipped deep
into his reserves of purple prose to describe the arrival at the
border of the 'small but brilliant retinue' of the Mounted Police:
'Their red uniforms and red and white pennants affixed to their
lances contrasted beautifully with the monotonous dun colour of

the plains around them.' The U.S. Cavalry escort was left
behind at the border and the commissioners were led to Fort
Walsh by Macleod's contingent, arriving towards sunset. Jerome
Stillson painted the picture for his New York readers:

> Suddenly Fort Walsh came into view, lying low in a charming
> valley. No more romantic spot, no wilder scene could impress
> a traveller at the end of a monotonous journey than the one
> that met our eyes. . . . Whitewashed on every part except the
> roof, the fort nestles between the surrounding heights. A
> scraggly but picturesque settlement adjoins it.

The conference was set for the next day, 17 October 1877, in
the officers' mess at the fort. Crowded behind two small tables
were the two American commissioners, General Terry and A. G.
Lawrence, the official recorders and the two newspapermen. After
being subjected to the indignity of a search for firearms at the
insistence of the Americans, the Sioux chieftains, led by Sitting
Bull, entered the room and made themselves comfortable on
buffalo robes spread on the floor opposite the commissioners'
table. They ignored the Americans. Sitting Bull wore a wolfskin
cap, a black shirt with large white dots, a blanket round his waist
and richly beaded moccasins. Alongside him was the striking
figure of Spotted Eagle, the war chief of the Sans Arc Sioux,
naked to the waist, his body daubed with white paint, a cartridge
belt across one shoulder, a single eagle's feather in his hair, and
a buffalo robe around his waist. Also present were several less
important chiefs and one woman, the squaw of the chieftain The
Bear That Scatters. Since women were invariably excluded from
Indian councils this was a calculated insult to the Americans and
indicated that the Sioux's minds were already made up. This
became even more apparent when Commissioner Macleod, Walsh
and some other police officers entered the conference room.
Sitting Bull rose, shook hands warmly with them and continued
to ignore Terry's group.

The council was opened by Terry, a distinguished veteran of

the American Civil War, quiet-spoken and of impressive bearing – he was 6ft 6in. tall and sported a flowing moustache and 'Uncle Sam' beard. He told the Indians that the American president desired to make 'a lasting peace' with them; that full pardons would be granted to them if they surrendered their horses and arms and returned to an Indian agency in the United States. During the general's speech, the handsome Spotted Eagle winked at the Mounted Police group.

Sitting Bull was the Sioux spokesman. He rose to his feet, threw back his blanket and strode to the centre of the room, beginning his speech with a review of the wrongs committed against his people by the Americans. Warming to his theme he told the commission, 'For sixty-four years you have treated my people bad. We could go nowhere so we have taken refuge here.' He broke off to cross the room and shake hands again with Macleod and Walsh, before turning to Terry and accusing, 'We did not give you our country, you took it from us. See how I live with these people, look at these eyes and ears; you think me a fool but you are a greater fool than I am. You come to tell us stories and we do not want to believe them. I will not say any more, you can go back home.'

After several other chiefs had endorsed Sitting Bull's comments, the squaw of The Bear That Scatters rose to speak; the interpreter paused for several moments before leaning over to Terry and telling him in a lowered voice, 'She says, General, you won't give her time to breed'. Next a chief called The Crow hugged the Mounted Police officers and told Terry's group, 'That is the way I like these people. How dare you come here to talk to us? This country is not yours. You can go back where you came from and stay there.' There was no more to be said, by the Americans at least. One of history's briefest and least-productive conferences was ended. Afterwards, however, Macleod had a meeting with Sitting Bull and told him that as long as he and his people behaved themselves they would not be driven out of Canada. But he added a warning, 'You must remember that you will have to live by the buffalo on this side of the line and that the buffalo will not last for ever. In a few years they will all be killed. I hope you have thought well on the decision you have given today, not only for yourself but for your women and children.'

While the Indian chiefs stayed at Fort Walsh several more days, being royally entertained in the police messes (one, Bear's Cap, ate so much plum-pudding at one sitting that he was taken severely ill with acute indigestion) the American newspapers officially wrote off Sitting Bull. Jerome Stillson's *New York Herald* said, 'We wish the Great Mother joy of her new subjects', and the *New York World* agreed: 'With him [Sitting Bull] we need deal no more, since Great Britain is responsible for his conduct.'

Chapter 8

THE PRAIRIE LIFE

WITH the Sioux in such massed strength on Canadian soil, two-thirds of the Mounted Police command, some 200 men, were soon concentrated in the frontier area around Fort Walsh and the Wood Mountain post, a cluster of mud-roofed log-shacks which even the police didn't bother to grace with the title 'fort'; furniture was almost non-existent, and the beds were merely buffalo-hide hammocks stretched between one wall and a row of stakes driven into the earth floor. According to Inspector Leif Crozier, Wood Mountain offered 'neither accommodation, comfort nor defence'.

When Swan River was abandoned as headquarters of the police and the proposed capital of the North West Territories in 1876, it was decided to move the infant government of the Territories to a place known as Telegraph Flat, at the junction of the North Saskatchewan and Battle rivers, about 300 miles north of Fort Walsh. In honour of the occasion the place was given the more attractive name of Battleford, and a police post was built there. Another rough barracks was set up in the beautiful Qu'Appelle Valley, about 200 miles north-east of Wood Mountain, but the garrisons were small indeed. Every man who could be spared was on duty near the Sioux; inevitably, in 1878 the headquarters, too, was shifted to Fort Walsh from Macleod.

It was to Fort Walsh that most of the recruits came to replace the steady drain of men whose three-year terms had expired, or who had been invalided, discharged or had deserted. (In 1877, for instance, eighty-two policemen took their discharge at the

124

expiration of their term of service, five were dismissed, nine invalided, two purchased their discharges, two deserted and one man drowned while travelling from Battleford to Fort Walsh. To replace this loss of 101 men, ninety-seven were recruited and thirty-two time-expired men decided to re-engage.) Since Sitting Bull and his Sioux were rapidly making the name of the Mounted Police a household word in North America there was no lack of applicants. The Canadian House of Commons was told that there had been more than 800 men seeking vacancies. But since French's departure medical examinations had slipped back to perfunctory routines. Robert Patterson, an Irishman from Templemore, Tipperary, described his medical as 'very cursory, consisting of the baring of my legs with trousers tucked up; the doctor just looked at me and said I was all right'. From Fort Macleod Surgeon George F. Kennedy was forced to invalid an asthmatic recruit named Zwick who had been told by the doctor who passed him fit to join the Force that the climate of the Canadian West would be excellent for his condition. 'His disease has grown perceptibly worse since his arrival,' Kennedy reported. 'I do not regard this country as a sanatorium for asthmatics and would respectfully recommend that in future, examining physicians be strictly cautioned on this point.'

The recruits travelled from eastern Canada by train through the United States as far as Bismarck, North Dakota, and then by steamer up the Missouri to Fort Benton and overland to either Fort Walsh or Fort Macleod. One of the recruits, Simon Clarke, was so annoyed about the rigours of the trip that his indignation outstripped his spelling ability:

Man, talk about the burning sands of Egyption. This could not be any worse. I took my tin cup before rolling myself on the prairie for bed and filled same with slough water for the night drink and it was covered with a green scumb and bitter. This we met in a good many places . . . we all got over it in time.

Clarke's group also ran into hordes of snakes on the march from

Fort Benton: 'They would croll into our blankets at night for warm places and kept us pretty busey.'

Perhaps Clarke should have addressed his comments to London, where *The Times* was cheerfully dispensing the worthless opinion that 'in every sense of the word the North West Mounted Police is a *corps d'élite*. The pay is good, the uniform handsome, the term of service short and life congenial to adventurous spirits.'

In fact, the quality of the uniforms was a continuing disgrace during the Force's early years. In 1876, in an attempt to cut costs, the Canadian government had the police clothing and boots made of inferior materials by inferior craftsmen – the inmates of Kingston Penitentiary in Ontario. One constable reported that when he got his prison-made boots wet he was unable to remove them when they dried, so he had to soak them again before being able to get them off. The officers fared little better with their uniforms, supplied at hefty personal expense from London by the firm of Maynard, Harris & Grice, who received a withering complaint from Commissioner Macleod early in 1878:

> I regret very much to have to inform you that the uniform lately supplied by you to the officers of the NWMP is made of the most miserable material. The lace is little better than tinsel and the workmanship so bad that many of the articles are coming to pieces. Several of the officers inform me that their trousers have split across the knee on the first or second time of wearing. The helmets are not the pattern which I ordered and I don't think a single one arrived with the gilt edging perfectly attached. . . . Hoping soon to hear from you about the matter, as the manner in which you have fulfilled our very large order is a very great disappointment to us all.

The scarlet jacket pulled in every direction when it got wet, and buttons placed too far apart gave a scalloped appearance to the front of the tunic. Pointing out the uniform's entire unsuitability for everyday work, one officer complained, 'If anything is required to handicap the freedom and efficiency of a mounted man's movements on the prairie I can with confidence recommend a tight tunic and a helmet.' Hardly any of the police would wear their heavy white helmets, except on formal parades. For prairie work they preferred cowboy-type felt slouch hats, purchased at their own expense; the helmets were pressed into service as water-carriers, feed bags for horses or a stow-all for pipe, tobacco and personal belongings. The ludicrous little pill-box cap was even more useless during the prairie summers, affording little protection from the sun. It had one other crippling deficiency which ensured that it would hardly ever be worn: the rumour got around that it made men go bald. Even the stable uniform was castigated as a 'cross between the Confederate Army and the Mennonites'.

The police horses were in little better condition than the uniforms during the late 1870s, when there was a strong danger of the Mounted Police not being mounted any more. The severe losses sustained during the march west in 1874 had never been made good, and four years later there were only 201 animals to carry out the diverse and exacting police duties. Horses had to be continually loaned from one division to another, and Inspector William Jarvis noted sadly that his small command at Fort Saskatchewan possessed 'only three horses fit for the saddle'.

Because of a combined shortage of funds, building materials and skilled workmen, the standard of living at the forts improved little during the hectic years of the Sioux problem. At the Qu'Appelle post snow drifted in through the cracks in the log walls and, according to Frank Fitzpatrick, 'it was not an uncommon sight to see someone using a shovel to take the snow off an occupant of a corner bed near the door'. Bitter winds blowing through the gaps in the walls of the new barracks at Battleford were responsible for many colds and much rheumatism, and on 19 December 1879 Battleford's commanding officer, Inspector James Walker noted, 'This morning, with the thermometer thirty-seven degrees below zero, water was frozen on top of the stove in my bedroom, notwithstanding there was sufficient fire in the stove to start the morning fire.' It was little wonder that Walker resigned soon afterwards to become manager of the Cochrane ranch, the first in the Canadian West.

Officers' families fared little better. At Fort Saskatchewan the wife of Inspector Arthur Griesbach, who had been the first man to enrol officially for the police in 1873, adapted packing-cases into washstands and dressing-tables to supplement the basic stove, rough table and benches provided as furniture for the married quarters. Griesbach's son recalled

> A few coloured prints from *The Illustrated London News* and other magazines were tacked on the wall and standing around artistically arranged were the photographs of our relatives and friends in their Sunday best or in full uniform. When we arrived at Fort Saskatchewan we occupied a log building, the walls of which had been covered with cotton tacked onto the logs over which paper had been pasted. A nest of snakes got in behind the cotton and used to appear either in the ceiling or wriggling on the floors. The assurance that they were harmless did not, however, make them any more welcome.

In addition to knocking together furniture, Mrs Griesbach also made clothes for her children out of the high quality outer canvas material of flour sacks 'taking care to snip round the supplier's brand name'. Her son, who wore the flour-sack suits, considered them 'quite snappy'.

Despite the hardships, most of the Force cheerfully made the best of their life. At Christmas, 1876, the garrison of Fort Macleod were blessed by the arrival of the warming chinook wind. The woodcutting squad worked stripped to the waist and William Parker described the weather on the last day of the old year as 'delightful, so warm and the sun shining so brightly, it is like a spring day'. On Christmas Day the entire garrison sat down to dinner with civilian guests from the nearby settlement. 'And a bully spread we had,' recalled Parker. It consisted of turkey, wild geese, antelope, buffalo tongues, plum pudding, California raisins, nuts and a milk punch – for which a special liquor-permit had been obtained. Parker wrote home to Kent, 'My voice is completely gone from singing "He's a Jolly Good Fellow". At the

10. (*Above*) A mounted constable, James Schofield, in prairie patrol dress

11. (*Above left*) Superintendent Sam Steele

12. (*Left*) Inspector Cecil Denny

13. (*Above*) Fort Walsh in 1878

14. (*Below*) A group at ease outside East End outpost, 1878

toasts I sang "Roast Beef of Old England" twice. So you see, dear mother, we were bound to enjoy ourselves and I think we succeeded pretty well.'

In October of 1876 the police at Fort Walsh had celebrated the first anniversary of their arrival in that area with a cricket match and an evening concert, which were fully reported in the *Manitoba Free Press*. The unpredictability of the prairie wicket was illustrated by the fact that the first four batsmen in Staff-Constable Homan's XI all failed to score, while byes accounted for almost half the total (93) of Sub-Constable Nedham's XI 'owing to the swift bowling of Sub-Constable Uniacke'. Homan's team won by twenty-five runs. A horse race planned to take place after the cricket match had to be postponed when one of the riders was thrown and severely injured. But it was the evening which was the most resounding success. The *Free Press* reported:

> In the evening an entertainment, the first given in the country, was got up by Staff-Const. Dunne. The performance began by Feats of Legerdemain by Staff-Const. Dunne, who has performed before the Earl and Countess of Dufferin. His tricks were splendid and very neatly done, surprising most of the audience. The second part of the performance was opened by Sub-Const. Nedham's playing a composition of his own, the 'Fort Macleod Gallop'. Several songs were given, with very nearly each one getting an encore. The entertainment was very good, and owing to the haste with which it was got up, Staff-Const. Dunne and the performance deserves great credit. The following is the programme of entertainment:

PART I

Overture – 'Poet and Peasant' . . . Sub-Const. Nedham
Feats of Legerdemain . . . . . Staff-Const. Dunne

An interval of fifteen minutes

PART II

Fort Macleod Gallop . . . . . Sub-Const. Nedham

Quartette – 'See Our Oars' . .	{	Staff-Const. Oliver
		Staff-Const. Dunne
		Sub-Const. Stone
		Sub-Const. Shepard

Song (Comic) . . . . Sub-Const. Wilson
Reading . . . . Staff-Const. Homan
Song (Comic) – 'The Blighted Shepherd' Sub-Const. Seymour
Song – 'Rocked in the Cradle of the Deep' Sub-Const. Stone
Song (in character) . . . . . . Sub-Const. Patterson
Song – 'Fifty Years Ago' . . . . . Sub-Const. Adams

God Save the Queen!

Admission Free.

The police had a splendid capacity for arranging their own amusements. One civilian, who sheltered under the initials J.S.M., attended a New Year's Ball at Fort Calgary, and wrote about it to the *Manitoba Free Press* (letters to this newspaper were almost the only source of public information about events in the north-west in the early days of the police):

> I was surprised to find that an entertainment so grand could be got up in such an out-of-the-way place. . . . The dancing hall was a spacious room, neatly fitted up with festoons of ever-greens, relieved by the Union Jack at one end and the crown of our Sovereign at the other, the whole being lighted up with three large chandeliers. The programme, which consisted of songs, recitations and dancing, was lengthy but not at all tedious. After enjoying the dance for some time, supper was announced when all repaired to the dining hall, where was found a sumptuous repast, the tables groaning beneath their loads of delicacies. Supper being over, the dancing hall was again resorted to when the rest of the night was pleasantly passed.

In some cases, special arrangements were made for guests to stay overnight in the posts. At Fort Saskatchewan one of the smaller barrack rooms was prepared for the use of women visitors after one dance. The floor was thoroughly scrubbed, the men's rough wooden beds were softened by pillows and sheets provided by the energetic Mrs Griesbach and the room was decorated with festoons of pipe-clayed ropes and artistically arranged evergreen branches. Under each bed, properly aligned on the same latitude, were chamber pots. Washstands were set up with towels, basins and mirrors which, like the chamber pots, had been hired for the occasion from merchants in nearby Edmonton. A non-dancing man – who was also a married man – was detailed to act as sentry over the women's quarters.

The shortage of women was a constant problem at the dances. Frank Fitzpatrick, who joined the police in 1879 and was sent to Fort Walsh, wrote that 'no white woman was in the country, at least not in our neighbourhood. I never saw one for three years.' So all the available half-breed girls – and sometimes Indian squaws – were invited for the occasions. Cecil Denny considered the half-breeds 'well-dressed, and some very, very good-looking'. So good, in fact, that he took one of them for himself. A police-man commented after a dance at Calgary, 'The belle was Capt. Denny's woman, a half-breed.' It was, in fact, his womanising which ended Denny's police career. A Fort Macleod settler named Percy Robinson brought a civil action for $10,000 damages against Denny, claiming the officer had enticed away his wife. Though the case was dismissed because of insufficient evidence, Irvine commented, 'The sooner Denny is gazetted out of the Force the better,' and he resigned shortly afterwards to become an Indian agent and then a rancher. So the Mounted Police lost their first aristocrat. Denny remained in the West but never made a com-mercial success of any of his ventures. He died penniless in 1928 at the age of seventy-eight ($57 had to be donated from a police trust fund to pay his funeral expenses). Denny never married and was the last of his line. The headstone over his grave in Edmonton records that Cecil Edward Denny, the sixth baronet of Tralee Castle, was an 'explorer, pioneer, adventurer and author. He knew not fear, a born optimist.'

The police's association with the native women around Fort Walsh grew to such proportions that Lieutenant-Governor David Laird complained to Macleod: 'Reports are brought to me that some of your officers are making rather free with the women. It is to be hoped that the good name of the Force will not be hurt through too open indulgence of that kind, and I sincerely hope that Indian women will not be treated in a way that hereafter will give trouble.' Macleod stoutly denied that there was anything like 'a regular brothel' at Fort Walsh, but there was no denying the truth of David Laird's accusations. Frank Fitzpatrick recalled, 'Some of the men – a few I must say – did fall for the charms of these sometimes pretty maidens and married them Indian fashion. In some cases they retained them as their lawful wives but in other cases, just as in civilised parts of our country, they discarded them without much further thought.' Mostly, however, the bachelor policemen contented themselves with letters to their loved ones at home, or with the occasional advertisement such as the one which appeared in the *Montreal Star*: 'Two lonely Mounted Policemen desire to correspond with a limited number of young ladies for mutual improvement.'

Others sought to escape the stunning boredom of pioneer prairie life by drinking whatever liquor or other intoxicating substitute they could lay their hands on. Joseph Francis, the Crimean War veteran who was a constable in the Force, noted, 'At Wood Mountain they drink Florida Water, cologne, pain-killer, bay rum and even mustang liniment in cases of great emergency.' Another policeman claimed that bay rum diluted with water and flavoured with pain-killer made 'a most excellent drink', while the *Fort Benton Record* reported that the police 'by dint of continued long experiments, have acquired knowledge of several substitutes which, although injurious to health, possess a sufficient stimulating power and succeed admirably in stealing away the brain'. Occasionally the officers responsible for enforcing prohibition were guilty of bringing liquor into the country. A trader in Fort Macleod ordered 'three gals your best whiskey' from a man named J. H. McNight at Fort Shaw, Montana on behalf of Inspector Crozier with the instructions, 'Send it to him with bill, packed securely . . . he is all right on the pay.' In general, however, the other ranks drank revolting substitutes or did without in the 1870s, as this plaintive anonymous letter from a Mountie to the *Manitoba Free Press* shows:

> I can assure you that if we could get a glass of beer or grog occasionally there would be fewer anathemas uttered against our lot than at present. . . . I am neither a lover nor a hater of strong liquor but I have discovered that a sojourn of two winters and two summers in the North West without stimulants is quite enough to try the constitution of any white man.

It was fortunate that their constitutions were generally sound, since medical treatment was at the best rudimentary and at the worst non-existent. When a constable called Donaldson was taken ill with stomach cramps while on patrol in 1879, William Parker detailed the treatment his companions devised: 'We heated rocks, rolled them in our shirts and placed them on his stomach, but it had no effect'. A passing group of traders were able to provide a little brandy (the police patrol forbore to mention that this was illegal) and this stimulating restorative did the trick. 'In an hour we were able to proceed.'

Sam Steele, who had been promoted to inspector in 1878, recorded an unusual cure for snow blindness, from which he was suffering agonies in the winter of 1880, lying in a darkened room with a handkerchief over his eyes and applying the traditional remedy of tea leaves 'with no apparent effect'. Steele was visited by an old trapper who told him to make a pot of strong black tea, cover his head with a silk handkerchief and look into the pot. 'I took his advice, got instantaneous relief and was quite well in a couple of days'.

The most serious health problems existed at Fort Walsh, where there were recurring cases of a typho-malarial infection known in the western mining-camps as mountain fever. During 1879 an average of eight per cent of the garrison were suffering from the fever, while in the surrounding settlement nine people out of a population of about a hundred died from it, among them William Walsh, a former policeman and nephew of Inspector James

Walsh. Before he was stricken with the disease himself, John Kittson, the police surgeon at Fort Walsh, tracked down the source of the trouble – a swampy area littered with the carcasses of buffalo and horses. In rainy weather this swamp overflowed into Battle Creek, which provided the water supply for fort and settlement. A well was sunk inside the fort, which immediately checked the incidence of fever, and Kittson urged that the settlers also 'should be made to build a well. Their filthy habits of throwing refuse matter, offal and wash-water into the stream should be prohibited and any offender promptly and severely dealt with. It would be an easy matter to keep typhoid fever out of the fort were there no settlers about it.' The following summer the garrison camped out in tents near a clear spring of water for two months while the fort was thoroughly whitewashed and fumigated, and floors taken up and relaid on a higher foundation. The Indians around Fort Walsh were ordered to move some distance downstream. The beneficial effect of these moves was neutralised by the non-co-operation of the weather. 'During the whole time we were under canvas rain fell almost every other day, and at intervals snow varied the monotony,' Kittson reported. The tents in use were old and sieve-like; consequently colds, coughs, rheumatism and throat infections replaced the fever. As soon as they moved back into Fort Walsh, cases of fever flared up again, and in October it claimed the life of thirty-six-year-old Inspector Edmund Dalrymple Clark, one of the Force's 'originals' and the first officer to die in Mounted Police service. Kittson pronounced Fort Walsh 'provocative of disease' and claimed that its use as headquarters handicapped the efficiency of the police.

But for the time being Sitting Bull's presence in the vicinity ensured that it would continue to be the most important police post in the west. Ceremonial, partly designed to impress the Indians, was an important part of the garrison's duties, and competition was so fierce to present the smartest constables when guard was mounted each day that rival barracks used to carry their representative over the dusty square to the parade area so that he wouldn't get even a fleck of dust on his glittering person.

Another great diversion at Fort Walsh was the raising of pets. At various times the fort boasted a tame buffalo calf, a baby antelope and an assortment of dogs, but the most famous pet was a goose which belonged to a Constable Hardy. It used to strut alongside the police when they were drilling, and every night perched on a flat stone outside the guard-room, staying there until the reveille bugle. On cold nights it would tap on the guard-room window with its beak until allowed inside to warm itself by the stove; it was a favourite with the sentries since it would warn them by honking and flapping at men creeping back into the fort late from pass. It also used to chase Indian dogs, an unfortunate habit which eventually cost the goose its life.

A glimpse of barrack life at Fort Walsh is provided by a letter from Constable Tom LaNauze to his mother in Ireland: 'I scribble to you now in the long room, containing 50 beds, the fellows on each side of me playing cards and further on a fellow at the flute, others singing and talking so it is not easy to write proper.' But LaNauze managed to get enough down on paper to indicate to his mother that he didn't think much of the Indians he had met: 'I don't see much of the noble savage about them; the squaws put me much in mind of the West of Ireland people, going about with various coloured blankets, and their general appearance much resembles the pictures one sees of the distressed Irish. . . .'

In 1878 there was a change of Canadian government. Alexander Mackenzie's Liberals were swept from power and at the age of sixty-three Sir John Macdonald led the Conservatives back into office. One of the first changes made by the new regime was to simplify the cumbersome police ranks and titles. Inspectors were to be known in future as superintendents, sub-inspectors became inspectors, sub-constables became constables, constables took up the title of sergeant, and staff constables that of staff sergeant.

Even the new titles didn't suit most of the Force, however. They liked to think of themselves as a military organisation, though they weren't, and the rank of superintendent (which sounded too much like a collector of tickets on the railways) was usually re-referred to as 'Major' – as in Major Walsh. Inspectors were often called 'Captain', and the Commissioner and his assistant were invariably addressed – even in official correspondence – as 'Colonel'. The habit percolated to the ranks, where constables often addressed each other as 'Private'.

The second change made by the new government was a good deal less harmless. Rates of pay were slashed, at a time when the police were a vital – and badly underpaid – peace-keeping factor in the Canadian West. All those constables who wished to re-engage when their terms of service expired were told that their pay would be cut from seventy-five cents a day to fifty. This produced a remarkable anomaly: valuable veterans of the Force were being offered twenty-five cents a day less than the latest batch of green recruits from the east, though the pay rate on enrolment quickly fell too – to forty cents. The effect of this remarkably stupid move was pointed out by Sam Steele: 'None of the old hands would re-engage to get less pay than the recruits . . . the result was that the Force was given a blow from which it took some years to recover.'

Chapter 9

'SITTING BULL'S BOSS'

ON THE whole, police relations with the Indians were extremely good during Commissioner Macleod's four-year term. This was due not only to the firm benevolence with which the police administered the law, but also because the Canadian West was almost empty of white settlers, the buffalo herds were still to be found on the plains, and the Indians were – if not well fed – at least free from the spectre of starvation for the moment. Most of the problems involving police and Indians had to do with the stealing of horses. Because the horse was a prized possession among the Indians (the explorer William Francis Butler had reported in 1871, 'I regret to have to write that possession of a horse is valued before that of a wife') the theft of these animals from other tribes became an honoured Indian activity. The successful abduction of a horse achieved the triple purpose of weakening and humiliating the enemy tribe, strengthening his own stock and elevating the thief in the eyes of his fellow warriors. The white man's laying-down of the Medicine Line along the 49th Parallel was regarded by the Indians as a delightful addition to the fun of raiding herds. Since it was a wholly artificial boundary drawn across an open plain the Indians cheerfully ignored it, safe in the knowledge that they could not be pursued across it by Canadian police or American soldiers.

Superintendent Leif Crozier, a vigorous man, felt that vigorous methods were needed to halt the stealing. 'When the Indians are made to understand that the mere fact of hopping across the line does not exempt them from punishment there will be a much greater guarantee of their good behaviour. Now they call the boundary the Medicine Line because, no matter what they have done upon the one side, they feel perfectly secure after having arrived upon the other.'

Unfortunately, Canadian frontiersmen did not regard the game as funny. To them, stealing horses was a hanging matter – or certainly a case for justified murder, as had happened at Cypress Hills in 1873.

With the depositing of what the Canadian author Wallace Stegner has called 'an ethnic junk heap' over the Canadian border between Cypress Hills and Wood Mountain, the situation worsened immediately. Despite the solemn promises of their chiefs, war parties of young Sioux raided into the United States and among the Canadian tribes on horse-stealing expeditions. And the Sioux, in their turn, were robbed. The North West's few settlers and new ranchers were frequent victims, and Commissioner Macleod was asked in all seriousness by an American who had set up home on Canadian soil if he was entitled to shoot any Indian who approached his home, as he had been able to do in the United States.

When they were called upon to recover stolen horses, which happened more and more frequently, the harassed and overworked police on boundary duty used to take the most enormous risks. On one occasion, after some Sioux reported the theft of horses, Assistant Commissioner Irvine and a squad of seven men traced the animals to a large Assiniboine camp of 250 lodges. They rode into the camp, demanded the missing animals and were given them. Irvine dismissed the incident by reporting, 'I gave them a good lecture and they promised to behave themselves in future.'

The arrival at the Cypress Hills of a large band of American Assiniboines from Montana at the end of May 1877 gave the dashing Walsh another opportunity to shine. The Assiniboines, under a boastful chief named Crow's Dance, had roughed up a small camp of Salteaux, demolishing tepees, killing dogs, terrifying women and children and bullying the small band of warriors. When the Salteau chief Little Child (who, paradoxically, was six feet tall) said he would report the matter to the Mounted Police, Crow's Dance struck him and said, 'We will do the same to the police when they come.' When Little Child arrived at Fort Walsh to complain, Walsh set off the same night with fifteen men, a guide and Surgeon John Kittson – just in case of bloodshed – realising that failure to support Little Child would invite more abuses of police authority.

The police party arrived at the Assiniboine camp in the early hours, to find it formed in the shape of a war camp with the lodge of Crow's Dance in the centre. Dr Kittson and three constables were left behind to build a barricade of stones on a small hill nearby.

At first light Walsh and the rest of his tiny party checked their guns, entered the Assiniboine camp 'at a sharp trot' and surrounded the war lodge. Crow's Dance, another chief named Crooked Arm and twenty other Indians were arrested and hustled out of the now-swarming area to the defensive position prepared by Kittson. 'It was now 5 a.m.; I ordered breakfast,' reported Walsh later. While his men were eating, Walsh sent a message to the Assiniboines saying he would meet the remaining chiefs in half an hour; at this confrontation Walsh lectured the Assiniboines and told them that thirteen of the arrested men were being taken to Fort Walsh for trial. The next day Assistant Commissioner Irvine sentenced Crow's Dance to six months' hard labour and Crooked Arm got two months; the remaining eleven Assiniboines were released with a warning.

Irvine wrote to Ottawa, 'I cannot too highly write of Inspector Walsh's prompt conduct, and it must be a matter of congratulation to feel that fifteen of our men can ride into an enormous camp of Indians and take out of it as prisoners thirteen of their head men. The action of this detachment will have a great effect on all the Indians throughout the country.' The *Fort Benton Record*, that keen observer of police activities, found its own way of congratulating Walsh: 'Custer's charge was not a braver deed.'

139

Walsh's swoop on the Assiniboine camp in fact set a pattern for nonchalant behaviour in the face of overwhelmingly superior numbers of Indians in similar situations over the next six years.

The prosperity and well-being of the Canadian Plains Indians had always been a hazardous affair, depending as it did on the presence of the buffalo in their country. In 1876, a year before he had signed Treaty No. 7, the Blackfoot chief Crowfoot had prophesied that 'the day is coming when the buffalo will all be killed and we shall have nothing more to live on'. He added hopefully, 'I know . . . that the Great Mother will not let her children starve.'

The ruthless way in which the buffalo were being hunted to extermination is shown by the fact that in 1877 export duty was paid on 30,000 buffalo robes in the tiny settlement of Fort Macleod alone. Two years later the figure had fallen to 5764. The arrival of more-sophisticated weapons of destruction carried by professional buffalo-hunters on the American plains hastened the end of the herds, but both the Indians and half-breeds in Canada were guilty of reckless killing. Though the meat was often dried and converted, especially by the half-breeds, into a highly nutritious preserved food known as pemmican (which according to the Catholic missionary Father Albert Lacombe tasted 'almost as good as a candle'), the prairie people lived mainly for the day. William Francis Butler wrote that 'No man can starve better than the Indian – no man can feast better, either. For long days and nights he will go without sustenance of any kind; but see him then if you want to know what quantity of food it is possible for a man to consume at a sitting.' In thirteen days Butler watched seven Indians put away 1700 pounds of meat, a daily average of eighteen pounds a man, and Inspector Sam Steele claimed that he sat in on an Indian supper where twenty pounds of buffalo meat per Indian was eaten.

As the herds began to disappear the Canadian Indians blamed their misfortune on the Sioux refugees. Crowfoot promised, 'If you will drive away the Sioux and make a hole so that the buffalo may come in we will not trouble you for food; if you do not do that, you must feed us or show us how to live.' Though the influx of American tribes merely hastened the inevitable end of the buffalo, it brought starvation to the Canadian West at a critical time, before the treaty Indians could be taught how to become self-supporting farmers and stockbreeders. Commissioner Macleod pointed out, 'Not only have the Sioux killed off an immense number of animals which would have been available for our own Indians but they have also driven the large eastern herd south to occupy the very gap left by the Sioux when they left their old hunting grounds.'

At its first session at Swan River in March 1877 the newly formed North West Territories Council passed an ordinance to protect the buffalo, making it unlawful to kill calves, or to slaughter any buffalo purely for sport, and imposing a closed season on cows between 15 November and 14 August. Although designed to protect the Indians it succeeded only in puzzling, then annoying them, and was a miserable failure. The idea of a man being sent to prison for killing a buffalo was totally beyond the understanding of the Indians; they cheerfully defied the regulations which were quietly repealed after sixteen months.

The starvation years were triggered by a mild winter in 1877–8. Macleod reported that 'week followed week with the same genial sunshine'. The snowfall was light and by early spring the dry prairie grass was ablaze for mile after disastrous mile, driving the buffalo far to the north or down into the United States. Early the following spring another series of prairie fires sprang up along the boundary line from Wood Mountain westward to the Rockies – set alight deliberately by Americans to keep the buffalo south of the line, according to some Canadian officials. When Canadian Indians sent parties into the United States to hunt for food they were turned back by the soldiers of General Nelson A. Miles.

By the summer of 1879 game had been completely swept from the plains by the desperate natives. 'Not even a rabbit track is to be seen anywhere,' wrote a Hudson's Bay Company official from Fort Carlton. The once-proud hunters of buffalo and bear were reduced to eating mice and picking clean the putrid remains of rotting animals. They ate their dogs and, when the wretched animals became too weak to be of any use, they killed and devoured their horses too.

Macleod wrote, 'during the spring and early summer the condition of our Indians was deplorable in the extreme'. Every police post and settlement in the North West was besieged by starving Indians begging for food. At Fort Calgary Inspector Cecil Denny issued police meat rations to parties of starving Blackfoot who were eating grass to keep themselves alive. He recalled, 'It was a pitiable sight to see the parties bringing in their starving to Fort Calgary, some of them being mere skeletons. I have seen them, after I had an animal killed, rush on the carcase before the life was out of it and cut and tear off the meat, eating it raw.'

At Fort Macleod thousands of emaciated Indians were issued with small quantities of beef and flour every other day from the police's own supply; at one stage Superintendent William Winder was reduced to six bags of flour for the use of his command. The police post at Battleford was surrounded by a mixture of Crees, Blackfoot, Assiniboines, Sarcees, Bloods and Sioux, all so weak that they couldn't be bothered to quarrel or fight with their hereditary enemies. Inspector James Walker, known to the Indians as 'The Eagle That Protects', managed to feed them small quantities but went in continual fear of his fort being burned. 'Large bands were continually in and about the barracks, wandering about the buildings, smoking in the vicinity of the stables and hay yards, to the great risk of the whole quarters.' Nowhere, of course, was the situation worse or the Indians thicker than around Fort Walsh, which was besieged by about 5000 Crees, Blackfoot, Bloods and Sioux. 'To all of them provisions had to be given,' Superintendent Leif Crozier noted, 'otherwise hundreds certainly would have starved to death.' The Indian horses were too weak even to carry the small bags of food from the fort to nearby camps, and police wagons were kept continually on the road, meeting and feeding starving Indians.

The police helped whenever and wherever they could. One patrol from Fort Saskatchewan was approached by a group of Indians who watched the police make camp and eat their meal before pouncing on the left-overs, and scraping and even licking the dishes and cooking pots. While on their way from Qu'Appelle to Fort Ellice to collect treaty money for payment, Sergeant Frank Fitzpatrick and his companion, Constable Moffatt, came across a group of some thirty starving Indians. Fitzpatrick wrote

Their appearance was most heart-rending. They looked like a delegation from some graveyard. There were men, women and children with their eyes sunk back in their heads and all with the look of despair about them. At first we threw them a few pieces of hardtack but imagine our feelings when we saw the men jump on the children to take away from them the few biscuits they were able to gather in the scramble. So we made them form a line. I took my post at one end with drawn revolver. They were told that I would shoot the first one who took a biscuit away from another, then Moffatt gave them a biscuit each and this he repeated until all the children had had their fill. We then gave them all our remaining biscuits and some other provisions and proceeded on our way.

But the most harrowing incident concerned a tall, heavily built Cree named Swift Runner who, in the spring of 1879, was arrested at Fort Saskatchewan on suspicion of having eaten his mother, brother, wife and five children. At first Swift Runner claimed that the others had died while he had survived the starvation winter in his lonely camp by boiling and eating his moosehide tepee; but when an investigating party under Inspector Sévère Gagnon found the tepee hidden in a tree, and the grisly evidence of skulls and bones scattered around the camp-site Swift Runner confessed and was sentenced on 8 August by Stipendiary Magistrate Hugh Richardson to be hanged at Fort Saskatchewan for cannibalism.

While awaiting execution the Indian became a Catholic. On the

morning of his execution, five days before Christmas, those
relatives of his who had survived his cooking pot and some local
chiefs sat in a circle around the scaffold in bitterly cold weather
singing the death song. Swift Runner was attended by a priest,
Father LeDuc, and before being pinioned by a local rancher and
former gold-miner named Jim Reid, he made a short speech
acknowledging his guilt and thanking the police and priests for
their consideration. He ended by reprimanding his guards for
keeping him waiting in the cold. Then, in the words of Jean
d'Artigue who watched the execution, 'the bolt was drawn and
Swift Runner launched into eternity'. Afterwards Reid remarked
cheerfully that it was the prettiest hanging he had ever seen, and
it was his thirty-first. But for the Mounted Police the execution
of Swift Runner was a landmark. It was the first legal execution
in the North West Territories.

Though most of the Indians accepted their miserable lot with
resignation, there were occasional outbursts. A group of starving
men broke into the Fort Qu'Appelle storehouse and made off with
flour and provisions left over from previous treaty payments
which they considered their own; and settlers complained with
increasing frequency that their cattle were being killed by hungry
Indians. Despite searching inquiries in his area, Superintendent
William Winder was able to make only one conviction at Fort
Macleod, 'and that was a case with the most extenuating circumstances'. A Stony Indian, Little Man, who had killed a cow to
feed his family, went to the farmer concerned and offered his
horse in payment. But the settler chose to prosecute and Little
Man, after being under arrest for some time, was fined $20, the
value of the cow.

At the end of the year Macleod reported to Ottawa, 'Hungry
men are dangerous, whether they be Indians or whites, and I
think it is a wonderful thing how well the Indian has behaved
under all the circumstances.' In their terrible plight most of the
Indians had managed to cling on to one thing, their dignity, as

Superintendent James Walsh observed: 'The conduct of those starving and destitute people, their patient endurance, their sympathy and the extent to which they assisted each other, their strict observance of law and order would reflect credit upon the most civilised community.'

The fear of violence was never far away, however, and in November 1879 came the blow that many policemen had been expecting for some months – the murder of one of their number by an Indian. The victim was a nineteen-year-old named Marmaduke Graburn, who had been in the Force less than six months. On his way back from herd duty he turned back alone to recover a forgotten axe. He failed to return to Fort Walsh that night, and next morning a search party led by Jerry Potts pushed out into the snow-covered hills to look for him. Potts soon found bloodstains in the snow, an indentation where Graburn had fallen from his horse, and a mass of hoof and moccasin prints. An hour later his body was uncovered in a ravine. He had been shot in the back of the head. Not far away lay his horse, two bullets in its brain. Rapidly melting snow made the tracking of Graburn's murderer impossible.

It seemed a motiveless affair and six months passed with no news of Graburn's killer. Then two Blood Indians under arrest at Fort Walsh for horse stealing admitted that they had been camped nearby at the time of Graburn's death. Afraid that they might be accused of the murder, the two Indians made a break for freedom while exercising outside the fort, but Superintendent Leif Crozier and Inspector John Cotton, who were playing tennis at the time, chased after them, rackets in hand, and kept the escapers in sight until a mounted squad recaptured the pair. The two men then asked to see Crozier that night in his quarters and, after the windows had been blacked out with blankets, they gave him the name of the man they said had killed Graburn – a fellow Blood called Star Child, who was at that moment away in Montana hunting. Another year passed before the police were able to get their man. When it was learned that Star Child had returned to a Blood camp about twenty-five miles from Fort Macleod a detachment of four police and Jerry Potts swept into the camp at dawn. As Star Child darted from his tepee with a rifle in his hands he was overpowered and disarmed by Corporal Robert Patterson. In the scuffle the rifle went off, rousing the rest of the camp. As his friends tried to pull him free, Patterson grabbed Star Child by the throat, snapped handcuffs on his wrists, swung into the saddle with the half-choked Indian under his arm and shouted to his colleagues, 'Ride, boys'. Patterson's bravery was wasted. At Star Child's trial in October 1881 the jury of six white settlers were out for nearly twenty-four hours before returning a verdict of not guilty because of lack of evidence. Inspector Sam Steele considered, 'There is no doubt that the jurymen who were for acquittal were afraid that conviction would bring on an Indian war, or cause the Bloods to kill their [the jurymen's] stock out of revenge.'

Although they had been slow to appreciate the Indians' plight, the Canadian government acted promptly enough when the starvation stories reached eastern Canada. Supplies were rushed to Fort Macleod and Fort Walsh; in addition to the normal flow of food guaranteed under the treaties, they forwarded 500 head of cattle, 91,000 lb of bacon, 100,000 lb of beef, 20,000 lb of pemmican and 800 sacks of flour, insisting at the same time that the relief was only a temporary measure and that the Indians were expected, to borrow a contemporary phrase, to stand on their own two feet as soon as possible. Between June 1879 and June 1880 the government spent $66,500 to relieve destitute Indians, in addition to the $100,000 handed out at annual treaty payments. They also took the first step towards having Indian interests officially represented in government circles by appointing the forty-four-year-old Edgar Dewdney as the first Indian Commissioner. Dewdney, who had been born in Devon, and had been a resident of Canada for the past twenty years and a Canadian MP since 1872, was given sweeping powers to operate on the spot in

146

the North West Territories. Dewdney met the leading chiefs and vigorously attempted to persuade them to settle on their allocated reserves of land and become self-sufficient as soon as possible. Until that time, he assured them, the Great Mother would see that they did not starve.

But there were no government hand-outs for the Sioux – though the police did not bother to discriminate between one Indian group and another at the height of the starvation. The small garrison at the Wood Mountain post cut down on their meals and saved all table scraps to be handed out to Sioux women and children. 'I do not think that one ounce of food was wasted at Wood Mountain,' wrote Walsh. 'Every man appeared to be interested in saving what little he could, and day after day they divided their rations with those starving people.' According to the American newspaper correspondent John Finerty of the Chicago *Times*, 'It was the intense humanity of Walsh that absolutely kept the wretched people from eating their horses.'

Walsh was the one white man in whom Sitting Bull had implicit trust. Before taking any decision he was always anxious to hear what Walsh had to say about it. This attitude fed Walsh's ego enormously. He referred to the Indian chief casually as 'Bull' in official correspondence and affected a dashing dress to go with his new image as a friend of the Sioux. One of the men who served with him described it as 'rather a bizarre style of uniform, a straight peaked cap like an infantry officer's, but with a heavy gold band, or else a wide-brimmed light fawn sombrero, a cavalry patrol jacket, Bedford cord breeches and U.S. Cavalry boots with the fronts reaching above the knees'. He also grew a goatee beard, which was copied by many of his men in B Division. Nothing pleased Walsh more at this period than the constant references to him in the American press as 'Sitting Bull's Boss'. (At Christmas, 1878, a picture of Walsh hung in the Fort Walsh mess, encircled by evergreens and pieces of harness, with the words 'Sitting Bull's Boss' underneath.) He was known to the Sioux as 'Long Lance',

though the Fort Benton *Record* rather spoiled the image by reporting that the true translation of Walsh's name was 'Little Ass'.

Walsh, in turn, had a tremendous admiration for Sitting Bull:

> In my opinion he is the shrewdest and most intelligent living
> Indian, has the ambition of Napoleon and is brave to a fault;
> he is respected, as well as feared, by every Indian on the plains.
> In war he has no equal, in council he is superior to all. Every
> word said by him carries weight, is quoted and passed from
> camp to camp.

But, much as he admired him, Walsh was against giving Sitting
Bull a reservation in Canada, since 'he would be joined by a great
number of disaffected Indians at present in the U.S. agencies . . .
and would, I fear, prove injurious to our settlers and Indians'.

It was an eminently sensible attitude, since the Sioux – despite
their promises – were drifting at will into the United States,
hunting buffalo, stealing horses and, occasionally, attacking
soldiers and settlers. When the United States government protested at these incursions Sir John Macdonald commented that
Canada 'might just as well try to check the flight of locusts'. In
April 1879 Assistant Commissioner Irvine read to the assembled
Sioux at Wood Mountain a warning from the new Governor-
General, the Marquis of Lorne, about raiding into the United
States. 'I read the message three times over to them . . . as I
wished them thoroughly to understand it.' But Irvine might have
saved his breath. Soon afterwards the Indian agent at Fort
Belknap, Montana, was complaining that his area 'besides being
covered with Sioux, is also overrun with British Blackfeet and
Piegans'. He reported that his agency Indians were practically
debarred from hunting on their own territory by the presence of
'hostile British subjects'.

In July 1880 an army column under General Nelson A. Miles
attacked a band of 400 Sioux, who fled back into Canada. Twice
afterwards Miles was visited by Walsh who insisted that the
Indians had not crossed the border with hostile intent, but merely
in search of buffalo. When the Americans again protested to the

British government, the Foreign Office summoned up its coolest phrases in asking the British Ambassador in Washington, Sir Edward Thornton, to point out 'that the Dominion suffers at least as much inconvenience from the presence [of the Sioux] in British territory as do the United States. It seems unreasonable that, if the authorities of the United States are powerless to restrain the Indians from crossing to the British side of the border, they should expect the Canadian authorities to prevent them from re-crossing into the United States.' The truth was that neither Canada nor the United States wanted the Sioux living as free men in their country. The Canadians realised that if good terms could be extracted from the Americans, the Sioux would be glad to abandon their bleak, uncertain existence in the North West and go home. But with a public determined to be rid of Sitting Bull, the United States was forced to adopt an inflexible attitude – the Sioux must return as prisoners, surrendering their guns and horses, and with them, of course, their freedom.

There were complaints, too, from Canadian citizens about the roaming Sioux. When a bunch of Teton Sioux drifted as far as Prince Albert, more than 250 miles north of Wood Mountain, in search of food it was reported that they had killed a tame buffalo belonging to the local magistrate, Captain H. S. Moore, slaughtered two oxen and had been guilty of persistent begging and trespassing around the homes of Prince Albert residents. Superintendent James Walker was ordered from Battleford to investigate the Prince Albert incidents and found the alleged depredations 'very much exaggerated'. What had in fact happened was that the starving Sioux had offered to trade their horses for the buffalo and oxen. For lack of an interpreter, the settlers assumed the Indians were trying to pay for animals they had already killed.

The narrowness of the margin between uneasy peace and disaster was illustrated by two incidents at Wood Mountain. In the first, a constable struck a Sioux and threw him off police property for 'obstructing him in his work'. The offended man's camp, about 200 lodges strong, prepared to raid the Wood Mountain post in retaliation. Getting his priorities right, Walsh readied his defences before sending for the camp's headmen. The incident was smoothed over when Walsh mocked them for becoming so disturbed over a personal quarrel, but he promised to discipline the policeman involved.

The second affair was not so easily put down. A Sioux was arrested on suspicion of having stolen a horse belonging to the Wood Mountain trader, Jean-Louis Legaré. A group of angry Indians, led by Sitting Bull, attempted to prevent the prisoner being taken into the police post. Walsh ordered his pathetically small garrison of twenty to arms. For some time a fight seemed imminent, until Walsh talked 'very sharply' to Sitting Bull, who stalked off in a sulk saying that he was going to the United States. For several days the police stayed barricaded in at Wood Mountain until, in the words of Walsh, 'Bull came and apologised for his conduct and asked my forgiveness, which I granted him.' The accused Sioux was released after a hearing, perhaps diplomatically in view of what had happened.

However, Walsh was under no misapprehension about the Sioux's generally good conduct, which he felt was due to 'their fear of being sent back to the United States'.

Despite this fear, some Sioux, starving and sick, began to drift back across the frontier in 1880, surrendering to General Miles's troops posted just south of the line. Sitting Bull promised to place no obstacles in the way of those of his people who chose to return. But Sitting Bull himself was still implacably opposed to surrender. A Wood Mountain trader, Edwin Allen, considered the Sioux chief 'the most suspicious Indian I have ever met. He is in constant terror of some unseen plan being made to entrap him across the line. This one idea haunts him night and day.' Sitting Bull even refused to allow the missionary Father Joseph Hugonard into his camp to treat six children in case the priest should suborn his followers. But he had reckoned without Catholic determination. Father Hugonard managed to see a few dying children by telling their mothers that he had a good medicine, which was in fact baptismal water in a scent bottle. Pretending to treat the children he managed to baptise them instead, saving their souls if not their lives.

Despite Sitting Bull's intransigence, more and more of his followers went back to the United States in 1880, drawn by the promise of food. By April the remainder were congregated at Wood Mountain; their horses were in such poor condition that when a small buffalo herd was discovered seventy miles away the Sioux could not get to them. By early summer Sitting Bull's camp was reduced to 100 lodges; the great chief himself vacillated, waiting to see what his friend Walsh would advise. But Walsh's star was on the wane. Many people, including the American General Miles, considered Sitting Bull was under Walsh's influence and that their alliance was delaying the Indian's return. When word of this reached Ottawa, Sir John Macdonald decided to transfer Walsh from the border region to command of the comparatively unimportant police post in the Qu'Appelle Valley.

In July Walsh handed over command at Wood Mountain to Leif Crozier. He planned to go on leave to his home at Brockville, Ontario, prior to taking over at Qu'Appelle. Just before Walsh left, Sitting Bull visited him, gave the policeman his war bonnet and pleaded with him to attempt to secure a home in Canada for the Sioux. Walsh wrote later, 'I explained to him that it would be a waste of labour on my part to undertake any such task, and a waste of time on his part to await the results.' So the Indian switched tacks, and asked if Walsh would intervene with the American President, Rutherford B. Hayes, to get the best conditions possible for his return. This plan appealed to Walsh's recently inflated sense of self-importance and he promised to undertake the task if his government would permit it. He kept his promise, writing to David Mills, the Minister of the Interior, offering to go to Washington and adding, 'I believe if he [Sitting Bull] were assured by the President that he would not receive harsh treatment and if a few concessions were extended to him I could induce him to surrender.'

151

Walsh's letter infuriated the politicians. Sir John Macdonald sent for him and told him bluntly that he would not be allowed to go to Washington 'or interfere in any way'. The Prime Minister considered that Walsh had made his offer 'in order to make himself of importance. He is, I fear, primarily responsible for the Indian's unwillingness to leave Canada' – a harsh judgement on Walsh's hard and faithful work. So Macdonald extended Walsh's leave in eastern Canada and issued orders that 'Sitting Bull's Boss' was not to return to Fort Walsh under any circumstances.

Walsh's successor, the overbearing and uncompromising Crozier, immediately set out to break Sitting Bull's influence and authority among the remaining Sioux.

> I spoke to the people generally, telling them not to allow any one or any set of men prevent their accepting American terms of surrender. I explained how much their women and children would benefit by such a step. These and similar arguments soon began to have an effect upon the camp. . . . Sitting Bull and his soldiers had to prevent the lodges leaving several times by force.

Twice, in October 1880 and again in January 1881, Sitting Bull crossed the frontier, ostensibly to hunt but actually to sound out the American authorities about conditions of surrender. On the second occasion the Sioux camp was attacked by the American Army and Sitting Bull fled back to the safety of Canada. In April he made a final, desperate attempt to obtain a home on Canadian soil, trekking 160 miles north-east to the Qu'Appelle Valley in search of his old friend Walsh. But Walsh was still in eastern Canada. Instead he met Inspector Sam Steele (who had acquired the nickname Smoothbore among his command) and he found Steele no more disposed to friendship than Crozier had been. The Indian Commissioner Edgar Dewdney hurried to Qu'Appelle for a conference with Sitting Bull, who told him, 'I gave Major Walsh my fine clothing and told him to speak for me, and that is what I am waiting for. . . . I know the reasons why all of you want me to go back, my carcase is nothing but gold, they would give a good deal for my carcase.' After rejecting Sitting Bull's request for a reservation at Qu'Appelle, Dewdney authorised the issuing of a limited amount of rations from the police post in the area. But, in order to get enough food to live, the Sioux were forced to trade five horses and assorted souvenirs taken from dead American cavalrymen at Little Big Horn in exchange for a few bags of flour from that enterprising missionary, Father Hugonard.

Dewdney was so impressed by Sitting Bull's determination to cling to Canada that he reported to Ottawa, 'I feel certain that their surrender can only be brought about by actual starvation.' It was an opinion which the government were coming increasingly to share. Sir John Macdonald, acutely aware that the Canadian Pacific Railway was beginning to inch across the prairies and that it would bring a rush of settlers in its wake, urged that the Sioux be persuaded to return to the United States 'as the only alternative to prevent the death by starvation of themselves, their wives and their children'. Lord Lorne agreed. He suggested that the American and Canadian governments should 'leave hunger to do its work'.

Hunger was certainly beginning to do its work. Sergeant Frank Fitzpatrick, who was based at the Qu'Appelle post, wrote, 'We received orders that we were no longer to trade with, feed or even talk to them [the Sioux]. When I imparted this information to Sitting Bull he said that the white men had gone back on him and that sooner than return to the United States he would drown himself.' The Sioux at Qu'Appelle, according to Fitzpatrick, were in a pathetic condition. He took pity on two of Sitting Bull's children, a daughter of about fifteen, whose Indian name meant 'The Girl Who Winks At You As She Walks Along', and a boy of six, and undertook to feed them.

Empty-handed and in a furious temper, Sitting Bull trekked back to Wood Mountain, where he asked Inspector Archibald McDonnell for food. When the policeman refused, Sitting Bull said he would take what he wanted by force, to which McDonnell – known as 'Paper-Collar Johnnie' because of his dress habits – replied that he and his band would receive nothing better than a ration of bullets. In utter despair, the chief cried, 'I am cast away.' McDonnell told him, 'No, you are not cast away. You have been promised a pardon and food and land if you return to the United States. I advise you to go.' Sitting Bull could take no more: he agreed to go. But, typically, he prevaricated until the very end. Appropriately, the commissary arrangements for Sitting Bull's return were in the hands of the Wood Mountain trader Jean-Louis Legaré, the first white man to deal with the Sioux when they had crossed the Canadian border nearly five years previously. At his own expense, Legaré prepared thirty-nine wagons to carry the women, children and supplies for the six-day journey to Fort Buford, Montana. Sitting Bull first delayed the departure by demanding that another ten bags of flour be loaded for the trip, then when the Sioux struck south towards the United States, accompanied by a small police detachment under Inspector McDonnell, Sitting Bull and a band of warriors feigned to go north instead, and followed Legaré's wagons at a distance. At the United States line the party was met by American soldiers. Constable Edward Barnett, one of the Mounted Police escort, described the scene:

> The Americans swung in between us and the Indians, bunched them like sheep into a compact body. How they wailed and cried, for the poor Indian felt he had made his last stand. The last I seen of Sitting Bull he was stretched as high as he could get, roaring at the top of his voice prevailing on his people to go quietly along and give no trouble.

On 21 July 1881, Sitting Bull surrendered at Fort Buford with the wretched remnants of his followers, fewer than two hundred. He made one final, bitter protest: 'This soil I am trampling upon is always mine; I never sold it nor gave it to anybody.' He insisted on being the last to hand over his rifle, via his small son, and told him, 'If you live you will never be a man because you will never have owned a rifle or a horse.' That said, Sitting Bull covered his face with a blanket as the surrender ceremony proceeded. His fears about his fate were well founded. Despite the promises of a pardon, Sitting Bull was imprisoned for two years. After his release he toured briefly as a star attraction in Buffalo Bill Cody's famous Wild West Show, but left the show to help the Sioux fight to preserve their reservation lands, which were threatened with encroachment. As a mark of friendship Buffalo Bill presented him with a performing horse, trained to sit down and raise a hoof at the sound of a shot. Towards the end of 1890 Sitting Bull's arrest was ordered again as 'a fomenter of trouble'. Just before dawn on 15 December Sitting Bull's log cabin on the Standing Rock agency was surrounded by Indian police mercenaries under Lieutenant of Police Henry Tatankan Bull Head. Though Sitting Bull agreed to go quietly, some of his followers attempted to free him; shooting broke out and at the end of it five policemen and eight Indians lay dead, including Sitting Bull and the police chief Bull Head. As the bullets flew Sitting Bull's horse, the gift from Buffalo Bill, began to go through its tricks.

James McLaughlin, the Indian agent at Standing Rock, could hardly conceal his pleasure at Sitting Bull's death. He suggested an allowance for the families of the dead Indian police 'to show that the government recognises the great service that has been done for the country' and thought that the Indian policemen's 'determination in maintaining the will of the government is most gratifying'.

The career of 'Sitting Bull's Boss', James Walsh, ended ingloriously. Discredited by his attempt to intervene with the American President on behalf of Sitting Bull, Walsh lingered a further two years in unimportant posts. In a harsh, biased confidential report in 1880 Irvine destroyed what was left of Walsh's police career: 'I regard him as both utterly incompetent and untrustworthy. He does not command respect from officers or men and is in my opinion unfit to hold a commission in the Force.' In September 1883 Walsh retired, taking with him his horse, for which he paid the government $150. The only thanks he got for his work among the Sioux was a lump sum of one month's pay for each of his ten years of service. Walsh went into the coal business near Winnipeg, though he was destined to make a dramatic and unhappy reappearance among the Mounted Police during the Klondike gold rush in the Yukon fifteen years later. Helping the Sioux was a distinctly unprofitable venture. Jean-Louis Legaré, the man who had played such an important part in finally persuading the Sioux to go back, had to wait six years to get from the United States government the money he had expended on provisioning the Indians for their return. And then he had to sue the government before the Court of Claims to obtain judgement for $8000.

A year before Sitting Bull surrendered to the U.S. Army, the North West Mounted Police lost their second Commissioner, James Macleod. His double burden of head policeman and leading member of the North West Territories council was a heavy one indeed. There were signs of irritation with Macleod's performance soon after the Conservatives regained power in 1878 when Sir John Macdonald complained to the Commissioner about his lack of economy in running the Force, saying that the police expenditure 'would not stand investigation. This would involve discredit on all concerned. I brought you into the Force and am much interested in your success and therefore act the part of a real friend in giving you this most serious warning.' Though Macleod strenuously denied this charge of inefficiency, the long knives were out again and he was relieved of his post as Commissioner in June 1880 – officially to allow him to concentrate on his position as stipendiary magistrate.

Macleod, described by a friend as 'a happy combination of the gentleman of the old school and the man of the world and affairs', was appointed Judge in the newly organised Supreme Court of the North West Territories in 1887 and held the post until his death at the age of fifty-eight in September 1894. James Farquharson Macleod, soldier, judge and gentleman, was given an impressive military funeral.

PART THREE

Acheson Gosford Irvine

Pass the tea and let us drink
To the guardians of our land
You can bet your life it's not our fault
That whiskey's contraband.

— *Mounted Police Song*

Chapter 10

RAILWAY DAYS

MACLEOD's successor, Acheson Gosford Irvine, was the first Canadian-born Commissioner of the Mounted Police; he came from a distinguished Quebec family of soldiers and politicians and, like Macleod, had joined the police via the Canadian militia. A slight man with a closely trimmed reddish beard, Irvine was known in the Force as 'Sorrel Top', and the opinion of one of his officers that he was 'a thorough gentleman' was shared by many under his command. Unfortunately, Irvine seemed unaware that all other men were not necessarily gentlemen, and Major-General Selby Smyth considered him 'almost too good-natured to command obedience'.

In anticipation of his appointment Irvine was sent to England and Ireland early in 1880 to learn about the management and organisation of the Transport Corps at Aldershot and study the Royal Irish Constabulary. Deeply impressed by what he had seen, Irvine returned to Canada in an enthusiastic mood of reform. Immediately he pressed for a bigger force – a minimum of 500 men, instead of 300. In justification he pointed out that the police had jurisdiction over 375,000 square miles of territory – as vast as Spain and Portugal combined – which contained 27,000 Indians, most of whom were being forced by starvation and the ceding of their lands to turn their backs on the habits of a lifetime. Irvine predicted, quite accurately, that there would be trouble: 'Discontent may, in fact more than probably will, break out particularly among the young men.' The rapid settlement of the Canadian West was another reason for strengthening the Force.

'The experience of our neighbours to the south of the boundary line cannot be without its lessons. In their case the military had no trouble with the Indians until settlers appeared on the scene.'

Irvine also recommended that a training depot be set up for recruits, where they could be thoroughly drilled in what he termed 'soldier-like conduct and general bearing', instead of being recruited in the east of Canada and shipped west without any form of preparation. Things had changed in the six years since Inspector Ephraim Brisebois had silenced an irate whiskey-smuggler by telling him, 'We make up the law as we go along.' The Mounted Police now needed a sound base from which to administer a developing territory. And after he had visited the north-west in the autumn of 1881 Canada's Governor-General, the Marquis of Lorne, agreed with Irvine. The following year the strength of the Force was increased to 500 and authorisation given for the establishment of a training depot.

Lord Lorne was the first Governor-General to see the West; when he left Ottawa he was accompanied by his own chef, surgeon and chaplain, as well as an impressive array of aides, assistants, advisers and a retinue of newspaper correspondents in keeping with his office and his importance as Queen Victoria's son-in-law (Lorne was married to H.R.H. Princess Louise). The Governor-General's party made their way west by steamer, canoe and barge, and where possible along the completed stretches of the newly built Canadian Pacific Railway as far as the end of the line at Portage La Prairie, just beyond Winnipeg. Elaborate arrangements were made to soften the West's rigours for the distinguished visitor. The railway provided a guard's van converted with carpets, sofa and easy chairs and an open wagon furnished with seats and awnings.

Winnipeg, the first big prairie settlement they visited, profoundly depressed Charles Austin, the correspondent of *The Times* accompanying the group. He described it as 'an odd, unsightly jumble of shabby shanties and showy stores, of cabins

15. (*Above*) A parade at Fort Walsh 1880

16. (*Below*) Fort Calgary in 1878. A group of Blood Indians can
be seen in the foreground. Inspector Cecil Denny sits, isolated,
behind them

17. Crowfoot, Chief of the Blackfoot

18. Sitting Bull, the Sioux victor of the battle of the Little Big Horn

and would-be palaces in ill-matched confusion as if they had been tumbled half-finished out of a bag onto the flat plain and somewhat damaged and knocked out of shape by the fall'.

From the end of the railway line Lord Lorne travelled by steamer up the Assiniboine River to Fort Ellice, where he was welcomed by the twenty-strong Mounted Police detachment under Superintendent William Herchmer which was to escort him for the remainder of the tour. At Fort Ellice the party encountered their first Plains Indians. According to Charles Austin one of them was 'a striking likeness of Mr Gladstone, and was happily named "He Who Is Always Right"'. But in the main the Indians impressed *The Times* man no more than Winnipeg had done: 'It is certainly disenchanting to find the Indian dressing as no decent scarecrow would ever voluntarily submit to be dressed, and it is positively painful to find that he never opens his mouth except to beg that something may be put into it.'

In addition to escorting the Governor-General, the police detachment acted as general lackeys to the party, unloading wagons, pitching tents and foraging for wood and water. From Fort Ellice they travelled to Qu'Appelle, 120 miles west, where Lorne met an assembly of more than a thousand Crees and Salteaux. At a formal pow-wow the chiefs addressed their visitor as 'brother-in-law' since they regarded themselves as children of the Great Mother, Queen Victoria. The Indian Commissioner, Edgar Dewdney, joined the group at Battleford, capital of the North West Territories, and the Cree chief Poundmaker undertook to guide them to their next major stopping-point, Calgary, in exchange for a suit of European clothes. Poundmaker was an extremely handsome Indian, and Charles Austin commented on his 'finely cut, aristocratic face, fascinating smile and thick plaits of magnificent black hair which would be worth their weight in gold to many a professional beauty'. But Poundmaker's performance as a hunter was not nearly so impressive as his looks:

Heading our procession today he viewed some wild ducks and at once paused to gather himself for the warpath. I watched him with keen interest, hoping that with a slight pressure of the knees he would start his war pony at lightning speed and, swinging himself around under its belly, shoot the leader drake through the off eye just to show his skill. Instead of this he solemnly dismounted, took a long careful aim, fired into the flock of birds sitting – and missed, just as any civilised Cockney might have done.

Poundmaker's performance was no better when the party ran across a small band of buffalo a few days later. Lord Lorne declined the invitation to take part in one of the West's last buffalo hunts, saying that since the expedition was short of fresh meat it was important to make sure the animals were killed by experienced hunters. Three buffalo were shot, but none fell to the blazing gun of Poundmaker. Totally unabashed, the Cree chief cut out a kidney from one of the dead animals and, according to Austin, 'ate it raw and reeking, slicing it with his knife as a schoolboy slices an apple'. In the opinion of *The Times* man 'the proceedings somewhat diminished his usual grace of manner and fascinating smile'.

The highlight of the tour came at Blackfoot Crossing, scene of the signing of Treaty No. 7 four years previously, where several thousand Blackfoot, led by Crowfoot, gathered to greet Lord Lorne. Lack of food and insecurity were temporarily forgotten as Crowfoot's tribe staged a series of displays of dancing and horsemanship, one of which ended with the cheerful unleashing of a volley over the heads of their guests. This so unnerved Lord Lorne's secretary, Lieutenant-Colonel Frederick de Winton, that he asked Superintendent Herchmer in a low voice, 'Are your men loaded?' At the great council afterwards one of the main Indian speakers, appropriately named Loud Voice, harangued the Governor-General at great length. When he sat down all heads turned to the police guide Jerry Potts for a full translation. Not for the first time, Potts's English failed him: he hesitated a moment, then said to Lord Lorne, 'He wants grub.'

The police's escort duties on the exhausting tour, covering 1229 miles in thirty-five days, ended at the American army post of Fort Shaw, Montana, from where Lord Lorne was to be taken by U.S. soldiers to Helena to return east by railway through the United States. The Americans had polished their know-how for the occasion. An army band playing 'Hail to the Chief' diplomatically changed in mid-tune to 'God Save the Queen' as the Governor-General's carriage swept into the fort through a specially built arch. One of the army wives at the post, Mrs Frances Roe, gushed in her diary about 'the gorgeously dressed police with their jaunty, side-tilted caps' but she wasn't so impressed with the hard-driven police-horses ('wretched little beasts'). Mrs Roe and other officers' wives watched discreetly from behind curtains as Lorne's contingent was officially received on the parade ground:

> Presently . . . the first notes of 'God Save the Queen' were heard. Instantly the head of every Englishman and Canadian was uncovered – quietly and without ostentation. . . . They were at a military post of another nation, in the midst of being introduced to its officers, yet no one failed to remember and to remind that he was an Englishman forever.

When he took his leave of the police escort the Governor-General shook hands with every man and thanked each one for his hard work. He considered them 'as fine a troop as I ever saw', an opinion which was shared by *The Times* man Charles Austin, who found them 'always cheery, most willing, hard working fellows'. There was no doubt that Lord Lorne also agreed with Austin's statement in one of his articles that 'They are ludicrously underhanded for the ground they have to cover and the number of Indians and white men, often more unmanageable than the Indians, whom they are expected to keep in order.'

The increase in size of the Force in 1882 came only just in time, coinciding as it did with the explosion of settlement and a boom in land values along the route of the Canadian Pacific Railway. Winnipeg's population, for instance, doubled in twelve months. The spread of 'civilisation' complicated police work enormously.

It caused deep resentment among the Indians and half-breeds, resurrected the dormant liquor-problem and pushed up the crime rate.

There had been talk of a trans-continental railway for many years; scandal over its financing had brought down the Macdonald government in 1873, two years after the far western territory of British Columbia had joined the Dominion on the understanding that a railway to link them to the rest of Canada would be completed within ten years. Ten years later the work was just beginning in earnest, but once under way the rails thrust relentlessly across the prairie. The 830 miles separating Winnipeg and Calgary were spanned in a mere two years.

The railway was the making of Calgary. Only ten years after the police had broken the first ground to build their fort at the junction of the Bow and Elbow rivers, there now stood stone buildings, a theatre, town hall, banks and churches. But the C.P.R. crippled other communities. In Montana, Fort Benton's business with Canada withered as rapidly as it had flourished, the golden days of overland freighting wrecked by the railway. Fort Benton was incorporated as a city in 1883, just in time to preside at its own death ceremony. The rip-roaring community lapsed into more decorous ways and when one of Fort Benton's female residents fired off a gun 'just for fun' she was fined $20.

The railway also doomed the territorial capital, Battleford. A change in the planned route took it well to the south of the town, and in 1882 – amid much political manœuvring – it was decided to site the new capital on the railway line at an old buffalo hunters' camp ground known to the Indians as Pile of Bones. Obviously, a more becoming name was needed for the capital, and Princess Louise, wife of the Governor-General, was invited to suggest one. With regal lack of imagination she nominated Regina ('What a name,' lamented one Ottawa politician when he heard the decision). Unfortunately, Regina was saddled with more serious defects than an unsuitable name. As one author commented, 'No city with the possible exception of Sodom and

Gomorrah has ever been founded in less congenial surroundings.' Perhaps as a compromise between the claims of other rival communities, or possibly because he owned 480 acres of land in the vicinity, Edgar Dewdney – who had just succeeded David Laird as Lieutenant-Governor of the North West Territories – managed to convince his good friend Sir John Macdonald that the government should build a new community in one of the flattest, bleakest parts of a desolate plain. Yet only a few miles away lay the beautiful and fertile Qu'Appelle Valley, where there was already a settlement, trading post and police fort. The new town struggled with a succession of problems and even ten years afterwards Flora Shaw, *The Times*'s famous colonial correspondent, considered it 'about on the level of an Australian bush township'. The North West was also divided at the same time into four districts, Assiniboia, Saskatchewan, Alberta and Athabasca, but this was mainly for postal convenience: the territory remained unrepresented in Parliament.

At the end of 1882 the Mounted Police also decided to set up a new headquarters and training depot at Regina alongside the territorial government. With the departure of the last of the Sioux in 1881 the main reason for keeping Fort Walsh as headquarters of the police was gone. Commissioner Irvine consistently criticised the location as altogether unsuitable and urged the fort's abandonment. He wrote to Lieutenant-Governor Dewdney from the fort, 'I wish to goodness we were out of this hole. It is a bad situation in every way. From a military point of view the situation could not be worse, the place invites attack . . . we are surrounded and commanded by hills on all sides. It is a most unhealthy place and the buildings are in a wretched state.'

There were two other reasons why Irvine wanted to abandon Fort Walsh. It was attracting settlers to what he considered poor farming country and it was also encouraging Indians to leave their reservations, hang around the police post subsisting on government hand-outs and plan raids across the American border.

Again it was the arrival of the railway which brought the crisis to a head. The Canadian government wanted all Indians moved to reserves north of the track so that they would find it difficult to trek south into the United States; the indigenous Indians, for their part, objected to the line being driven through what they considered their land around the Cypress Hills. Immigrant workmen felling timber for the railway were terrified by the occasional appearance of armed warriors demanding payment for the wood, or provisions; the railway company's horses were frequently stolen and once a tomahawk was found wedged between two rails.

Piapot, an arrogant Cree chief who styled himself 'Lord of Heaven and Earth', took particular objection to the coming of the Iron Horse. He uprooted survey stakes and finally camped his tribe in the path of the construction gangs. The nearest available Mountie was an English corporal and ex-Guardsman, William Brock Wilde. He gave Piapot and his followers fifteen minutes to clear away their tepees. When the time was up Wilde strode into the Indian village and kicked out the centre poles of the lodges, collapsing them on their startled inhabitants. Bravery bordering on foolishness had again overawed the Indians.

Commissioner Irvine himself went to explain to the Indians the terms of the Vagrancy Act, warning that the government would not allow them to loiter near the railway. But neither the police nor the Indian agents were within their right to insist that the Indians stayed on their reserves. Freedom to hunt through the tracts of surrendered land had been heavily stressed as part of the Indian treaties, and was one of the main reasons for their ready acceptance of them. Now they were being asked to leave their homes in Cypress Hills and settle on unknown reserves far to the north. Only the fact that the Indians were utterly destitute enabled the police to bribe them away from the Fort Walsh area with wagonloads of provisions.

The police's pathetic lack of numbers was illustrated when the job of escorting more than 1000 Assiniboines from Fort Walsh to their allocated reserve near Battleford, 250 miles north, was given to *one* constable, a stocky twenty-three-year-old named Daniel Davis whose fondness for canned fruit had earned him the nickname 'Peach'. A generous number of supply wagons enabled Davis to keep the Indians eating their way steadily northward; in a little over three weeks he was able to deliver his party to the Indian agent at Battleford, get an official receipt for them and burn his verminous clothes before returning to Fort Walsh. Irvine attached so little importance to Davis's accomplishment that he didn't even mention him by name in his report of the move. Cool behaviour in the face of staggering odds was an everyday matter, it seemed.

The police could not congratulate themselves for long. By the late summer of 1882 many of the tribes had drifted south again to Fort Walsh. Piapot said he didn't like the land his people had been given at Qu'Appelle; returning Assiniboines told Irvine they wanted to be where their dead were buried and friends were living. By that winter, with a change of police headquarters imminent, the situation was as bad as ever, with almost 300 tepees sprinkled around the walls of Fort Walsh. So the government again adopted the expedient of starving out people who were unwilling to leave their homes. Inspector Frank Norman at Fort Walsh was forced to issue the Indians two days' rations every seven days. Inevitably, slow starvation and a bitter winter totally disheartened the Indians. By the spring of 1883 they had all been escorted north again and in May Fort Walsh was demolished.

Irvine was only too well aware of the inhumanity behind many of the forced moves. 'These Indians have always looked upon the Cypress Hills as their home. It is not, therefore, to be wondered at that I had considerable difficulty in inducing them to accept a new and northern reserve.'

Chapter 11

'OFF TO CHARM
ALMIGHTY GOD'

THE site of Fort Macleod was also in some danger early in the
1880s. The original fort and settlement had been built in a loop
of the Oldman River, but the river changed course in 1881 and
Fort Macleod was marooned on an island which was steadily being
washed away. As one of his first duties after founding the *Fort
Macleod Gazette* (which, until an engine could be installed, had a
dozen Blood Indians cranking a handle to supply motive power
for the printing press), a former policeman named Charles Wood
reported to the community, 'Each succeeding Springtime the
betting is almost even that the whole concern, fort, town and
inhabitants will form a stately procession on the watery road to
Winnipeg.' In the spring of 1883, with the river lapping almost
at the gates of the fort, it was decided to build a new community
on higher ground about half a mile away.

This time the work of building the fort was contracted out.
More than a million feet of lumber went into the new barracks,
and Surgeon George Kennedy was particularly pleased with the
post's hospital, which he considered 'probably the best in the
North-West'. Health, too, improved considerably with the move,
'a fact which cannot be a source of wonder when we consider the
difference between the foul-smelling and ill-ventilated log buildings of the old fort and the spacious, airy, well-lighted and comfortable quarters of the new', reported Kennedy.

Though the new town received scathing comment from John

Higinbotham, just arrived from Ontario to become its first chemist – 'decidedly ramshackle and distressing' – and another visitor described its main street as 'a wide, muddy lane with a row of dirty, half-finished shanties flanking it', Fort Macleod did possess one of the few hotels in the territory. The building was owned by that old squaw thief, Harry 'Kamoose' Taylor, whose arrest by the police for whiskey smuggling had not dampened his sense of humour. Taylor, educated for the ministry in England, had come to the West as a missionary but abandoned the cloth for the financially more rewarding business of selling liquor. Since his arrest he had become a legitimate businessman. Some of the hotel regulations ('adopted unanimously by the proprietor') were:

In case of FIRE the guests are requested to escape without unnecessary delay.

The BAR in the annexe will be open day and night. Day drinks 50c each; night drinks $1 each. Only regularly registered guests will be allowed the special privilege of sleeping on the Bar Room floor.

Quarrelsome or boisterous persons, also those who shoot off without provocation guns or other explosive weapons on the premises, and all boarders who get killed will not be allowed to remain in the house.

No kicking regarding the quality or quantity of meals will be allowed. Assaults on the cooks are strictly prohibited.

Meals served in rooms will not be guaranteed in any way. Our waiters are hungry and not above temptation.

Guests are forbidden to strike matches or spit on the ceiling. Spiked boots and spurs must be removed at night before retiring.

Two or more persons must sleep in one bed when requested to do so by the management.

Dogs are not allowed in the bunks, but may sleep underneath.

All guests are requested to arise at 6 a.m. This is imperative as the sheets are needed for tablecloths.

And so on. . . .

It was unfortunate for the recruits who were to bring the strength of the Force up to 500 that they were engaged before the opening of the new training depot and headquarters at Regina. Nearly all of them were examined in Toronto by Dr Augustus Jukes, an elderly general practitioner from St Catherine's, Ontario, who had unwisely allowed himself to be persuaded to take over the post of senior surgeon when John Kittson resigned. Jukes accompanied the 214 recruits, commanded by a newly appointed superintendent, Alexander McKenzie, when they left Toronto for the overland journey to Fort Walsh through the United States. The Toronto *Globe* reported: 'A number of the very young lads seemed at the last moment to wish that they might stay behind, and even tears were seen to roll down the cheeks of some as they bade their friends adieu.' The fact that they marched from their assembly point to Toronto railway station to the tune of 'John Brown's Body' was a prophetic start to a disastrous journey.

Superintendent McKenzie was taken ill three days after their departure, had to be left behind and subsequently died, while on a crowded and uncomfortable thirteen-day steamer-trip up the Missouri river a recruit named Adam Wahl fell overboard and was drowned. Poor Jukes was pressed into service as doctor for the 170 civilian passengers who, in addition to the police contingent, were crammed with cattle, horses and sheep on the steamer *Red Cloud*. According to Jukes, 'This entailed an amount of labour, anxiety and responsibility which I can never forget, and which seriously impaired my own health and strength.' For the overland journey from Fort Benton to Fort Walsh a covered wagon had to be converted into an ambulance to carry the most seriously ill recruits. An exhausted Jukes commented, 'On 13 June, the day after my arrival at Fort Walsh, I entered upon the active duties of surgeon.'

Though he was considered by one officer 'a very fine old gentleman and also a very competent practitioner', Jukes's memory was unreliable and he was bewildered by the mass of paper work which confronted him. 'Everything as far as I am concerned is shrouded in mystery and always has been since I joined the Force,' he grumbled in his personal diary. And when winter came to Fort Walsh his spirits sank below freezing: 'I had three pairs of blankets over me and a railway rug tucked across my shoulders to keep the wind from rushing down under the bed-clothes and a buffalo robe over all, with a red woollen night cap pulled well on over my ears, and towards morning I was colder than I have yet been in bed since I came here.'

But even Jukes's gloom could not equal that of one recruit who spent all his 237 days as a policeman in hospital. He arrived at Fort Walsh with his legs so badly ulcerated that he could scarcely walk, 'yet I was sworn in just the same as though I had been a sound man'. He entered hospital on 23 September and left it the following May. He detailed his experiences to the *Manitoba Free Press*:

Now what do you think they did with me? Out of my 40 cents a day they took 25 cents for every day I was in the hospital for 'stoppages' as they call it. For 237 days I got 15 cents a day, which was just about enough to pay for my washing . . . all the time I was in hospital I hadn't anything in the shape of extra comforts. Nobody had in fact. All hands got the same rations in hospital as if they were out. The regular rations are a pound and a half of bread, a pound and a half of 'meat' – and such meat, too. Yes sir, I wish you could see and smell some of the meat we got. At one time it was so bad it was perfectly unendurable and in spite of the terrorism which prevailed, we hospital patients entered a protest and called the doctor's attention to the matter. An investigation ensued and the whole lot of the meat was condemned and the doctor ordered it thrown away. That's the sort of stuff they were feeding sick men on all winter.

On 16 May I was discharged and generously presented with ten dollars and a ticket to home. Ten dollars was supposed to pay my board and expenses *en route* but anybody knows that it's not near enough. My ten dollars was up even before I got across the prairies and I would have been strapped completely if I hadn't sold a couple of blankets that I beat the government out of.

Another thing that don't strike me as right was making the

171

invalids in hospital work. We had to rub down frost-bitten Indians, light fires and do a thousand and one things we had no right to do and which invalids in no other hospital in the world are required to do.

From 1883 the railway simplified the westward journey of the bunches of recruits, but their first sight of headquarters must have come as a blow – a huddle of rough prefabricated shacks two-and-a-half miles from the Regina town site. Needless to say, the portable barracks shipped from eastern Canada were no match for the fierce prairie winters. The roofs leaked, badly connected sections of the buildings became separated and the floors warped. Water froze in basins and bathtubs, and clerks muffled to the ears bent their pens on solid ink.

To combat the mud, which was of a particularly tenacious quality, the police laid their own four-foot-wide boardwalk around the barrack square and, since the water in a small creek nearby was undrinkable, they had to sink a well six feet in diameter and sixty feet deep, and then pump water by hand.

When one recruit, John Donkin, was deposited at Regina station he felt that 'any homesick youth would have fairly broken down at the dismal scene; all around lay a great muddy expanse, while a soaking rain fell from a leaden sky. A few unpainted wooden houses all stood in open order with dismal spaces of clay and puddles intervening. The great prairie stretched away as far as the eye could see, flat and cheerless, like a ghostly sea.'

Though he joined the Force later, when Regina was more established as a training depot, Charles Dwight provides a fascinating glimpse of what life must have been like for recruits in those days. On eating, for instance:

At the sound of a bugle call everyone made a wild scramble from the barrack room to the mess room door. After a few moments the door was thrown open by the cook, which was the signal for a mad rush through to the other side of the room. Here was a table on which rested a great pile of plates, and a rough counter behind which a brawny individual with sleeves

172

rolled up was, with the aid of a huge butcher's knife, rapidly slashing chunks off a huge roast of beef and slapping them on the galvanised iron plates as they were held out. I managed to procure a plate after several ineffectual efforts and, holding it forth, received a huge triangular chunk of burnt meat. With my well-earned trophy I now walked proudly towards the tables in the centre of the room, on which were huge pots of steaming potatoes, and forthwith commenced an assault upon my dinner. It was certainly plain and rough fare – in fact the plainest and roughest I had ever sat down to, but one possesses great powers of conformity at times.

The same manœuvres were gone through for the evening meal, which consisted of tea, cold beef and dry bread, while breakfast – served after a ninety-minute session of stable cleaning and horse grooming – was coffee, more dry bread and a concoction called 'Mystery' – the remains of the previous day's dinner, a conglomeration of meat, grease and potatoes. The men gladly contributed ten cents (twenty-five per cent of their meagre daily pay) to run their own mess and bring in 'luxuries' such as milk and butter, pies and puddings.

On his second day in the Force, Dwight was assigned a horse, though on his own admission his only previous knowledge of that animal 'had been gained by observation on the front platform of a streetcar'. Each day the recruits were put through an hour's foot drill and then an hour's riding, without stirrups. In common with other inexperienced horsemen, Dwight suffered badly from saddle sores. When they reported to the medical officer they were told to ride the soreness off. Dwight commented, 'This I found a trifle galling, to say the least when, in compliance with this advice, I discovered that my saddle on a number of occasions was dyed a deep vermilion with my own blood.'

When he joined the police as an inspector in the summer of 1883, Richard Burton Deane, a former Royal Marine officer, considered his new comrades 'an armed mob'. Forewarned by friends in eastern Canada about the lack of home comforts, Deane carried to Regina with him a folding bed 'which I had used in the

Ashanti Campaign of 1873–4', and until accommodation was available he slept on this in Commissioner Irvine's quarters.

Deane's first job, as a former Marine division adjutant, was to draft some Standing Orders for the police. He was astonished to find that the Mounted Police had been in existence for ten years without possessing 'a single standing order or regulation of any kind'. In the book he wrote about his life in Canada, Deane gave an example of 'the go-as-you-please manner' in which the Force was being run in 1883:

> One of the officers had been detailed for railway duty and he used to travel on a pass and to talk mysteriously about the people with whom he used to come in contact. After I got to know him better he told me he did not know what his duties were, and that he had never received any orders on the subject. To my knowledge he never made a report, and his chief object in life seemed to be to buy [land titles] . . . cheaply from the half-breeds.

It was little wonder that the Force was badly organised in view of the times it had changed hands at ministerial level. It was successively under the Departments of Justice, Interior, State, Interior again, Indian Affairs and even Railways and Canals; in its first eighteen years the police had seven ministerial heads. One officer considered, 'The Children of Israel might never have reached the Promised Land if their leaders had been changed with such devastating frequency.'

Once Deane had prepared his Standing Orders life became a good deal more regimented, especially at Regina. The headquarters in those days contained the only prison in the North West (until then the police had been forced to ferry their sentenced prisoners to Stony Mountain Penitentiary, twelve miles north of Winnipeg – a journey which often took a month each way from the western forts) and squads of four took it in turn to do a solid week's prison guard, bidding farewell for that time to what little society Regina possessed. The four men took it in turn to sleep on the one wooden bed, but were not supposed to remove any article of clothing for the entire week. Constable John Donkin recalled

> When the week was completed and other unfortunates took your place, what a blessed relief it was! To remove the spur strap across the instep and draw off the boots was bliss! To cast aside your under-garments of cobwebs and assume a change of clothing was rapture! And to stretch your legs between clean sheets at night was simple ecstasy.

Other guard duties and even Sunday church parades were also heartily detested by the Regina unfortunates. One Irish sergeant on his way to church parade told an officer's wife that he was 'off to charm Almighty God with pipe-clay and brass'. Another policeman recalled, 'From our boots to the tip of our helmet spikes we all had to be in a state of perfect cleanliness and order.'

The excess of spit and polish, the poor food, wretched accommodation, worse pay, long and demanding hours of work and the tedium of cold winters took its toll of health and spirits. In 1883, twenty-seven men were invalided out of the Force, twenty-five more deserted and there was a steady stream of men attempting to buy themselves out or misbehaving in the hope of being discharged free of cost. Word was spreading, too, about the not-so-glamorous Mounted Police life. Superintendent Sam Steele reported from Winnipeg in the same year. 'There are no recruits offering themselves for engagement. . . . I think the prospect of getting many this winter is slight.'

Sick mothers, dependent families, urgent business . . . all sorts of excuses were put forward by those wanting to get out of the police. Perhaps the most original application came from a Constable Garratt at Battleford, who applied for discharge as an invalid – and got it – by reporting that he was unable any longer to do his duty as a trumpeter because 'blowing strains the nerves of my eyes'.

An anxious Welsh father, John William James, wrote from Merthyr Tydfil asking Sir John Macdonald to intervene for the release of his son Robert who was at Calgary and suffering, according to his father, 'from heart affection and frostbite'. Constable James got his discharge mainly because his commanding officer, Sam Steele, felt that 'for reasons too numerous to mention' he was not a worthwhile policeman. Agreeing with Steele, Assistant Surgeon George Kennedy pointed out that James's system was 'weak and wanting in tone due to habits of self-indulgence. His heart participates in this want of tone, but is organically sound.'

Eleven men ran away from Fort Macleod during March 1884 and desertion became such a serious problem that the Police Act was again amended, doubling the term of imprisonment for the offence from six months to a year. But the strange sequence of unpunished mutinies continued at Macleod in September 1883. The garrison drew up an impressive list of complaints for their commanding officer, Superintendent Leif Crozier: for seven months they had been existing on bread and beef so rotten that they were forced to eat out at their own expense to avoid starvation; replacement uniforms were in such short supply that they were having to buy their own clothing and some men had been punished because their only pair of trousers was not smart enough for guard duties; a shortage of men meant too much work and – the greatest blow to their dignity – 'it has been the custom at this post when strangers arrive for men to be detailed off to act as grooms and bootblacks for them, which is not the duty of constables'.

By the next day, a Sunday, when Crozier had failed to act on their complaints, the garrison refused to mount guard or assemble for church parade with the comment, 'If the commanding officer does not do *his* duty we will not do *ours*.' This brought Crozier hurriedly into action for a meeting with the dissidents' spokesmen. According to Constable Robert Wilson, Crozier 'admitted he had overlooked some things and pleaded ignorance of others; all our requests were granted and grievances removed'.

But if the food in the larger forts was stodgy and inedible, there were often better times to be had in the network of small outposts beginning to appear between the C.P.R. line and the American border. At St Mary's River, ten miles north of the frontier, a small group of police watching for horse thieves, cattle rustlers and whiskey smugglers varied their regular diet with a steady supply of prairie chickens. When one constable returned to St Mary's from a trip to Fort Macleod he noted in his diary, 'The boys found a cache of whiskey and I found them all pretty full.' From the slightly more sophisticated surroundings of Qu'Appelle William Parker wrote to his sister Annie in Kent

> We are living very well here. Today we had white fish for breakfast washed down by about as good a cup of coffee as I want to drink. For dinner a brace of prairie chickens, served with bread sauce and potatoes and coffee to drink, then for tea, roast beef followed by grand-looking plum pudding with a cup of tea. We have a cow and, not making butter, put all the cream into the coffee, so you see we bachelors know how to live.

At an outpost known as East End, seventy miles east of Cypress Hills, they supplemented their bacon, pemmican and beans with the occasional venison, prairie chicken and even bear, which Frank Fitzpatrick found 'entirely too oily and greasy for my taste'. But he praised the whitefish, netted from a nearby lake and fried in bacon fat, as 'indeed fit for a king'.

In some cases, however, the outpost detachments did not even possess a roof over their heads, and tent life on the prairie, even in summer, tended to be rough and unpredictable. John Donkin was one of a group of seven living in two tents at the Souris River. They managed to eat fairly well by exchanging some of their police rations for what he termed 'delicacies such as butter and eggs and preserves' with local settlers, one of whom had two daughters – 'strapping Highland lassies' – who baked bread for the police group. But all summer they were plagued by insects.

> The mosquito, like the poor, was always with us. The small black flies came upon the scene shortly after our arrival and were very severe upon our poor horses ... they clung in clusters around the eyes of the frantic animals, and we had to

guard against a stampede. After swarming in dense masses for three weeks they suddenly disappeared. Then came the bulldog species, a huge creature that would take a comfortable bite out of you, causing the blood to spurt like an ornamental fountain. This voracious brute was followed by the flying ant, who generally made for your neck. To wind up the procession, the house fly came in squadrons, and continued until November.

Then they had to contend with the weather's vagaries. One night Donkin awoke during a thunderstorm to find a torrent of water rushing through his tent, which shortly collapsed beneath the downpour and was blown away. He and his soaked companions joined the others in the remaining tent:

> How we survived that night I do not know. We could only sit with our elbows on our knees and our chins in our hands, though we laughed and jested as though it were a lively spree. The floor of the tent was a pond, and the other fellows were sitting in boots and cloaks upon their respective rolls of bedding in the water.

Every Monday, sunburned or saturated, the Souris River detachment sent a small patrol westward to a spot called Buffalo Head – merely a buffalo skull placed on a pile of stones – where they met a patrol moving east from the nearest inhabited point, Willow Bunch, 200 miles to the west of them. Donkin considered these routine patrols 'hideous in their monotony'. In camp there was nothing to do but 'lie down and smoke, and dream of home, or read'. No wonder Donkin compared his existence to that of a castaway: 'It takes the spirit out of you, and ages you before your time.'

Boredom was one of the police's biggest enemies. Superintendent Deane sent in a request on behalf of his men for books 'not exclusively of a scientific or religious character' to pass the winter evenings, while an eighteen-year-old recruit named Algernon R. Dyre from Manotick, near Ottawa, wrote to thank his brother for sending a copy of *Under Two Flags* and urged him to forward more reading matter 'even if it is only Webster's Unabridged, as times are rather dull here now'. Times were rather livelier, however, when Dyre attended a dance given by his colleagues at Fort Calgary for local civilians:

> We had the barrack rooms decorated with beadwork, mottoes made of cartridges, revolvers and rifles on the walls. Music was two violins, a flute and banjo. . . . There was only one white woman, and she was Dutch with hair like my tunic, and she had one side of her dress tucked up so as to show her white petticoat, but it showed her leg as well, up to the knee when her partner gave her an extra strong swing.

Perhaps stimulated by the sight of a Dutch knee, Dyre enthused in the same letter, 'I *do* like Calgary better than either Walsh or Macleod, as it is in a very pretty part of the country, and another thing, the Commissioner calls us his pet troop, and it's no slouch of a thing to be among the pick of 500 Mounted Policemen, if I do say it myself.'

By the mid-1880s there was an awareness of the need for off-duty facilities. The new headquarters, Regina, had a recreation room in which the principal Canadian newspapers, together with popular British publications such as *Punch* and *The Illustrated London News* were available, alongside draught boards and a bagatelle table.

Also popular with the Regina garrison was a nearby canteen which contained a billiard table 'of uneven tendencies' and where, according to John Donkin, 'There was a flash bar, gorgeous with mirrors and photographs of American *danseuses* with elephantine legs and busts, surpassing in development the wildest imagination.' It was as well the place offered some stimulant, for its bar sales consisted of nothing heftier than non-intoxicating cider or hop beer.

In the main, the police made do with their own company – partly by choice and partly because of the wretched rates of pay. As Donkin said, 'My comrades were more like a band of brothers than merely a chance medley. . . . We nurtured a most thorough contempt for civilians.' Perhaps it was their very dissimilarity which bound them together. Donkin's barrack block, for instance, contained a former militia officer, a colonial governor's son, a major-general's son, a medical student from Dublin, an Oxford B.A., two ex-Scots Greys and 'several ubiquitous natives of Scotland', while the Canadians were a mixture of descendants of families of wealth and influence 'as well as several from the backwoods who had never seen the light till their fathers had hewn a way through the bush to a road'. Donkin considered another of his colleagues, the brother of a Yorkshire baronet, the best amateur contortionist and comedian he had seen. He and an ex-circus clown from Dublin used to give spontaneous performances, using the rough barrack-room furniture as acrobatic props.

On joining the Force, all recruits were required to provide testimonials of good character. But, as a well-bred young English drifter named Roger Pocock pointed out, 'in my time a third of the crowd were broken-down gentlemen, a third were Canadian bucolics, the rest promiscuous desperadoes, old soldiers, cowboys, sailors and hell-rake adventurers from all ends of the earth. Not one of us had the least difficulty in proving our good moral character.'

At Fort Saskatchewan the cook was a former London policeman, Sam Taylor, who grew one thumbnail to an extraordinary length and used it to nick the eyes out of potatoes, and the mess orderly, a member of the Plymouth Brethren named William Maitland, always wore his pill-box cap on the crown of his head; wearing it over the right ear was an unseemly form of vanity, he claimed. The police also enrolled an English gentleman, Sir John Granville Louis Temple, a former Sandhurst cadet who had been a lieutenant in the Lancashire Fusiliers. When he applied to join the Mounted Police the examining doctor reported, 'He is evidently a gentleman by birth and education though now, for reasons known only to himself, is dead broke.' Temple, known as 'Jakey', was several times charged with drunkenness and eventually dismissed, though he later re-engaged as a special constable and was given the job of night watchman at the Prince Albert post. He died shortly afterwards of cancer, leaving $238 in cash and a silver watch and chain.

Chapter 12

STRIKERS AND SMUGGLERS

THE settlers brought west by the railway enormously complicated the work of the police in the early 1880s. Many of them had ideas of getting rich quickly; unaccustomed to the habits and manners of the half-breeds and Indians, they often lacked the necessary tact and patience in their relations with the original inhabitants of the country. One settler, an ex-policeman named Stuttaford who should have known better, found a Cree leaning on his garden fence and struck him in the face. When the man's tribe heard that Stuttaford had been fined only $3 for assault they descended on his garden and began to trample down his plants. Irvine noted that 'but for the timely arrival of the police much more serious consequences would have followed'.

There was certainly plenty of sympathy for the sort of attitude voiced by the *Fort Macleod Gazette*: 'If we are obliged to fight the Indians to stop their depredations let the entertainment commence.' But there was much truth in the statement of *The Times* correspondent Charles Austin that white men were causing the Mounted Police as much – if not more – trouble in the West than the Indians. There was indignation when hungry Indians occasionally killed cattle, which they simply regarded as the natural successor to the buffalo; yet American-owned cattle drifting north from the overstocked Montana ranges in search of richer pastures in Canada caused the police far more trouble. There was considerable evidence that some of the bigger American ranching concerns herded thousands of cattle to within a few miles of the

181

boundary, then turned them loose into Canada, for them to fatten and be returned by the police – a practice which was only stopped when the border was fenced at the turn of the century.

Problems literally flared along the railway line. The engines, spouting sparks and occasionally walnut-sized lumps of coal, started more prairie fires than the combination of all other causes such as lightning, carelessness and malice. Police constantly patrolled the railway, but fires – often fanned by high winds – burned over much of the plains area. Frank Fitzpatrick was out all night with one police group fighting a blaze and recalled, 'We finally got the best of the fire and came back to the fort at about 5 a.m. a sorry-looking lot – eyes red, faces blackened and the soles of our shoes nearly burned off. At 5.30 a.m. reveille sounded and we answered the call as usual.' In an attempt to curb the menace heavy fines were levied on offenders, with half the fine going to the informer, but the weakness of this method was exposed when a hay contractor reported that a fire had been started by the carelessness of one of his employees, paid the man's fine of $100 and then demanded – and received – $50 back as the informant.

Serious trouble with the Blackfoot over the railway was averted by the diplomacy of a French-Canadian Catholic missionary, Father Albert Lacombe, when the government – with total lack of foresight – permitted construction gangs to push into Indian reserves without even bothering to inform the natives. Father Lacombe, who was then fifty-six, had been working among the Indians of the north-west for thirty years and was much loved and respected. When the Earl of Southesk had hunted his way through the West in the 1860s he met Lacombe and described him as 'a perfect gentleman', adding: 'What an advantage Rome has in this respect – Protestants constantly send vulgar, underbred folk to supply their missions. Rome sends polished, highly educated gentlemen.' The polished Lacombe held a council with Crowfoot and, assuming an authority which the government had not granted him, offered the Blackfoot generous grants of additional land in compensation if they would allow the railway to pass through their reserves. The matter was amicably sealed by a splendid piece of public relations work by the C.P.R.'s general manager, an astute American named William Cornelius Van Horne who presented Crowfoot with a lifetime pass on the railway, a metal tag which the chief always wore proudly afterwards on a chain round his neck. And the invaluable Father Lacombe was not forgotten by Van Horne either. He was made president of the railway company for the duration of a special lunch, served in his honour in a private carriage at Calgary.

It fell to the Force to control and assist the thousands of railway construction workers, many of them European immigrants, who were being overworked and underpaid by ruthless sub-contractors. There were countless complaints about non-payment of wages, each one of which had to be carefully investigated and, if possible, settled on the spot by police diplomacy. Occasionally the police were used as strike-breakers by the company. In December 1883 drivers and firemen went on strike for more money, and police were called in by the Canadian Pacific to ensure that trains carrying passengers and mails were not 'interfered with', as the company put it, by the strikers. Drivers were brought in from the east, police guarded every train against possible sabotage and the strike collapsed.

As the railway moved into the Rocky Mountains and the province of British Columbia (where the Mounted Police had no official jurisdiction) a detachment under Superintendent Sam Steele was empowered by the Canadian government to accompany the construction gangs as they cut their way towards a union with the rails being driven east from the Pacific coast. Steele was well aware that he and his tiny command faced a hard time. 'Large numbers of gamblers, whiskey men, in fact almost every description of criminal who had been plying their trade on [the American railways] . . . were establishing their dens on every little creek along the line.' One of the first anomalies which Steele faced was the fact that the police were only given jurisdiction over a stretch ten miles wide on each side of the railway route. Even inside this zone it was only the sale, not the consumption, of liquor which was forbidden.

Outside the ten-mile limit shanty bars, saloons and brothels proliferated. As Steele pointed out, 'The greatest obstacle in our way was the determination of the government of British Columbia that the province should not be deprived of its internal revenue. It therefore issued to all comers licences to sell spirituous and fermented liquors, even within ten miles of the construction work.' But they had reckoned without Steele's determination. He persuaded Ottawa to enforce a forty-mile-wide belt of prohibition along the line of construction, and to increase the penalty for second offences of selling liquor inside the zone to imprisonment.

The construction work was pushed forward with great determination. Nearly every worker averaged ten hours a day, seven days a week, and if progress was held up by bad weather the Swedes among the gangs used to make up for it by working by moonlight and clocked fourteen-hour days. Steele's command set up winter quarters at the end of the track at a place called Beaver River, west of the Kicking Horse Pass, and a settlement soon arose around them. 'We had a great deal of trouble with gamblers and toughs of every description,' Steele wrote. Night after night drunks had to be imprisoned to protect them and their bankrolls from the toughs who preyed on the camp. According to Steele, 'No people in the world earned the title of "night hawk" more honestly than we of the Mounted Police at the Beaver. We were rarely to bed before two or three a.m., and were up in the morning between six and seven.'

Serious trouble was avoided until March 1885, when bunches of construction men complained to Steele that they had not been paid for some time. Despite Steele's plea for patience – an appeal made from a sick bed where he was laid up with a severe attack of fever – more than a thousand workers went on strike and there was talk of destruction of railway property if they were not paid their due wages. The action of the police (whose detachment at the Beaver numbered only eight) in guarding with drawn rifles the tracklayers who wished to continue working incensed the strikers, and when one notorious character named Behan attempted to incite the crowd to attack the police a constable named Kerr bravely but foolishly tried to arrest him singlehanded and was roughed up. Directing operations from his sick bed, Steele ordered Sergeant Billy Fury – described as 'a determined, bulldog little man' – to take three men and arrest Behan at all costs. Soon Fury returned, his uniform in ribbons, with the news that the mob had snatched the police's prisoner from them a second time. Fury was told to arrest his man and to shoot anyone who attempted to interfere, which he did – wounding a rioter in the shoulder.

Hearing the shot, Steele rose from his sick bed, just in time to see two constables dragging the wildly struggling Behan over a bridge towards the police post while a woman – appropriately clad in scarlet – dogged them, shrieking and cursing, followed by an angry mob. Seizing a rifle, Steele ran towards the bridge yelling at the crowd to halt or he would open fire. As they paused, Steele ordered Behan and the woman in scarlet taken into the cells, then went across the bridge to the mob where, backed by his tiny group of eight, he had the Riot Act read to them, underlining it with the threat to 'shoot the first man of you who makes a hostile movement'. Next day Steele reported, 'All along the line was as quiet as a country village on Sunday.' Behan and other ringleaders were fined $100 each: the following week the overdue wages were paid and the railway avoided what could have been a crippling strike.

Six months later, to the immense relief of the Mounted Police, the converging lines were united at Craigellachie in British Columbia. William Van Horne of the Canadian Pacific had earlier written to Commissioner Irvine acknowledging the debt of gratitude his company owed the police: 'Without the assistance of the officers and men of the splendid force under your command it would have been impossible to have accomplished so much as we did. On no great work within my knowledge where so many men have been employed has such perfect order prevailed.'

The police thoroughly deserved Van Horne's compliments. In addition to shepherding his line to completion, they were also acting as postal clerks on the trains as well as undertaking all sorts of other tasks, menial as well as manual, to help the railway run on time and to patrol the vastness of the North West. Frank Fitzpatrick summed up the work of the police in those days:

> We acted as magistrates, sheriffs, constables, collectors of Customs, postmasters, undertakers, issuers of licences. We married people and we buried people. We acted as health inspectors, weather bureau officials, Indian treaty makers; but above all as diplomats when it came to dealing with either Indians or half-breeds.

As Fitzpatrick rightly pointed out, 'It was strange, but our Force seemed to possess men who could do almost anything when the occasion demanded it.'

There was, for instance, the case of that remarkable Kentish vicar's son, William Parker, who performed a prairie version of the pentathlon in pursuit of a prisoner who had escaped from him. Parker was escorting the man – a Norwegian half-breed named Nelson, sentenced to five years for assaulting an elderly woman – by rail to the Stony Mountain Penitentiary near Winnipeg when the prisoner leapt from the moving train and sprinted away. By the time Parker managed to get after him Nelson had a mile start on a fiercely hot day. 'As I did not appear to be gaining on him I sat down and pulled off my top boots, opened my tunic and started on again in my stockinged feet, going to within a quarter of a mile of him.' But when the escaper reached the concealment of some woods Parker ran back to the railway line where he had previously noticed a gang of workmen.

By the time he reached the group his socks were worn out and his feet raw and bleeding. 'When I reached the men I could not talk to them as my tongue was swollen in my mouth, so I grabbed their kettle of cold tea, took a big drink and slumped on the ground.' Once recovered, Parker persuaded the men to pump him along the line in their handcart to the nearest station, Dundurn, where he commandeered a bottle of pain killer to drink, socks and moccasins for his aching feet and the station's only horse. He rode fifteen miles back towards where he had last seen his prisoner, alerting settlers and ranchers along the way and stopping to drink 'about half a gallon of beer' which was offered to him at one ranch.

Eventually he encountered a woman who said that Nelson had called at her home and asked for a file. Not having one she had sent him to a neighbour's house. Parker and his growing following of helpers surrounded the place. 'We were none too soon as we caught him in the stable filing off the end of the light chain attached to his ankle,' said Parker. 'Nelson turned as white as a sheet when he saw me. I think he thought it was my ghost. He never uttered a word, although I gave him a bit of my mind.'

Though not quite so athletically impressive, a Corporal Hogg managed a minor masterpiece of his own in his report of the occasion when he was called to a disturbance at a railway hotel in North Portal:

> I found the room full of cowboys. One Monaghan, or Cowboy Jack, was carrying a gun and pointed it at me, against Sections 105 and 109 of the Criminal Code. We struggled. Finally I got him handcuffed behind and put him inside. His head being in bad shape, I had to engage the services of a doctor who dressed his wound and pronounced it as nothing serious. To the doctor, Monaghan said that if I hadn't grabbed at his gun there would have been another death in Canadian history. All of which I have the honour to report.

Strict enforcement of prohibition had helped to speed the building of the trans-Canada railway across the prairies. Paradoxically, it was the very arrival of that railway which threatened to inundate a 'dry' country with alcohol. In 1874 when the police had marched into the North West the white population could be numbered in hundreds. Ten years later it had swollen to 35,000 on a flood tide of immigrants thirsting for other things besides a new land. As the settlers poured in, one thing quickly became obvious: the system of strict prohibition existing during the 1870s was impossible to sustain.

When he was appointed Lieutenant-Governor of the Territories in 1881, Edgar Dewdney attempted to alleviate the growing problem by introducing a permit system for the importation of liquor. Application had to be made to Dewdney in writing for permission to bring alcohol (usually limited to a maximum of five gallons) into the country 'for medicinal or family use'. It was the duty of the police to cancel the permit once the shipment was delivered, a task which vastly complicated the work – and endangered the hard-won popularity – of the Force. During Dewdney's seven-year term as Lieutenant-Governor the annual number of gallons legally imported into the Territories shot up from 3000 to 56,000. So Dewdney's permit plan complicated, rather than alleviated, the liquor question.

Obtaining drink legally was a laborious process. First the permit application had to be considered by the police or local civic officials, then – if there was no objection – it was forwarded to the territorial capital (first Battleford, later Regina) for Dewdney's approval. The owner of the precious document then sent it, with a pre-paid order, usually to Winnipeg, a lengthy process even after the arrival of the railway. As Sergeant Frank Fitzpatrick recalled:

A permit was known and recorded for months in advance and the neighbours (I mean by neighbours anyone residing within a radius of 200 miles) was sure to have received the good tidings at least three months in advance; and believe me, they were all in at the death. The records show the life of a permit never exceeded 24 hours; its funeral was in some cases the occasion of a grand dance. After the celebration and before departing the guests would make a note of the date of the next permit, the arrival of which would be attended at whatever the cost of travel.

This laborious law roused the white inhabitants of the North

West to fury. One of them complained to the prairies' latest news-paper, the *Regina Leader*, that prohibition was 'never intended for civilisation but for the suppression of a nefarious traffic amongst the Indians'. Even such a stern upholder of the law as Superinten-dent Sam Steele agreed that prohibition should not have been enforced 'against the will of the majority. . . . We soon learned that compulsion will not make people sober. The prohibitory law made more drunkards than if there had been an open bar and free drinks at every street corner.'

There was widespread disregard of the regulations. The *Mac-leod Gazette* commented, 'The law is daily broken by the entire population from the highest to the lowest. There are few people in the world who are more law-abiding than those of the North-west, and at the same time there are few countries on the face of the earth where any one law is so openly and universally violated.' It was an opinion with which Commissioner Irvine was forced to agree:

> Men who were law-abiding citizens in the old provinces think it no crime to evade the liquor law and do so on every oppor-tunity. If such men are not caught the police come in for abuse from temperance quarters. If on the other hand conviction follows, so much the worse for the police, for in nine cases out of ten the conviction gives birth to the most unsparing abuse, not of the law but of those whose duty it is to enforce it.

For instance, when the *Regina Leader*'s editor, the fiery Nicho-las Flood Davin, was fined $50 for bringing in liquor without a permit, he lambasted the police in his columns, accusing them of seeking revenge for articles he had written criticising the Force.

As Irvine pointed out in his annual report to Ottawa, 'The suppression of this traffic is the most disagreeable duty the police are called upon to perform.' And since most of the police them-selves were drinkers it was easy to understand Constable John Donkin's assertion that 'whiskey hunting is not popular in the corps, and a man who persistently prosecutes for this offence is

189

looked upon with contempt'. With patronage being widely exercised by Dewdney in the issuing of permits the police were rarely over-zealous in seizing the occasional bottle from some humble, thirsty soul who lacked a permit.

Once, when Inspector Arthur Griesbach was tipped off that a bootlegger was on his way to Edmonton with two wagonloads, he decided to handle the arrest himself and seized the cargo successfully. When the would-be customers – a group of leading citizens who had gathered in a hall for the celebration – heard the news they were so infuriated that they actually complained to the Minister of Justice in Ottawa, and for some months after that they refused to speak to Griesbach because he had carried out his duty.

The smuggling of liquor was spectacular in its variety, and Irvine considered the ingenuity 'worthy of a better cause'. Alcohol entered the North West inside imitation bibles and dummy eggs, tins of fruit and produce, salt and sugar barrels, false-bottomed buckets, the hollow soles of boots, and on one famous occasion in a coffin carried past the lowered heads of a police patrol. Police intercepted a consignment of liquor labelled as canned apples and addressed to a Justice of the Peace named Davidson at Qu'Appelle, and opened two barrels of oatmeal destined for the Rev. Leo Gaetz to find that each contained ten gallons of whiskey.

There was also the occasional spectacular theft: a wagonload of alcohol which had been left overnight in a Calgary siding was found to be almost empty when it reached its destination. Holes had been bored through the bottom of the wagon and into the barrels. The police's task was a hopeless one. In the opinion of the *Macleod Gazette*, 'For every gallon of this illegal liquor which is seized, there are thousands of gallons which get safely in.'

The liquor which the police managed to intercept was supposed to be spilled in the presence of an officer. But this practice was open to abuse, too. Constable John Donkin described how half-breeds and Indians used to assemble at any winter spilling of liquor and afterwards 'would reverently gather up the precious snow and devour it eagerly'. It wasn't only the Indians who enjoyed whiskey-flavoured snow. When two smugglers were caught near Fort Macleod their fifty-gallon haul was ceremoniously spilled into the snow near the police post. 'The boys soon gathered it up and took it into the kitchen and made punch of it,' one constable noted in his diary. 'Before night there was hardly a sober man in the fort.' In summer the police neatly overcame the lack of snow by burying trays beneath the piece of turf selected for spilling.

Though they disliked hounding the civilian population, the police were unflagging in their efforts to subdue the resurgent smuggling of dubious liquor from across the American border. Constable Robert Wilson's diary records the capture – and partial consumption – of a wagonload of alcohol while on patrol near the American border with Corporal Tom LaNauze, Constable Callaghan and that ardent whiskey-fan and guide, Jerry Potts, in February 1882:

In the afternoon, with the aid of field glasses we could distinguish two objects coming towards us. We laid low for a couple of hours and a man on horseback rode past us. We made him prisoner, then waited a few minutes longer and a man with a team and wagon drove up, containing 20 gallons of pure alcohol in five-gallon coal-oil cans. The owner was an old ex-policeman Cochrane, who had been smuggling for some time. ... The other was an American named Davis.

The night was bitterly cold and we had no blankets but those under our saddles. The two prisoners and Jerry [Potts] were soon howling drunk and the rest of us managed to keep from freezing by taking frequent doses of alcohol diluted in water. About midnight a priest who was camped not far from us came over and was persuaded (?) to take a drink for his stomach's sake. It was not long before he and Tom LaNauze became very jolly and were toasting each other, drinking out of two old fruit cans and touching them together at every sip. Callaghan had long retired, crawling in between Davis and Cochrane who were too drunk to prevent him and before morning I had the honour of being the only sober man in camp, although I must admit that I took quite enough to keep the cold out. At daylight we saddled up and after each man had taken a cup of alcohol for his breakfast we started off.

One legal alternative to hard liquor was an allegedly innocuous beverage called hop beer. Richard Burton Deane, the former Royal Marine officer, reported that it was extremely popular with Hungarian immigrants. 'When they lay themselves out for a day's enjoyment they empty several dozen bottles at $1.50 a dozen into a tub, sit round and drink and soak their bread in the mixture.' When one of these sessions was followed by a riot, Deane was puzzled to know how anybody could get drunk enough to want to fight on such a harmless brew, so he conducted an experiment. He bought two dozen bottles of hop beer and called for a police volunteer to drink them. One man was chosen from the swarm of applicants, locked in a room and ordered to drink the lot. Deane noted that 'when he had consumed his 18th bottle the man showed unmistakable signs of inebriation'. The Indians, who were permitted to buy hop beer, soon found a way to inject a lethal wallop into it by boiling it with tobacco.

The police found it almost impossible to obtain liquor convictions against white settlers. Despite the practice of paying the informant half the fine levied, few people chose to inform. A contributor to the letters column of the *MedicineHat Times* considered it 'a low, mean and infamous piece of business to inform on a fellow citizen' and warmed to his theme with such further phrases as 'despicable, degrading ... depraved ... and devoid of all honour'. Even when the police did manage to bring a case it had little chance of standing up in tiny communities where the magistrates might be trying a friend, customer or client. After a hotelkeeper in Moosomin had been fined $50 for selling liquor without a permit this advertisement appeared in the local paper:

INDIGNATION MEETING

A meeting will be held in the Orange Hall tomorrow night to protest against the late mean and despicable action taken by the police in subpoenaing respectable and worthy citizens to give

19. Commissioner Lawrence Herchmer

20. Commissioner A. G. Irvine

21. Gabriel Dumont

22. Louis Riel

evidence as whiskey sneaks, thus interfering with the liberty of free-born subjects. Every one should attend and protest against such an iron-heeled law, to bear which is to suffer worse than the slaves in Siberia. Arouse ye all!

Picking up half of a substantial fine was often a good way of supplementing the low police-pay, and young Constable Algernon Dyre wrote home from Calgary, 'I live well and make plenty of money capturing the festive whisky trader and maudlin drunk.' Eventually it was decided to halt this practice, since the police were being accused of prosecuting purely for mercenary purposes.

Soon after becoming Commissioner in 1880, Irvine had made a gentle request to his command in which he 'earnestly trusted' that he would receive the 'hearty support and co-operation' of every man to suppress intoxication within the Force. But it had little effect. Although the young English recruit Roger Pocock had most of his tongue in his cheek when he commented that 'it became incumbent upon the Force to drink or destroy all liquor lest the Indian tribes and civil population should be demoralised', there is no doubt that discipline was severely undermined by the drinking that went on. The Prime Minister, Sir John Macdonald, no mean man with a bottle himself, dismissed parliamentary criticisms of the police's behaviour with the comment that it would be impossible to expect a corps of saints, but the thousands of dollars collected in fines from the policemen's scanty pay supported one constable's comment that 'we were as God made us, and oftentimes even worse'.

The police themselves were guilty of violating the law they had sworn to uphold by importing liquor into the North West at every opportunity. On his way to join the Force at Regina, John Donkin travelled with a policeman who had a hefty haul of whiskey stowed away in his luggage 'for distribution to the boys'. Donkin considered this 'a pretty commentary upon the prohibition law'. Among the police a strict code of honour applied about personal belongings. The exception was alcohol. 'It was no crime to steal it from each other,' recalled another English recruit, E. A. Braithwaite (who was a teetotaller). 'If you had it you had to run the risk of losing it.'

The deterioration of discipline under Irvine is indicated by the rise in drunkenness among both officers and men and by the slaphappy attitude towards the problem. When Constable W. W. Alexander, a hospital steward at Calgary, took to drinking tinctures from the medicine cabinet, Superintendent John H. McIllree (known as 'Easy-Going Old John Henry') merely made Alexander pay for the tinctures and pushed the problem on to somebody else by posting him to Regina.

There was a high incidence of insobriety at Ford Macleod under the benevolent administration of Superintendent William Jarvis, hero of the long march from Roche Percéé to Edmonton in 1874. Irvine complained to Ottawa, 'There is not the slightest doubt that illegitimate liquor traffic was carried on directly under his eyes, either by his knowledge or as a result of a glaring neglect of duty.' There was also heavy drinking at Fort Walsh just before it was abandoned. James Livingstone, the hapless recruit who spent his entire police career of 237 days in hospital at the fort, told the *Manitoba Free Press*:

> The amount of drinking is something that you would hardly credit. Alcohol is the general tipple. They get it over from Fort Assiniboine on the Yankee side of the line. The doctor writes a permit for so many gallons of alcohol for hospital purposes, it comes in, is mixed with water and is drank. Then we have a lot of brandy for hospital use but the poor devils of invalids never get a taste of it. Alcohol and water is good beverage for them and the brandy is saved for the officers to drink on select occasions.

At Christmas 1882 the Fort Walsh hospital orderlies, Acting-Sergeant Alex Bethune and Constable Charles Scott, broke open the medicine cabinet and stole nine gallons of whiskey and brandy, sharing it among their comrades and some civilians who were attending a dance at the fort. Both men were sentenced to four months' hard labour, and five of the civilians were fined the cost of the missing liquor. The same Christmas the N.C.O.s' mess at Battleford concocted a party punch out of ether. According to the post commander, Superintendent William Herchmer, 'The effect was most disastrous, Sergeant Waltham for the time being was a regular lunatic.' The unfortunate sergeant lost his stripes.

Reduction in rank was a frequent punishment for drunkenness. It was said of one N.C.O. named Toby O'Brien that he 'rose and fell like the Roman Empire. Today a sergeant, tomorrow a corporal, and so on. He was clever and well-educated but his main objective in life was whisky, or rather liquor, for he polished it off quite impartially when he could get it. He was finally dismissed.'

There were, however, occasional instances when the use of liquor was authorised in the Force, as these extracts from Constable William Metzler's diary show:

10 Feb. 1884: Got a bottle of whiskey from Capt. Cotton and Sgt. Shaw hauled out my teeth for me.
11 Feb.: Got some more whiskey and had some of the roots taken out.
9 April: Got a set of teeth, $30.

Chapter 13

SLIDING TO DISASTER

THE circumstances in which Francis Jeffrey Dickens became an inspector in the Mounted Police might have made an interesting plot for his father, the novelist Charles Dickens. Francis was born, the fifth child and third son of Dickens, in January 1844, a month after the publication of *A Christmas Carol*, and was named after Lord Francis Jeffrey, the Edinburgh literary critic, who had been fulsome in his praise of Dickens's latest work. Francis Dickens, nicknamed 'Chickenstalker' by his family, was a frail boy who suffered from a stammer and partial deafness. He was sent to a private school in Boulogne, where his father requested that he be given a glass of porter every evening with his dinner to help build his strength.

Though he had hoped to become a doctor, Francis decided that because of his speech impediment 'all professions are barred to me', whereupon he announced to his father his desire to become a gentleman farmer in Australia or Canada. 'With my passage paid £15, a horse and a rifle I could go two or three hundred miles up country and in time be very comfortable.' Charles Dickens had no faith in Chickenstalker or his dreams and commented, 'The first consequence of the £15 would be that he would be robbed of it – of the horse that it would throw him – and of the rifle that it would blow his head off.'

Francis returned to England from Boulogne to become a businessman but could not tolerate the work; so he decided to visit India to see his brother Walter, who died while Francis was in mid-voyage. Stranded in India, Dickens joined the Bengal

Mounted Police and served for nine years, returning to England on his father's death in 1870. Though he had inherited his father's gold watch his timekeeping was atrocious. He overstayed his leave in London and lost his commission in the Bengal Police. So he made his way to Canada where, through the patronage of the then Governor-General, Lord Dufferin, he was offered a commission in the Mounted Police in November 1874. Again his sense of punctuality deserted him, however. He went adrift in Toronto and it cost him $200 out of his own pocket to rejoin his detachment in the North West.

A small, morose, introverted man who suffered increasingly from deafness and a heavy addiction to drink, Dickens (known as 'Little Charlie' to his fellow officers) created an unhappy impression wherever he served. After touring the police posts in 1875, Major-General Selby Smyth considered Dickens 'a very poor officer of no promise, physically weak in constitution, his habits not affording a good example'. Things had not improved five years later, in the opinion of Commissioner Irvine: 'I consider this officer unfit for the Force – he is lazy and takes no interest whatever in his work. He is unsteady in his habits. I am of the opinion that his brain is slightly affected.'

The beginning of 1881 found Dickens safely tucked away at an undemanding job, in charge of a detachment of twelve men at Blackfoot Crossing, scene of the great treaty-signing four years previously. Against all expectation, trouble erupted on the second day of the year when an Indian Department employee named Charles Daly accused a minor Blackfoot chief, Bull Elk, of stealing a beef head from the slaughter pen. Though Bull Elk insisted he had paid for the head, Daly took it from him. The infuriated Indian went home for his rifle, an old flintlock, and took a pot shot at Daly; fortunately he missed.

When Dickens, Sergeant Joseph Howe and two constables arrested Bull Elk on the reservation they were surrounded and jostled by a horde of young braves. By the time they got to the frozen Bow River, which they had to cross to reach the safety of the police post, the group was almost submerged by a mob of angry Indians. Sergeant Howe recalled:

> An Indian caught me by the right arm, another came up behind me and tripped me up; the constable on the left was treated in the same manner; as soon as I fell an old squaw snatched the prisoner's gun out of my hand before I could recover myself. I still held onto the prisoner with my right hand while Inspector Dickens kept the Indians back in rear with his revolver. I could hear the young Indians loading their carbines. One of them discharged his carbine and I heard the bullet whistle over my head.

The harassed contingent managed to get Bull Elk into the police post, where they were immediately besieged by some 700 Indians and cut off from water and food. Dickens had overlooked the need to put the detachment in a state of defence before setting off to arrest Bull Elk; now, he realised, his position was desperate. Chief Crowfoot was summoned, and he agreed to be responsible for Bull Elk until the dispute could be officially heard before a magistrate. When Crowfoot emerged from the hut with the freed chief it was regarded by the Indians as a great victory. 'Such discharge of firearms and such yelling was never heard', according to Sergeant Howe. Dickens knew that he had acted weakly and, more important, had lost face with the Indians by his lack of firmness. In his report of the incident he wrote, 'If my conduct is considered blameable I respectfully ask for a full inquiry.'

But police authority had to be restored, and by more urgent means than the holding of an inquiry. As soon as he heard of the trouble, Superintendent Leif Crozier hurried from Fort Macleod to Blackfoot Crossing with twenty extra men. He immediately prepared the police post for a battle; bastions were raised at each end of the building and the walls were lined with sacks of flour and oats.

Crozier admitted, 'I had determined to arrest the offender' – though at that point he had not even spoken to Bull Elk. Crozier's obvious determination overawed the Indians: 'I had no trouble after my arrival,' he reported. 'They were evidently greatly impressed with the preparations I had made. Crowfoot asked if I intended to fight. I replied, "Certainly not, unless you commence".' The Blackfoot decided not to commence. Bull Elk was given up quietly, taken to Fort Macleod, convicted and imprisoned.

The Bull Elk incident was typical of the deteriorating relations between Indians and police in the early 1880s, following the starvation years. With the exception of the Cypress Hills area, the native tribes had wisely been given their choice of land for reservations, but initially were utterly unable to settle down to raising crops and cattle. One Indian told Sir John Macdonald, 'We are the wild animals; you cannot make an ox out of a deer.' Old habits died hard. When a carefully nurtured turnip-and-potato patch on a reservation at Battleford was raided by some non-treaty Indians the reservation occupants, unable to resist the temptation, joined in the fun, stealing their own crops.

Attempts to stop tribal dances further antagonised the Indians. When he became Governor-General of Canada in succession to the Earl of Aberdeen, Lord Minto (who was a Scot) was sympathetic to complaints about the suppression of traditional dances. 'Why should not these poor people dance?' he wondered. 'It is their only amusement and sober beyond words in comparison to a Scottish reel. The wish to cut it down on the part of narrow-minded authorities makes me sick.' But opinion was unanimous among white officials and police about halting the religious festival known as the Sun Dance, at which young Indian males were made into warriors. The Sun Dance, a macabre type of maypole celebration, usually took place in a rotunda about fifty feet in diameter made of small trees and branches roofed over and joined to a large tree or pole in the centre of the ring. The young constable, Algernon Dyre, described a Sun Dance in a letter to his brother back home in Ontario:

A big fellow with nothing but a breech cloth on and all painted from head to foot came into the ring, climbed up the post in the centre and fastened his lariat to it and came down again, standing like a statue till another buck caught hold of his right breast with one hand while he shoved a knife through it with the other and then poked a stick into the hole. The same was done with the left breast and the lariat fastened to both sticks. The poor cuss's part was not yet played, for until he broke the flesh through he could not call himself a Sarcee warrior. He stepped back as far as the line would let him and began to jerk and tug and throw himself on the ground in a vain effort to burst free. At last, when the rest saw he could not get free, one heavy old brave jumped on him and bore him to the ground. When he got up he was as stoical and calm as ever. The sticks were dangling to the lariat and two great gashes in his breast told that he was a warrior. He never uttered as much as a groan through it all and the blood flew and spurted, all around and over him. He just looked at it as indifferently as if it was water running in a creek. We waited for no more, but got our horses and rode home thinking of several things, but what damn fools Indians were in particular.

There were equally gruesome variations. Youngsters who were being blooded sometimes had the thongs under their chest muscles attached to a pony and were dragged around the ring until the flesh gave way, or buffalo skulls were hung on ropes passed under the back muscles. The unfortunate victim then had to dance until the weight of the skulls tore loose the bindings and the flesh. When a youth could not free himself and was in danger of disgracing his family by not becoming a warrior, a relative – often his mother – would add weight to the exhausted victim's tuggings until he was torn clear.

Inspector Richard Burton Deane felt the Sun Dance 'brings out all the bad qualities of the Indians'. Superintendent Sam Steele agreed: 'Old warriors take this occasion of relating their experiences of former days. . . . This has a pernicious effect on the young men; it makes them unsettled and anxious to emulate the deeds of their forefathers.'

Since the young braves could no longer take to the warpath any longer, they did the next best thing and indulged in an orgy of horse-stealing. As with the American Indians, the favourite ploy was to cross the frontier, steal as many horses as could be rounded up and then race back across the 'Medicine Line' as quickly as possible. Half-breeds were also guilty of many thefts and the situation was further complicated by the presence in the Canadian West of an increasing number of white vagrants who were not averse to a bit of horse-stealing, either. The Canadian side of the line was popular among American Indians and white desperadoes since, in the words of Commissioner Irvine, they did not have to face 'the contingency by bullet or rope which attends the exercise of their calling in the United States'.

The prospect of catching horse-thieves crossing the border, in either direction, was slight so long as the police were stretched thinly, and the thefts grew more and more daring. In one case some American Peigans stole horses from a stable in the settlement of Fort Walsh, right under the noses of the police. Soon the farmers and homesteaders in the North West were having to bed down with their horses every night. Even this didn't prevent them from losing their animals. There were examples of settlers harnessing their horses with a lariat and passing the other end of the rope around their own bodies, only to awake in the morning clutching a cut rope. But the police were able to make some spectacular recoveries of stolen American animals, none better than on the occasion when a Blackfoot war party stole thirty-four horses from the I. G. Baker Company of Fort Benton. The Company's promptness in reporting the loss to Fort Walsh was matched only by the police, who recovered all the stolen horses within twelve hours. And when an American settler from the Marias river, Montana, trekked to Fort Walsh with the description of eleven horses abducted from his farm the Mounted Police scoured the Indian camps until all had been found and returned 'taking care that no expense was incurred by the man who had suffered the loss'.

Irvine made strong representations to his government that the offence of horse-stealing should be made extraditable, pointing out that the police usually managed to recover most of the American horses stolen by Canadian Indians but the local horses taken by Americans 'are almost without exception never returned'. Though the American Army did their best to help, Irvine criticised the U.S. Indian Department for not being interested in retrieving stolen Canadian horses.

There was much bickering and ill-feeling on both sides of the border. When an American rancher arrived at Fort Macleod in search of fifty horses taken by Blood Indians he carried a letter from that man of many parts, John J. Healy, who after losing his job as editor of the *Fort Benton Record* had become sheriff of Chouteau County, Montana. Sheriff Healy warned the police that 'should this missive prove futile serious consequences are liable to follow, as the people of Montana have tired of being harassed by the marauding hordes of the north and will wreak vengeance upon all war parties caught this side of the line, and not knowing Blood from Peigan are liable to strike many innocent men by mistake'.

This sort of threat was a red rag to the bull-like Leif Crozier, who complained to Irvine, 'Considering the tone of Mr Healy's letter I would bring to your notice the fact that during the past summer there has scarcely been a ranchman or horse owner in this section of the country who has not lost horses by means of American horse-thieves.' Crozier managed to recover almost half of the missing horses and arrested eight Blood Indians suspected of the theft. Though they were found guilty the Bloods were released with a caution, 'the court taking into consideration the Indians had not heretofore been punished under this Act and what they had done was not considered by them an offence'.

But this lenient attitude soon hardened. Two years later a Cree called Mis-as-quat got five years' hard labour for stealing horses, and two white men, John McDonald and F. Watson, were each sentenced to four years. Even this sort of punishment was not considered severe enough by most of the white settlers. Thomas Bland Strange, a former major-general in the British Army who had fought in the Indian Mutiny and was now ranching on 70,000 acres near Calgary, lost some of his horses to the Blackfoot. He managed to recover all except one, and accompanied Sergeant Billy Fury and an interpreter to arrest the suspected thief, whose name was Dried String Meat ('he certainly would have become *strung-up* meat if Judge Lynch had had him on the other side of the line,' raged Strange). The Indian was taken to Calgary, and by the time Strange got there to give evidence Dried String Meat had been released. Insult was added to Strange's injured pride when 'the amiable magistrate assured me that the prisoner was willing to give me the kiss of peace, which he did, taking me unawares'.

Strange, the sort of man who would have sent a gunboat to the prairies had he been able to, fumed, 'With all savages, leniency has no meaning but cowardice, and is followed by contempt.' He was a good deal nearer the mark, however, when he wrote that 'the presence of the Mounted Police has alone prevented these matters being squared by the settlers themselves in the short and decisive way they manage it over the border'.

A noisy minority of settlers arrogantly assumed that the police had nothing to do other than search for their missing horses. One settler sent a telegram: 'Piapot's Indians stole team of horses from me last night; will you please find them. Answer.' After much effort the horses *were* recovered but when the rancher was told he would be required to give evidence when the Indian responsible was arrested he was most indignant at the prospect of wasting his valuable time in court.

The reputation of poor Francis Dickens dropped another notch after he again sidestepped a confrontation with Indians while on a mission to recover stolen horses from the Blood reserve. Dickens, accompanied by several Montana ranchers, managed to pick out fourteen stolen animals from the Blood herds but as the search continued the Indians became restless and in turn accused the Americans of stealing their horses. Then, according to Dickens, they 'commenced howling and yelling' and tried to seize the ranchers, so he abandoned the search. 'I thought it best to get both men and horses as far away from the reservation as possible.'

Fortunately for the preservation of their hard-won reputation, not all Mounted Policemen were so meek. Dickens might have taken a few lessons from his energetic fellow-Englishman William Parker, who set off from Battleford by canoe with a constable and an interpreter to arrest two Stony Indians, Thunder Horse Son and Little Buffalo, on suspicion of horse thefts. Thunder Horse Son was detained first, then Parker entered the tepee of Little Buffalo, leaving the first Indian with his colleague:

> Just then, the constable outside calling for help, I with the interpreter jumped out and found the two wives of Thunder Horse Son trying to tear him away from the constable. Just as we had pushed the squaws off and put the handcuffs on the Indian I heard a voice from the tepee saying, 'Look out mister, you will be shot.' I turned round and found Little Buffalo putting a cartridge into his rifle. I jumped at him, threw the rifle out of his hands, caught him by the collar, jerked him up in the air and landed him on his head through the round tepee door at the feet of the other prisoner. I knew what would happen then. He wanted to shake hands with me, but instead the handcuffs hanging on my belt were snapped on him. I just had time to thrust my head in the tepee and ask 'Who are you?' An old grey-headed woman sitting close to the door said in good English, 'I am Mrs McKenzie, widow of an old Hudson's Bay officer'. I thanked her for the warning and as there was not a minute to lose gave the order to run for the boat about 200 yards away, driving the two prisoners ahead of us and chased by the two squaws.

Yet Parker was also capable of great consideration towards the Indians. When he was stationed at Qu'Appelle he invited the local natives to a New Year's Day party ('Currant buns and a large kettle of tea') in his quarters. He wrote to his sister Annie, 'About 9 a.m. they commenced to flock in thick, not only Indians but whole gangs of half-breeds. I tell you, we had to fly around and crack our heels together to wait on them all ... I am sure you would never kiss me again if you could only see some of the old beauties that kissed me.'

Parker's friendly, occasionally firm but always fair attitude was shared by most of his comrades. Typical of this was the action of Constable Robert Wilson, who was in charge of five Indian prisoners exercising outside Fort Macleod. Four of them made a break for liberty. 'I could have killed them all if I had wanted to', Wilson wrote afterwards, 'but I did not try to hit any of them because a policeman has no orders that would justify him in killing an escaping prisoner.' Instead, Wilson alerted the fort and fired warning shots over the heads of the Indians, only two of whom were recaptured.

Inexorably, inevitably, the Indian situation slid towards disaster. In the space of a few years the tribes of the Canadian West had suffered a crippling series of calamities – smallpox, rotgut liquor, loss of their lands, and starvation. War-making, horse-stealing, polygamy and firewater were forbidden to them, the Sun Dance was discouraged. In the opinion of many Indians, they had lost much and gained nothing.

To set the seal on their misery Sir John Macdonald's government, as part of a series of economy measures, slashed the allocation of funds to the Indian Department in 1883 and 1884. Rations and supplies were reduced, and there was a wholesale dismissal of the Department's employees in the North West. The experience of Cecil Denny, who after leaving the police had become an Indian Agent for the tribes of Treaty No. 7, was typical. His staff consisted of a clerk, storekeeper, interpreter and a teamster to look after the horses. At the end of 1884 he received a letter telling him to dismiss his clerk and storekeeper 'as you ought to be capable of performing all the office work in your agency as well as supervising the issue of supplies from the store'. Denny wrote back to the Department telling them 'The work of a clerk in my office takes all his time from one month's end to the other, and I cannot do this and look after my treaty.' He resigned.

It had been starvation which forced the Indians on to reservations. Now, their nomadic life over, they were starving again. Superintendent Leif Crozier was one of the first police officers to warn of the dangers of reimposing starvation on a desperate people: 'Considering all that is at stake it is poor, yes, false economy to cut down the expenditure in connection with the feeding of the Indians . . . such a policy will be far the most expensive in the end.'

The continuing reduction in rations was the direct cause of an incident which seriously undermined the prestige of the Mounted Police. It happened on the Salteaux reserve of Chief Yellow Calf at Crooked Lakes, about eighty miles east of Regina. Farm Instructor Keith was ordered to issue government food only to the aged and infirm. An eruption was inevitable. Yellow Calf and some two dozen armed followers broke into the storehouse on the reservation, knocked down Keith and carried away sacks of bacon and flour and barricaded themselves in an untenanted building nearby.

Inspector Richard Burton Deane and ten men were sent from Regina to bring in the offenders. The weather was bitingly cold, $-30°F$, when Deane, Keith, Sergeant Bliss and an interpreter approached the house where the Indian group was sheltering. It was a one-roomed hut, about thirty feet by eighteen. 'The place was literally packed with Indians,' Deane reported. 'When I first went in at the door I stepped into an excavation and very nearly came a cropper, at which there was a general guffaw.' Deane lectured the Indians about the Great White Mother's displeasure, but to this group at least Queen Victoria's opinions meant nothing any more. They were hungry, they said. Their rations had been stopped. What were the police going to do about it? The sympathetic Deane promised to take up their case and advised the ringleaders of the storehouse break-in to surrender themselves for trial. Yellow Calf replied that they might as well die there and then as starve slowly, but promised that they would consider what Deane had said. The police officer found them 'perfectly respectful and friendly from first to last'.

206

Next day Deane's tiny detachment was joined by Superintendent William Herchmer and another ten constables from Regina,
and just after noon they all started for the Indian-occupied house
again, this time accompanied by the local Indian Agent, Colonel
Allan McDonald. According to Deane

> When we came in sight of the house we could see there were a
> number of armed Indians round about it ... every Indian
> present had a firearm of some sort. Col. McDonald, who had
> not spoken to the Indians, wanted to talk but Herchmer would
> have none of it. He told me to fall in the men, and I did so.
> Then he said 'You had better draw pistols'. Instantly the heel of
> a butt was applied to the window sash, which fell out with a
> crash, and the cavity bristled with muzzles. Indians simultane-
> ously appeared round the corners of the house, all being ready
> to shoot. Finding remonstrance useless, Col. McDonald
> whipped up his horse and drove off in his sleigh, saying 'I'll
> have nothing to do with it'. Herchmer suddenly said, 'Well,
> I suppose we'd better go right in', and started off by himself.
> Everyone who knew Billy Herchmer knew that, whatever his
> failings, lack of courage was not one of them, and he presumed
> that bluff would carry the day ... Herchmer had taken no more
> than a couple of paces towards the door when a big, fine-looking
> and determined Indian, who was guarding the door, presented
> his double-barrelled shotgun full in his face at a distance of
> something like two feet. Herchmer stopped dead, as in my
> opinion he was well advised to do, for there was certain murder
> in the dusky ruffian's eye.
> The other Indians followed his example, and we were all
> covered. A movement on the part of any one of us would have
> precipitated a climax. I do not know what Herchmer proposed
> to do in the house even supposing the Indians had admitted us
> all. We had no warrant to arrest anyone – no information had
> been laid and neither of us knew who the guilty parties were.
> We were, in effect, provoking the Indians to commit wilful
> murder by threatening to thrust ourselves into premises into
> which we had no right to force our way. If disaster had befallen
> us, as for two or three seconds seemed extremely probable, our
> blood would have been upon our own heads.

Finally, after two days of talks, four of the Indians, including

Yellow Calf, agreed to stand trial at Regina. The indictment against Yellow Calf was dropped; the other three, charged with larceny, were convicted but discharged on suspended sentences by the stipendiary magistrate, Hugh Richardson. Deane commented, 'It was practically understood from the first that this was to be the outcome of the trial.'

Crooked Lakes had proved that the old Walsh-style bluff which had served so well since the days of the Sioux did not work any more against desperate, hungry Indians. News of the event spread through the camps like a prairie fire. More defiance was the inevitable corollary to Crooked Lakes.

The outbreak came four months later on the reserve of the Cree Chief Poundmaker, about forty miles from Battleford; there was an assembly of nearly 2000 Indians for the annual Thirst Dance ceremony, a modified version of the Sun Dance; it was a convention of disaffected chiefs and their followers bent on a test of strength with the police and the government.

Trouble erupted when a visiting Cree named Man Who Speaks Our Language demanded rations for his sick child from the local farm instructor, John Craig. When Craig not only refused but pushed him out of the storehouse, the Indian seized an axe handle and struck Craig on the arm. The police were sent for. That experienced douser of flames, Leif Crozier, came hurrying from Battleford with twenty-five men into an ugly situation; as the police contingent passed the vast camp the Indians staged a mass demonstration, firing off their rifles and yelling. 'They did not fire at us,' Crozier reported drily. 'At least, the bullets went over our heads.'

Crozier immediately sent for reinforcements and, as he had done three years earlier during the Bull Elk incident at Blackfoot Crossing, worked all night emptying the storehouse and fortifying the Indian Agency building on the reserve. Next morning sixty more police arrived and Crozier moved out in strength towards the Indian camp, accompanied by John Craig to identify and arrest Man Who Speaks Our Language and by William McKay, a Hudson's Bay Company official from Battleford who was popular with the local Indians. The warriors surged from their tepees towards the police line, and a group of homeward-bound Indians under Chief Sweet Grass climbed a nearby hill for a ringside view of the clash. The Cree Chiefs, Poundmaker and Big Bear, offered themselves as hostages, but Crozier was interested only in the Indian who had assaulted Craig. The situation grew unbearably tense, with the Indians pulling and jabbing at the police's guns and uniforms attempting to provoke them into firing first. Wandering Spirit, war chief of Big Bear's tribe, tried to drag William McKay into the Indian ranks, not to harm him but – as he explained later – to prevent him from being killed when the inevitable fight broke out.

Eventually, Man Who Speaks Our Language stepped to the front of the Indian line screeching defiance at the Mounted Police. Fearlessly, Crozier plunged in: 'When I was about to put my hand on him to arrest him he said, "Don't touch me". I said "I shall not touch you if you come with me". This he refused to do. Then I seized the prisoner, at the same time ordering men to my assistance.' Surrounded by infuriated Indians the police group retreated step by step to the fortified Agency building, their rifles levelled. As the warriors swarmed towards the hut the police threw out sacks of supplies, and the hungry natives temporarily forgot their anger while they scrabbled for food. Man Who Speaks Our Language was rushed away to Battleford while his tribesmen were fighting over the food, and received a one-week prison-sentence for the assault on Craig.

In his report of the incident, Crozier wrote, 'It is yet incomprehensible to me how someone did not fire, and it is more than fortunate they did not.' Fred Bagley, the original bugler boy who had now risen to sergeant, was one of the participants in the struggle to arrest Man Who Speaks Our Language, and was full of admiration for Crozier. He considered it 'another of those many instances of courage, resource and determination, in the face of apparently insurmountable obstacles, shown by that gallant officer'.

But the bloodshed had merely been postponed. Big Bear, Wandering Spirit and the handsome Poundmaker were soon to become wanted men and Leif Crozier's fearlessness would spill over into rashness, with disastrous results. The consequences of the government's indifference and stupidity were not to be much longer delayed.

Dissatisfaction was not restricted to the Indians. The half-breeds, and particularly the French-speaking mixed bloods, the *métis*, were deeply disturbed by the spread of civilisation. The extinction of the buffalo herds had wrecked the nomadic lives of the hunters among them, and the arrival of the railway destroyed much of their lucrative freight-carrying operations. For years the half-breeds had been a vital buffer-race between the Indians and the white traders without ever really belonging to either community and there was much anxiety about their ability to survive the inevitable settlement of the North West. The explorer William Francis Butler found the half-breeds 'gay, idle, dissipated, unreliable and ungrateful' – an opinion which was shared by many – and considered them 'a hopeless prospect as a future nationality'. Yet the Earl of Southesk, during his hunting trip in the 1860s, thought 'in all respects they are like civilised men, not more uneducated, immoral or disorderly than many communities in the Old World', and a policeman expressed the opinion of the majority of his colleagues when he said the *métis* were 'as a whole lawabiding and loyal, so long as they were fairly dealt with'.

As Canada's frontiers rolled back, many half-breeds had retreated westward from their settlements around the Red River and founded new communities along the north and south branches of the Saskatchewan River. They were soon overtaken again by officialdom and regulations, none more irksome than the unimaginatively imposed Land Surveys. The *métis* preferred to settle on a narrow strip of river frontage with their property running back for two miles or more. This permitted the maximum number of people access to water, and had the additional advantages of providing a compact community life and an effective front against would-be attackers. (These narrow-fronted holdings can still be seen in operation along the St Lawrence River near Quebec City.) The government's surveyors began to carve up the North West in rectangular chunks, along American township lines, with total disregard of water rights or geography. Eventually, swamped by complaints and petitions from half-breeds, the government compromised, permitting the river-frontage division of land in established communities, but insisting on the imposition of the method of rectangular division in new developments. The situation was complicated because many of the *métis* had never been near enough to a government office to file legal claim for the land on which they squatted.

Eventually, their homes and property in danger and their way of life threatened, they turned to the man whose personality and organising ability had made such an impact in the half-breed uprising at Red River fifteen years previously. They decided to send for Louis Riel.

Chapter 14

THE '85 FOLLIES

LOUIS RIEL's life since he had fled from Garnet Wolseley's troops at Fort Garry in 1870 had been unhappy and unsatisfactory. After being expelled, in his absence in the United States, from the parliamentary seat to which he had been elected by his Manitoba followers, Riel was granted an amnesty in 1874 by the Liberal government of Alexander Mackenzie – but only on condition that he stayed out of Canada for a further five years.

Riel wandered aimlessly about the United States, depending heavily on charity and living occasionally in half-breed communities near the Canadian border. He became bitter, disillusioned and, eventually, mentally unbalanced. After he began tearing his clothes, threatening suicide and interrupting Masses in church he was smuggled back into Quebec under a false name and spent almost two years in mental asylums there. A consoling letter from Bishop Ignace Bourget of Montreal during his confinement telling him that 'God . . . will not abandon you in the darkest hours of your life, for He has given you a mission' was an act of benevolent short-sightedness; the letter became Riel's most treasured possession.

On his discharge in 1878, certified as 'cured – more or less', Riel moved to Montana and a succession of jobs – Indian trader, interpreter, woodcutter, purchasing agent and, after his marriage to an illiterate *métis* named Marguerite Monet, a schoolteacher. He became an American citizen in 1883 and, his period of exile long ended, occasionally visited his family in Manitoba. But he remained convinced (after all, had not Bishop Bourget himself said it?) that he had 'a mission' in life. That mission, as far as Riel was concerned, was the struggle for the betterment of his fellow *métis*. In June 1884 came the call for which Riel had been waiting and which confirmed his extraordinary hold over Canada's half-breeds: a four-man delegation representing the English and French mixed-bloods of the Saskatchewan country travelled 700 miles to Riel's home at St Peter's Mission in Montana and asked him to lead them in their attempts to gain redress for their grievances. Riel accepted at once.

The enthusiasm with which he was received, even by white settlers (who felt he could also help their fight for political recognition and economic assistance) quickly resurrected Riel's ambitions. He undertook a speaking tour of the settlements and began to organise opposition to the Canadian government along the successful lines of 1869 in Red River. A Bill of Rights was sent to Ottawa requesting the issue of land titles and grants to half-breeds, the sale of Dominion lands to raise money for half-breed schools, hospitals and agricultural implements, and the reservation of lands for children of half-breeds. Sir John Macdonald's government and his complacent administrators in the North West took practically no notice of the petition.

Gradually Riel's movement gathered power, and soon the more conservative elements in the territory, particularly the Roman Catholic Church which saw its own influence being undermined, were speaking out against Riel. His fiercest critic among the prairie clergy was Father Alexis André, who reminded one policeman of a mendicant Greek priest: 'He wore a lofty cap of beaver and a greasy cassock very much the worse for wear. In addition he sported an uncared-for beard of iron-grey.' Father André wrote to the Lieutenant-Governor of the North West Territories, Edgar Dewdney, 'I think it is really the duty of the government to get Riel out of mischief as soon as possible,' and suggested that Riel, who had no means of support, could be bribed to return to Montana. Dewdney passed on the suggestion to Ottawa but

213

Macdonald flatly rejected it: 'We have no money to give Riel and would be obliged to ask for a Parliamentary vote. How would it look to confess we could not govern the country and were obliged to bribe a man to go away? This would never do. He has a right to remain in Canada, and if he conspires we must punish him, that's all.'

Riel was certainly conspiring. His speeches and actions became daily more belligerent and emotional and, early in 1885, he determined to repeat his Red River tactics and form a provisional government, take possession of the country around the Saskatchewan rivers and force the Canadian government to take notice of his demands.

Heeding the repeated warnings of officers like Leif Crozier, Sévère Gagnon and Joseph Howe, the police opened new posts in the area and rented Fort Carlton, twenty miles from the principal settlement, Batoche, from the Hudson's Bay Company. Small reinforcing parties were dispatched from Regina bringing the strength in the Saskatchewan area up from eighty to 200. Constable John Donkin was one of a group of twenty who marched the 300 miles from Regina to Prince Albert in appalling weather at Christmas 1884. On the journey Donkin claimed he saw milk being carried in nets and two dogs standing by the trail, frozen in their tracks. The group spent Christmas Eve at the lonely mail station of Hoodoo, 'a most abominable hole'. The occasion was not particularly festive: 'We slept upon the floor as well as we were able. A disreputable crowd we looked (on Christmas morning). Our fur coats were ornamented with hay seeds and straw. Our chins, noses and cheeks were raw with frostbite and smeared with vaseline.' Their Christmas dinner consisted of bacon 'hauled from its bag in a solid block', biscuits and tea.

Riel's hysteria, instability and repeated references to 'striking a blow' and 'ruling the country or perishing in the attempt' eventually alienated the white settlers and English-speaking half-breeds, but most of the *métis*, exasperated by the government's lack of reaction to their demands, followed him faithfully; Riel also made persistent attempts to persuade dissident and unsettled Indian chiefs like the Cree, Big Bear, over to his side. Riel scored a decisive coup when he chose to speak to an assembly of chiefs on 15 March 1885, a day when he knew there was to be a partial eclipse of the sun. Riel told the chiefs that, in order to sanctify his words, the Great Spirit would throw a shadow over the sun. After that master-stroke, Riel was 'big medicine'. Next day Riel told a Dr John Willoughby in Batoche that he intended to divide the North West into seven parts for the Indians, half-breeds, Irish, Germans, Poles, Italians and Bavarians. Inside a week the Mounted Police would be 'wiped out of existence', he said, adding that the Red River Rebellion 'would not be a patch upon this one'.

Gradually the urgency of the police warnings began to register. Inspector Arthur Griesbach telegraphed from Fort Saskatchewan that the half-breeds were about to take up arms and that the Indians in his area were 'very uneasy and saucy'. On 13 March Crozier wired from Battleford 'Half-breed rebellion liable to break out at any moment. If half-breeds rise Indians will join them.' While Crozier made preparations to cope with the uprising he had forecast so accurately, Commissioner Irvine hurriedly assembled every available man at the Regina headquarters to march to the Saskatchewan. E. A. Braithwaite, an English medical student who had twice failed his examinations, and who had emigrated to Canada in disgust and joined the Mounted Police, was detailed by Irvine to take medical charge of the column. The failed student replied that he was neither qualified nor competent, but since there was nobody else with even his limited talent he agreed to undertake the job.

On 18 March, the day that Riel's followers cut the telegraph wires at Batoche, ransacked government stores and seized employees as hostages, Irvine marched north for Prince Albert, the most important white settlement in the Saskatchewan River country, with ninety police, sixty-six horses and a long train of sleighs. He left behind a headquarters manned by only thirty-two men and so short of horses that they had to borrow ponies from the Indian Department. Despite deep snow, bitter cold and howling winds Irvine set a fierce pace, covering forty-three miles the first day and keeping up that average for the next six days. The column marched into Prince Albert on the evening of 24 March.

Though twenty-two men had been treated by the unqualified Braithwaite for snow-blindness on the journey, the appalling weather inflicted only one serious casualty. A young English constable, Roger Pocock, ignored the advice of more-experienced colleagues that he should occasionally run alongside the sleighs to restore circulation, replying that he would rather freeze like a gentleman than run like a dog. Accordingly, he froze like a gentleman. When frostbite was diagnosed in Pocock's feet, Braithwaite put them in a bucket of ice water for the rest of the trip, and he was propped up in a sleigh and bundled in horse robes. Pocock was carried into the barracks at Prince Albert with each foot a black mass, and though he was invalided after the amputation of all the toes of his right foot he overcame the handicap in spectacular fashion, riding alone in 1899 down the mountain spine of North America from Fort Macleod to Mexico City, and going on to become a Boer War soldier, a missionary in Africa and New Caledonia, and a round-the-world yachtsman. But Pocock never again underestimated the cold. Thirteen years after losing his toes he wrote in an English magazine, 'Woe to the idiots lazy enough to spend the day in a sleigh. . . . There was more than frostbite to fear – the chilling of the brain and of vital organs, delirium, coma, death.'

Irvine wasted no time at Prince Albert. The day after his arrival was taken up with 'a thorough inspection of men, arms and horses', and at 2.30 the following morning, 26 March, the Commissioner set out with the eighty-three fit survivors of the dash from Regina, plus twenty-five civilian volunteers from Prince Albert. His plan was to reinforce Superintendent Crozier at the rented Hudson's Bay post of Fort Carlton, fifty miles up the

216

North Saskatchewan River, and only twenty miles from Riel's headquarters, Batoche.

When news was received that the *métis* had seized hostages and supplies, Crozier organised a civilian defence force in Battleford, then set out with fifty police and a seven-pounder gun for Fort Carlton. On his arrival he appealed to Prince Albert for civilian backing; there was such a swift response that he was joined the same night by eighty men from the hastily formed citizen army, the Prince Albert Volunteers.

Louis Riel, seeking to overawe the government by the capture without a struggle of Fort Carlton, sent a letter to Crozier demanding surrender. He promised to set the police garrison free 'on your parole of honour to keep the peace', and added ominously 'In case of non-acceptance we intend to attack you . . . and to commence, without delay, a war of extermination upon those who have shown themselves hostile to our rights.' He signed the letter, with a pompous flourish, Louis 'David' Riel, *Exovede*. David, after the Hebrew King, was a name he adopted at the outbreak of the rebellion; *Exovede* was a pseudo-Latin word coined by Riel to indicate that he was 'chosen from the flock' to lead his people.

In attempting to intimidate Crozier, Riel had picked the wrong man. The policeman's only reply was to demand, in turn, that the *métis* responsible for the recent outrages should surrender at once. On 26 March, as Riel dithered about commencing his 'war of extermination' and with Irvine's column on the way to Fort Carlton, fate and his own impetuosity played Crozier into the hands of the *métis*. A trader named Hilliard Mitchell arrived from the half-breed settlement of Duck Lake, thirteen miles from Carlton, with the news that he had hidden his ammunition and food supplies to keep them from falling into rebel hands. Sergeant Alf Stewart was sent to Duck Lake with some horse-drawn sleighs with an escort of seventeen men to collect the badly needed provisions and bullets. On the way they were halted by armed *métis* accompanied by a few Indians, who tried to provoke the police into opening fire; two half-breeds jumped into a sleigh and attempted to drive it away. Sensibly, Stewart's small contingent retreated towards Fort Carlton. When an advance rider brought the news to Crozier, the man who had outfaced Indians in a dozen tricky situations reacted in typically vigorous fashion. He immediately ordered the seven-pounder gun which had been dragged from Battleford to be limbered up and called for volunteers for a punitive column. Eager police had to be restrained from jumping into the sleighs for what they cheerfully termed 'a picnic'; eventually, to the cheers of those who couldn't find room, Crozier led out ninety-eight men (fifty-five police and forty-three Prince Albert Volunteers) into the sticky snow and weak sunshine of an early spring morning. Because of the deepness of the snow, the party was confined to the narrow trail. About two miles outside Duck Lake they found themselves among rebel positions carefully chosen on a brush-covered hill by their military leader Gabriel Dumont, a thoroughly experienced hunter, horseman and scout whose ability was highly respected by the police. The column halted in what one policeman called 'a wretched position, in an exposed hollow, surrounded on three sides by scrubby brush'.

Two Indians appeared and indicated a wish to parley. Superintendent Crozier moved forward, accompanied by a Scottish half-breed interpreter Joe McKay, but it quickly became obvious that the natives were merely playing for time to allow their colleagues to take up ambush positions. As Crozier turned away, telling McKay, 'We can do nothing here', the older of the Indians, Asseeweeyin, tried to grab Crozier's revolver, telling him, 'You have too many guns, grandson. Give me this.' As the pair struggled, McKay shot the Indian. The battle of Duck Lake had begun.

Crozier admitted that Dumont's rebels, whose strength has been variously assessed between a hundred and four times that number but never truly established, 'had their disposition most skilfully made'. The furthest distance between the contenders was 150 yards, and in places it was considerably less. The rebels poured in a deadly fire from three sides as Crozier's column scrambled for cover behind overturned sleighs. Constable Thomas Gibson was shot through the heart as he wrestled with the seven-pounder gun, which was rendered partially ineffective by the depth of snow and the fact that it was on wheels, and put out of action completely after firing only three shots when a frenzied gunner rammed home the shell before the charge.

The contest was palpably one-sided. A Prince Albert Volunteer, William Laurie, recalled, 'We could see nothing but hats and caps just over the top of the snow. We all tried our best to puncture the heads beneath them but, alas for our inexperience, there were none, for we learned afterwards the hats were set up on sticks planted in the snow while the owners were in each case several yards away.' There were pathetic instances of bravery. Constable George Arnold, a former U.S. Cavalry scout, was shot through the chest, leaped to his feet with an oath and blazed away at the rebel lines until he was felled by bullets in the leg and groin. For no particular reason Corporal Hugh Davidson suddenly jumped on top of one of the sleighs and led his comrades in 'three British cheers', though it is difficult to understand what there was to cheer about. Constable George Garrett was shot through the left lung and mortally wounded. Corporal Tom Gilchrist, his hip broken by a bullet, yelled for the surgeon, Robert Miller. Eventually, in desperate pain, Gilchrist shouted at his commanding officer, 'Crozier, tell that damned fool of a doctor I'm bleeding to death.' When Miller arrived and took his surgical case from his pocket he found a bullet embedded in his instruments.

After half an hour the police broke off the disastrous battle. Nine Prince Albert Volunteers and one policeman lay dead. Two more constables died the next day of their wounds and another dozen members of the ill-fated party were wounded, including Crozier himself, who received a flesh wound in the right cheek, though he never mentioned this in his reports or casualty lists. The police had lost twenty-five per cent of their group and only the refusal of Louis Riel (who had watched the fight armed only with a large crucifix which he waved in the air as the bullets flew) to allow the rebels to follow up prevented them from annihilating the routed column.

Four *métis* and one Indian lost their lives and another three were wounded, including their leader Gabriel Dumont, whose scalp was furrowed by a bullet.

An hour after Crozier's group limped through the gates of Fort Carlton, Irvine arrived from Prince Albert. If only Crozier had waited for Irvine's reinforcements he would probably have ended the day a hero rather than a scapegoat. Irvine's anger showed through the official jargon in his report on Duck Lake:

> I cannot but consider it a matter of regret that with the know-ledge that both myself and command were within a few miles of Fort Carlton, Supt Crozier should have marched out as he did, particularly in the face of what had transpired earlier in the day. I am led to believe that this officer's better judgement was overruled by the impetuosity displayed by both the police and volunteers.

Irvine's immediate problem was to decide whether to dig in at Fort Carlton or retreat to Prince Albert, the strategical centre of the Saskatchewan River territory. Ignoring Crozier's suggestion that the police should attack the *métis* again, Irvine checked on the defensibility of Fort Carlton. The fort had been built principally with trading in mind; its stockade was dilapidated and the place was dominated by hills. The amateur doctor, Braithwaite, who had arrived with Irvine's column, considered it 'a beautiful spot for sharpshooters to pot at us as we walked about'. Irvine also faced the problem that the civilian volunteers, their thirst for action more than assuaged, were anxious to get back to their families in Prince Albert. Irvine decided to extricate his column, abandon the fort and fall back on Prince Albert, the capture of which would have been a major triumph for Riel.

All day on 27 March preparations were made to abandon the Hudson's Bay post. The police were given *carte blanche* to take away what they could carry or eat. Everything else was soaked in coal-oil to prevent its use by the rebels. Constable John Donkin recalled, 'The whole place was looted. Suits of clothing, blankets, tobacco, and even perfumes were taken possession of. . . . Tins of preserves, lobsters, sardines, and boxes of fancy biscuits were carried off to the rooms; and there was a general picnic on the beds.'

That evening the three police victims of Duck Lake, Gibson Arnold and Garrett, were buried by lantern light outside the fort walls, 'Col. Irvine reading the most beautiful service of the Church of England in a most impressive manner; whatever was wanting in the ceremony being made up for by the real grief of those who stood about.'

The funerals and the loading of the sleighs with supplies and hay for the comfort of the wounded and of the women and children, refugees from local farms, delayed the departure from the fort until the early hours of 28 March. In the middle of the preparations fire broke out in a hospital room when some loose hay ignited near a stove. The wounded were hurried out into the cold. Braithwaite told how he and a sergeant moved Corporal Tom Gilchrist, whose hip was broken. 'The sergeant got hold of Gilchrist by the head and shoulders and I the feet. In removing him I had to back into the room which was on fire. The sergeant called to me to look out and gave me a kind of jerk to pull me out. The broken hip apparently came out of its setting and we had to carry him to Prince Albert in that condition.'

Afraid that the fire would attract a rebel ambush the column moved out immediately, abandoning most of the articles plundered from the Hudson's Bay stores. They marched in a dangerously exposed line, encumbered by laden sleighs, wounded men, and women and children, but were left alone by the *métis* and got to Prince Albert that evening.

Two days later – and four days too late – the Canadian government appointed a parliamentary committee to investigate the halfbreeds' claims and petitions.

Prince Albert had been founded in 1866 as a Presbyterian settlement by a Glaswegian missionary, the Rev. James Nisbet, and named after the Prince Consort. The town straggled along the bank of the North Saskatchewan River 'like a disjointed snake' according to one policeman.

The core of the defence plan was the brick-built Presbyterian church and manse. A wooden fence nine feet high was thrown up around the buildings and into the stockade flocked terrified refugees from nearby homes and farms, swelling the town's population from 700 to 1800. The defence force consisted of 225 police, several of them wounded at Duck Lake, and just over 300 home guards. Though they were woefully short of arms – some of the civilians patrolled the stockade ramparts carrying wooden clubs – the garrison was large and determined enough to discourage half-breed ambitions against Prince Albert.

In the first apprehensive days after the Duck Lake débâcle, the scene inside the stockade was one of utter confusion. The church was 'a vast nursery of noisy children and screaming females', according to Constable John Donkin. Two lines of improvised dining-tables stretched the length of the church while a detachment of cooks toiled in a tent outside the building preparing 'everlasting bacon' for the refugees. 'Of course, it was quite impossible to wash,' Donkin reported. 'And food had literally to be fought for.'

Safe, if uncomfortable, inside the stockade, police, home guards and their families waited and wondered what was happening elsewhere.

The Duck Lake victory had temporarily strengthened the *métis* cause and swayed uncommitted Indian tribes towards Riel. Immediately after the battle he wrote to several chiefs (addressing them as 'dear relatives') praising God 'for the success He has given us' and urging the Indians, 'Capture all the police you possibly can.' Riel also advised his half-breed followers: 'Murmur, growl and threaten. Stir up the Indians. Render the police of Fort Pitt and Battleford powerless.'

The most important chiefs to go over to the rebel side were the Cree pair, Poundmaker and Big Bear. Though he had guided Lord Lorne's party during their tour of the North West years previously, Poundmaker had grown increasingly resentful about the restraints of reservation life. And it was around Big Bear, a slight elderly man with a deeply seamed face and an impressive voice and manner, that had gathered those Crees who were determined not to lose their identity and way of life to the white man. Big Bear's independent attitude and ability to extract rations from government agents while avoiding the farming work which treaty tribes were forced to undertake in exchange for food, unsettled other bands.

The majority of the Indians stayed firmly, if uneasily, on their reservations, however. Peace among the Blackfoot nation was ensured when Chief Crowfoot promised, 'We are agreed and determined to remain loyal to the Queen', a message which produced cheers when it was read out in the House of Commons in Ottawa. The influential Catholic Father Lacombe, was asked to travel among the Blackfoot tribes with soothing words, and the government authorised the issue of extra rations to keep them docile, if not contented. There were other, more flamboyant examples of loyalty to the Great Mother. The Cree chief Moosomin stalked around Fort Macleod with a tattered Union Jack draped around his shoulders; and when the civilian volunteers underwent drill instruction at Prince Albert one Indian ('the principal recipient of our bounty from the kitchen', according to John Donkin) paraded with them in full war paint.

Battleford, a hundred miles from the start of the insurrection at Duck Lake, was the first settlement to suffer from marauding Indians. On 29 March, as the bands of Poundmaker and Little Pine approached, the civilian population fled into the police fort which stood apart from the town. Nearly 600 people were cooped up inside the barracks, two-thirds of them non-combatants. The police garrison numbered only forty-three, under Inspector William Morris. William McKay, an officer of the Hudson's Bay

223

Company post at Battleford, spoke to the Indians, who offered to return to their reserves if they were given food, clothing and ammunition, but while he was attempting to obtain government permission to bargain with the Indians looting broke out in the abandoned town. Stores and houses were emptied and destroyed. Painted warriors tore off their own clothes and cavorted through the streets in top hats, silk shirts and bonnets. Furniture was smashed, feather mattresses torn up and set alight. Pigs, chickens and pets were killed. Out of rifle range, the police and refugees watched as Battleford was torn apart. One resident said afterwards, 'It was just like taking a lady's trunk and pulling both ends two miles apart, with all between them.' Nearby farms and homesteads were ransacked and burned, and a marauding band of Assiniboines killed their farm instructor and a white settler. Finally, their cupidity and frenzy exhausted, the Indians imposed a desultory siege on the police fort, intent on starving out the occupants but unaware that there was a three-month supply of food inside.

As soon as news reached him of the depredations at Battleford, the energetic Inspector Arthur Griesbach at Fort Saskatchewan, near Edmonton, took swift steps to improve the defences of a police post which was exceedingly dilapidated. Though Griesbach had only twenty men, the rotten stockade was strengthened, bastions built and a well dug. Some thirty civilians armed with guns 'of various descriptions' and seventy-nine women and children were admitted to the fort. When he had ensured that his post was in good defensive order Griesbach travelled to Edmonton 'where I found the citizens assembled at a meeting and much excited'. He advised them to take refuge inside the Hudson's Bay fort and rejected requests that he and his tiny command should move to Edmonton to protect a community which had enough men and arms to protect itself. 'I received a large amount of abuse for not complying with their wishes,' he reported.

Edmonton boasted two ancient four-pounder brass cannon, minus mountings or ammunition. Griesbach, who was noted

23. Poundmaker

24. Superintendent Leif Crozier

25. Charcoal, killer of Sergeant Wilde, with handcuffs hidden by his hat

26. Almighty Voice, killer of three policemen

mainly by the locals as a keen horseman and snappy dresser (he sported the first bowler hat ever seen in that part of Canada) showed improvisational flair by mounting the guns on wagon wheels and uncovering in the Hudson's Bay storehouse salmon tins which fitted the bore of the cannon. When filled with scrap metal and soldered, these tins were tested and found to make effective canister shot. Next, Griesbach sent a courier 200 miles south to Calgary, asking for aid. Then he sat back to await attack – or assistance.

But it was in the area commanded by the unfortunate Inspector Francis Dickens that the next Indian blow fell. Dickens had been sent to the Hudson's Bay post of Fort Pitt with a detachment of twenty-five men late in 1883 to supervise Big Bear and his restless followers, who had finally signed a treaty with the government but still equivocated about settling on a reservation. Built by the Hudson's Bay Company in 1831, Fort Pitt had admirably served its purpose for more than fifty years as an intermediate point of call between Edmonton, 150 miles to the west, and Fort Carlton, a similar distance in the opposite direction. Like many others in the Canadian West, it was a fort in name only and possessed neither a defence wall nor a stockade. It had been sited with trade and shelter, rather than war, in mind, was dominated by hills and stood near the north bank of the North Saskatchewan, which at that point was 400 yards wide.

A further thirty-five miles north lay the tiny settlement of Frog Lake in the middle of a large Cree reservation. After arguments between the Frog Lake Indian agent, Thomas Trueman Quinn, a lanky American from Minnesota, and some of Big Bear's starving, destitute followers over Quinn's 'no work – no rations' policy, a handful of police under Corporal Ralph Sleigh was sent there. When news of the Duck Lake defeat reached him at the end of March, Dickens offered to strengthen the Frog Lake police guard, but Quinn was convinced that the presence of police was likely to inflame the unsettled Indians in his charge. In any case,

Quinn pointed out, their numbers were so few that they would be powerless to keep any uprising in check. So, at the agent's request, the police returned to Fort Pitt on the last day of March with the words of Quinn ringing in their ears, 'They might kill me, but they can't scare me.'

Two days later, the Thursday before Easter, 2 April, Indians in war paint interrupted a Mass in the Frog Lake Catholic mission, looted the Hudson's Bay store and ordered all the whites in the settlement to their camp as prisoners. When Thomas Quinn refused to lead the way, Wandering Spirit, the war chief of Big Bear's band, his eyelids and lips thickly coated with yellow ochre war paint, shouted 'I tell you – go', shot Quinn dead and called on the Indians to kill all the other whites. Big Bear himself, who had just returned from a hunting trip, ran among his braves vainly crying 'Stop, stop.' In addition to Quinn two Catholic priests, five other whites and a French half-breed were murdered.

The only survivors at Frog Lake were Henry Quinn, an Indian Department blacksmith and nephew of Thomas Quinn, William B. Cameron, the Hudson's Bay agent, and the wives of two of the murdered men, the farming instructor John Delaney and a settler John Gowanlock. Henry Quinn, warned by a friendly Indian, made his escape on foot through snow and slush thirty-five miles to Fort Pitt with news of the massacre, but Cameron and the two women were made prisoners.

To judge from his terse diary notes, Francis Dickens seemed no more galvanised by the terrible affair at Frog Lake than he had been by other alarming incidents in his undistinguished police career. His entry for Good Friday, the day Fort Pitt heard the news, started 'Fine weather'. Fortunately, William J. McLean, Hudson's Bay agent at the fort, has left a better account of the terror which must have gripped the inhabitants of the lonely outpost:

> Everyone in the fort felt horrified at the dreadful occurrence and at our fearful prospect. We at once commenced to barricade the windows and doors of all the buildings with sacks of flour

... the following day we pulled down outlying buildings which might afford shelter and cover for the Indians, who were expected hourly to rush upon us ... we set up a sort of barricade between the buildings. It was a very poor defence but the best that we could hurriedly set up.

Every civilian in the fort was sworn in as a special constable by McLean, who was Justice of the Peace for the area; everyone took a turn at sentry duty, including McLean's three eldest daughters (Corporal Ralph Sleigh noted, 'The Misses McLean show great courage and each, rifle in hand, stands at a loophole'). But the situation was hopeless. The tiny police garrison had only forty rounds each, there was no water supply nearer than the river 400 yards away and, in any case, the fort was totally vulnerable to a determined attack by superior numbers. Even Dickens realised this quickly and switched the energies of the handymen among the defenders to the construction of a large boat to carry them all down the North Saskatchewan River to Battleford.

Ten days went by without a sign of the marauding Crees and on 13 April Dickens decided to put out a three-man patrol to discover the Indians' whereabouts, despite McLean's protests that he would be presenting three horses and rifles to the rebels and losing three men. Those chosen for the assignment were two police constables, David Cowan and Clarence Loasby, and the young survivor of Frog Lake, Henry Quinn.

Only a couple of hours after the scouts had departed, Big Bear and about 250 mounted Indians appeared to the north of the fort from the direction of Frog Lake. Big Bear sent a letter, written by one of his white prisoners, demanding the police's surrender and on the same page pleading for tea and tobacco, together with a blanket for himself, complaining that he was 'very cold'. The goods were sent but the surrender demand was rejected. Later that day a Cree aptly named Miserable Man delivered another demand for surrender and supplies. This time the Indians wanted kettles to make tea in, and Miserable Man, who was almost naked and blue with cold, asked for a shirt and trousers, 'all of which he got', noted William McLean. Though Dickens again refused to surrender his arms and command he was already beginning to waver. 'I told them that if they would go away we would leave.'

Since the Indians seemed more concerned about their comfort than war, McLean walked out, alone and unarmed, to their camp for talks. He returned to the fort later but next day – 'without telling me of his intentions', according to Dickens – went out again for a further council. In the middle of this, however, the three police scouts returning to Fort Pitt blundered into the Cree camp. Constable Cowan was killed almost immediately, Henry Quinn – who seemed to be leading a charmed life – again got clean away into nearby woods, and the other policeman, Clarence Loasby, had a miraculous escape. Making for the fort, his horse was shot from under him and he sprinted for safety. Though shot in the back he staggered on, only to be ridden down by a mounted Indian, Lone Man, who shot him again. Loasby fell and lay still. When the Indians were driven off by fire from the fort Loasby crawled into the makeshift stockade.

After the excitement McLean now found himself a prisoner in the Indian camp. Wandering Spirit, the Cree war chief who had instigated the Frog Lake massacre, approached the Hudson's Bay agent excitedly and told him to hold up his arms. 'I thought my time had come . . . he then said I must swear by the Great Spirit that I would not desert them and they would spare my life.' Having no choice, McLean promised. The Indians, seeking more hostages, offered to take care of the remainder of the two dozen Fort Pitt civilians if they wished to surrender. Mrs McLean sent her husband a message that Dickens was 'so confused and excited he did not know what to suggest, nor how to act'. Eventually all the civilians decided to go to the Indian camp rather than take their chance with the Mounted Police, 'believing it to be the safer course', in the words of McLean.

Dickens maintained later that the surrender of the civilians was 'entirely owing to the pusillanimity of Mr McLean' (a statement which McLean himself rejected as 'inconsiderate and un-kind'); but, with the responsibility for the non-combatants removed, Dickens was now free to abandon Fort Pitt. The evacuation took place that night in bitterly cold weather across a river which had only recently broken up and was full of ice. The police destroyed what arms they could not take with them and, carrying the badly wounded Loasby, embarked in the makeshift boat, which leaked badly. 'By dint of hard baling we got across the river, although I thought she would sink under us,' Dickens wrote later.

The party passed a most wretched night encamped about a mile down the North Saskatchewan from Fort Pitt. Next morning the final entry in the diary of Francis Jeffrey Dickens – who would have been the first to admit that he wasn't his father's son when it came to writing – stated simply: 'Very cold weather. Travelled.' Corporal Ralph Sleigh was more explicit: 'Snowing fast and very windy. Several men frost-bitten. Clothing frozen on our backs, and some narrow escapes from ice jams.'

The same morning Henry Quinn's luck finally ran out. After again escaping from Big Bear's followers, he shivered through the night in a hole he had dug in the river bank. Unaware that the police had evacuated it, he approached Fort Pitt at dawn, only to be captured by the Indians who had occupied the buildings during the night. Though he survived his period of captivity, the ordeal left Quinn with severe rheumatism, and eventually he went blind.

The Crees pillaged the settlement, loaded all the abandoned wagons with plunder and marched their herd of prisoners to join the other hostages and their own families back at Frog Lake.

Dickens's laden boat was six days on its perilous journey down the North Saskatchewan. Cramped and frozen, constantly stopping to repair their craft and to haul it over shoals, they finally reached Battleford, whose besieging Indians had become bored and with-drawn to their reserve, on 22 April. The garrison turned out and presented arms and a police band played them into the fort, a welcome totally out of keeping with Dickens's miserable performance. Corporal Sleigh noted in his diary, 'Enthusiastic greeting. Ladies gave us a grand dinner.'

Astonishingly, the wounded Loasby not only survived the rigorous trip but lived to a ripe age. Staff-Sergeant J. Widmer Rolph, in medical charge at Fort Pitt, reported that Loasby, 'suffering two severe flesh wounds, bore the journey well, showing how large a factor pure fresh air is in the treatment of wounds. It was impossible to dress his wounds properly, he had to be carried on and off the boat whenever we landed, often up steep banks and on an impromptu stretcher and yet after six days of such usage his recovery was as rapid as any cases of similar severity which came under my notice.' One of the bullets which wounded Loasby had passed through his body and lodged in his underclothing. He had it mounted on a signet ring as a memento of a truly remarkable escape from death.

But the experience of Fort Pitt completely shattered Dickens. When Battleford was relieved two days after his arrival there, Superintendent William Herchmer found Inspector Morris still in command, though Dickens was his senior. Dickens had to be ordered to take over. The following year, on the grounds of his worsening deafness, Dickens was retired. He spent a month in Ottawa vainly trying to extract $2000 which he claimed the government owed him in back pay, eventually ran out of money and had to sell the prized gold watch bequeathed to him by his father. To raise funds he decided to tour the United States lecturing on his experiences in the North West Rebellion.

His first engagement was to speak to a literary group known as the Friday Club in Moline, Illinois. He went to dine first at the home of the editor of the local newspaper, arrived thirsty after a dusty carriage-ride and drank a glass of iced water. A few minutes later he complained of feeling unwell, lay down to rest and died.

Moline gave an elaborate funeral to 'the third son of the renowned author' and an appropriate epitaph in its Riverside

Cemetery for the morose introvert who was habitually unpunctual: 'Take Ye Heed, Watch and Pray, For Ye Know Not When the Time Comes.'

The fall of Fort Pitt was the peak of the rebels' success. The police and white settlers were bottled up in Prince Albert and Battleford, Dickens's meek abandonment of his fort persuaded more Indians to follow the seemingly invincible Riel and Big Bear and provided the Indians with easily obtained hostages and supplies. But massive retribution was on its way from the east to crush the *métis* and their Indian allies.

Chapter 15

A CURIOUS LITTLE WAR

WHEN news of the uprising reached Ottawa, the government reacted with a promptness not previously apparent in their dealings with the inhabitants of the North West Territories. The sixty-year-old Major-General Frederick Dobson Middleton, commander of the Canadian Militia, was appointed leader of the punitive expedition and despite his portly build (chest 43 in., waist 43 in.) he too exhibited some untypical hustle. Middleton got his orders on 23 March and arrived in Winnipeg four days later. That same evening he was on his way west by rail with 260 men of Winnipeg's 90th Battalion of militia, known as the 'Little Black Devils' because of their dark uniform.

Middleton, born in Belfast and educated for a military career at Sandhurst, had joined the British Army at seventeen and served in the Maori War and the Indian Mutiny. He arrived in Canada only a year before the outbreak of the rebellion as commanding officer to the Canadian Militia. This custom of appointing a British officer over the Canadian forces was an outdated relic of colonialism. Middleton, erect and white-whiskered, was an anachronism in other ways too. Obsessively infantry-minded, he still fought and thought in Indian Mutiny terms, and he had all the contempt of a regular for non-professionals, referring to his part-time army as 'raw soldiers'.

In return, the volunteers – and others – thought little of the general. Uncomplimentary adjectives like pompous, egotistical, stupid, stodgy and brusque were used to describe him. And there seems little to contradict the comment of one writer that during the North West Rebellion Middleton's courage was more in evidence than his intelligence.

Although it was badly executed, Middleton's campaign strategy was well conceived. Using the Canadian Pacific Railway as a line of swift communication and a springboard, Middleton planned to launch three columns north from the railway line into the heart of *métis*-controlled country. He would lead the main force against the rebel headquarters, Batoche; a second column under a Canadian Militia colonel, William Dillon Otter, would relieve Battleford; and another veteran of the Indian Mutiny, Major-General Thomas Bland Strange, agreed to leave his ranching business near Calgary, take over the third brigade and pacify the country between Calgary and Edmonton. After subduing the *métis*, Middleton and Strange were to converge on Fort Pitt to rout the dissident Indians of Big Bear and Poundmaker.

Middleton's overall strength (excluding the Mounted Police already in the area) was more than 5000, made up mainly of militia troops from Quebec, Ontario and Manitoba. The problem of shuttling these eastern troops to the west at the worst period of the year, the tail-end of winter, was a vast one. William Van Horne, general manager of Canadian Pacific, promised the government he would deliver them in twelve days, although there were still four gaps in the line, totalling eighty-six miles, in the wild, broken bush country along the north shore of Lake Superior.

Because of the haste with which the troops were assembled, supply arrangements were often ludicrously inadequate. The first detachment to leave Ontario was told to bring its own lunch; others had to provide their own clothing, and one group set off with its kit in brown-paper parcels because of a shortage of knapsacks. Clutching donated New Testaments and temperance leaflets warning of the perils of strong drink, the inexperienced and ill-equipped militiamen cheerfully headed for what was to be easily their worst experience of the campaign.

Van Horne had worked swiftly to provide transportation to

span the gaps in his tracks. Horse-drawn sleighs and dog teams were commandeered to ferry the soldiers over the uncompleted stretches, but often the amateur troops were forced to struggle through on foot in blizzards and temperatures of $-25°F$. The last section of seven miles across the frozen edge of Lake Superior to where the uninterrupted railway lines commenced took some of the contingents six hours to cover; this terrible country claimed as casualties of frostbite and snow blindness more men of Middleton's militia than did the combined efforts of *métis* and Indians.

By mid-April all had arrived at their jumping-off points – Qu'Appelle station, about thirty-five miles east of Regina; Swift Current, 130 miles west of the territorial capital; and Calgary. This unprecedented speed in transporting a military expedition to the west was the decisive factor in localising the rebellion and persuading uncommitted *métis* and Indians that they would be joining a doomed cause.

The first success was marked up by the Canadian militiaman, Colonel William Otter. He left the Swift Current railway halt on 13 April with more than 500 men, including a Mounted Police detachment under Superintendent William Herchmer, and eleven days later marched unopposed into Battleford.

After a four-day layover at Qu'Appelle to give the Winnipeg volunteers target practice 'as I found that many of the men had never pulled a trigger', Middleton marched for Batoche on 6 April with the earliest of his militia arrivals, leaving the others to catch up. Fiercely cold days and nights – tent pegs frequently had to be chopped out of the ground with axes in the mornings, and the boots of those lucky enough to be mounted froze to the stirrups – alternated with spells of milder weather which reduced snow to slush and turned trails into quagmires, but in less than two weeks his column of 800 had struggled 200 miles to Clarke's Crossing on the South Saskatchewan River and only forty miles south of Batoche.

Meanwhile, forty miles north of the rebel headquarters, Commissioner Irvine and his police sat in Prince Albert waiting for

234

news and orders. Since the loss of Fort Carlton there had been no alarms and precious little activity for the town's garrison, and Constable John Donkin recalled, 'Why we did not march out and attack the rebels was the daily – nay, hourly – subject of speculation.' The police were carrying out only limited patrolling near Prince Albert and since their scarlet tunics were too conspicuous for these duties they improvised a uniform from the town's clothing stores consisting of slouch hats, brown jackets, moleskin riding-trousers and brown canvas bandoliers. According to Donkin, they looked like 'a cross between a Montana desperado and a Sardinian *chasseur*'.

Irvine had merely received notice that he was to take orders from the overall field-commander, Middleton, and after witnessing the disastrous consequences of Crozier's hastiness at Duck Lake the Commissioner intended to sit tight and guard Prince Albert until he received further instructions. He was well aware, in addition, that the threat of a raid by his command was a constant worry to Louis Riel in Batoche. Finally, on 16 April, two messengers reached Prince Albert from General Middleton informing Irvine that Batoche would be attacked on 18 April. Middleton obviously expected little resistance; he did not ask for Irvine's support in a joint operation but merely instructed him to 'look out for flying half-breeds'. In fact, Irvine moved out towards Batoche on 19 April with 200 mounted men, but abandoned the push when scouts told him that Batoche was not under assault as Middleton had promised. In any case Middleton had decided to leave Irvine and his police out of the reckoning when he was told by his returning messengers that the Commissioner seemed unwilling to leave Prince Albert.

Before moving from Clarke's Crossing to attack Batoche, Middleton unwisely divided his command into columns to push up each bank of the South Saskatchewan. The move almost proved disastrous when on 24 April – the day Battleford was relieved – Middleton only just avoided blundering into a *métis* ambush laid by Gabriel Dumont and a force of 150 at Fish Creek, seventeen miles south of Batoche; he was hard-pressed for a time until the troops on the wrong side of the river could be ferried over to his assistance. Middleton lost ten killed and forty-three wounded before the *métis* broke off the fight. (A cairn at the battle site tells the modern traveller, with a poor sense of accuracy, history and taste, that 'the rebels were defeated and driven from the field'.)

Middleton, who admitted he 'could not help having a feeling of admiration' for the pluck and fighting skill of the *métis*, came close to death himself at Fish Creek as he directed operations in full view of the enemy. One bullet holed his fur cap and another grazed his horse. Middleton's bewilderment about who had really won at Fish Creek was reflected in his report: 'We had a very sharp brush with the rebels and I am almost inclined to think that we have given them a lesson which may materially affect the whole affair.'

It was almost two weeks before the hesitant Middleton was ready for the final push on Batoche. On 7 May, three weeks *after* the date he had given to Irvine, Middleton moved off. Strangely, for such a cautious and unimaginative man, he had prepared what he hoped would be a surprise for the *métis*. He had brought with him a 'battleship' – the *Northcote*, the first steamer on the Saskatchewan, which had been plying the river for eleven years. At Gabriel's Crossing, the home of the *métis* leader Gabriel Dumont was destroyed and the *Northcote* was fortified with timber from his house and sacks of flour; thirty-five infantrymen were placed aboard and on the morning of 9 May the vessel floated downstream towards Batoche in what was intended to be a co-ordinated attack. But the rebels were ready: the soldiers on board were pinned down by fierce fire from both banks, a wire ferry-cable stretched across the river carried away her funnels and mast and the crippled *Northcote* had swept past Batoche before the North West Field Force was anywhere near the settlement, anchoring out of firing range and taking no further part in the fight – an inglorious end to the only naval engagement in the history of the

Canadian prairies. The *Northcote* crept back upstream four days later just in time to sound its whistle at the victory celebrations following the fall of Batoche.

While Middleton had been preparing for the decisive contest, Louis Riel and his 'cabinet' – the 'Exovedate' – were preoccupied with such vital matters as proposing new names for the days of the week. Riel regarded himself as a man of God, a man with a mission, but not a man of war. Defence was left in the hands of Gabriel Dumont who, despite a crippling shortage of men and ammunition, had devised a cunning series of rifle pits which gave the militia nothing to shoot at as they advanced through the broken countryside towards the shabby wooden settlement of Batoche. After the battle Middleton inspected the pits and expressed astonishment 'at the strength of the position, and at the ingenuity and care displayed in their construction'.

It was not until the eve of the battle that Riel seemed to realise his own future and that of his people was about to be decided. Accordingly, he addressed an urgent message to his Maker in his diary on 8 May: 'O my God, do not permit England to get the better of me, for she would annihilate me, together with my nation. . . . O my God, hasten to help me. Do not delay.'

Middleton began a cautious probing attack the next morning; he lost two killed and ten wounded that day before retiring his command, with true Sudan War mentality, to a *zareba*, a fortified stockade of supply wagons. The next two days followed the same pattern, with the troops trudging off to war in the morning and coming back to the *zareba* for their supper in the evening, minus an occasional dead or wounded comrade. The *métis*, safe in their rifle pits, suffered no losses, though shellfire caused some casualties among non-combatants in Batoche itself.

On the fourth day the exasperated troops waited until General Middleton returned to the *zareba* for his lunch then, led by an Ontario militia colonel, A. T. H. Williams, charged the rifle pits head on; the *métis*, so short of ammunition that they had been firing metal buttons, rusty nails and pebbles from their ancient

237

muzzle-loaders, were routed before Middleton, vainly trying to halt the triumphant advance, could get to the scene. One of those killed in the overrun pits was a ninety-three-year-old named Joseph Ouellette. Among the militia dead that day was Captain John French, brother of the Mounted Police's first Commissioner, shot in the chest as he dashed into a building. Middleton's command suffered eight killed and forty-six wounded in the four-day fight. *Métis* casualties were sixteen dead and thirty wounded. Colonel Williams, instigator of the charge, survived the battle only to die of fever two months later.

Both Gabriel Dumont and Louis Riel got away from Batoche. Dumont, an experienced plainsman and hunter, evaded his would-be captors and reached the safety of Montana (and later toured Europe as an attraction with Buffalo Bill Cody's Wild West Show) but Riel gave himself up to two Mounted Police scouts and a half-breed guide three days after the fall of Batoche. One of them, an American Indian-fighter named Robert Armstrong, offered Riel a lift into Middleton's camp on his horse. Riel accepted, at the same time politely removing a .22 revolver from his hip pocket and saying that it would 'perhaps be better' if the scout took possession of it. In order to forestall any possible violence against Riel, the scouts announced as they entered camp that the prisoner was Riel's cook. The *métis* leader was taken to General Middleton's tent. 'I found him a mild-spoken and mild-looking man with a short brown beard,' the general wrote. 'He had no coat on and looked cold and forlorn and as it was still chilly out of the sun I commenced proceedings by giving him a military greatcoat of my own.'

Next stop for Middleton on what had now become a triumphal procession was Prince Albert, which was 'relieved' by his column on 20 May. Commissioner Irvine made the mistake of turning out his Mounted Police in their finest scarlet to welcome him. According to Constable John Donkin, the Field Force's uniforms were 'a dingy purple' by comparison, a colour which was matched by Middleton's face when he saw the spick-and-span police guard of honour. 'Look at my men, sir,' he spluttered at Irvine. 'Look at the colour of their uniforms, sir.'

Middleton's dismissal of the Mounted Police as 'gophers' (a prairie animal that retreats into a hole at the first sign of danger) had been widely quoted in Canadian newspapers, and the inevitable repercussions of Irvine's handling of his command were soon felt. A telegram from Ottawa asked for a full report from Crozier about the Duck Lake fight and ordered Irvine to explain 'why you abandoned Carlton and why you did not go to Duck Lake; why you did not scour the country around Prince Albert and why you did not join General Middleton'. In other words, why had Irvine remained inactive in Prince Albert during the fighting?

Irvine defended himself vigorously. He had already forwarded a long letter of explanation about the reasons for retreating from Fort Carlton. As for the other criticisms, Irvine explained, 'The country around Prince Albert was thoroughly scoured; result, no houses pillaged or burnt. Received no order to join General Middleton, which rather surprised me as I am sure from my long service in the country and my knowledge of Indians and half-breed ways I would have been of great service to him.' Irvine claimed that the work of his force in and around Prince Albert had been 'as important as it was successful'.

The magazine *Illustrated War News* defended both Crozier and Irvine. It said of Crozier, 'He has always been deemed one of the best and most popular officers of the Mounted Police, in which estimation he should continue to be held until the full particulars of the Duck Lake disaster are known.' When the full particulars *did* become known Crozier was finished. He had been promoted to Assistant Commissioner in recognition of his undoubted bravery at Duck Lake. But when his equally undoubted stupidity at that battle became general knowledge the following year he was superseded by Superintendent William Herchmer as the Force's second-in-command; Crozier went on a long leave of absence, then resigned.

Of Irvine's conduct, the *Illustrated War News* said, 'Circumstances have been unfavourable to his opportunities of earning distinction during the recent campaign. . . . Colonel Irvine, while by no means a strict disciplinarian, has never failed to elicit the confidence and respect of those placed under his authority.' But it added ominously – and accurately – '*It is quite possible, however, that he has shown less vigour than many officers would have exercised on the eve of a serious outbreak.*'

Crozier excepted, the criticism of 'lack of vigour' could be directed at quite a few of the Mounted Police. Irvine himself had certainly shown little initiative or enterprise, being content to await orders from a general who was keen to do everything himself; Dickens's meek abandonment of his civilian charges and Fort Pitt was one of the most humiliating episodes of the North West Rebellion, and Inspector William Morris had hardly distinguished himself by watching from the shelter of his fort while Poundmaker's Crees pillaged Battleford. When Batoche fell the police were holding their garrison sports-day at Prince Albert. And at the Pincher Creek outpost William Metzler noted on 1 May, 'Everything quiet around here, except some of the chaps getting full on cider.'

On the day the 'chaps' at Pincher Creek were filling up on cider, Colonel William Otter moved out from Battleford to attack Poundmaker's camp, which had been located by scouts about forty miles west of the town at Cut Knife Creek in the Eagle Hills. After the routine and unexciting relief at Battleford, Otter was keen to teach Poundmaker and his tribe a lesson and, by striking at their camp, discourage them from any plan to join up with Big Bear. Unlike Irvine, Otter did not bother to consult General Middleton, who had ordered him to 'sit tight' at Battleford until he joined him. Instead, Otter secured the approval of Lieutenant-Governor Edgar Dewdney for the assault and marched out with 320 men – including seventy-four Mounted Police – two seven-pounder guns and a Gatling machine gun.

Otter's plan to surprise the Indian camp at dawn on 2 May succeeded, but his advance troops failed to press home the advantage. The guns and wagons were bogged down on the far side of Cut Knife Hill and his force was exposed on the skyline to the Indian marksmen below. As the Crees worked their way round the sides of the hill Otter was in danger of being surrounded; the gun carriages, rotten with age, collapsed, the operators of the Gatling could see nothing to shoot at, and the force suffered heavy casualties in driving back the Indians' flanking movements. Only the fact that the Indians were armed mainly with old muzzle-loaders and in some cases bows and arrows kept down the losses to eight dead and fourteen wounded. Among the killed were Corporal Ralph Sleigh, who had escaped death at Frog Lake, at Fort Pitt and on the bitter river-retreat with Dickens to Battleford. He was shot through the mouth charging an enemy position. Two other police, Corporal Talbot Lowry and Trumpeter Paddy Burke, died next day of wounds. Poundmaker's casualties were never officially known, but after the rebellion Superintendent William Herchmer found fresh graves on Poundmaker's reserve and 'several tepees filled with the bodies of Indians recently dead'.

Whatever the Indian losses, there was no doubt that Otter had suffered an ignominious defeat. As his disorganised column straggled away from Cut Knife Hill, Poundmaker – who was anxious to end his conflict with the government – held back his warriors who were eager to cut the retreating troops to pieces, and the exhausted and battered force got back to Battleford that evening after a round trip of eighty miles in thirty hours, bringing to a close another inglorious episode in the rebellion.

As General Middleton prepared to move from Prince Albert to Battleford by the river steamer *North-West*, Irvine reported that he had 175 fully equipped and mounted men ready to take up the chase of Poundmaker and Big Bear. Middleton, upset by Irvine's failure to take a more active part in quelling the uprising, curtly

241

rejected the offer and ordered him to remain in Prince Albert. The Commissioner wrote to Ottawa

> You can picture my amazement. . . . Like myself, every member of the Force was most anxious to secure active employment, the nature of which was familiar to us in every detail – such work, in fact, as we had been successfully performing for years. We were able to travel twice as fast as the militia troops General Middleton had with him. In addition to this, we not only knew the country and the habits of the Indians but even the men in the ranks knew and could recognise at a glance the chiefs, headmen and others against whom operations were being conducted.

But Irvine was left behind to fume in Prince Albert as, on 22 May, resplendent in white helmet, grey tweed shooting-suit, long boots and spurs, Frederick Dobson Middleton sailed away to Battleford with a military band on deck playing 'The Girl I Left Behind Me'.

By now Poundmaker had heard of the fall of Batoche and Riel's capture, and Middleton's steamer was met by a released prisoner of Poundmaker's in a rowing-boat carrying a letter requesting Middleton to 'send us the terms of peace in writing'. The general was in no mood to discuss terms. He pointed out that he had 'utterly defeated' the *métis* and added, 'I have made no terms with them, neither will I make terms with you. I have men enough to destroy you and your people, or at least to drive you away to starve, and will do so unless . . . you meet me at Battleford on 26 May.'

With civilians and soldiers lining the river banks for a mile to welcome him, Middleton reached Battleford on 24 May, and celebrated Queen Victoria's birthday with a troop parade. Two days later Poundmaker's Crees and some Assiniboines arrived to hand over their arms, plunder and prisoners. Middleton, seated on a camp stool, faced a semi-circle of headmen, all of whom had plenty to say in explanation of their conduct. An old squaw even attempted to plead for mercy for the warriors, but Middleton shut her up, 'saying that we did not admit women to our councils in wartime and that I could not listen to her. When this was translated to her the dirty but crafty old woman shrewdly remarked that we ourselves were ruled by a woman. In answer I allowed that this was the case but our Gracious Queen only spoke on war matters through her councillors, among whom there were no women. The old lady did not seem to see it and she was dragged away grumbling loudly.'

Two Assiniboines, Ikta (wearing a woman's stolen black straw hat with green plumes for the occasion) and Wawanich, stepped forward and admitted killing their farm instructor and a settler. They were handed over to the Mounted Police, and were joined by the forlorn Poundmaker in handcuffs.

When news of the Duck Lake defeat and the Frog Lake massacre reached Calgary, the citizens of that prospering community pleaded with their distinguished soldier-turned-rancher Major-General Thomas Bland Strange to organise the defence of the area. Strange, who had served with the Royal Artillery at the siege of Lucknow and had never lost his taste for action or excitement, agreed at once. He made an impressive figure with his monocle (the Indians called him 'White Chief With One Eye Open'), huge black beard, artillery trousers with a broad red stripe, long jackboots, a dark blue frock coat, felt hat with the brim pinned up at one side, Australian-fashion, and a sword.

Strange's attitudes matched his dashing appearance. Unlike Middleton, he was fully alive to the importance of cavalry in such open country: he immediately enrolled all the volunteers he could talk into enlisting – 'Some were Americans', he recalled, 'but they took the oath of loyalty to the Queen without flinching and served her faithfully' – and detachments sprang up with names like the Rocky Mountain Rangers and Alberta Mounted Rifles. When Sam Steele came down from his railway-minding duties in the mountains Strange named another formation after him – Steele's Scouts. The Indian Mutiny veteran then agreed to lead the third column of Middleton's punitive expedition, to be known as the Alberta Field Force, from Calgary to the relief of Edmonton, which had sent a panicky plea, 'Indians on the warpath. Send us men and arms immediately. Can't you help us at once?'

On 20 April, his local militia strengthened by the arrival of the French-Canadian 65th Rifles of Montreal, the 9th Voltigeurs of Quebec and the Winnipeg Light Infantry, Strange led the first of three relief columns on the 200-mile march north to Edmonton. The 'eyes' of this force were Steele's Scouts, made up of twenty-five Mounted Police, about a hundred settlers and cowboys, that tough prairie parson the Rev. John McDougall, and four Stony Indians. Since Strange complained that the police's scarlet tunics 'used to make my eyes ache' Steele dressed his men in brown clothes and cowboy-type slouch hats. But Strange admitted that 'Steele himself, a splendid-looking fellow, could not give up the swagger of his scarlet tunic and I did not ask him to make the sacrifice.'

After an exacting but incident-free march, Edmonton was reached on 1 May. The excited citizens wheeled out the home-made cannon of Inspector Arthur Griesbach to fire a salute of welcome as the troops prepared to ferry across the North Saskatchewan. The gunner, a half-breed dwarf known as John Collins, became confused and was still ramming home a charge of powder when someone else ignited the gun; the rammer sailed through the air and fell among Strange's column, bringing the battery's performance to a summary end. And Edmonton's home guard, after being cheerfully disbanded, was hastily re-enrolled when the townspeople realised that they had been relieved by French-Canadians.

Strange's next objective was Fort Pitt, where he had received orders to join up with General Middleton's forces for a combined operation against the last active hostile band, the Crees of Big Bear. Again Steele's Scouts pushed ahead overland, while the rest of the troops were ferried down the North Saskatchewan in hurriedly built boats. Near the burned ruins of Fort Pitt a grue-

244

some sight met Steele and his men – the mutilated body of Constable David Cowan, the police scout who had been killed trying to ride through Big Bear's camp after the Frog Lake massacre. Cowan had been scalped, his heart cut out and impaled on a stake and his wrists manacled with a pair of handcuffs found by the Indians at Fort Pitt.

There was no love lost between Strange and Middleton, though both had served in India and knew each other. Anxious to get news of Middleton's movements, Strange sent a police sergeant named Borrowdaile by canoe from Fort Pitt to Battleford. Borrowdaile arrived safely but had lost his revolver *en route*. When Middleton ordered him to take back some messages to Strange, including a letter addressed to Big Bear demanding his surrender, the policeman asked for another gun. Middleton refused and told him, 'Pouf, you don't need a pistol, you could walk through the country where General Strange is with a good stick.' Strange wasn't above sarcasm either, noting that 'Middleton's letter addressed to Big Bear for various reasons – among others the deficiency of pillar postboxes – failed to reach that gentleman'.

Big Bear's white prisoners, numbering about forty, had led a strange life in captivity as the Crees wandered aimlessly around the vicinity of Fort Pitt arguing endlessly about what they should do. Eventually, when messengers arrived with the news of Poundmaker's battle with troops at Cut Knife, Big Bear harangued his camp: 'You were in a hurry to commence trouble and now you have it.' Then he retired to his lodge and refused to attend any more of the interminable meetings (at which the Indians flew, upside down, the Hudson's Bay flag they had stolen from Fort Pitt). Leadership of the tribe was shared between the war chief Wandering Spirit and Big Bear's eldest son Imasees, 'a man of venomous disposition', according to William McLean, the captured Hudson's Bay agent. Under their new leaders, the Indians returned to Fort Pitt, removed all the remaining provisions and then set fire to the settlement. But on 26 May scouts reported troops in the vicinity and Big Bear's band fled, camping near a high, conical hill known as Frenchman's Butte twelve miles east of Fort Pitt.

The soldiers sighted were Steele's Scouts, who had picked up Big Bear's trail. On 27 May they had a skirmish with a Cree war party, killing two. When they came across a recent camp site with almost 200 dead fires Strange was informed, and at once set out from Fort Pitt with 197 infantry, 27 cavalry, a nine-pounder gun which had been dragged all the way north from Fort Macleod by a police contingent, and three days' rations. At Frenchman's Butte Strange found the Indians 'occupying a very advantageous position on the slopes of a thickly-wooded ridge, interspersed with ravines'. After pumping a few shells into the hillside the soldiers bedded down for battle in the morning.

Next day, 28 May, the fight began in earnest. In front of Strange's troops lay a 500-yard-wide swampy valley, and beyond and above were the Indian rifle pits. Streamers of red and white calico, the spoils of Fort Pitt, drooped from the branches of trees above the Indian positions in the still morning air. When Strange began to shell the crest of the hill he drew a heavy response of bullets. Infantry trying to cross the swamp sank to their waists, so Strange ordered Steel's cavalry to outflank the Indian defences and try to drive them towards the North Saskatchewan River, where Middleton's column from Battleford was expected at any time. Instead, the more mobile Crees began to encircle the soldiers and Strange – wary of what he called 'committing Custer' – decided to break off the short, fierce but almost bloodless engagement. 'The affairs at Duck Lake, Fish Creek and Cut Knife made me cautious,' he admitted.

The caution was obviously for his command and his reputation rather than his own life, which he casually risked to bring back a dying French-Canadian militiaman lying exposed near the Indian positions. When Strange reprimanded the man's commander for leaving him, the officer replied, 'General, I have been shot at quite enough today, and I am damned if I go down there again.' So

246

Strange himself went into the swamp, accompanied by two stretcher bearers and Father Prevost, priest of the 65th Rifles, crucifix in hand to administer the last rites. Strange recalled

I must admit some impatience which the good priest did not seem to share during the confession of sin, and suggested to the brave padre the desirability of lumping the lot, which he did; putting the dying man into the stretcher the party moved up the hill, and I brought up the rear with the man's rifle. The fire grew hotter as we ascended the hill; the rear man dropped his end of the stretcher and I took his place.

There were other instances of bravery. Constable D. McCrae, the only police casualty at Frenchman's Butte, refused to be brought out of the front line until he had fired away all his ammunition though he was badly wounded in the leg and bleeding heavily. And Constable Algernon Dyre, who had fumed from an out-of-the-way detachment earlier in the year about being unable to get into action against 'that scheming, copper-coloured devil Riel', finally had his wish for action granted at Frenchman's Butte. He wrote to his brother, 'I did not tell them at home half the danger I was in at times as I knew it would upset Mother . . . a bullet grazed so close to the hand I was holding my rifle with as almost to burn it, while others struck the ground between my long legs and whistled round my head like devils let loose.'

Frenchman's Butte was an inconclusive affair, which astonishingly ended with both sides retreating precipitately at the same moment – Strange to Fort Pitt for supplies and reinforcements, and Big Bear to the safety of the swamp and lake wilderness to the north. The Hudson's Bay man William McLean, who as a captive had an Indian's-eye view of the fight, was convinced that 'General Strange had won this battle, although he had no knowledge of it'. He maintained that, if Strange's men had pressed their attack, Big Bear's tribe would have surrendered that evening. In the confusion during the fighting some of the white prisoners slipped away, to be picked up later by police patrols. The rest were forced to trek with the fleeing Crees through country so appalling that one squaw hanged herself from a tree. 'From this time our great-est physical hardships began,' McLean wrote afterwards. 'We were without transport of any kind, we had little or no bedding and no provisions whatsoever.' The prisoners trudged steadily northwards in wet weather, wading waist deep through swamps and swollen streams and sleeping in their saturated clothes.

Strange sent Steele and his scouts after the fugitive Indians again, while he remained at Fort Pitt to meet General Middleton, who arrived by steamer from Battleford with 200 men on 3 June. At Loon Lake (where a present-day historic marker grandly pro-claims the site of the 'last military engagement' fought on Cana-dian soil) Steele caught up with Big Bear's band and charged them, killing several before the Indians escaped across the narrow neck of a lake. It was here that the police suffered their final casualty of the rebellion when Sergeant Billy Fury was wounded in the chest. The demoralised Indians were anxious to surrender, but fearing they would be shot out of hand they sent back their prisoner William McLean to negotiate with the pursuing troops:

> Taking a piece of white cotton I fixed it to a long pole and commenced to wave it. I called as loud as I could in both English and French but I received no attention. The only response was a volley from their rifles. I kept calling and waving the flag until a lot of earth and leaves was thrown up in my face by a bullet which struck the ground in front of me. One of the Indians, creeping up behind me, said, 'Come away, we do not want you to be shot.' . . . My feelings of disappointment then can be better imagined than I can describe them. I was filled with regret at my failing to be peacemaker and put an end to such wretched warfare. I returned to the camp with the Indians a truly sorry man.

Pursuit through impossible country was called off in favour of starving out the Crees, who eventually decided to release their remaining twenty-seven prisoners on 18 June ('The anniversary of the Battle of Waterloo,' William McLean noted). They were given a few guns and horses, a little food and some moccasins by their captors, who asked them to plead for mercy on their behalf.

Back-tracking to Loon Lake, the ragged and starving whites met a small search-party who had thoughtfully brought along a trunk of fresh clothing as well as food. They got back to Fort Pitt on 24 June.

Gradually the refugee Cree were rounded up or surrendered. Wandering Spirit, who had started the Frog Lake massacre, gave himself up at Fort Pitt and attempted to stab himself to death after telling his fellow-tribesmen, 'All who wish to look on me once more, come now.' But he was patched up and preserved for the scaffold.

On 2 July Big Bear surrendered after a final gesture. Accompanied by his twelve-year-old son Horse Child and a councillor All And A Half, he travelled many miles right under the noses of police and troops to reach Fort Carlton, where a police sergeant named Smart, one of the few people for hundreds of miles around who wasn't out searching for Big Bear, found him lying exhausted at a camp fire. Big Bear was taken to Prince Albert 'in a pitiable condition of filth and hunger' according to Constable John Donkin. 'He was given a good scrubbing in a tub at the barracks. . . . Big Bear's horror of the cleansing process was comic. His breech-clout had done duty for a decade and was as black as the ace of spades which, by the way, it rather resembled.' Donkin described Big Bear as 'a little shrivelled-up looking piece of humanity, his cunning face seamed and wrinkled like crumpled parchment'.

With the capture of Big Bear Canada's curious little war was over. There remained only the formal revenge. Eleven Indians were sentenced to death at Battleford for murder. Three were reprieved but the remaining eight – among them the would-be suicide Wandering Spirit – were hanged from a communal scaffold in the police barracks in November. Eighteen *métis* were convicted of treason-felony at Regina and given terms ranging from one to seven years, while the two Cree chiefs, Big Bear and Poundmaker, each received three years on the same charge. When the sentences were read out Poundmaker pleaded, 'Hang me now. . . . I would rather you kill me than lock me up for three years'. However, the authorities at Stony Mountain Penitentiary granted the handsome Poundmaker one concession: he was permitted to keep his fine long hair while in captivity. Both chiefs were released after serving two years. Both died within six months of leaving prison.

Although there was pressure to have the trial switched to the east, Louis Riel, a Catholic French half-breed, faced a charge of treason in a cramped, rented building converted into a courtroom at Regina towards the end of July before stipendiary magistrate Hugh Richardson and a jury of six settlers, all white Anglo-Saxon Protestants. Riel's counsel, paid for by public subscription in Quebec, pinned their hopes of acquittal on Riel's undoubted mental instability, but Riel himself undermined this course with an impassioned speech insisting that he was sane. When Inspector Richard Burton Deane, who had been in charge of Riel during his confinement at Regina, was asked if he had ever seen anything to indicate the prisoner was not of sound mind, Deane replied, 'Nothing whatever.' As he passed the dock on his way out of the witness box Riel said to Deane, 'Thank you, Captain.'

The jury needed only an hour and twenty minutes to find Riel guilty though they added a recommendation for mercy. He was sentenced to be hanged on 18 September. An appeal was lodged but the sentence was upheld, and a further appeal to the Privy Council in England was also rejected. During the appeals three doctors – the senior Mounted Police surgeon Augustus Jukes, F. X. Valade and M. Lavell – inquired into Riel's mental condition. Jukes felt that apart from his 'peculiar views' on religion Riel was 'a sane, clear-headed and accountable being, and responsible for his actions before God and man'. Valade considered that Riel 'suffers hallucinations on political and religious subjects, but on other points I believe him to be quite sensible and can distinguish right from wrong'; Lavell's report paralleled Valade's.

Prime Minister Sir John Macdonald thought the sentence 'satisfactory' and stood firm as controversy raged in eastern

Canada about Riel's fate, with the Catholics defending Riel as a patriot and the Protestants vilifying him as a traitor. 'He shall hang though every dog in Quebec bark in his favour,' Sir John maintained. Petitions for clemency poured in from all over the world, and Riel himself, who had become an American citizen while living in Montana in 1883, addressed one on his own behalf to the American President, Grover Cleveland.

According to Constable John Donkin, who was regularly assigned to guard duty on the *métis* leader, 'Everyone expected that Riel would be pardoned and in all probability pensioned, so that he did not at first receive the many delicate attentions which were later lavished upon him.' Donkin found Riel 'most studiously polite and painfully deferential'.

'He occupied the cell next to the guard-room. Writing was his continual employment, when he was not praying or at exercise. A shelf formed his bed and a small table stood alongside. In front of him was a metal statuette of St Joseph (patron saint of the *métis*) and when he was telling his beads he would carry this little image in his hands and hug it.'

The execution day, 16 November 1885, dawned brilliantly sunny, the prairie covered with hoar frost. A large crowd from Regina had gathered outside the police barracks, which was ringed by armed policemen. Riel had spent most of the night in prayer with Father Alexis André, and on his last walk he was joined by another priest, Father Charles McWilliams. As Father André stumbled on the way to the scaffold Riel reassured him, 'Courage, mon père.' Riel was pinioned by his executioner, Jack Henderson, who had once been a prisoner of Riel's during the Red River uprising fifteen years previously, and Father Mc-Williams and Riel stood in the centre of the group on the gallows saying the Lord's Prayer together. When they got as far as *Deliver us from evil* the trap was sprung and Louis Riel dropped to his death.

The body was removed to the Catholic Church in Regina and was watched over by Mounted Police in plain clothes. Just before its removal to his home in St Boniface, near Winnipeg, for burial, ugly rumours began to spread that after the body had been cut down a policeman had stamped his boot in Riel's face. To scotch these stories the coffin was opened in the presence of Commissioner Irvine and leading Regina officials. 'A few locks of hair had been taken from the brow but there was no trace of disfigurement of any kind,' reported Inspector Richard Burton Deane.

Though the controversy over Riel's hanging raged – and still rages – in Canada, the Mounted Police officially relegated him to just another entry in the record book. In their annual return of criminal cases tried during 1885 Riel's name is wedged between William Lockey, accused of selling intoxicating liquor (dismissed) and A. Van Lundten, accused of indecent assault (also dismissed).

When he returned east, General Middleton was made a Knight Commander of the Order of St Michael and St George and the Canadian Parliament voted him $20,000 for his services (though one policeman considered him 'simply an egotistical, lying old hog, no more worthy to be knighted than I am'). Middleton resigned his command of the Canadian Militia in 1890 after sordid accusations had been levelled at him in Canada's Parliament of appropriating furs belonging to half-breeds during the rebellion. He returned to England, and in 1896 was appointed Keeper of the Crown Jewels at the Tower of London. He died two years later.

Every militiaman who served in the North West Field Force was awarded a campaign medal and entitled to a free land grant of 160 acres. The Mounted Police received nothing, with the possible exception of abuse, though they had suffered eight killed and eleven wounded. Police who had been under fire were granted medals in 1888, but it was not until 1902 that the remainder of the Force in the North West Rebellion got their medals.

The outcome of the uprising had been inevitable once shots were fired and people killed. By following Riel the *métis* were not only defeated, but lost for ever their hopes of independence and identity. One Catholic missionary, Father Clovis Rondeau, lamented that the rebellion was 'an unfortunate prank which definitely caused their ruin'.

The rebellion was also the ruin of Commissioner Irvine. In a private letter to Edgar Dewdney, Sir John Macdonald indicated his intention to 'get rid of Irvine as soon as possible'. In March 1886, a year after the Duck Lake disaster, Irvine 'resigned' and became an Indian agent on the Blood Reserve. Six years afterwards he was appointed Warden of Stony Mountain Penitentiary near Winnipeg. He died in Quebec City on 9 January 1916 and was buried there.

PART FOUR

Lawrence William Herchmer

This is the law of the Yukon, and ever she makes it plain:
'Send not your foolish and feeble; send me your strong and your
   sane.
Strong for the red rage of battle; sane, for I harry them sore;
Send me men girt for combat, men who are grit to the core. . . .'

Robert W. Service
'The Law of the Yukon'

Chapter 16

CRACKING THE WHIP

ON Irvine's departure several of the more experienced superintendents obviously considered themselves in line for promotion to the Commissionership or the second-in-command position still held, though tenuously, by Crozier: men of the 1873 'originals' like Sam Steele, John McIllree and Arthur Griesbach, or later arrivals who had impressed by their ability such as Richard Burton Deane and William Herchmer. But Sir John Macdonald turned to none of them. First he offered the job to Lord Melgund, who had come to Canada in 1883 as military secretary to the new Governor-General, Lord Lansdowne, and had served as General Middleton's chief of staff during the North West Rebellion. But Melgund, who as the Earl of Minto later became Governor-General of Canada himself, declined the police job on the grounds that he would be compelled to spend too long away from his wife.

Macdonald's next choice was even more astonishing. He appointed the unknown Lawrence Herchmer, brother of Superintendent William Herchmer, as Commissioner. The Herchmer family were United Empire Loyalists and friends and neighbours of Macdonald when he lived at Kingston, Ontario. Herchmer's father, a Church of England clergyman who had been to Oxford University, insisted that all his children should be born in England, so his wretched wife, a niece of the painter J. M. W. Turner, crossed the Atlantic thirteen times to deliver her offspring. Lawrence Herchmer, like his brother William, was born in the Oxfordshire village of Shipton-on-Cherwell. Educated in England, he served three years in Ireland and India as a British Army

257

ensign before travelling to Canada at the age of twenty-two to take up property he had inherited near Kingston. He had experience of the North West Territories as commissariat officer of the Boundary Commission which laid down the U.S.–Canada border. Next he founded the Redwood Brewery in Winnipeg and ran it for ten years before becoming Indian Agent for Manitoba. He was forty-six when he accepted the appointment as the Mounted Police's fourth Commissioner in April 1886.

Stubborn, opinionated and dedicated (in his fourteen years as Commissioner he took only two weeks' leave), Herchmer was fiercely determined to eradicate the laxness of the Irvine regime and to instil pride in the force he had so surprisingly been chosen to command. One of Herchmer's first acts, and one which was hardly guaranteed to endear him to the disgruntled officers who felt they should have had the job, was to appoint his brother William (or 'Colonel Billy' as he was invariably known) Assistant Commissioner in place of Crozier. Having thus assured himself of a loyal second-in-command, the new Commissioner pitched enthusiastically into his mission.

First, Herchmer announced that he proposed to reverse the current trend by making the Mounted Police hard to get into and easy to get out of, tightening up medical examinations, dismissing drunkards and dead-beats, and attempting to encourage many of the experienced veterans to stay in the Force by introducing a pensions plan and improving living conditions. He was only just in time. In the year following the Riel Rebellion, discipline had reached rock bottom. In order to control the Indians and *métis* the size of the Force had been hastily doubled to 1000 – nine divisons of 100 men in the field and a depot division at Regina – and many unsuitable and unqualified men had been enrolled.

There was an immediate opportunity for Herchmer to show his firmness when the most serious mutiny in the Force's brief history occurred at Edmonton, where the new G Division were temporarily housed at the Hudson's Bay trading post. Their sleeping-quarters were old and infested with bed bugs and fleas,

and when a newly appointed corporal attempted to give orders to
some old hands they ignored him; apart from looking after their
horses they performed no duties, and some of the malcontents
even hauled down the Union Jack and ran up a home-made skull
and crossbones. Superintendent Arthur Griesbach, anxious to
avoid bloodshed, made no attempt to arrest the ringleaders until
he received reinforcements from Regina. Then he persuaded the
mutineers to take out their horses on an exercise ride; on their
return they were surrounded by armed men and arrested. Nineteen were sent to Regina for trial: six went to prison for a year
and the rest were dismissed from the Force.

The lesson was not lost on Herchmer. He redoubled his efforts
to reinforce discipline. Unfortunately he antagonised, rather than
inspired, his subordinates, scattering waspish notes and needling
memoranda all over the North West Territories.

Herchmer's most implacable enemy was Superintendent
Deane, the former Royal Marine officer, whose outrage rapidly
replaced his astonishment when Herchmer, and not he, was made
Commissioner. One of Herchmer's first memos was to Deane,
who was Adjutant at Regina: 'Constable Hutchinson states that
he is liable to lose heavily through your ordering him away so
suddenly, as he had bought a lot of pigs from you. . . . How did he
manage these pigs on patrol?'

Deane and Herchmer fought running battles on almost every
conceivable subject, wasting prodigious amounts of time and
paper. Occasionally the accusations and counter-accusations
reached a hysterical pitch. After thay had had a heated row on
the very day that the Comptroller of the Force, Frederick White,
was visiting Regina from Ottawa, Deane was removed from his
adjutant's job, sent on a recruiting mission in eastern Canada, and
given command of Depot Division on his return to Regina. Deane
considered the change 'much more palatable. . . . I had dry-
nursed [Herchmer] for a full year and was heartily sick of the job.'
Even when Deane was posted out of the way to Lethbridge the
feud simmered on. Herchmer reported Deane to Ottawa for

'insubordinate correspondence' and complained that Deane couldn't be bothered to write his own monthly report ('which is not only insubordinate but flippant and irrelevant all through'), entrusting the job to his orderly-room clerk.

Deane was not the only sufferer. After a bad case of drunken behaviour at Maple Creek, Herchmer wrote to the commanding officer, Superintendent William Antrobus, 'Your division affords me more anxiety than any other, and there are more serious breaches of discipline than in all the other divisions together. I cannot but ascribe this to your weakness and want of tact. . . .'

Fred Bagley, the former boy bugler who had risen to the highest non-commissioned rank, staff-sergeant, was reduced to sergeant by Herchmer for neglecting to see that the Church of England members of the police band at Regina attended choir practice. Bagley was a Roman Catholic.

Herchmer took a lively interest in every detail: the purchase of oats and hay, the painting of married quarters, equipment inventories. But he reserved his special attention for the liquor offences and cases of drunkenness within the ranks. 'It is to be distinctly understood that a fine of not less than ten dollars is invariably to be awarded in every case of drunkenness in addition to such other punishment as may be inflicted,' he ordered. 'In all cases of drunkenness full particulars will be forwarded for my consideration.'

But it was hard going, even for Herchmer, to curb the deep-seated drinking problem in the Force. At Maple Creek the bugler, Constable W. Martin, fell over while attempting to play the Last Post. 'I was standing behind him when he blew "Last Post",' Sergeant Robert Ince testified. 'He could hardly stand up; as for blowing the calls, you could hardly tell what they were.' Martin got three months' hard labour and was fined ten dollars. A Constable Wood was sentenced to four months for being drunk on a train and, in the words of Herchmer, 'making a beast of himself.' To halt the hoarding of alcohol at Battleford instructions were given that all cellars under barrack rooms were to be nailed down.

In 1888 four men of H Division at Fort Macleod were dismissed for drinking; four years later there were twelve cases of drunkenness at the same post, drawing down on Superintendent Steele's head the testy comment from Herchmer, 'I regret to hear that such a large proportion of your command are drunkards.'

At Fort Calgary just before Christmas 1887 a two-gallon keg of whiskey, seized from an empty compartment on an immigrant train, was taken to the orderly room and disappeared within half an hour in circumstances which were termed 'discreditable to the Calgary command'. Constable C. P. Sheppard, in charge of the guard-room in the next building, got six months' hard labour and Staff-Sergeant Billy Fury – the wounded hero of the North West Rebellion – was reduced to sergeant over the affair.

Herchmer was particularly strict with officers who violated his code of behaviour. After being found drunk at Maple Creek, Inspector S. G. Mills was given the choice of resigning or being dismissed: he resigned. Inspector William Brooks, accused of being drunk during a murder investigation, was suspended and finally resigned. And Herchmer urged Superintendent McIllree to persuade another officer who had been drinking to leave the Mounted Police and the country: 'If he agrees, purchase a ticket for him and see that he leaves.'

Perhaps the most spectacular example of erratic conduct among the officers was provided by Superintendent Archibald Macdonell. At a banquet at Fort Macleod Macdonell tried to sing 'Scots wha' hae', insisted on making a speech and, when he was reprimanded by the chairman, launched into a war dance. Surprisingly, he escaped with a censure. Herchmer even investigated Sam Steele's conduct after complaints that he and Inspector C. F. A. Huot had been drinking and making a noise in a hotel. Herchmer reassured Steele that there had been no foundation for the rumours, but gave some sound advice: 'I think it would be advisable to meet your friends in a private house where practicable when you propose to spend a social evening. Certain parties in this country are only too happy when they can get the slightest chance of vilifying the police, and it behoves us to be circumspect.'

Yet Herchmer himself was hardly circumspect in the amount of drink he imported by permit for personal consumption. In sixteen months from January 1887 to April 1888 the Commissioner received twenty-two gallons of whiskey, nine of wine and 316 of beer. Even this figure was exceeded by Superintendent Deane. During the same period he was authorised – and presumably drank – fifty-six gallons of whiskey, five of gin, two of wine and sixty-four of beer. Eventually, Edgar Dewdney, the Territories' Lieutenant-Governor, was asked by the Police Comptroller, Frederick White, to be strict about issuing liquor permits to officers where there was so much ill-feeling over liquor in the west.

Predictably, the new Commissioner's insistence on rigid discipline brought in its wake disaffection and desertion. Recalling the 'endless succession of drills, parades, picquets and guards', Constable R. G. Mathews said that 'the daily performance of mounting the guard at Fort Macleod would have done credit to St James's Palace and was worth a better setting than the wide-flung expanse of lonely prairie in which it was staged'. Another of the Macleod unfortunates described how Sam Steele 'drilled us morning, noon and night. . . . Some men will stand almost anything but there were twenty-four who couldn't or wouldn't stand Old Sam and his methods – for that number deserted in one month. The international boundary wasn't very far away and none of them were caught.'

There was ample evidence that pursuing parties were not over-anxious to overhaul their deserting colleagues. One policeman commented, 'It was quite usual for the deserter to get safely across the line and wait for his pursuers to come up, when he would turn over what government property was in his possession. Desertion was not an extraditable offence. Taking stolen property into the States was, so this little arrangement got around that difficulty nicely.'

Men were tempted away by the high wages being offered in the mines and on the railway construction gangs in Montana;

Constable Bainbridge took his musical talents into the United States to join a minstrel show; Constable Wilson carried off the Calgary mess funds; a recruit called Fleming was involved in a fight at Lethbridge with five civilians who made fun of his scarlet tunic, then deserted out of shame for having got into trouble. Men who managed to get home leave in England or Ireland almost invariably deserted; others never came back from leave in eastern Canada.

Some were considered good riddance. When Constable J. A. Clarke deserted from Fort Mcleod, Steele noted, 'He was quite unfitted for the Force, being what is commonly known as a "sport".' And the Commissioner was untypically philosophical about the loss of Constable Conway, who had been a policeman only forty-eight days before failing to return from a group excursion to Winnipeg: 'He was a railroad man and they never remain in the Force.'

In 1890 there were twenty-one desertions. The following year the figure rose to thirty-six but in 1895 the number of dismissals (forty-seven) far exceeded the desertions (seven) when the size of the Force was reduced to 750 after complaints in Parliament about the heavy expense (one politician even proposed that the Mounted Police should be reduced in size annually until they disappeared). Herchmer was thus able to get rid of the policemen he considered undesirables. He also persuaded the government to adopt a pension plan, to increase the term of service from three to five years, to hand out more money (a constable's pay went up to seventy-five cents a day) and eventually to introduce a two-month probationary period of service for recruits which effectively sorted out those who didn't like the Force, as well as those the Force didn't like. 'The knowledge that they can get away if they do not like the work seems to have a very beneficial effect,' Herchmer noted. The practice also grew of employing 'special constables' for specific and unattractive jobs such as cooks, labourers and dog drivers. It was a useful innovation since, as Superintendent Deane put it, 'Those who are not satisfactory are easily discharged and those who want to retain their employment take pains to do so.'

In the early years of Hermer's reign it was the sheer monotony which persuaded most deserters that Mounted Police life was not for them. Herchmer was well aware of the need for improved conditions and worked hard to bring them about, but when R. G. Mathews signed on at Regina in 1887 barrack life was still decidedly rough and ready:

> There was no great danger of becoming effeminate. . . . For a bed you got three boards and a pair of wooden trestles and a canvas tick (which you filled from the haystack if you felt inclined to). A table, two benches and a syndicate stove completed the furniture, with a rifle rack at one end of the room. All round the room ran a shelf, and on this at the head of his bed each man's kit was laid out. . . . Under the bed you were allowed to stow your kitbag – officially that was all the baggage you were supposed to have but most men also possessed a wooden chest.

Washing facilities were equally primitive; each barrack had half a dozen basins in a long sink. Water had to be scooped from a nearby zinc-lined box which was filled daily by water cart. 'If you wanted a bath you had to open up negotiations with the troop barber, who presided over the solitary bathing receptacle,' Mathews recalled. Conditions were little better for the officers. At Fort Macleod Superintendent Percy Neale complained, 'The officers' mess consists of a bare room with a deal table and half a dozen common chairs, so that the officers . . . have no place but their bedrooms to ask their friends into.'

Beds proved literally the most painful memory of police life for many men. From the inception of the Force its members had slept on planks laid across wooden trestles and this spine-jarring arrangement ('The most uninviting couch on which it has ever been my misfortune to seek repose', according to one recruit) stayed in use almost until the end of the nineteenth century, despite the vociferous complaints of Herchmer and other officers. As Herchmer pointed out, 'The finest body of men in the country still sleeps on boards and trestles while the Indians at the industrial schools have iron beds.' At Moosomin the town sheriff permitted police to use the jail's iron bedsteads when they weren't needed by prisoners. Herchmer admitted that he was ashamed to show strangers over the barrack rooms 'on account of the very disparaging remarks they invariably make on our sleeping accommodation'.

Slowly conditions improved. In 1888 Herchmer opened a canteen at Regina which sold a relatively harmless brew known as four-per-cent beer (or near-beer). It was a sensational success. Charles Dwight recalled how his colleagues used to relax in the evenings 'with pipes lighted and schooners of four per cent beer flowing galore', though the *Qu'Appelle Progress* labelled it 'a bastard beverage pleasant to none'.

The beer cost only five cents a pint, a third of the price charged in Regina's saloons, and the canteen finances flourished. Within two years the canteen committee had paid out from its profits $180 to various messes for the purchase of luxuries, $30 for rifle-match prizes, $250 towards reducing the cost of a railway excursion to Winnipeg (on which the ungrateful Constable Conway deserted), $100 to the Regina band for instruments, $100 for a new billiard table and $50 for refurbishing the old one, and $400 on a gymnasium. In addition, a bowling alley costing $1600 was being built from canteen profits. The canteen was also a vital safety valve: Herchmer reported to the government that since its inception there had been no police defaulters of any consequence at Regina.

The following year a canteen was opened at Calgary, selling four-per-cent beer, cigars, tobacco, cigarettes, soap, blacking, biscuits and cheese. Six years later the Calgary canteen was housed in a new cedar-clad building and had nearly $1500 worth of stock on hand. Other posts soon had their canteens, all equally useful and profitable. From Lethbridge Superintendent Deane reported, 'We are in a position to pay for everything we buy. The men recently decided to buy an edition of the *Encyclopedia*

Britannica now being issued by the *Daily Mail*, London, and sent a draft for £17 sterling.'

Battleford boasted one of the best libraries in the Canadian West, established and maintained by voluntary monthly subscriptions of twenty-five cents and containing more than 600 books; the Prince Albert garrison built their own recreation room, with a stage and a library, and also formed cricket, dramatic, rifle, lacrosse and baseball clubs. Calgary was the first post to have electric light installed (in 1891) and four years later electricity, telephones – and even those long-awaited iron bedsteads – had arrived at most of the larger barracks, though at Fort Saskatchewan Superintendent Arthur Griesbach was still asking for modern beds in 1898, 'it being almost impossible to keep wooden beds free from vermin'.

The question of better arms for the Force was a saga almost as long-running as the problem of beds. On his appointment in 1880 Commissioner Irvine had criticised the Winchester rifles with which his men were armed. Although it was a favourite with cowboys and prairie men generally, he considered it too frail to stand up to the rough treatment it received at the hands of the police. Twenty years – and many complaints later – the same rifles were still in use. Superintendent John Cotton suggested from Battleford in 1898 that the Winchester carbines and Enfield revolvers were, 'to put it mildly, out of date'. Superintendent Deane considered that 'accurate shooting with them is out of the question'; Sam Steele complained, 'It is quite impossible for men to make good practice with the Winchester and they constantly grow disheartened'; and Superintendent John McIllree dismissed the arms of his command at Calgary as 'more or less honeycombed and sights not true'. Inferior ammunition worsened the situation. The Dominion Cartridge Company's ammunition was officially described as 'useless': of 45,000 cartridges tried in different rifles at Calgary only 760 would enter the Winchester bore without being forced in, and American bullets had to be imported so that the garrison could have target practice. There were 161 misfires during annual revolver-practice at Fort Macleod, and Herchmer told the Canadian government, 'It would be criminal to send any force into action with such wretched cartridges.' In 1895 the police received an experimental issue of 200 Lee-Metford rifles, enabling Herchmer to discard the worst of the Winchesters, but the old carbines and Enfield revolvers were not finally phased out until 1905, twenty-five years after their introduction.

Long-overdue changes in the uniform were equally slow in coming, though Superintendent A. Bowen Perry claimed quite rightly that the scarlet uniform was 'suitable only for men in barracks' and recommended the adoption of sensible clothing for prairie work. Most of the other officers agreed. Superintendent John McIllree urged the introduction of felt hats (which most police bought privately anyway for use on patrol), pointing out that 'helmets are too conspicuous and heavy for constant use and forage caps are no protection whatever from the sun'. But it was not until 1900, when Perry became the Force's fifth Commissioner, that the hopelessly outdated uniform was restyled. Pipe clay and blacking were discarded; out went the pith helmet, forage cap, white gauntlets and black boots. In came the sensible Stetson hat, easily cleaned brown boots and gauntlets, prairie service jackets and waterproof capes.

Fortunately for the health of the Mounted Police, improvements in medical and hospital facilities eventually matched the modernisation of their barracks, though in the years following the North West Rebellion conditions were still poor. At Maple Creek the water supply was so impregnated with alkali and other highly corrosive minerals that it decomposed wood and ate through kitchen utensils and stoves in a few weeks. Understandably, it was also a source of constant diarrhoea among the garrison. 'It is so bad', reported hospital steward J C. Holme, 'that a diarrhoea mixture is as necessary to a recruit as any part of his kit – he is not complete or safe without it.' Maple Creek's hospital was small, badly constructed and totally inadequate and the doctor in charge, Hugh Dodd, warned, 'Should any serious case of illness arise I could not be considered responsible for the recovery of the patients.' It was so cold inside the building that drugs froze on the shelves, and when a Staff Sergeant McGuinnis was admitted to Maple Creek hospital with malarial fever he was cured but as soon as he was well enough to sit up in bed he caught a cold and suffered a relapse.

Though most of the Mounted Police who died in service were victims of fever, drowning or freezing there were occasionally other bizarre fatalities and injuries. Sergeant Alfred Taylor died after falling from a horizontal bar while practising gymnastics at Calgary, and another member of the Calgary garrison, Constable Reading, broke his spine in three places when a horse fell on him ('We all felt his death very much,' said Superintendent John McIllree. 'He was our best cricketer. . . .'). Staff Sergeant Kirk, one of the Force's 1873 'originals', died at Battleford of 'cerebral deterioration due to alcoholism', and Constable Craig was discharged from Calgary because he was 'an opium eater'. At Maple Creek Corporal Anderson dislocated his right shoulder while attempting to walk on his hands; at Calgary Constable F. A. Morgan shot himself in the right leg while crawling across the prairie in search of coyotes; and in 1891 a thoughtless constable named Thompson spoiled what would have been a clean year for hospital treatment at Maple Creek when he entered a building at Medicine Hat in search of a gas leak while smoking a pipe. He scorched his face and hands badly and burned down the building.

The senior surgeon Augustus Jukes (soon to be pensioned off because, according to Herchmer, his failing memory 'made it almost impossible to transact business with him') castigated most of the men who were sent to him at Regina from the prairie posts for discharge as 'impudent malingerers' who were trying to work themselves an invalid's ticket. 'Out of one batch of twenty-five sent from Battleford and Calgary to be invalided for various nominal diseases fourteen were given the choice to return to full duty forthwith or to go to the guard room at hard labour. They elected the former.'

Gradually, however, pride in being a member of the North West Mounted began to outweigh the desire to get out of the Force. Although conditions of service were still far from good in 1888, Herchmer was able to report, 'I am deluged with applications from all parts, even the Old Country and the United States, for admission to our ranks', and the following year only thirty-three of the 122 police whose time had expired chose to leave. Sam Steele considered that by 1888 the Force 'had arrived at a very high state of efficiency'.

Unfortunately there was also an equally high state of unhappiness about the personality of Lawrence Herchmer, the man responsible for the improvement in efficiency and living conditions. Herchmer's hasty – and frequently unsound – judgements, improper language and arbitrary conduct alienated most of the officers who had to bear the brunt of his many memos and orders.

Herchmer took a dislike to Superintendent John Cotton of Regina's depot division and tried to drive him away ('Circumstances having arisen which render your retaining your position disagreeable to me as well as yourself, I would suggest that you write me officially asking to return to command of A Division'). Cotton declined, accusing Herchmer of imposing on him, 'without any cause whatsoever, gross personal abuse and outrageous insult'.

The Commissioner was involved in a sordid row with Inspector A. Ross Cuthbert after Cuthbert's wife and Mrs Herchmer had a disagreement about who should have the services of a Constable Pitts as a servant-stoker. When Herchmer reported Cuthbert to Ottawa for being 'insubordinate' (his favourite accusation), the Comptroller of the Force, the Birmingham-born Frederick White – who had been appointed to the post in 1878 and filled it with distinction for forty years – showed clear signs of testiness with Herchmer: 'If the wife of the Commanding Officer is to repeat to her husband conversation which transpires between herself and the wives of other officers of the Force, and the Commanding

Officer is to hold the officers responsible for such conversation, it cannot be expected that friendly relations will prevail or that discipline will exist.' And, quite rightly, White threatened to investigate the extent to which constables were being withdrawn from regular police duty 'for the convenience of the families of officers'. One blatant example of this occurred at Maple Creek. Charles Dwight was posted there as orderly-room clerk but on his arrival was given the job of sweeping chimneys in the officers' quarters.

Herchmer attempted to justify his actions by stressing his loyalty and trying to incriminate those he considered his enemies. He claimed that, since he had become Commissioner, 'a determined and most underhand effort has been made by certain officers to embarrass me in every way possible', and became so obsessed about the matter that he wrote, but did not send, a letter to White charging, 'My life is hardly safe while certain officers remain under my command.'

Safe or not, Herchmer continued to act vigorously. Superintendent William Antrobus was suspended from duty at Battleford, accused by the Commissioner of 'the most disgraceful and dishonourable conduct and repeated drunkenness which has been the common talk of not only the settlers but the members of the police at that place'. He also castigated Antrobus's successor, Inspector Joseph Howe, for 'deliberately and foolishly' ignoring orders over the purchase of oats.

Herchmer continued to hound his enemies even after they had left the force. Assistant Surgeon J. Widmer Rolph, a veteran of the Fort Pitt evacuation, was dismissed in 1887 for some heinous but unspecified crime. When Rolph went to Vancouver and applied for the post of doctor aboard the steamer *Parthia*, Herchmer wrote to the manager of the company, 'It would be unfair to ladies and children using your line to have such a man coming in contact with them', and attempted to wreck Rolph's chances of getting any work in the area by telling the Attorney-General of British Columbia that Rolph had been dismissed for 'the most disgraceful conduct', and adding, 'I do not think he should be allowed to remain in the province.'

Herchmer instructed Inspector James Wilson to move from Pincher Creek to Regina though Wilson's wife was pregnant, and when the inspector objected Herchmer commented, 'In future I'll have to order married officers to send in monthly reports as to their wives' condition before I can order them to move.' He ordered that Constable E. Dubois be shackled with a ball and chain during his twelve months' imprisonment for deserting from Battleford; in front of a parade he threatened to report Inspector Frank Norman to the Prime Minister if his division did not drill better; and he promised to post some officers from Regina for refusing to organise a dance when he requested them to do so.

Herchmer's clashes were not confined to the police. He continually wrangled with Nicholas Flood Davin, editor of the *Regina Leader* (and, when the Territories gained parliamentary representation, an M.P.) and Charles Wood, the ex-policeman who edited the *Fort Macleod Gazette*. In Parliament Davin accused Herchmer of being arrogant and overbearing, 'strutting and flaunting' on the railway station at Regina, drinking to excess, passing out harsh sentences, being pro-Protestant and anti-French-Canadian – and of interfering with elections by confining to barracks the policemen he suspected intended to vote for Davin.

Eventually, with Herchmer pressing for an investigation to clear his name after Davin's accusations, it was announced that there was to be an inquiry into Herchmer's management of the Mounted Police, starting at Regina on 18 January 1892. On New Year's Day the Commissioner's younger brother, William Herchmer, who also faced some minor charges in the inquiry, died suddenly of a heart attack, and his post as Assistant Commissioner went to Superintendent McIllree, 'Easy Going Old John Henry', the Sandhurst-educated son of a British Army Surgeon-General, who had enlisted as a constable with the first batch of recruits in

1873. McIllree held the second-in-command position for nineteen years until his retirement in 1911 after thirty-eight years' service.

When the inquiry opened before Mr Justice Edward Ludlow Wetmore, Commissioner Herchmer faced a total of 137 complaints, eighty-nine of them by the *Fort Macleod Gazette* editor Charles Wood. Herchmer's former servant and stoker, ex-Constable F. A. Pitts laid another twenty complaints, two M.P.s – Nicholas Flood Davin and D. H. McDowall – put forward four each; Superintendent John Cotton made four charges, and the rest were from an assortment of civilians and former and serving policemen, mainly about Herchmer's harshness, arrogance and improper language. A hundred of the complaints were either withdrawn, abandoned or thrown out by Judge Wetmore. Of the remaining thirty-seven charges he found fourteen proved and twenty-three proved in part, involving illegally interfering with and dictating to officers, improperly sentencing constables, using threatening, insulting and abusive language, and hasty, arbitrary actions.

In his report Judge Wetmore stressed that none of the charges which he had found proven affected in any way the Commissioner's honesty, business capacity or the efficiency of the Force under his command. He ruled that the charges did not amount to misconduct by Herchmer. He was guilty of an excess of zeal and misapprehension of his powers. 'A very large proportion [of the charges] are attributable to infirmity of temper, brusqueness of manner or hasty conduct,' said Judge Wetmore. 'I found the relations existing between the Commissioner and a large number of officers of the Force very much strained. I am not, however, prepared to state on whose shoulders the blame lies for this state of things.' When he forwarded the Wetmore report to the government, Comptroller Frederick White stressed that, in his opinion, these strained relations were 'the keynote of the troubles'. White then made a firm bid to get rid of the evil-tempered Herchmer:

There are faults on both sides and even if a whitewashing order were issued reprimanding all round and starting with a clean slate I fear the truce would not be of long duration. If it could be found possible to provide for Herchmer in some other branch of the public service where his unfortunate infirmity of temper would be less taxed a better feeling would prevail throughout all ranks of the police force.

Though Herchmer's great benefactor Sir John Macdonald had died in June the previous year – being succeeded as Prime Minister by Sir John Abbot – Herchmer was reprieved and whitewash *was* lavishly applied by the President of the Privy Council when he decided to take no action over the Wetmore report in the pious and naïve expectation that 'harmony and good feeling will be thoroughly re-established among all members of the Force in the early future'.

Though considerably chastened, Lawrence Herchmer survived to command the Mounted Police for a further eight years.

Chapter 17

'THE LAW IS A DISGRACE'

LIKE his predecessor Irvine, Herchmer found the enforcement of the liquor laws 'the most disagreeable and trying' of the Mounted Police's duties. It was rendered doubly disagreeable when, in 1888, Joseph Royal succeeded Edgar Dewdney as Lieutenant-Governor of the North West Territories. Royal, a French-Canadian, decided on a new, liberal policy to check the abuses of the permit system. He began to issue permits freely and introduced a licence system for four-per-cent beer, hoping to eliminate the demand for smuggled liquor. Instead he brought about a near-total collapse of the liquor laws and the police's ability to supervise them.

Herchmer's men were vilified by the drinkers for what they regarded as over-eager enforcement of the laws (though generally the police were extremely unwilling to prosecute because of the unpopularity it earned them), while the temperance advocates – with a good deal more justification than the drinkers – attacked the police for not enforcing the country's laws. The Press was solidly against the police. The *Prince Albert Times* announced that if the Force considered the enforcement of liquor laws its basic work 'it has outlived its usefulness', and the *Fort Macleod Gazette* pronounced loftily, 'Why any Mounted Police officer should dictate to any Canadian citizen as to what and when he should drink is more than any fellow can tell.'

It was certainly more than the Calgary judge Charles B. Rouleau could tell. In a succession of startling rulings he totally undermined police authority. One case concerning illegal possession of liquor was thrown out because, in Rouleau's opinion, it did not come within the province of his court to presume that whiskey was an intoxicant. Rouleau also ruled that, once admitted to the country on a permit, liquor could be held by anyone and not only the original applicant.

Understandably, Calgary soon became a roaring liquor-town. The Toronto *Mail* told its readers that there were fourteen saloons in operation where liquor could be bought for twenty-five cents a glass at any hour of the day or night. Every saloon-keeper held a sheaf of permits, some of them so old that the original holders had died. Whenever police searched a saloon the proprietor would produce a fistful of permits for whatever amount was found on the premises. As Superintendent John McIllree complained, 'What is the use of searching saloons under this system? It is simply a waste of time? It was also a waste of time to prosecute, as McIllree discovered. In 1888 he brought fourteen prosecutions; only one was successful. 'It does not matter if a man is caught with a lot of liquor in his possession and is convicted; he will appeal,' said McIllree. He cited the case of a man who was discovered by police locked into a cupboard on a Canadian Pacific train with a ten-gallon keg of whiskey. Though convicted, he appealed, and McIllree confessed, 'It is hard to see how it will end.'

Things were just as bad in other developing towns. At Fort Macleod, Sam Steele reported, 'The town abounds in saloons and dives where liquor is sold openly across the counter.' When a Corporal Greenacre seized a quantity of liquor in D. P. Smith's saloon he was presented with twenty-one permits, only two of them in Smith's name, 'covering sufficient liquor to supply the needs of a large community'. And when the same corporal seized some liquor in James Murphy's saloon, Murphy – not having a permit handy – crossed the road and borrowed one from an obliging friend. The frustrated Steele asked Herchmer, 'Are we to go on or are we to leave the liquor question alone?' The Commissioner, who damned the law as 'a farce and standing disgrace', ordered his officers, 'If you find that you cannot obtain a conviction in a whiskey case make it as uncomfortable for the dealers as you can by frequently searching their places at inconvenient hours.'

The difficulties under which the police operated were highlighted at Prince Albert when Constable Archibald Leslie, wearing uniform and side arms, was detailed to watch for liquor at the Queen's Hotel where a dance was being held. The hotel owner, who testified later that Leslie 'had the look of a sneak thief' had him arrested by the Town Constable of Prince Albert and the unfortunate policeman was fined twenty-five dollars by the local magistrate, Colonel Sproat, for 'vagrancy'. The conviction was overthrown on appeal, when the Deputy Minister of Justice, Robert Sedgewick, criticized Sproat for 'an evident intention to ... throw discredit upon the Mounted Police in their honest endeavours. . . . Colonel Sproat has not hesitated to prostitute the forms of law and has, without evidence and in spite of the clearest proof of innocence, convicted a police constable for simply doing his duty.' Sedgewick wanted Sproat relieved of his legal duties, but since his term of office was almost up Sproat escaped with a warning.

That wasn't the end of the affair, however. A week after Leslie's arrest a public meeting in Prince Albert decided to send a letter to Sir John Macdonald complaining about the conduct of Superintendent A. Bowen Perry and his men of F Division. The vindictiveness of the accusation and its wording is clear indication of the bitterness which existed between public and police, at least in Prince Albert:

It is the common practice of the constables under Supt Perry's command, without any grounds of suspicion, to go about private and public houses at night looking through windows, listening at doors, wandering through stable yards and lighting matches in haylofts, and to stop vehicles in the dark of night and roughly search the persons driving and their goods.

A system of espionage, conducted at all hours of the day and night and without regard for ordinary good feeling and courtesy, is arousing deep feelings of resentment amongst people of all classes. No man feels safe from insult, and there is a growing belief that detailing of certain constables as spies in order to mulct citizens in fines, the profits of which they share, is a direct invitation to them to involve, by their own acts, innocent citizens.

Two days later a counter-petition, signed by every man in F Division, pleaded with the government to keep Perry in Prince Albert, claiming that 'the wish for his removal from the district arises wholly from the fact that under all circumstances he has impartially carried out his duty'. Perry, an honours graduate of the Canadian Royal Military College, a police superintendent by the age of twenty-five and one of the Force's outstanding young officers, ignored what he termed 'the jeers and flaunts' and stayed in Prince Albert.

Herchmer himself was charged by businessmen in Regina with violating the law by importing 1000 gallons of near-beer for the police canteen without written permission. The case was dismissed. And William Parker, one of the most zealous members of the Mounted Police, received painful indication of his unpopularity when he played in a Christmas Day Police *v* Civilians football match: 'It was a tough game all right, played in snow a foot and a half deep and ten below zero. . . . As I expected the civilians made a dead set against me, tore my shirt clean off. I was kicked in the nose, the blood flowing freely and just at the end of the game sprained my ankle but we had the satisfaction of winning the game.'

At Regina the garrison entered a tug-of-war team for a sports day and defeated the hotly fancied town team to win the event. A fist fight immediately erupted. Superintendent Richard Burton Deane tried to break it up. 'I ran into the fray and the first man I came across was a hot-headed Irish corporal who held a townsman by the throat and was choking the life out of him. I ordered him to let the man go but he affected not to hear me, so I took hold of his face with both hands and said, "If you don't drop that man this instant I'll give you six months tomorrow morning." He let go of the man, fell back and saluted.' Deane then marched his group back to the barracks, where he congratulated them for their 'magnificent exhibition of discipline' in breaking off the fight.

Occasionally the harassed police were granted divine intervention, such as the time when a notorious whiskey-smuggler Gus Brede was struck by lightning while on a 'business trip' in Montana.

The unworkable liquor-permit system was finally abandoned in 1892 and replaced by wholesale and hotel licences. Simply, this now meant that, in theory, alcohol was widely available to all but the Indians. In practice, it ensured that Indians were again able to lay their hands on strong drink – supplied to them by their half-breed relatives who were legally entitled to buy. So the police were back where they had started nearly twenty years previously, trying to keep Indians and alcohol apart.

The appointment of civilian licence-inspectors relieved the police of much of their previous distasteful work and after an initial surge of convictions for drunkenness following the introduction of the new laws – there were thirty-eight convictions in Regina in the first six months, more than in the previous six years – things quietened down when the novelty wore off. The following year Sam Steele was able to report, 'There is much less liquor sold now . . . and there is much less drunkenness among the public than when the permit system was in force,' though there was evidence around Prince Albert that some half-breeds were selling their cattle and household possessions to raise drinking-money.

Astonishing, after all the fuss that had gone before, when a liquor plebiscite was held in the North West Territories in 1898 the voting was two to one in favour of prohibition.

With few exceptions the white settlers were guilty of no offences more serious than cracking an illicit bottle or two. After the violence of 1885 it was amazing that only three years later Herchmer was able to congratulate himself on 'a most remarkable absence of crime', adding, 'Apart from criminals from the United

States, we have made no important arrests in our territory.' From Battleford Inspector Joseph Howe reported, 'Crime is a thing almost unknown here.'

There were rare murders during Herchmer's fourteen-year reign. Dave Akers, the gaunt cowboy who had welcomed James Macleod and his column to Fort Whoop-Up at the end of the great trek west, was shot dead after an argument over a cattle deal. His killer, an elderly ex-whiskey and gun runner, was sentenced to three years for manslaughter. In a situation which Fellini might have relished, an Italian knife-grinder Giovanni Battaralla was murdered as he tramped eastward along the railway line towards Winnipeg. Two of his compatriots, itinerant musicians named Luciano and Dejendo, were convicted of the killing; Luciano was hanged at Regina, but the death sentence on Dejendo was reduced to life imprisonment. Two half-breeds, James Gaddy and Moise Racette, also went to the Regina scaffold for the murder of a settler, Hector McLeish. The pair had escaped into the United States but were arrested there and extradited. When Inspector Gilbert Sanders went to Fort Benton to collect them he was warned by Herchmer to take the greatest care that they did not escape on the return trip, 'but if it is impossible to hold them you must shoot them at once, taking care to ensure the necessary evidence in support of your action'.

The clumsiest murder attempt was made by a man named Charles Forward on his brother William at Saltcoats two weeks before Christmas 1894. While William was preparing a meal at their cabin Charles struck him on the head with an axe, slashed him with a carving-knife, battered his face with an iron pot and doused him with coal-oil. Then he tried to set fire to the house but succeeded only in burning himself to death, while his intended victim managed to crawl to safety.

The robbing of stagecoaches, that highly popular pastime in the American West, made only the briefest of appearances in Canada. There were two recorded cases, both in the year following the Riel Rebellion. In July a man named Garnett, who didn't even bother to wear a mask, held up a stagecoach near Qu'Appelle with a double-barrelled shotgun, tied up and robbed the passengers, then borrowed a knife from the driver to cut open mailbags and steal the registered letters. Garnett got away with about $1300 but was at liberty less than a month before he was recognised in Prince Albert by the coach driver and sent to prison for fourteen years. Five days after Garnett's arrest the Edmonton-to-Calgary stagecoach was held up by two men, one of whom used a small Union Jack as a mask. The passengers were robbed, but the mailbags contained nothing of value. The pair got away, and for a time forced the police to escort the coaches over this route.

There was also an isolated case of what Superintendent Deane called 'lynch law' in Lethbridge in 1895. Charles Gillies, unemployed and a heavy drinker, committed suicide. Deane recalled, 'It was reported to me he had blown his brains out. I went to his house and found that the report was in no way exaggerated, as brains were scattered all over one of the walls of his bedroom. He had put the muzzle of a Winchester rifle into his mouth and pressed the trigger with his great toe.' Gillies had complained to friends that his wife was having an affair with their lodger, James Donaldson, who went to live with his brother after the shooting. Two nights later a band of masked and armed men broke into the Donaldsons' house; James Donaldson was pulled from bed, tarred, feathered and dragged by rope to Mrs Gillies's house and thrust through the front door. Among the gang later identified were a Mounted Police sergeant named Hare and an American, Charles Warren. Because of the townspeople's dislike of Donaldson the trial of Sergeant Hare and Warren was switched to Fort Macleod, but the night before he was due to appear in court Hare, who was undergoing hospital treatment for a broken arm, deserted into the United States. According to Deane, a subscription of $100 was raised for the policeman 'by the persons most interested in his absence'. When Warren was released on bail until the delayed trial he, too, fled over the border.

The railway was a constant source of work for the police.

Vagrants and tramps were arrested on it, a man who chose to sleep across its rails was run over by a train, and once a corporal and constable travelling near Moose Jaw arrested a one-legged negro passenger they recognised as Peg-Leg Brown, wanted for murder in Ontario, only to discover to their embarrassment that he was already a prisoner in charge of the man sitting next to him.

Perhaps the chief reason for the absence of crime in the Canadian West was the intricate and highly efficient patrol network established by Herchmer to ensure the country's pacification after the Rebellion of 1885 – though one policeman considered that the peaceful settlement of the west was equally due to the fact that 'when people had taken up land they were too busy to get into trouble'. By 1889 the line of police outposts along the frontier extended 800 miles from Gretna – twenty-eight miles east of the Red River in Manitoba – to the Rocky Mountains. Regular patrols went out in all weathers to visit farmers and settlers, a service which was sometimes not as much appreciated as it deserved to be: one man ordered a police patrol off his land because their horses were eating his valuable grass. 'This patrol was sent solely for the protection of the ranchers,' reported Superintendent Percy Neale. 'The men naturally feel very sore at the action taken.'

The amount of territory covered by the patrols was prodigious. In 1895 Sam Steele recorded that his division at Fort Macleod had travelled 447,894 miles with 166 horses, and in 1892 the 100 horses of B Division based at Moosomin patrolled an average of 2950 miles each. One year the Assistant Commissioner William Herchmer covered 15,818 miles on inspection tours: 10,461 by rail, 900 by water, 3620 on horseback and 200 on snowshoes.

The police occasionally paid a high price in suffering and discomfort. In 1891, close to the spot where the two constables Baxter and Wilson had been frozen to death during the Force's first winter in the west, Constable James Herron, alone on patrol, got lost in a blizzard, went snowblind and anticipated death by shooting himself with a revolver.

After one winter patrol William Parker wrote, 'The icicles on my moustache stuck out beyond the tip of my nose and to prove how intensely cold it was I happened to put out my tongue and, on it coming in contact with one of the icicles, it froze to it and before I could get it in again it pulled the skin off'. Chasing stolen horses one winter night, Corporal R. G. Mathews arrived with four companions at the Standoff detachment post at 6.30 a.m. to find a thermometer hanging beside the door registering −56°F. 'However, not one of us had even a little toe frozen,' he recalled. 'But it was a tough trip on the horses. They looked more like polar bears. Long icicles hung from their nostrils, while the bridle reins were stiff enough to stand up by themselves.'

There were other hazards than severe weather. In a camp near Fifteen Mile Lake one man had his boots eaten by foxes, and skunks were so numerous and obtrusive that the policemen were afraid of treading on them when getting out of bed. One night Superintendent Deane counted seven skunks and a fox in the camp and wrote, 'The skunk seems to have a keen appreciation of the art of minding his own business but woe betide any unlucky knight who is betrayed into any gesture giving him cause for alarm.'

Patrolling did not decline until just before the turn of the century with the heavier settlement of the prairies. Increasing population, the ploughing of the plains and the cutting of roads also brought a welcome drop in the number of disastrous prairie fires which plagued the country. In 1894, a particularly dry year, eighty-five fires around Regina alone burned 7000 square miles of prairie. But the worst year was 1889 when the plains were ablaze almost continuously from March until November. Inspector Gilbert Sanders reported from Maple Creek, 'A day and night have scarcely passed during which we could not see somewhere on the horizon the columns of smoke or at night the lurid glare in the sky of a prairie fire. . . . No sooner were they put out in one place than they sprang up in another. Besides this, the unusually high winds which prevailed most of the time rendered the extinguishing of fires an almost hopeless task.' One fire entered the Cypress Hills at the west end and burned its way through to the east in two weeks, destroying on its way what little remained of old Fort Walsh. The entire country around Lethbridge was burned over, and a huge blaze which swept the country south-east of Calgary in April was not finally put out until the autumn. It did thousands of dollars' worth of damage to property, homes and grazing-land: the man who started it was fined $100.

Railways engines remained the most common cause of fires. The sparks from one cattle train started eight fires in twelve miles; in 1893 Superintendent Perry wrote from Regina, 'There was scarcely a day during August that fast passenger trains did not set a fire,' and Inspector James Wilson reported from Estevan, 'I personally saw six fires started by an engine within a distance of five miles.' Though railway officials fitted safety screens on the smokestacks it was not until firebreaks were ploughed, one hundred feet wide on each side of the tracks, that the incidence of fires was checked. Some farmers were suspected by Herchmer of setting fire to the stubble in their fields and paying the fine rather than go to the expense of clearing their own acres, and Superintendent Deane claimed that Indians who made a living selling buffalo bones were also guilty of burning the prairie so that they could spot the bleached bones more easily on the blackened ground.

There was much bitterness among the police about the unwillingness of many settlers to fight fires. Herchmer grumbled, 'Unless a fire is actually at their own door they will not generally turn out to help until they are made to do so by the police.' One inspector reported, 'After fighting fires day and night we would come across farmers in bed with the fire burning all round them.' Perhaps they had heard of the case of one man who obeyed police orders to fight a blaze and returned home to find his own farm burned to the ground.

The passing of the era of the prairie fire ended the sort of ghastly drudgery outlined in one report by Superintendent Steele: 'A party left Fort Macleod at 1 p.m., rode 30 miles to the fire, worked all night at it and returned to barracks by noon the following day, making a ride of 60 miles without rest.'

The Police were always ready to assist settlers in other ways. A group of German and Austrian families settled near Maple Creek in a community they christened Josephburg. Since none of them could speak English Herchmer arranged to have a German-speaking constable named Halenbach specially stationed at Josephburg to assist them.

And when the Mormons settled at Lees Creek (now Cardston) in 1877 the police turned a blind eye to their polygamous activities since they were such hard-working and otherwise law-abiding people. Sam Steele recalled that whenever police called on the Mormons they were 'hospitably received, sometimes with hymns of welcome, the result being that the fatigued traveller is quite prepared to blind himself to their faults, the worst of which are concealed as much as possible, the extra women going to other houses for the period of the traveller's visit'. The police documented the case of a Miss Legerman who joined the household of the Mormon leader Charles Ora Card and changed her name to Mrs Taylor. Card built an extra room on his house, 'which room Constable Kirkman states he has seen him use without regard for the privacy of Mrs Taylor', who was soon pregnant.

Police were called to the defence of the Chinese, the hardest-working but least popular of immigrants, who had aroused the fury of an already-hostile Calgary population when one of their number recently arrived from the Pacific coast was found to have smallpox. Though the laundry building in which he worked was burned with its contents, nine cases were soon confirmed and there were three deaths. Indians, who as we have already seen were particularly susceptible to this disease, were warned to keep clear of Calgary by police patrols, but when the outbreak was ended there were rumours that the Chinese population was to be driven out by 'aroused citizens'. Although Calgary by then had its own town constables, quite separate from the Mounted Police, it was the latter who broke up the crowds and went out to collect the terrified Chinese who had fled into the countryside. 'For some nights afterwards at sundown a procession of Chinamen could be seen making for the barracks,' said Inspector Ross Cuthbert. 'Night and day patrols were provided in Calgary and the Chinese returned to permanent possession of their dwellings after three weeks when everything was quiet.'

In addition to acting as guardians to refugee Chinese the Mounted Police undertook a bewildering variety of duties. They tracked whiskey smugglers and cattle thieves, guarded the country against prairie fires, issued seed grain and relief to indigent settlers, patrolled the border to round up and turn back stray American cattle, treated sick animals, acted as timber and game guardians, looked after the insane, guarded prisoners and provided escorts for distinguished visitors. They were Customs, census and quarantine officers, and – of necessity – had to become trained carpenters, blacksmiths, wagon and harness repairers, and raisers of their own crops.

As Superintendent Perry pointed out, 'It does seem that at times the most important reason for the existence of the Force is overlooked. If the North-west Territories had no Indian population it would need no Mounted Police Force.'

Chapter 18

THE ALMIGHTY VOICE
AFFAIR

THE spirit of the restless Indians had been broken by defeat in the North West Rebellion, and soon Superintendent Perry was reporting from Prince Albert that the followers of the rebellious Beardy had fenced their lands and were successfully raising crops, while even White Cap's nomadic Sioux were turning their hand to farming. There were occasional cases of cattle-killing and horse-stealing, but these offences were committed more frequently by white men than Indians, and by 1889 Herchmer was able to extol the success of his patrolling system: 'Horse-stealing, even among Indians, has almost totally disappeared from the list of crimes.' There was an indication of how conscious the natives had become of the white man's law when the Blood chief Red Crow surrendered his own son to the police for being concerned in the theft of horses from American Indians in Montana.

Surprisingly, it was among the normally peaceful Kootenay Indians of British Columbia, whose land lay 100 miles west of Fort Macleod over the Rockies, that the worst trouble erupted. A succession of early travellers through that part of Canada had commented favourably on the Kootenays' honesty and truthfulness. The Edinburgh geologist James Hector, who visited the area with the John Palliser expedition in the late 1850s, also found them fully converted to Christianity by Roman Catholic missionaries: 'Frequently, and at stated times, a bell is rung in the camp and all who are within hearing at once go down on their knees and

286

pray.' But in 1887 anger replaced piety in the Kootenay camp. They objected to being herded onto reservations and losing what they rightly regarded as their country to miners and settlers; and when an Indian named Kapula was jailed at Wild Horse Creek accused of the murder two years previously of two white miners the prison was broken open by the Kootenay chief Isadore and his followers and Kapula was released. There was further trouble when the British Columbia government sold a stretch of foothills land to a British army colonel, James Baker. Isadore claimed that the land was his and refused to move off it.

Since British Columbia was outside the territorial jurisdiction of the North West Mounted Police, they were not permitted to enter the province except by permission of, or at the request of, the British Columbia authorities, who had been anything but grateful for police supervision of railway construction through the Rockies. The Assistant Commissioner, William Herchmer, was instructed to make an unofficial visit to the Kootenay area and report to the Canadian government on the difficulties, taking care not to alert the local authorities about his movements. Herchmer found 'a very uneasy feeling' among the settlers. 'The older Indians are anxious for peace but the young men, who are all great gamblers and have no stake in the country are a bad lot and ready for mischief at any moment.' He reported a Kootenay fighting strength of about 350 well-armed men, and recommended the dispatch of a peace-keeping force to the area as soon as possible.

No immediate action was taken but when Indians prevented miners from working in the Kootenay River area that spring Colonel James Baker asked the Canadian government for the protection of seventy-five Mounted Police 'without delay'. In mid-June 1887, with the permission of the British Columbia government, Sir John Macdonald authorised the dispatch of Superintendent Sam Steele and seventy-five men of D Division to the Kootenay land, and by early August they were constructing their own barracks (named Fort Steele) on an ideal site at the junction of the Kootenay River and Wild Horse Creek. The

287

building work was cruelly hard and soon three deaths through fever, plus sickness, desertions and discharges had cut Steele's tiny command by twenty per cent. He pleaded for reinforcements, pointing out that after deducting necessary men for the running of the fort he could muster no more than twenty-eight police in an emergency. 'The effect on the minds of Indians and whites alike would be more beneficial if I could make a better showing,' he felt.

Eventually Isadore handed over the freed prisoner Kapula and another murder suspect to the police, but both were released by Steele because of lack of evidence against them. As the negotiations with the chief about his dispute with Colonel Baker dragged on Steele – who had originally found Isadore 'the most influential chief I have known' – began to get irritated and referred to him as 'stubborn, crafty and a persistent grumbler'. Finally, early in November, Isadore gave in. He agreed to waive his claim to land occupied by Colonel Baker in exchange for $1000 to improve the remainder of his property, and Steele clinched the deal by promising that his men would dig Isadore an irrigation ditch – yet another in the long list of strange tasks performed by the North West Mounted Police.

By the following summer, with the district settled and all reason for remaining in British Columbia gone, Steele was ordered to abandon his barracks and return to Fort Macleod with his detachment. As a farewell gesture Steele organised a sports day, inviting all the local whites and Indians to attend. To impress Isadore, Steele opened the sports with an official march-past at which Colonel Baker officiated. 'The colonel did not care to do it', Steele recalled, 'but as I felt that it would place him in an important position with the Indians he consented.' Marquees were pitched, food and overnight accommodation were provided and the Indians were delighted to win several events, including the one-mile horse-race, although the victorious jockey weighed in at fourteen stone. At the close of the two-day sports, Isadore and his tribe assembled to say goodbye to the men of D Division, whom the chief praised for their 'manly and moral behaviour'. After

27. Big Bear, Chief of the
Plains Crees

28. (*Below*) A trading group
at Fort Pitt. Big Bear is
standing fourth from the left

29. A working detachment during the construction of Fort Steele, 1887

30. (*Below*) A group of officers at Regina, 1895. Inspector Constantine is standing second from the left and Inspector D'Arcy Strickland second from the right. Commissioner Herchmer is seated, centre, with Assistant Commissioner John H. McIlree on his right.

Isadore's speech every Indian filed past Steele and shook hands with him. On 7 August 1888, almost exactly a year after arriving in the Kootenay land, Steele and his command rode out eastward for Fort Macleod.

In April 1890 Crowfoot died. The majestic chief of the Blackfoot had presided over the most momentous period of change in the history of his people, and it was due to his wisdom, patience and foresight that this transition had been a peaceful one. Dr Henry George of Calgary visited Crowfoot as he lay on a bed of buffalo robes in his tepee, surrounded by armed and painted warriors and medicine men. The nervous Dr George, who recalled, 'Every eye was upon me', dropped and broke his thermometer as he removed it from Crowfoot's mouth – an evil omen as far as the Indians were concerned. The doctor offered Crowfoot brandy and eggnog as a stimulant but the chief refused it, not wishing to become drunk and disgrace himself in front of his people, even on his death bed.

Dr George spent five nights in the Blackfoot camp attending Crowfoot; finally two Indians roused him with the news that their chief had 'died and come back to life again'. Crowfoot had in fact fainted and his followers, believing him dead, had launched into the tribal death ritual. Crowfoot's favourite horse was shot outside his tepee and his three wives each cut off one of his fingers. Mercifully, Crowfoot's recovery of consciousness was brief. On 25 April 1890, on the heights above the beautiful Bow Valley where thirteen years earlier he had signed his nation's treaty with Canada, Crowfoot died. A rough slab over his grave bore the inscription 'Father of His People'.

As the turn of the century approached the Canadian Plains Indians had almost entirely abandoned their nomadic life. The grim starvation years which followed the disappearance of the buffalo were long behind; now the more enterprising Indians were carving a good living from their land. In a decade they had changed from buffalo hunters to competitive businessmen, winning many lucrative contracts – with the police among others – to supply hay and coal. Commissioner Herchmer reported 'a grow-ing inclination to make money' which was keeping the able-bodied men of most tribes at work. He also praised the Indians' be-haviour: 'While a few Indians have been arrested for being drunk and disorderly and for gambling ... in most cases they elect to pay their fines and pay up much more promptly than many whites. They quite understand their responsibilities and stand punish-ment with much better grace than the settlers.'

Gradually, too, the white man's customs and clothes were adopted. The Stony Indians under the energetic Rev. John McDougall said their prayers morning and evening, and the ubiquitous blanket gave way to European clothing. An Indian brass band was formed at an industrial school near Calgary. Treaty money was increasingly invested in household items in-stead of liquor as the Indians, moving from their traditional tepees to wooden houses, bought bedsteads and washstands. Perhaps the most striking example of this 'progress' was the house belonging to the Blood chief Red Crow. When Sam Steele visited it in 1895 he found it 'very comfortable'. The house was well carpeted throughout, had white sheets on the beds, stoves polished, windows cleaned 'and in fact compares favourably with the residence of the average settler', said Steele.

After visiting the Sarcee and Blackfoot reserves in 1900 Lord Minto wrote to Queen Victoria:

> The Indians have made great advances and though they met me with all their old barbaric pomp, bead-work, feathers and tomahawks, I am told I am probably the last Governor-General who will receive such a welcome, and that my succes-sors will have to be content with chiefs in tall hats and black coats. I suppose one must not regret the coming change, but I confess the wild red man has charms for me.

According to Superintendent Percy Neale the Indians now had a thorough respect for the police 'and I have no difficulty in mak-ing arrests, even in the large camps on the Blood reserve'. Neale and other officers were considerably helped in this work by a ruling from Sir John Thompson, the Minister of Justice, that the police were entitled to arrest Indians 'at any time or place' following complaints from chiefs that Indians had been seized on the reserves.

The chief danger, as Herchmer pointed out, was in isolated incidents where 'excitement or the natural cussedness of a few young Indians may precipitate serious trouble'. He might have added the word 'despair' as a further reason for the occasional act of violence by an Indian. After the death of his ailing son, a Blackfoot named Scraping High killed Frank Skynner, the rations agent on his reserve who had refused him extra food for the child. Scraping High was shot the same day while resisting arrest. Three Indians were empanelled for the coroner's jury at their own request and expressed themselves 'perfectly satisfied' at the manner in which their fellow tribesman had been dealt with.

But the Bloods were far from satisfied over another shooting incident. Police scout Bob Giveen, searching for an escaped prisoner named Deerfoot, shot and wounded his brother Bad Dried Meat in a case of mistaken identity. Blood chiefs complained to Fort Macleod about the incident, throwing in a few other stock grumbles about the poor quality of the tobacco they were issued, the inadequacy of their reserves, and the fact that they didn't get enough to eat. In a reference to government letters refusing their request for an increase in rations, one chief said, 'The Great Mother only sends us bad letters, we never get any good ones. Anyway, it is no use for us to write to her, she is a woman and all women get jealous of each other.'

There was more trouble when a police patrol from Standoff, searching for whiskey smugglers, stumbled across a group of Bloods who had just killed some cattle. As Constable Alexander galloped forward to make the arrest, an Indian named Whetstone shot him in the neck at point-blank range and Constable Ryan shot Whetstone through the back, the bullet passing through a lung and coming out at the left breast. Alexander's wound, miraculously, was minor and he soon recovered. So did Whetstone who, scorning all offer of medical treatment, paid a medicine man ten ponies to ensure his recovery. 'Strange to say in a fortnight's time he was riding around,' Superintendent Steele reported. When he was well enough, the Indian was given two months at hard labour. Constable Alexander had been lucky, but the days of the renegade Indian were to end, unhappily but perhaps predictably, in tragedy.

The terrible affair of Almighty Voice began harmlessly enough. A Cree Indian, he was arrested by Sergeant Charles Colebrook on 22 October 1895 charged with killing a cow and locked up in the police guard-room at Duck Lake. He broke out of captivity, however, and swam to freedom across the icy South Saskatchewan River. But Colebrook tracked him down again inside a week. Accompanied by a half-breed scout named Dumont, the sergeant caught up with Almighty Voice and a thirteen-year-old squaw with whom he had eloped. Though the Indian waved a double-barrelled muzzle-loader to warn him away, Colebrook rode ahead of Dumont towards the exhausted Indian couple, his right hand raised as a sign of peace, his left hand gripping a revolver hidden in his overcoat pocket. Almighty Voice shot him in the neck at close range, and Colebrook died within seconds. The Indian took the sergeant's horse and got away. One colleague felt that Colebrook was 'a brave Mountie in wanting to take his man alive but made a grave error in not keeping Dumont with him to hold a parley with the Indian. With a good explanation he would probably have surrendered.'

The police offered a $500 reward for Almighty Voice's capture. Though his description was extremely detailed ('About 22 years old, 5ft 10in in height, weight 11 stone, slightly built and erect; neat small feet and hands; complexion inclined to be fair, wavy dark hair to shoulders, large dark eyes, broad forehead, sharp features and parrot nose with flat tip, scar on left cheek running from mouth towards left ear, feminine appearance'), the hunted

292

Indian eluded his pursuers for more than eighteen months. Criticism of the police's failure to catch Almighty Voice nettled Herchmer, who hit back by pointing out that it took Australia's police two years to hunt down Ned Kelly's gang: 'If the Australian police sometimes have such trouble to arrest white men with the advantage of moderate weather all the time, how much more difficult must it be for the Mounted Police to follow and arrest an Indian in an equally difficult country surrounded on all sides by his own relatives and with the climate we have to contend with.'

Though the police were warned to exercise the greatest care in arresting fugitive Indians, the Colebrook tragedy was repeated in almost exact circumstances a year later. On 13 October 1896 the body of a Blood Indian, Medicine Pipe Stem, was found in a cattle shed, shot through the head. There was no clue to his killer until a Blood informed the police that an Indian named Charcoal, also sometimes known as Bad Young Man, had admitted the crime. Despite his second name, Charcoal had been an inoffensive Indian until he murdered Medicine Pipe Stem, who was having an affair with one of his wives, Pretty Wolverine. Realising that he would hang for murder, Charcoal apparently decided to leave behind a reputation as one of the mightiest Blood warriors. The same day he fired at and wounded a farm instructor named McNeil, and announced his intention of gunning down the local Indian Agent James Wilson and the Blood chief Red Crow (who was so terrified that he slept on the newly carpeted floor of his house until Charcoal was caught).

Charcoal fled into the bush, taking with him his four wives and two children. A police patrol caught up with him once but he escaped, abandoning two of the squaws and one child. The chase dragged on for four weeks, during which time Charcoal took a pot shot at a police corporal on his way to stables at the Cardston detachment one evening.

Eventually a patrol from Pincher Creek, led by Sergeant William Brock Wilde, overtook Charcoal late in the afternoon of 11 November in deep snow and bitter weather. The police group had already travelled thirty miles that day and all their horses except Wilde's were exhausted. Wilde, a tall ex-Guardsman whose fearlessness with Indians had been demonstrated when he kicked down the tepees of Piapot's tribe because they were blocking the Canadian Pacific Railway line, pushed on ahead of the others, ignoring his own earlier instructions to the patrol that, if sighted, Charcoal was to be shot at fifty yards' range if he refused to surrender. When the patrol's interpreter, Charles Holloway, called out to Charcoal to stop the Indian turned round and challenged, 'Come on.' Holloway leapt from his horse and aimed at Charcoal at a range of 100 yards but his rifle misfired twice. The intense cold had frozen the oil and clogged the breech.

An unarmed settler named John Brotton who was rounding up cattle only fifty yards away was an uncomfortably close eye-witness of what happened next. Sergeant Wilde rode up level with Charcoal, his rifle across the saddle as a peace sign. But, as he leaned over to make the arrest, the Indian swerved round and shot him. The bullet entered Wilde's body on the right side and was afterwards found inside his left gauntlet. As Wilde fell from his horse, Charcoal – who according to Brotton was shouting and singing – shot the policeman a second time in the abdomen, took his horse and rifle and galloped off into the gloom.

Charcoal travelled seventy miles to seek refuge at the home of his two brothers, Left Hand and Bear's Back Bone who, in common with other members of the family, had been arrested by the police and forced to promise to help arrest Charcoal in exchange for their freedom. The two men overpowered him and, when he tried to commit suicide by slashing his wrists with an awl, they staunched the flow of blood with flour, binding up the wounds with sacking. When he was transferred to police custody Charcoal at first refused to eat and had to be forced to swallow, but later took nourishment 'readily and regularly'. He was chained to the floor of his cell, not allowed a knife or fork for his meals, and escorted on exercise in leg irons by two guards.

At Wilde's funeral at Pincher Creek, which was attended by the leading Indian chiefs of the area, one of Wilde's two dogs refused to let the pallbearers near his master's body and had to be shot. The horse he was riding when murdered was taken to London the following year as one of the Mountie contingent to attend Queen Victoria's diamond jubilee celebrations and was presented afterwards to the Life Guards unit in which Wilde had formerly served.

Charcoal was tried for murder at Fort Macleod in January 1897, found guilty and sentenced to death. During imprisonment he lost the use of his legs as a result of the hardships he had experienced in the bitter cold during the hunt for him. When he was executed, at 7 a.m. on 16 March, Charcoal was tied into a chair and hanged from that position.

Two months later Corporal Bowridge and a scout named Napoleon Venne, investigating a cattle killing near Duck Lake, stumbled upon the elusive Almighty Voice. Venne was shot in the left shoulder and Almighty Voice tried to catch his horse and dismount him, but the scout had just enough strength left to spur his horse free, escaping with no further damage than a second bullet through the brim of his hat. A detachment of a dozen men set out from Prince Albert under a veteran Irish inspector, John Beresford Allan, to hunt down Almighty Voice. Allan was a remarkable man. His father had served at Waterloo and Allan himself had fought in the American Civil War. He trekked to the Sudan in 1884 with the Canadian contingent of the Gordon relief expedition, was a Boer War volunteer at the age of sixty-two, tried to get into the First World War but was rejected since he was seventy-six at the time, and died in 1927 aged ninety.

Almight Voice was spotted the next day with two companions, and the group took refuge in a clump of poplars. Apparently undeterred by the deaths of Colebrook and Wilde, Allan's group chased the Indians into the trees. Allan's horse was shot from under him and his right arm was shattered by a bullet, and Sergeant Raven was wounded in the thigh. Allan, who at this stage still considered it 'more desirable to make prisoners than corpses', came dangerously close to being a corpse himself. He wrote about his escape afterwards:

> For the space of a minute or two, minus the use of my right arm, I was unable to gain an erect position. Pulling myself through the twigs to a small stump I was enabled thereby to come to my feet, only to find myself looking into the barrel of an old pattern Winchester. Almighty Voice had covered me . . . he lacked ammunition and demanded my belt, to which he pointed. I signified my refusal and awaited the end of a one-arm struggle with doubtful results.

But Allan's life was saved by one of his constables, who fired at Almighty Voice. The Cree ran deeper into the trees, which were quickly surrounded by the rest of Allan's detachment and a group of armed civilians who had arrived from Duck Lake. Allan was taken to a nearby farmhouse where his arm was treated. The police surgeon Hugh Bain was assisted by William Parker, who recalled: 'I held the Captain's arm for nearly an hour while Dr Bain took from it a heaped saucerful of splintered bone. The doctor wanted him to take a drink of brandy but he refused, just gritted his teeth and when the operation was over called for his pipe.'

After an attempt to set fire to the copse failed because the wood was too green, Corporal C. H. S. Hockin – in command during Allan's absence – made a suicidally foolish decision to rush the Indians in their entrenched position. Hockin took with him eight constables and Ernest Grundy, the postmaster of Duck Lake. As the ten men dashed blindly forward Grundy and Constable J. R. Kerr were shot dead and Hockin himself mortally wounded. When one of the Indians, Tupean, stood up to get a better aim he was shot through the head by Constable O'Kelly.

Just before sunset Superintendent Sévère Gagnon arrived with eight men to strengthen the circle of rifles around the two remaining Indians. More help was on the way: a special train rushed Assistant Commissioner McIllree, twenty-four men and a nine-pounder gun from Regina to Duck Lake in under six and a half hours. They went straight to the scene of action, seventeen miles away and were in position by ten o'clock the same evening. Another group from Prince Albert had dragged with them the ancient seven-pounder which had been used in the Indian Mutiny and had seen brief, inglorious service at Duck Lake during the Riel uprising.

About midnight the police were startled to hear Almight Voice call out, 'Brothers, we've had a good fight today. I've worked hard and am hungry. You have plenty of grub; send me in some. Tomorrow we'll finish the fight.' For his supper he received a salvo of shells.

The next morning, 30 May 1897, a large crowd of Indians, half-breeds and settlers had gathered to watch the last act. Among them was Almighty Voice's mother who sat on a low hill nearby, wrapped in a gaudy blanket, chanting her son's death song. Then both guns opened up on the Indians' hiding-place, 'making most excellent practice' as Commissioner Herchmer reported later. After the copse had been thoroughly sprayed with shells the police rushed it again, to find Almighty Voice and his companion Little Salteaux dead, killed by shell splinters. Almighty Voice had also had one leg shattered by a police bullet the previous day and had rigged up a makeshift splint with a lanyard taken from the body of Constable Kerr; the thirsty Indian pair had stripped and sucked the bark from nearby trees during the night.

Only six Mounted Police have been killed by Indians in the history of the Force. Almighty Voice, the Cree who made up his mind to die, carried three of them with him.

Chapter 19

GOLD! GOLD! GOLD!

MEN had known of the existence of gold in the Yukon for years before the Klondike stampede. In 1864 a young clerk at the Hudson's Bay Company post at Fort Yukon wrote to his family in Toronto: 'I had some thoughts of digging the gold here ... if I could only get time to make an expedition up the Yukon I expect we should find it in abundance. There is a small river not far from here that the Rev. McDonald saw so much gold on a year or two ago that he could have gathered it with a spoon.'

He and his colleagues of the Company cared only for furs, which they considered a far richer prospect. This encompassing interest was shared by the Russians, the first white men on the River Yukon in the 1830s. Yet it was this same river which was to be the main highway for the men who came to seek the gold – and for the police who came to enforce the law. The Yukon rises only fifteen miles from the Pacific Ocean before twisting its way northwards, crossing the Arctic Circle into Alaska, then turning abruptly south-west to expend itself eventually in the Bering Sea. The region was so poorly explored that in the 1880s globes were still being sold in London showing the Yukon emptying into the Arctic Ocean to the north.

The mining men reasoned that if gold had been found along the spine of North America from Mexico to British Columbia there was a strong chance that it also existed in the frozen loneliness of Alaska and the Yukon. So the gaunt, bearded professionals began to work their way northwards from the diggings in California and

British Columbia. Some trickled in across the thin coastal 'panhandle' of Alaska, which had belonged to the United States since its purchase from Russia in 1867, and over the Chilkoot Pass into the Yukon. Others came the long – but easiest – way round, by water all the way, northwards through the Pacific and the Bering Sea, then up the bleak, winding Yukon River until by the early 1890s there were probably a thousand miners working the country.

They found the fine 'flour' gold on the river's sandbars, and the easily mined 'placer' gold (after a Spanish word meaning pleasure, or delight, since it could literally be shovelled up). The first significant strike was made in 1887 on the Fortymile river, a tributary of the Yukon. A settlement straggled into being along the high bank where the Fortymile washed into the Yukon, a settlement which has been described as 'a community of hermits whose one common bond was their mutual isolation'. There was one other common bond: gold. The miners lived in tiny, foetid cabins, munched monotonous, unvarying, scurvy-provoking diets, flung themselves at the frozen earth and spent much of what they dragged from the ground in Fortymile's ten saloons, which charged fifty cents a glass for a rotgut concoction, Forty-Rod Whiskey (so called because it was attributed with powers to kill a man at that distance). A Mounted Policeman described how it was made:

> Take of sugar or molasses an unlimited quantity; add a small percentage of dried fruit or, in summer, berries; ferment with sour dough, flavour to taste with anything handy – the higher flavoured the better – such as old boots, discarded (and unwashed) foot rags and other delicacies of a similar nature. After fermentation place in a rough sort of still, for preference an empty kerosene tin, and serve hot according to taste.

Although the settlement was in Canadian territory its population was almost entirely American. United States stamps were used on letters and no Customs duty was paid on the American goods brought in. The only law was the grass-roots democracy of the miners' meeting, which had the power of life and death as it once demonstrated by hanging two Indians for murder. William Ogilvie, a Canadian government surveyor who was sent to the Yukon in 1887 to establish the boundary line with Alaska, warned of the dangers of this American community as early as 1889, and four years later again urged his government to establish authority in the area.

The Canadian government also received several letters from William Bompas, a tall, hook-nosed Church of England bishop who had left the comforts of London to live – and preach – in squalor in Fortymile. Bompas, a Cambridge graduate of scholarly tastes, complained that the miners were 'teaching the Indians to make whiskey with demoralising effect', and warned:

> Already one nearly fatal brawl has occurred among the Whites with dangerous stabbing and shooting. . . . Last winter Whites and Indians, men and women, passed nights of debauch drunken together, with brawls and constant discharge of rifles. Unless some restraint is placed on the Indians' manufacture of and traffic in whiskey I feel that I must myself leave the neighbourhood, as the instruction of the Indians is painful under present circumstances.

And finally John Jerome Healy, the man who had built Fort Whoop-Up, was once more a motive force in bringing the Mounted Police to an ungoverned stretch of Canada. After his Montana careers as whiskey trader, editor and sheriff, Healy had drifted north. He talked a rich American, Portus B. Weare, into setting up a transportation and trading company to service the growing needs of the Yukon, and established a post across the Fortymile river from the miners' settlement. Healy's habit of sending out bills promptly and refusing to extend the unlimited credit often expected in such remote areas made him unpopular with the miners. When a girl whom Healy employed as a servant stayed out late against his orders and Healy locked her out of his house, she complained to the miners' court, who ordered him to pay her a year's wages and her fare back home. He paid but, like Bompas, wrote to the Canadian government. This, added to the warnings of Ogilvie and Bishop Bompas, persuaded Ottawa to act. And since the Yukon formed part of the vast North West Territories the Mounted Police were given the job of investigating.

The man chosen by Commissioner Herchmer to carry out an inspection tour of the Yukon in 1894 was a Yorkshireman, Inspector Charles Constantine. He had been born in Bradford forty-five years previously, the son of a Church of England clergyman, and had emigrated to Canada with his family when he was five. He had taken part in the Red River expedition of 1870 against Louis Riel, became chief of the Provincial Police of Manitoba and when the North West Rebellion broke out he again opposed the *métis*, obtaining a commission in the Winnipeg Light Infantry. After the rebellion he was accepted straight into the Mounted Police as an inspector.

A blunt, no-nonsense man (described by one of his contemporaries as 'without exception the most colourful character I encountered during my 35 years of service') Constantine set off by train from Regina in June 1894 with one companion, Staff Sergeant Charles Brown. They boarded the steamer *Chilkoot* at Victoria, British Columbia and sailed north for Alaska on the route into the Yukon which was to be followed by hundreds of police and thousands of gold seekers in the next six years. The vessel touched at Wrangell and Juneau in Alaska before sailing up the fjord-like Lynn Canal to the end of navigation on the tidal mud flats where there were two small Indian settlements known as Skagway and Dyea.

Constantine planned to cross the coastal mountains by the Chilkoot Pass to the lakes which constituted the headwaters of the Yukon River, then hire a boat and float down to Fortymile. Though the total distance from Dyea was more than 600 miles, only the first forty miles of this would be on foot – up the trail from Dyea which led directly to the foot of the steep but short Chilkoot Pass, and down the other side to Lakes Lindemann and Bennett. The rest, theoretically, was a straightforward sailing job.

Fifteen years earlier the pass had been jealously guarded by the Chilkoot Indians, who had monopolised trade with the Indians of the interior and at the same time dominated and terrorised them. Yet if they were unscrupulous the Chilkoots were also shrewd. As the trickle of white men grew into a steady stream, they changed from defenders of the pass into its exploiters, charging heavy fees for transporting equipment and food into the Yukon. Their attitude earned the contempt of Constantine, who had little time for Indians. He wrote that the Chilkoots 'seem to take in but one idea, and that is how much they can get out of you'. His was an experience which many people were to suffer in the next four years.

When Constantine and Brown left Dyea on 1 July they were reluctantly paying porterage fees of fifteen cents a pound for their 800 lb of baggage to be carried the fourteen miles from Dyea over the Chilkoot. And Constantine's fury wasn't cooled when he and Brown were charged an extra twenty-five cents every time they had to be carried across the frequent icy streams they were required to ford. They got over the summit safely, though it was 'a hard and dangerous climb over bare rocks and soft snow most of the distance, sinking nearly to our knees at every step'.

There were no boats to be bought from the Indians at Lake Lindemann so Constantine and Sergeant Brown put together a crude raft and floated down to Lake Bennett where there was good timber. Here they started to build a boat for their river trip but the work was so back-breaking that Constantine christened the place 'Camp Misery'. They were about to abandon their efforts and try to float down the Yukon when, on Friday 13 July, they met two miners, a French-Canadian Joe Beaudoin and an American Jack Cawper, who offered to build their boat and help the two police-men through to Fortymile for $125. 'Steep price but no alterna-tive' was Constantine's comment. The construction work took a week and the four men set off in weather so calm that they were forced to row through the lakes ('Very tired and hands one mass

302

of blisters,' wrote Constantine in his diary) until they began to benefit from the pull of the current.

The first river hazard to be navigated was Miles Canyon, named after the American Indian fighter General Nelson A. Miles by Frederick Schwatka, a U.S. Cavalry officer who had been the first man to explore the river from mouth to source (under the impression at the time that it lay in Alaska for its entire length). At the canyon's entrance basalt walls a hundred feet high constricted the river into a third of its normal width – Schwatka had called it 'a diminutive Fingal's Cave' – and the water seethed through, falling fifty feet at its first drop, plunging on for a mile to a deadly whirlpool called 'The Squaw', racing a further two miles through deceptively calm water and then foaming onto the razor rocks of the White Horse Rapids. The experienced miners ran Constantine's boat through this maelstrom, but their own craft and all the supplies had to be portaged around the canyon.

There were further swiftwater hazards at Thirtymile and Five Finger Rapids, but Constantine was more concerned about the torrential rain which plagued their journey. On arrival at Fortymile on 7 August Constantine wrote, 'Am glad trip so far is done. Was well tired and sick of the everlasting river. Had just enough grub to see us through.'

As soon as Constantine stepped ashore in their midst the Fortymile miners realised that their free-and-easy days were over. His official title for the purposes of his visit was Agent of the Dominion Government, which gave him wide-ranging powers to act for every department. Constantine imposed Customs duties and an excise on locally manufactured 'hootch', reporting, 'Customs duties were distasteful and at one time it looked as if there might be trouble in collecting. Better counsels prevailed, however.' Miners arriving on river steamers from St Michael at the Yukon's mouth were angry when they were charged duty, claiming that Fortymile lay in disputed territory, but in the end they bowed to Constantine's firmness. Then, after arranging to purchase 320 acres of land for the future construction of a police post across the Fortymile river from the mining settlement and leaving behind his trusted Sergeant Brown ('He is a good man in every way') to spend the winter collecting Customs dues at Fortymile, Constantine sailed downriver by steamer on 3 September carrying $3248 levied from the miners. He completed the return journey to Victoria by a U.S. revenue cutter and the British warship H.M.S. *Pheasant*.

Constantine's report recommended the establishment of a police post at Fortymile the following year with a garrison of two officers, a surgeon and forty N.C.O.s and men. 'They should be of large and powerful build – men who do not drink.' Ottawa agreed to his proposal in typical government half-measure by halving the size of the force. Constantine was given command and also appointed Agent-General for the Yukon Territory with czar-like powers. On 1 June 1895, repeating the pattern set in the Canadian West when the police established themselves well in advance of the flood of humanity, the group left Regina for the Yukon. Accompanying Constantine were Inspector D'Arcy Strickland, Assistant Surgeon A. E. Wills (who for a long time would be the first and only doctor in an area the size of France), seventeen other ranks, Mrs Constantine and their young son Francis and Mrs Strickland and their baby. News of their going preceded them and when they pulled into Calgary station with a Union Jack flying from the carriage window they were cheered on their way by a huge crowd, although it was three o'clock in the morning.

They embarked at the American port of Seattle on the tiny tramp steamer *Excelsior*; besides the police's hefty supply of provisions and stores there were forty other passengers, nearly all miners, also heavily laden. There was so little room on board that the police had to be accommodated in a temporary shanty on deck. 'Certainly she would never have been allowed to leave any English port laden as she was,' wrote one of the police contingent, Sergeant Murray Hayne. 'It was a matter for congratulation that we had no really rough weather, for the first big sea would have washed our accommodation, and possibly ourselves, overboard.'

Owing to drifting ice the *Excelsior* did not arrive at the mouth of the Yukon River until 2 July. Next day the police transferred their supplies – a year's food and tobacco, portable stoves, building tools, and even window sashes already containing panes – on to the flat-bottomed stern-wheeler *Portus B. Weare*, named after John Healy's wealthy American partner in the North American Trading and Transportation Company. Sergeant Hayne thought the steamer resembled a Thames houseboat, except for its two funnels and three deck levels. On 5 July the *Weare* nosed upstream into the swift, grey current, tying up frequently to let passengers and crew ashore armed with axes to chop wood for the boat's voracious appetite. At first the policemen enjoyed the shore forays, but the constant stoppages became a bore and a nuisance. Hayne complained about

> the deadly monotony of our surroundings with idle hands and eternal daylight ... the hideous sameness of steaming up through barren, unlovely country with nothing whatever to do, and the speed decreasing every day as the current grew stronger. Although we were every hour getting nearer and nearer to the Arctic Circle the heat was unbearable, and the mosquitoes hovered over us like a cloud until we felt almost inclined to jump overboard to escape them. The natural heat, too, was increased tenfold on board by the heat from the boilers, which was absolutely insupportable. One could hear the logs crackling and roaring with an energy worthy of a better cause and which recalled mocking memories of Christmas at home. Anything soluble on board promptly melted; my valise was in a disgusting state.

At the end of their nineteen-day haul nearly 2000 miles up the Yukon River the prospect was just as barren when they landed at the riverside huddle of shacks and log stores and saloons that constituted Fortymile. Constantine's group immediately set to work clearing ground to establish the British Empire's most northerly military outpost – which quickly became known as Fort Constantine – across the river from Fortymile. The site chosen for the fort was a swamp, covered with eighteen inches of thick, saturated moss and overgrown with scrubby spruce trees. They managed to rent some shacks from John Healy and half the group started to clear space while the others chugged upriver in a chartered steamboat in search of suitable building timber. It was difficult to know which detachment had the least enviable job. The site clearers laboured alternately in pouring rain and 90°F. heat, up to their knees in icy water, while the log-cutting team – after three weeks of being pestered to distraction by clouds of gnats and mosquitoes and forced to sleep in their wet clothes on the sodden ground – assembled 400 logs into three huge rafts and floated them downstream to Fort Constantine, where their colleagues, owing to the lack of horses, had pressed into service a plough drawn by a team of dogs which had been shipped up the Yukon by a later steamer. Originally there had been four dogs, named Matthew, Mark, Luke and John. But the monotony of the river journey had been too much for John, who jumped overboard and drowned. And the dog-plough team suffered a further mishap one night when Mark and Luke ate Matthew.

Once the site had been cleared work progressed swiftly. The permanently frozen ground formed a firm foundation, the logs were manhandled into position and chinked with moss, which made an excellent draught-excluder as soon as it froze. Slabs of wood, covered with moss and a layer of earth, served for the roofs (though when the heavy spring rains came six months later they leaked so badly that oil sheets had to be hung over the beds to keep them dry). By the beginning of November nine buildings had been put up, one of them seventy-five feet long, forming a square with a surrounding stockade and a gateway facing the river. It had been a backbreaking slog. 'We cut and carried and squared all the timber ourselves,' said Constantine. 'Yes, our shoulders were raw.'

Before the guard-room was completed the police had their first prisoner. He was arrested by Sergeant Hayne after threatening to shoot another miner over a woman. While being taken to the police post under arrest he protested so violently that Hayne was 'obliged to knock him down by way of a gentle reminder that I was in charge of the case now'. The problem of where to keep the man was overcome by driving a large post into the ground inside one of the completed huts and handcuffing him to it. But there remained the further question of what to do with him since he was an American citizen. It was eventually decided to get rid of the prisoner who, according to Hayne, was 'a thorough-paced scoundrel and a coward into the bargain'. So the Mounted Police's first Yukon prisoner was put into a boat, handed a piece of bacon and pushed out into the swift Yukon current in the firm knowledge that he would quickly be carried down into American territory.

On 17 October the Yukon River froze over and, in the words of Sergeant Hayne, the tiny group of Mounties were 'as entirely shut off from the outside world as though we were on another planet'. Since the miners were, by and large, law-abiding and Constantine was prepared to make generous allowance for their free and easy mode of living, there was little in the way of official duties for the police, apart from the occasional foray to collect Customs dues. Just as well, since they spent most of the winter pushing ever further afield from their post foraging for firewood. As the thermometer plunged, the fuel expeditions became more urgent: during the months of December 1895 and January 1896 the temperature never rose above zero; in January it averaged −48°F – eighty degrees of frost.

The food was as monotonous as the existence. Sergeant Hayne recalled, 'Our staple food during the winter was bacon and brown beans. We mostly drank tea, with occasional bursts of execrably bad whisky – which was not, however, included in the rations supplied by the government. The only variation was when we were able to get fresh meat or fish from the Indians, and this was very seldom.'

To relieve the monotony the isolated garrison went through regular routines of arms and barrack inspection. For failing to carry out an order Constable Brothers was fined three dollars and confined to barracks for four days, a punishment which many of his colleagues condemned to wood gathering would have been pleased to share. There was a flurry of excitement in January when Mrs Constantine, out tobogganing with her son Francis, ran into a tree and suffered a compound fracture of the right leg; she was still unable to walk by midsummer.

In the same month Staff Sergeant Charles Brown became due for discharge and, rather than complete a second grim winter in the Yukon, trekked out over the ice of the frozen river. Constantine deplored the loss of such a hard-working N.C.O., particularly since he was profoundly unimpressed by his second-in-command, Inspector D'Arcy Strickland, a fat, twenty-seven-year-old Canadian. 'He has a taste for low company with a decided fondness for drink,' said Constantine in a confidential report. 'His conduct on [the journey up the Yukon River] was such that the men were even ashamed of him. . . . His saloon bill last month was $67, more than half his monthly pay.' Of Sergeant Murray Hayne, he said, 'His motto seems to be get all you can out of the government and do as little as you can in return.' And though he praised some of his command, particularly an N.C.O. named Webster, for their willingness he complained that some of the constables worked 'in a perfunctory way, looking forward to the time for going out'. Like conscripts everywhere, these men counted each day towards their discharge and ticked them off on calendars.

Eventually, in the spring of 1896, came the confrontation with a miners' meeting which Constantine had been expecting since his arrival nine months previously. Two prospectors had left the Yukon for the winter and sub-let their claim on Glazier Creek to another miner. This man hired others to work for him and then decamped with the proceeds of their labour. The workmen, owed two months' pay at ten dollars a day, demanded their wages from the original owners, who were brought before a miners' meeting. When they refused to admit liability their claim was confiscated and sold by auction to a man named Jerry Baker, who tried to register it with Constantine, whose many assignments included the post of Mining Recorder. When he was refused, Baker left 'breathing defiance and saying that the miners would see him through'. A dozen armed police were sent to Glacier Creek to back up the ruling, shattering for ever the authority of the miners' tribunals. 'I felt this was the turning point,' said Constantine. 'Should I give them their way or recognise them in any manner trouble would never cease.'

In mid-May, as soon as the river was free of ice, a party of police was sent upstream for more logs to repair the ravages wrought on Fort Constantine by the winter. By ironic coincidence the group did most of their cutting on the exact spot where the boom town of Dawson was to stand a few months later, at the junction of the Yukon with a fast-flowing stream with an unpronounceable Indian name, Thron-diuck – quickly corrupted to Klondike that summer by the miners. The police group even travelled up the creek soon to be known as Bonanza. 'I took a photograph of that golden creek,' Sergeant Hayne recalled. 'Needless to say, none of us had any suspicion of the pavement of gold that lay a few inches beneath our feet.' It was an ignorance soon to be remedied.

George Washington Carmack had a background as colourful as his name. He had been born near San Francisco, the son of a goldseeking pioneer who had travelled west with the California '49 stampede. He had gone to sea as a dishwasher aboard Pacific Coast steamers, jumped ship in Alaska, married a Tagish Indian chief's daughter named Kate and settled contentedly to the life of a squaw man, soon becoming proficient in the local dialects. Carmack, with his sleepy eyes, pudgy face and drooping moustache, even looked like an Indian and the miners nicknamed him Siwash George.

In August 1896 Carmack and two Indian relatives, Skookum Jim and Tagish Charlie, were camped at the mouth of the Throndiuck with their families catching and drying salmon. Skookum

Jim, a huge, handsome Indian and a fine hunter, had earned his name – an Indian word meaning strong – because he once carried 156 lb of bacon over the Chilkoot in a single trip for the surveyor William Ogilvie. Drifting into their camp one day by canoe came Robert Henderson, a Scots-descended lighthouse-keeper's son from Nova Scotia, who had trekked as far as Australia in search of gold. Henderson was a strong believer in the prospector's code of full exchange of news about gold. He had enjoyed moderate success, washing out some $750 that summer from a creek he called Gold Bottom and was on his way back to his diggings after collecting more provisions. Henderson landed at the camp to share his news with the bedraggled-looking white man fishing for salmon. This was the historic meeting of the pair who were to be known as the 'co-discoverers' of the Klondike. When Carmack asked about the chances of staking in the area Henderson encouraged him but, with a glance at his companions, said he didn't want any 'damned Indians' staking on his creek, a remark which was to cost him a fortune.

Wandering up the Thron-diuck, Carmack and his Indian relatives turned off before Gold Bottom Creek in order to cut logs and explore a tributary called Rabbit Creek. And there, on 17 August, they found gold lying 'like cheese in a sandwich' among protruding bedrock; Rabbit was swiftly rechristened Bonanza. Under Canadian mining law Carmack was entitled, as discoverer, to a double claim of 1000 feet. Skookum Jim and Tagish Charlie each staked 500 feet. Then, leaving Jim behind to guard the claims, Carmack and Charlie set off for Fortymile to record them, carrying a cartridge case filled with nuggets and telling everybody they met of their good fortune. But Henderson, the man who had pointed them in the right direction, was ignored. He paid a crippling price for his anti-Indian comment.

When the pair landed at Fortymile on 20 August, Carmack's nuggets and ready tongue swiftly emptied the saloons. Next day he crossed over to Fort Constantine and laid out fifteen dollars to register his claim with Inspector Constantine. Later that day

Sergeant Hayne went over to Fortymile, and found an empty settlement. Everybody had gone to the Klondike. Hayne reported 'an unending procession up and down the Yukon between the Klondike and Fortymile rivers by day and night . . . until the end of the first week in September'.

By then Hayne and some of his colleagues, including Dr Wills, had succumbed to the gold fever themselves. On 28 August, only a week after Carmack had recorded his claim, they took a week's leave and started upstream by boat, only to find most of the creek already staked. 'I had to tramp a long way up the creek before I came to the last claim and was able to stake one out for myself in the headwaters of the creek. I at once obtained enough colour [signs of gold] with my pan to be able to swear to for registering purposes.' All agreed there and then to take their discharge at the completion of their two years in the Yukon since, in Hayne's words, 'The prospects were better and "promotion" more sure.' In the meantime, the policemen who had managed to stake on Bonanza hired labourers among the latecomers to work their claims for them.

With admirable foresight, Constantine marked off forty wooded acres on behalf of the government at the junction of the Yukon and Klondike rivers. He was just in time. Soon building plots were selling briskly for $500 and within a year prime sites were fetching $10,000. The government surveyor, William Ogilvie, went to lay out the new town and named it Dawson City after George Mercer Dawson, a Canadian geologist. Gradually a ragged tent town sprang up. By the end of 1896 Dawson's population was around 500; six months later it had increased tenfold and by the summer of 1898 15,000 people jammed its streets. But for the time being winter froze within the Yukon the full news of the Klondike discovery.

Constantine, who had been so bored that he mused in his diary on 18 June, 'Battle of Waterloo fought 78 years ago. How many of those who fought there are left?', was swept off his feet by the rush of claims and counter-claims. He described his job as 'Chief

311

Magistrate, Commander-in-Chief, Home Secretary and Foreign Secretary'; he wrote to Herchmer and to Ottawa urging the establishment of civil courts and a registry office and the appointment of a gold commissioner, and told Herchmer, 'One man cannot do all the work there is to be done now. I have three tables in my room and a different kind of work on each. I walk from one to the other to rest.'

He pleaded for food and clothing, for a Maxim gun, a steam launch, trolley wheels to alleviate the grind of log-rolling, and for a coffee grinder. He pointed out that he had just received a ton of stationery, including government forms requiring him to register the number and disposition of farm animals in a country where there wasn't a single farm.

Constantine also pleaded for at least another eighty men. 'Unless the government are prepared to put a strong force in here next year they had better take out what few are now here.' Pointing out that 'the gold excitement is at fever heat', he wrote to Herchmer, 'It is pretty hard to hold the men.' He advised that Yukon recruits should be 'of a cheerful disposition, of good physique, free from any tendency to weak heart or rheumatism and above all sober and temperate'. He had also decided to get rid of Inspector Strickland by the first available boat the following spring and urged, 'If more officers are sent in, send single men and men who don't drink, if they are to be had.' Of his own health, Constantine commented laconically, 'I am well, not having time to be sick.'

Even the arrival of the newly appointed Collector of Customs, D. W. Davis, in the autumn of 1896 failed to cheer up Constantine. Davis, who had been John Healy's partner in the days of old Fort Whoop-Up, had prospered mightily since then and had served two terms as a Member of the Canadian Parliament. But Constantine commented, 'He is not the magnate he was supposed to be.' On New Year's Eve, still saddened by the summer departure of his son Francis to school in Toronto, he noted gloomily in his diary, 'Been a hard year – anxiety, worry, hopes and fears but we have pulled through ... who out of our little band may be above the sod to welcome 1898?'

With the blessing of the overworked Constantine, the miners approached the experienced and patently honest surveyor, William Ogilvie, who was wintering in the Yukon after his boundary-mapping duties, to attempt to resolve the welter of conflicting claims on and around Bonanza Creek. Ogilvie's measurings brought out some astonishing facts: one of the Mounted Police, for instance, instead of measuring off his permitted 500 feet in a straight line, as the law required, had followed the meandering line of the creek bed on Lower Bonanza with such lack of regard for geography that he actually finished twelve feet further up the valley than he had started. In other words, he had staked twelve feet less than nothing. Another 500-foot claim turned out, when carefully measured, to be only 150 feet. Another was 942 feet long: the owner lamely explained that he had stepped it off in the dark.

There was fierce argument over claims which had been staked but never recorded. Under Canadian mining laws these fell open again after sixty days. The most notable scramble for one of these claims came when a miner who had staked on Upper Bonanza left the Yukon without bothering to record it. News got around, would-be stakers began to gather days in advance, rather like January sales bargain hunters, and police were sent in to prevent trouble. So many miners were there that, as midnight of the final day approached, most realised the futility of disputing the claim with such a throng. Eventually, only two were left, a Swede and a Scots-descended Canadian with the distinctly un-Scottish name of Johnny Van Iderstein, who was known as Johnny Van.

At midnight a policeman gave a signal, both men drove in stakes at one end of the now-vacant land and sprinted 500 feet to the other end to repeat the formality. Then started the Great Claim Race to Fortymile, more than seventy-five miles away, an event which was incorporated by Jack London into one of his

Yukon novels. The two men stumbled on foot down Bonanza Creek in the dark to Dawson, eighteen miles away, where after a hurried breakfast they set off on the trek down the frozen Yukon to Fortymile by dog teams to register the claim with Inspector Constantine.

When, two or three miles from the police fort their dogs began to flag, both men abandoned the sleighs and ran the rest of the way. They went through the barracks gate neck and neck but the Swede, unfamiliar with the layout, made for the largest building – the officers' quarters. Johnny Van knew the recorder's office, reached the door first, opened it . . . and fell across the threshold shouting his claim number, which the Swede echoed as he fell over him a second later. When they had recovered, Constantine, Solomon-like, persuaded them to divide the claim. They could have saved their legs and their breath. It was worthless.

Occasional rumours filtered through to the outside world during the winter of a big gold strike on a river called 'Chandik, Throndak or some such name'. But it wasn't until the ice broke in the Yukon River that the full, incredible story came floating out. Aboard the river steamers *Portus B. Weare* and *Alice*, making their way downstream to St Michael, were fewer than a hundred prospectors carrying more than three tons of gold in nuggets and dust. Going out aboard the steamer – which had brought them into the Yukon two years earlier – were five of the Mounted Policemen who had staked claims and, after completing their term of service, had either sold their ground or left partners to look after it in their absence.

At St Michael the Pacific coast fur-trading vessels *Excelsior* and *Portland* were waiting to take the miners back to civilisation. The *Excelsior* completed its trip first, docking in San Francisco on 15 July and disgorging lean, bearded, tattered men dragging suitcases and bundled blankets bulging with gold. Two days later the *Portland* steamed into Seattle, to be greeted by a milling crowd of 5000 on the dockside pleading 'Show us the gold' to the miners

314

and Mounties lining the rails. Sergeant Hayne, who had sold his claim without making a fortune, recalled:

> The whole town turned out to greet us. The reporters were absolutely merciless ... they clung to us like limpets. 'For pity's sake', I cried, heading for the nearest hotel, 'I have been for two years in a country where the only drink is poison. Let me at least have a thimbleful of good Scotch whisky before I suffer the torment of an interview'. Six men accompanied me to the bar, and each one simultaneously planked down 25 cents on the counter and six voices exclaimed in chorus, 'Say miss, give this man a drink.'

The Seattle *Post-Intelligencer* carried a screaming banner headline 'GOLD! GOLD! GOLD! GOLD! 68 Rich Men on the Steamer Portland'. Within hours the whole of the western world knew of the Klondike. The last and greatest of the gold rushes was under way.

Fortunately the Canadian government had already taken Constantine's advice about strengthening the police contingent in the Yukon. On 8 April a group of twenty men under Assistant Commissioner John McIllree with Inspector William Scarth second in command sailed from Victoria aboard the *City of Topeka*. Scarth, a jaunty, monocled, ladies' man, was given to emerging unscathed from spectacular mishaps. On the voyage to Dyea a rope against which he was leaning gave way and Scarth fell head first into the ship's hold, only to emerge unhurt with his cap and monocle firmly in place. And on the river trip down the Yukon he was swept overboard by some low branches when trying to land his boat.

On arrival in Alaska McIllree handed over command to Scarth and returned to British Columbia, while the police party safely crossed the Chilkoot, which Scarth considered 'not by any means as bad as it is painted'. He noted, 'A larger number of fast women are coming in over this trail, and although the majority of the men seem respectable there are some tough-looking cases.'

By 9 May Scarth's force was camped at Lake Bennett preparing to fell timber and build three 24-foot boats. He quickly established a daily routine for his men: 'Reveille 6.30; Breakfast 7.15; Work 8; Dinner 12; Work 1.30; Supper 6. Daily, except Sunday, when I allow men to get up when they like. All blankets to be aired once a week, allow Sunday afternoon for washing etc.' On 24 May, Queen Victoria's birthday, two of the boats had been launched and the third was ready for caulking. In the evening the police celebrated by toasting the Queen in tea and singing the National Anthem. The party ended with 'three cheers and a tiger for Her Majesty'.

Four days later they set off. At Lake Tagish ('mosquitoes awful') they passed a deserted Indian-settlement. A note on the door of one hut explained, 'Gon to Youkon for two year. White man leave alone.' On 10 June Scarth bought seventy pounds of fresh moose-meat for six dollars from an Indian camp; the following day, on arrival in Dawson, he refused an offer of $100 for it. He handed over his party to Inspector Constantine 'in the best of health and condition'. Scarth's cheerfulness had not been affected in the slightest by the arduous journey. 'The whole trip has been a delightful one and the scenery along this route is unsurpassed by anything I ever saw,' he wrote. 'We were almost sorry when it was over.'

The sensational arrival of the steamers in the west coast American ports brought the swift organisation of further police detachments for Yukon duty. McIllree set off with another small party towards the end of July, to be followed a week later by a contingent under Inspector Frank Harper, a thirty-seven-year-old Londoner who had worked his way up from the ranks. By the end of the year the police force in the Yukon totalled eight officers and eighty-eight men. Twelve months later it had mushroomed to twelve officers and 254 men.

As the gold-seekers swarmed north the Yukon was hastily declared a judicial district by the Governor-General, the Earl of Aberdeen, and a well-known name was sought for the post of Commissioner of the territory. Clifford Sifton, the Minister of the

Interior, chose the former Mounted Policeman, James Morrow Walsh, 'Sitting Bull's Boss', and he came out of retirement in Brockville, Ontario, still spruce and fit at the age of fifty-four. Walsh's acceptance of the Commissionership was a grotesque mistake. By the time he undertook the job on 17 August it was already dangerously late in the season to plan a trip to the Yukon, and by the time he finally left Ottawa on 23 September there was no chance of completing the journey to the Klondike goldfields before winter closed in. With Walsh travelled Clifford Sifton himself, on a brief tour of inspection, and a party of officials chosen, according to Sifton, 'for the purpose of taking hold of matters as they might develop'. The group included Mr Justice McGuire of the Territorial Bench, a Crown Prosecutor Mr F. C. Wade, an accountant, two inspectors of mines, Walsh's private secretary Dufferin Pattullo (who later became Prime Minister of British Columbia) and his brother Philip Walsh.

A huge crowd of well-wishers greeted their train at Vancouver, where they were joined by yet another Yukon-bound contingent of police under Inspector Zachary Taylor Wood, a great-grandson of Zachary Taylor, twelfth president of the United States. With Wood's policemen travelled nine experienced dog-sleigh drivers, half a dozen Indians skilled in swiftwater navigation, seventy-eight dogs, twenty-five sleighs, two Gatling guns and several crates of rifles and revolvers. They dodged the frantic scramble for shipping space by sailing to Skagway aboard the government steamer *Quadra*.

Their arrival on 8 October plunged them into the centre of masses of frustrated men, terrified animals and colossal chaos. Skagway had mushroomed in four months from a conglomeration of tents into a roaring, wide-open town which, according to McIllree, had 'well laid out streets and numerous frame buildings of all sorts and sizes . . . very passable hotels, numerous saloons, gambling houses, dance houses and a population of about 2000'. Walsh didn't like what he saw, either of Skagway or of the preparations to get his party to the Klondike before winter. He had

317

expected to find provisions carried over the mountains and boats constructed to take them down the Yukon. Nothing had been done, which was particularly embarrassing since Walsh had the Minister of the Interior in his party.

Walsh immediately made arrangements to have his supplies moved inland and set off with Sifton and the surveyor William Ogilvie on a quick fact-finding tour of the White and Chilkoot passes, a nine-day round trip which included a visit to the newly established Canadian Customs post at Tagish, where Inspector D'Arcy Strickland – who had just returned to the Yukon at his own request after being sent out the previous spring by Constantine – was in charge of a corporal and five constables. Poor Strickland, whose scruffy group was miserably quartered in tents, was reprimanded by Walsh about the appearance of his police in this bleak wilderness: 'I told him as soon as clothing came they should be put in proper uniforms,' Walsh reported.

The Chilkoot, which leaps the mountain barrier by way of a thousand-foot climb up a thirty-five-degree slope, was too steep for pack animals to navigate. The White Pass, named after a former Canadian Minister of the Interior Sir Thomas White, was theoretically open for animals all the way to Lake Bennett, but was in fact a strength-sapping series of obstacles – swamps, precipitous hills and narrow, boulder-strewn trails. Though the photographs and films of the ant-like line of laden men inching their way step by step over the Chilkoot remain the instantly recognisable symbol of the Klondike stampede, most people chose to go into the Yukon by the White Pass, precipitating a wanton slaughter of the animals they had imported to carry their possessions – most of them utterly useless. One man, who said he was going to the Yukon 'just for a jolly good time', took with him thirty-two pairs of moccasins, a case of pipes, a case of shoes, two Irish setters, a bull pup and a lawn-tennis set.

One of the men who struggled over the White Pass in the autumn of 1897 recalled:

I saw a horse that had fallen and broken its leg a few minutes

318

before in a place where the trail passed between two large boulders. His pack had been removed and someone had mercifully knocked him on the head with an axe, and traffic had been resumed across the body which was still warm when I passed. When I returned that evening there was not a vestige of that horse left, except his head lying on one side of the trail and his tail on the other.

Walsh's description of conditions along the White Pass was equally horrifying:

Such a scene of havoc and destruction as we encountered can scarcely be imagined. Thousands of pack horses lay dead along the way, sometimes in bunches under the cliffs where they had fallen from the rocks above, sometimes in a tangled mass filling the mudholes and furnishing the only footing for our poor pack animals on the march often, I regret to say, exhausted but still alive, a fact that we were unaware of until after the miserable wretches turned beneath the hoofs of our cavalcade. . . . The inhumanity which this trail has been witness to, the heartbreaking which so many have undergone, cannot be imagined.

William Ogilvie thought that the stampeders were 'all mad with a common madness', and Walsh's secretary, Dufferin Pattullo, was one of several people who reported that suffering animals were trying to commit suicide on the White Pass by throwing themselves over cliffs rather than face the trail.

Sifton returned to Canada after his brief tour of the passes, while Walsh prepared to move off again with his full party towards the end of October. At this late stage of the season their attempt to reach Dawson before the Yukon froze over was more foolhardy than optimistic. They crossed the Chilkoot, at times up to their armpits in snow, and pressed downriver in seven open boats. Soon, however, cakes of ice pouring into the Yukon from its tributaries made travelling hazardous, and finally impossible. So Commissioner, judge, crown prosecutor, mining inspectors, Indian guides and police escort were stranded in two hastily assembled log cabins at the Big Salmon River's junction with the Yukon, about halfway between Lake Bennett and Dawson City.

Walsh, who only three months before had been comfortably at home in Brockville, now found himself marooned in a frozen wilderness, literally in the middle of nowhere, kept in sporadic contact with Skagway and the outside world by police messengers.

As Dawson flourished during the spring of 1897 Constantine decided to move the police headquarters from Fortymile and build on the government land he had reserved at the junction of the Klondike and Yukon rivers. First he had to remove a band of Indians who were squatting on the property at the instigation of Bishop Bompas after selling their cabins at exorbitant prices to prospectors. Bompas, an ardent defender of Indians at all times, clashed frequently with the blunt Constantine, who had little time for the local natives ('A lazy, shiftless lot,' he called them). But Constantine promised his superiors, 'When I want the place he and his Indians will go off. . . . I don't propose to be bluffed by an arrogant bishop who thinks the only people worth considering are a few dirty Indians too lazy to work and who prefer starvation.'

Three of the buildings were ferried upriver from Fort Constantine for the new barracks – named Fort Herchmer in honour of the Commissioner – but the other six had to be built from scratch. Because of the phenomenal wages – $15 a day for labourers and $20 for skilled men – the police, who were paid 75 cents a day plus a further ludicrous 50 cents cost-of-living bonus for Yukon service, undertook the construction. They were plagued by a desperate shortage of materials, particularly windows and nails, and hampered by the fact that all the logs and wood had to be moved and shaped by hand. Since most of the horses in the Yukon had been killed for dog food it cost $150 to hire a team of four, and Constantine grumbled, 'Had horses and a saw mill been furnished, the government would have saved a great deal of money.' But the work proceeded steadily. At the end of July he wrote to Herchmer, 'We are pounding away at the post. Hard work but all well and ready for sleep at night.'

31. (*Above*) The famous ascent of the Chilkoot pass, by
prospectors on their way to the Yukon

32. (*Below*) A NWMP detachment on duty at White Pass. Snow
has almost buried the hut immediately behind them

33. (*Above*) Street scene in Dawson City, bocm town of the Yukon gold rush

34. (*Below*) The first twenty men to go to the Yukon, photographed at Fort Constantine in 1895. E. M. Telford, from whose album this picture comes, is seated second from the right, front row. D'Arcy Strickland is in the white shirt, Inspector Constantine is on Strickland's right, with his son, Francis, next to him

By the end of the summer, when Fort Herchmer was ready for occupation, Constantine was reporting a plentiful supply of 'money, whiskey, whores and gamblers' in Dawson. 'I could fill the guard rooms but cannot spare the men or rations,' he wrote. For the increasing threat of starvation hung over them all, police and prospectors alike. The Mounties would arrest no one for a minor misdemeanour unless he had enough food of his own to see him through his prison term. Constantine informed Herchmer:

> The whole country is now covered with men travelling from creek to creek in search of gold. The population has jumped during the past few summer months from a few hundreds to at least 5,000. . . . The majority of the newcomers are from the United States, many of them could well be spared in any community. The rush has brought in toughs, gamblers, fast women and criminals of almost every type . . . a considerable number appear to be the sweepings of the slums and the result of a general jail delivery. Heretofore goods could be cached at the side of the trails and they would be perfectly safe, now a man has to sit on his cache with a shotgun to ensure the safety of his goods. Cabins in out-of-the-way places are broken into and everything cleaned out. In a great many instances the perpetrators have been arrested and in some cases given so long to leave the country. This was absolutely necessary as we could not feed them.

At one stage during the autumn of 1897 the police were reduced to four ounces of bacon and twelve ounces of flour a day each. Further supplies were difficult to obtain from local traders, who were naturally far more interested in selling their goods to miners for three or four times the authorised price. Constantine pressed the government to ship in its own supplies: 'There is grumbling all round,' he wrote. 'The traders because they say they are losing money, the miners because the police seem to get so much, and the police because they do not get more.'

Although they were assured of a steady, if small, ration the police suffered more than most when it came to buying extras and luxuries with their pitiful daily pay of $1.25. Dance-hall girls, who charged a dollar a waltz, were being paid $100 a night, and labourers earned more in a day than the police did in a week. Their daily allowance literally wasn't worth a candle, since these sold for more than a dollar each in Dawson. Eggs cost $1.50 each on the rare occasions they were available, milk was five times the price of whiskey and a good cigar was worth $50 in gold.

The police clothing, particularly footwear, was little better than the pay. The cavalry boots with which the men were issued were totally unsuited to the conditions and wore out quickly, and moccasins and thick socks were in such short supply that the police were forced to buy their own, paying $8 or more for a pair of inferior moccasins from the Indians, whose products were in heavy demand. The fur caps and thick jackets sent from Canada were meant to fit normal-sized men rather than the hand-picked giants the police had shipped to the Yukon. Inspector Strickland reported that the winter clothing was 'much too tight' and that the caps 'will not pull down over our ears'.

The cause of Dawson's food crisis was the influx of newcomers and the fact that supply steamers were stranded by low water at Yukon Flats, about 300 miles downstream. The few which did get through were pirated by hungry miners on the way upstream. When the *Portus B. Weare* steamed into Dawson through thickening ice on 28 September there was little left on board but whiskey and hardware. When, two days later, the *Bella* arrived with a similarly disappointing cargo, notices were posted in Dawson's streets, signed by Constantine, the Collector of Customs D. W. Davis and the newly-arrived Gold Commissioner, Thomas Fawcett, urging all those without sufficient food to make 'an immediate move' out of the country. The notice warned grimly, 'For those who have not laid in a winter's supply to remain here longer is to court death from starvation or at least the certainty of sickness from scurvy and other troubles. Starvation now stares every one in the face who is hoping and waiting for outside relief.'

Soon the very people who had struggled so hard to get to the Klondike before freeze-up were queueing to get out again aboard the last steamers sailing to St Michael. Others made their way out by boat and canoe downriver until the river froze, and then by sled. Constantine estimated that 600 people had fled Dawson after his starvation warning – and he considered the Yukon was well rid of most of them.

The exodus continued in a thin, pathetic straggle all winter, but most of those left behind decided to make the best of it in Dawson. Though the inexperienced newcomers and highly prized sled-dogs went hungry (one man had his lighted candle devoured at a gulp by a ravenous dog) few of the practised prospectors actually starved that winter. When Inspector Frank Harper visited Eldorado and Bonanza creeks he found their inhabitants well provisioned and comfortable. Indeed, he commented on their hospitality, saying that they entertained him 'in a princely manner, making one think that no such thing as starvation could exist in the Yukon'.

Chapter 20

A SHORT WALK TO THE YUKON

CLIFFORD Sifton had returned to Ottawa from his foray into the Yukon convinced that an all-Canadian overland route must be sought to the goldfields to overcome the problem of crossing American territory in Alaska. The most ambitious of these routes was from the village of Edmonton, which then had a population of 700, through the Peace River country and over the continent's spine into the Yukon. Though the distance was 1700 miles, Edmonton advertised itself as 'the back door to the Yukon' and people who should have known better told the public in eastern Canada that the Klondike could be reached in six weeks from Edmonton.

The Edmonton *Bulletin* trumpeted the virtues of the route – 'The money which has already been lost at the White Pass . . . would have established a good horse trail all the way from Edmonton to Dawson, would have opened up our own country and would have immeasurably benefited our home trade' – and an advert in the paper announced cheerfully, 'Off for the Yukon! All smooth sailing when you're supplied with a good and complete medicine chest from Macdonald's. Every gold-hunter should have a few necessary medicines.'

In fact, of the hundreds who stepped out jauntily from Edmonton many died, more turned back bitter and angry, and the few who trickled through to the Yukon found that the gold rush was over by the time they arrived. Of all the routes into the Klondike, this was the most difficult. One man who committed suicide on the trail left a despairing last note: 'Hell can't be worse than this.

I'll chance it.' But one party *did* get through. It was a police patrol led by a Scot, Inspector John Moodie, which set off from Edmonton on 4 September 1897 and arrived ragged, exhausted and half-frozen fourteen months later after the most incredible difficulties and hardships. The march is one of the epic stories of the Mounted Police.

The Edinburgh-born Moodie was just short of his fiftieth birthday when he was detailed by Commissioner Herchmer to take a small group from Edmonton to the Yukon to collect information on the best route for parties of gold seekers. Herchmer told Moodie in what must rank as one of the crassest understatements of all time, 'With fair luck you should be able to get to the Klondyke and back during the winter.' It seems that he too had been reading Edmonton's publicity hand-outs.

Moodie took with him only one policeman, Constable F. J. Fitzgerald, and three 'special constables', Richard Hardisty, son of a Canadian Senator, and two graduates of the Royal Military College, Frank Lafferty and H. S. Tobin, who were engaged for a dollar a day. Also with the group was a half-breed, Baptiste Pepin, in charge of twenty-five pack and six saddle horses, and an Indian guide who, according to Moodie, 'knew nothing of the country and was perfectly useless'.

Moodie's group rode across prairies and through forests, fought their way through bogs and vast areas of burned and fallen timber, plunged into coulees and canyons, and faced – with unwavering determination – floods and fog, ice and slush, heat of 90°F. and cold so intense that it froze the sap in trees until they cracked. They were often waist-deep in snow or knee-deep in mud. They fled from huge bush fires, and suffered dysentery, snow blindness, dog bites and the torments of clouds of mosquitoes and venomous flies as big as bees. On his return to civilisation Moodie reported, in all seriousness, 'We were most fortunate in having good health.' Yet Moodie himself was for a time snow blind, Fitzgerald cut his right hand so badly that he was unable to use it for a month, Tobin severely injured an eye and all went down with dysentery.

Yet no one was frostbitten, though 'wet feet with frozen moccasins and socks, from early morning to night camp, has been the rule and not the exception'.

At first the expedition made deceptively easy progress through the rolling Peace River country and arrived at the Hudson's Bay Company post at Fort St John on 1 November. Here, for reasons which Moodie did not specify, Richard Hardisty was left behind. Moodie set the local Indians to work making sleighs, snow shoes and moccasins and hired an Indian, Dick Eggs, who was reputed to know a way through the mountains to their next stopping-point, Fort Graham. Dick Eggs failed to last a month; on 22 December he announced that he was sick and was going back to Fort St John, provoking from Moodie the outburst, 'The Indians here are useless and quite unreliable but this man was, without exception, the worst I came across.' Four days after Christmas their horses had to be killed for dog meat and when the party arrived at Fort Graham on 18 January – having wandered considerably out of their way since the defection of Eggs – they were entirely out of food, so they spent the rest of the winter there. Moodie left Fort Graham for his next staging-post, Stuart Lake, on 1 April and plunged into an all-but-impassable wilderness. A typical entry from Moodie's meticulously kept diary reported:

27 June, reveille 4 a.m. Baptiste went after one horse which was missing last night and returned with him at 10.30. Sent two men on to cut trail this a.m.; they returned at 10 a.m. Had dinner and left at 1.15 p.m. Morning fine but the flies were very bad. Horses nearly crazy. When half through packing a heavy thunderstorm came on and wet us through in about three minutes. After about two hours of fairly good going we struck a big swamp covered with downed timber lying in every direction and had to bear west, then south-west and finally camped in thick downed burned timber at 5 p.m. about two miles from last night's camp having travelled almost in a circle.

Though he must have realised his mission was hopeless, Moodie made copious notes – as instructed by Herchmer – about which trails needed grading and where bridges were required for a road which would not be built for another fifty years.

Summer passed, the first anniversary of the patrol's departure came and went and winter began to close in again as Moodie's ragged band headed for the Pelly river, hoping to float down towards the Yukon and Dawson. To save time building a boat, Moodie paid $175 for a portable canvas canoe twenty feet long, which he considered 'a fair price'. They launched this frail craft – which they named Dreadnaught – on 4 October into a shallow river thick with floating ice, and by noon they had stopped half a dozen times to patch their torn and overloaded canoe. They also had to disembark frequently and lift the boat over sandbars–'cold work in running ice', Moodie commented. In four days they covered only forty-three miles and were running out of food.

Their luck was in when Moodie persuaded three prospectors to sell him a more solid canoe for $450, 'though the man asked $500 and did not wish to sell even at that,' Moodie wrote. 'Considering the cost and difficulty of taking it there, it was not really so dear as it appears at first; in any case it was a matter of absolute necessity, and without it some of us at any rate would most likely have left our bones up there.'

The party struggled on in their two canoes through a river full of slush ice. Several times they drifted for miles jammed among ice floes and when, on 22 October, they found the Pelly frozen over as far as they could see Moodie decided to cache the canoes and all the heavier equipment and set off on foot for the nearest inhabited point, Fort Selkirk, thirty miles away through snow-storms and heavy bush, carrying only a small amount of food and a blanket each. Moodie took along his precious diary and note-book, still detailing precisely the route they were taking. Two days later they stumbled – weary, starving and in rags — into Fort Selkirk, to the astonishment of the 200-strong garrison of Canadian regular soldiers known as the Yukon Field Force who had been sent north in the wake of the gold rush and had made Fort Selkirk, at the Pelly's junction with the Yukon, their headquarters.

327

Efficient to the last, Moodie supplied the Field Force's commanding officer with a detailed list of the goods he had cached with his canoes, requesting that they be recovered as soon as possible. But when he learned that a steamer from Dawson, the last of the season, was due at Fort Selkirk on its way upstream, the temptation was too great. Moodie sent a note to Dawson to Superintendent Sam Steele, who by this time was in charge of the Mounted Police in the Yukon, reporting his safe arrival and adding, 'As my instructions were to return east without delay and a steamer goes up in the morning I have taken passage on her without reporting to you in person, which I trust will be in order.'

In an understatement which matched that of Herchmer in his original orders, Moodie reported of the trail he had blazed, 'I should say it would never be used in the face of the quick and easy one via Skagway and the White Pass.' Sam Steele added a more forceful amen: 'It seems incomprehensible that sane men will attempt to get into the country that way.' But the experience did no lasting damage to Moodie's health. He lived to be ninety-nine.

Sam Steele, the Force's top 'troubleshooter', was ordered to the Yukon on 29 January 1898. Pausing only long enough to ensure that his family would be provided for in his absence, Steele was on his way to Vancouver within hours. Superintendent Deane, who had been given command of the Macleod district in Steele's place, travelled immediately to the barracks from Lethbridge – and was just in time to catch a glimpse of the energetic Steele disappearing towards the railway station. He left for Skagway on 6 February aboard the tiny steamer *Thistle*, crammed with men bound for the Klondike. Of his eight-day voyage Steele wrote:

> My berth was one of three situated above the screw, in a little cabin which had a strong odour of ancient cheese. The berths were so small that it was with the greatest difficulty that we could remain in them when the boat pitched in the heavy seas which she encountered during the voyage. . . . The food was coarse but well served and, as there were more than 200 to feed

in the little vessel, only 120 feet in length, the tables were crowded all day, only one-sixth of the passengers being seated at one time.

Steele disembarked at Skagway in a roaring gale with the temperature $-30°$F. He found the town roaring, too, and described it as 'a hell upon earth . . . about the roughest place in the world'. It must have been galling to such a rigorous enforcer of the law as Steele to find himself powerless in the middle of a scene of gambling, round-the-clock drinking and general lawlessness. He wrote of Skagway:

> Robbery and murder were daily occurrences; many people came there with money and next morning had not enough to get a meal, having been robbed or cheated out of their last cent. Shots were exchanged on the streets in broad daylight . . . at night the crash of bands, shouts of 'Murder', cries for help mingled with the cracked voices of the singers in the variety halls.

The Mounted Police shack which served as office and living-quarters in Skagway was frequently struck by shots. One Sunday morning Steele and Inspector Zachary Wood were awakened by a gunfight just outside the building and as they lay in bed bullets pierced the thin wooden walls just over their heads. 'But the circumstance was such a common event that we did not even rise from our beds,' recalled Steele.

The chief architect of all this fun and games was a soft-spoken American from Georgia, Jefferson Randolph Smith, better known as 'Soapy' Smith. A masterly confidence trickster, Smith had earned his nickname in the mining camps of America where he sold, for a dollar, cakes of soap which he had – in the eyes of the gullible – previously wrapped in ten- and twenty-dollar bills. On arrival in Skagway in the autumn of 1897, Soapy set up a slick organisation which plucked a fat living from the thousands of bewildered gold-rushers who were dumped ashore in Skagway. Since there was no law enforcement Smith's gang did as they pleased.

Steele's arrival in Skagway coincided with two momentous decisions, one taken by James Walsh from his winter headquarters deep in the interior, and the other from Ottawa. Having witnessed the suffering of the wretched refugees who had fled from starvation in Dawson and had stumbled into his camp at Big Salmon half-dead and badly frostbitten, Walsh decreed that nobody should be allowed to enter the Yukon unless he had enough provisions to sustain himself for a year; he fixed the minimum amount at a ton of supplies. Though this ruling meant heartbreak and backbreak for the thousands who were poised to cross the mountain passes, it was an eminently sensible move.

Ottawa's action was far more important. The exact location of the Alaska–Yukon border had been in daily dispute since the gold rush started, and when the Mounted Police set up a Customs Post at Tagish, sixty miles inland from the Chilkoot summit, the local Americans assumed that Canada had acknowledged United States sovereignty over the mountains and they even elected mayors and justices of the peace for the lake areas of Lindemann and Bennett. But in January 1898 Clifford Sifton ordered the police to set up posts at the mountain summits – an arbitrary action which Sifton later admitted had saved twenty years of negotiations. From Vancouver Superintendent A. Bowen Perry warned the Minister of the Interior, 'You are certain to hear a great deal about it; the Americans in Alaska hold that the boundary is thirty miles from tidal water', but Sifton persisted, and a year later the United States officially recognised Canada's right to establish the border at the peaks of the coastal mountains. In the absence of any other government officials, the overworked police became border guards and Customs officials, setting up their makeshift posts in the very worst weather of the winter.

Command of the White Pass border point was given to Inspector D'Arcy Strickland; and Inspector Robert Belcher, who had just arrived in Skagway with twenty police, was ordered to establish a post on top of the Chilkoot. Strickland and twenty men plodded from their inland quarters at Tagish to the summit of the

330

White Pass in a howling snowstorm on 13 February and pitched their tents on the ice. Since not even gold-crazed people would move in such weather, the immediate problem facing Strickland's squad was one of sheer survival. The nearest timber for fuel was twelve miles away and for ten days, as blizzards raged continuously, teams of police battled through the snow hauling the fuel and building materials. A tiny hut was erected by 27 February and at reveille that day Strickland hoisted the Union Jack. The makeshift White Pass Customs Post was open for business.

Belcher's group set off from Dyea on 9 February, carrying their own lumber. Two days later they had pitched their tents on the ice of Crater Lake near the summit of the Chilkoot and set about clearing a space for a twelve-foot-square building. On 13 February, working by moonlight, the police erected four walls. Next day a tarpaulin was stretched over the frame as a makeshift roof and the border post, such as it was, was ready for occupation. It was grandly styled The Customs House and Quarters for the Officer in Command. In the absence of dry lumber, one-inch planks of green wood had been used, and they shrank so much that fine snow constantly drifted through the cracks, wetting everything inside the building. And at night frost accumulated thickly inside the tarpaulin roof; when a fire was lit in the morning the place was, according to Inspector Belcher, 'like a shower bath until noon'. The corporal who shared the cabin with Belcher slept in wet blankets until the spring. Clothing, bedding and official papers were saturated until Belcher managed to have a wooden roof put on six weeks later.

Because of the hut's limited size, the rest of the Chilkoot detachment stayed in tents on Crater Lake, battered by a hurricane-force wind and driving snow for ten days non-stop. The conditions were appalling. Attempts to fetch firewood from the nearest source of supply seven miles away had to be abandoned because it was dangerous to move more than a few feet away from the tents. Those containing the supplies were blown down and the others were only kept upright by teams of men taking it in turn

331

to cling grimly to the support poles. To make things even more intolerable, the water began to rise on top of the frozen lake; soon the tents were six inches deep in water, blankets and bedding were saturated and the police crouched on sleighs above the water level trying to snatch some sleep. But on 26 February, the first fine day after the storm, the Union Jack was hoisted and Customs collections began.

Strickland soon fell victim to bronchitis and when Inspector F. L. Cartwright arrived in Skagway from Vancouver with another party of reinforcements on 20 March he was ordered to take command of the White Pass post, and Strickland was sent down to the drier and healthier climate of Tagish. Cartwright found the Customs detachment existing in the most miserable circumstances. He reported:

> On several occasions I went into the men's tents and could feel a wet drizzle which drove right through the tent. Now, not one man complained to me, nor do I wish to complain myself except to point out that stricter attention be paid to the selection of tents, especially as to the quality of canvas. It is certainly unreasonable to expect men to do duty in all kinds of weather, then ask them to sleep in blankets which are anything but dry.

The weather continued foul, with snowfalls so heavy that on one occasion eight men had to dig through the night's drifts before Cartwright could get out of the door of his Customs Post in the morning. Belcher's party on the Chilkoot fared no better. Another storm set in on 3 March and continued, with a few intervals of fine days, until the beginning of May. Cabin and tents were completely buried and doorways had to be kept clear, since they were quickly nine feet below snow level. When the snow began to melt in May the cabin rested nine feet above ground, one corner lodged against a rock and the other sides propped up.

Despite the weather, thousands of people crossed the passes that winter – some as many as forty times – freighting their statutory ton of goods into the Yukon on their own backs. With blizzards frequently making the trail impassable, it took some of them three months to haul their supplies over the summits and down to the head of navigation on the other side. Belcher estimated that 25,000 people ('a small percentage being genuine miners') crossed the Chilkoot that winter. Since most of them were Americans who had bought their supplies before leaving home, there was a howl of protest when the police began collecting Customs dues, an average of twenty-five per cent on the cost price of each article, even the canvas bags in which the goods were wrapped. American newspapers headlined such words as 'knavery' and 'extortion' and called for reprisals from Washington when those staggering to the summit of the Chilkoot even found themselves taxed thirty-five per cent on the vests and underpants they were wearing. Angry meetings were held in Alaskan territory, and one American called for a thousand volunteers to eject the Mounties from their posts; there were no takers. The American Press carried a story that a crowd of excited miners had hauled down the Union Jack on the Chilkoot summit. In fact, a drunken man in desperate need of a blanket was responsible for the temporary removal of the police's flag.

In Inspector Belcher's twelve-foot-square cabin much of the space was taken up by two beds, and a rough plank served as a counter for the collection of Customs dues. There was no safe to hold the money and at one stage about $90,000, mostly in gold coin, was stuffed in a kitbag under Belcher's bed. When the posts were withdrawn from the summits into the Yukon Valley and Canadian Customs officials took over at the end of June 1898, Belcher had collected more than $174,000 in four months.

Yet one Customs clerk, John Whiteside, accused the police at both posts of dishonesty, claiming there were irregularities in the entering of collections and that cash entries had been 'smeared with ink or torn out'. Unfortunately, Whiteside hadn't been at the posts during the frenzy of winter work when the police were logging collections on pieces of mouldy scrap paper in dripping huts and tents. The allegations were refuted and the police praised for their efforts in such terrible conditions.

As they funnelled through the White and Chilkoot passes all winter, the thousands of stampeders crowded together to form the world's largest tent-city. Every available piece of flat or sheltered ground was occupied, from the eastern end of the passes to lakes Lindemann and Bennett. The once-silent lakes and their beautiful, wooded shores were rendered hideous by the mass of humanity and ravaged for any timber likely to be useful for boat-building, since anyone who had not assembled some form of water transport by the time the lake ice broke would be left behind in the frantic scramble down to the Klondike.

Sam Steele, who arrived to take command around the lakes at the end of March, described the scene as 'unique, and not likely to be repeated on this earth again'. People swarmed in by the thousand every day, using every imaginable means of transport. Some packed the loads on their backs, others pressed horses, mules, oxen and dogs into service as sleigh animals. Some men even harnessed themselves to the sleds with their animals in the haste to get to the frozen lakeside. Steele saw one woman driving a team of goats hauling the equipment for a laundry which she intended to set up in Dawson.

For five months, from his arrival until he left for Dawson in September, Steele was rarely able to leave his office, which also doubled as sleeping-quarters. His furniture consisted of a trestle bed, a table of rough planks which served as a desk, another table for his assistant Corporal Tennant, a sheet iron stove and a few home-made wooden chairs for visitors. Here, almost around the clock, Steele was besieged by complaints, inquiries and seekers of advice and information:

My work began at 4 or 5 a.m. each day, and at 9 I breakfasted. At 10 I commenced interviews with Klondikers, who came all day and far into the night, asking advice and assistance in connection with every imaginable phase of their lives. . . . Every individual in the Police Force was considered a bureau of information, was questioned about everything and gave general satisfaction. The demeanour of all ranks was so soldier-like and obliging that they became universal favourites, particularly with American citizens.

They sorted out bitter disputes between partners whose friendship had failed to survive the back-breaking work of boat-building, dispensing the sort of Solomon's justice which sometimes saw boats divided in half or frying-pans chopped in two. There were occasional lighter moments, such as the arrival of an American couple who had decided to visit the Yukon for their honeymoon. Their selection of route was no better than their choice of holiday, and they were both soaked when they broke through the ice trying to cross a creek on the White Pass. But an obliging corporal placed his tent and wardrobe at the disposal of the bride, who completed her journey to Lake Bennett wearing a scarlet jacket and police trousers.

Among those waiting to get to Dawson were the managers and staffs of two banks, engaged in a private race to be the first to set up in Dawson. One of the managers asked Steele to look after $2 million in notes. 'I was obliged to stow them under my cot for safety, as there was no better place,' said Steele. Soon afterwards Steele was faced with another money problem – the question of what to do with the $150,000 collected at the White and Chilkoot summits. He decided to send it back to British Columbia in charge of Inspector Zachary Wood, whose report on his mission merely stated, 'I left Bennett, going out by the Chilkoot and Dyea, reached Victoria in due course and handed over the money.'

The reality of the journey was a good deal more exciting. Wood was given an escort as far as the Alaska border, but after that he had only enough men to carry the money, which was stowed in kitbags. The Chilkoot–Dyea route was chosen to avoid the worst elements of Soapy Smith's gang, and word was deliberately spread that Wood was returning with his luggage to duty on the prairies. All went well until Wood's party were crossing the bay between Dyea and Skagway, where the steamer *Tartar* was waiting to carry him to Victoria. A boat manned by a bunch of Soapy's men tried to ram Wood's craft and had to be held off at gunpoint. When Wood got to the dockside more of the gang, led by Smith himself, jostled Wood but found themselves covered by the rifles of the *Tartar*'s crew. The tension was eventually broken by Smith, who strolled over to Wood and with a smile invited him to 'stick around' Skagway for a while. The inspector thanked him for his thoughtfulness, declined politely and boarded the steamer, while Smith returned to easier pickings in his saloons. A month later he was dead, shot in a gunfight by a member of a vigilante group formed by the Skagway citizens to combat Smith's gangsters.

After his enforced winter of isolation at Big Salmon, James Walsh had decided that the job of Yukon Commissioner was not for him. Every message which had reached him from Dawson seemed based on avarice: claims disputes, liquor-permit requests, property squabbles. 'This all needs purging,' he reported to Ottawa, 'and I would like to give it the dose required. But I am not going to remain long enough in the country to do it.' Walsh attempted to resign in March 1898 but Sifton persuaded him to complete a year's service, telling him, 'I would rather lose $20,000 than have you come back without going to Dawson.'

Walsh set off downriver on 3 May but because rotting ice made river navigation difficult it took him eighteen days to get to Dawson. One of his first acts was to enforce the observance of Sunday: 'I found, on the first Sunday after my arrival, that the general weekday business was continued. I deemed it highly improper that the Sabbath should be desecrated and at once gave orders for its due observance.' Walsh also admitted that he had found in Dawson 'a great many questions awaiting solution'. His problems were about to be multiplied a thousandfold.

As May drew to a close, excitement mounted along the shores of Lakes Lindemann and Bennett. Seven thousand boats of every shape were readied for the massive regatta, with the Klondike's riches the expected prize for the swiftest. Steele ordered that every boat be numbered and the names of its occupants recorded by his police, ensuring that every member of that unique, erratic fleet was traceable all the way down to Dawson. Inspector Strickland registered more than 28,000 people and, considering the tough element to be expected among such a throng, he considered the absence of crime 'simply wonderful', reporting, 'No cases of stealing were brought to my notice, and in fact all I had to do was to settle a few petty squabbles, chiefly among partners.'

On 29 May the ice on the headwater lakes creaked, rumbled and broke and the exodus to the Klondike, 500 miles away, was on. Steele stood on the hill behind his police post at Lake Bennett to watch the start: 'At one time I counted over 800 boats under full sail on an eight-mile stretch of water.' Like an anxious mother hen, Steele followed them down through the lakes aboard the newly assembled forty-foot iron steamer *Kilbourne*, which had been freighted in over the mountains. The first checkpoint for the armada was the police post at Lake Tagish. Here every boat was halted for re-registration and examination of Customs clearances. Those who attempted to sail past had a shot put across their bows. Before the Yukon River proper could be reached there loomed ahead the mighty obstacle of Miles Canyon. By the time Steele and his little steamboat had reached the canyon many of the leading craft had attempted to shoot the rapids, with disastrous results. About thirty boats had been smashed to pieces and five men drowned. Steele immediately posted a detachment at the entrance to bar further foolhardiness, called a public meeting and told the mainly American gathering, 'There are many of your countrymen who have said that the Mounted Police make the laws as they go along, and I am going to do so now for your own good.' Steele nominated a number of experienced pilots to guide the boats through the raging water, appointed a group of police under Corporal Dixon to make arrangements for the safe passage of boats and passengers, and ordered that no women or children should be taken in boats which were shooting the rapids. If they

337

were strong enough to get this far they could certainly walk the five miles around the canyon, Steele said. Then he announced $100 fines for flouters of his on-the-spot regulations, turned round and travelled back upstream to Bennett. Of the thousands of boats taken through Miles Canyon afterwards, hardly one was lost. There were several grumbles about having to pay a pilot's fee, however. A man called Frank Dunleavy, who according to Steele was 'a professional agitator from Australia', complained that Corporal Dixon and Constable Fyffe were soliciting piloting commissions for themselves. It was typical of Steele's stern reaction to any complaint about his men that he had Fyffe taken to Dawson under arrest, where the charge against him was dismissed. At the end of the year Steele could report:

> More than 30,000 persons, every one of whom received assis-
> tance and advice, has passed down the Yukon. Over $150,000
> in duty and fees has been collected, more than 30 million
> pounds of solid food, sufficient to feed an army corps for a year,
> has been inspected and checked by us. We had seen that the
> sick were cared for, had buried the dead, administered their
> estates to the satisfaction of their next-of-kin, had brought in
> our own supplies and means of transport, had built our own
> quarters and administered the laws of Canada without one well-
> founded complaint against us.

As the fleet of fortune hunters pursued the ice downriver towards Dawson, massive steps were being taken to tame the main route into the Yukon for the summer wave of Klondikers. In January 1898 work had begun on a steam-powered fourteen-mile aerial tramway to the summit of the Chilkoot and, despite a disastrous avalanche which wiped out sixty-three people crossing the pass on 3 April, the tramway was in operation by spring, dumping nine tons of supplies an hour alongside the police's Customs hut. In May work started on a railway from Skagway to Lake Bennett via the White Pass. Although there was no lack of labourers for the project, there was plenty of difficulty in keeping a steady work force. Men abandoned the job whenever it snowed and stampeded off into the mountains at every rumour of new gold strikes, but the forty-four-mile track was opened a year later.

With the tramway's installation heavier materials were swiftly ferried over the Chilkoot, including the parts for several steamboats designed to operate on the lakes and the Yukon River. The first of these to take to the water were a couple of forty-foot stern-wheel, light-draught iron steamers, the *Goddard* and the *Kilbourne* (in which Sam Steele had followed the Dawson-bound flotilla as far as Miles Canyon at the end of May). Some were named as hastily as they were built: one batch of three boats was christened *Flora*, *Nora* and *Ora*. The *Nora* bustled back and forwards between Lake Bennett and Miles Canyon; *Ora* and *Flora*, which had run the rapids, did the other half of the run from White Horse to Dawson. Inspector Zachary Wood, logging the comings and goings of the steamers at Tagish, reported that hardly a day passed with a boat calling at the police post. 'There is no doubt in my mind that the trip down the lakes and rivers will become a favourite tourist route, for the scenery is grand,' he wrote.

Tourists as yet were few, but the number of inexperienced, gullible gold-seekers showed little sign of easing. Inspector Philip Primrose thought very little of the hordes he watched scrambling to get to Dawson: 'A large number had the idea that gold was to be picked up quite easily, probably on the hills or in the streets and some, I believe, would not have known gold had they seen it.'

Among these raw newcomers were many women, one of them a distinguished foreign correspondent of the London *Times*. Her name was Flora Shaw and she arrived in Skagway on behalf of her newspaper on 12 July 1898. An experienced and adaptable traveller, she set off from Skagway in the early evening and spent the night in the open rather than stay at the only hostelry, since 'there is no distinction of such trivialities as sex, and you may consider yourself lucky if you get a whole bunk to yourself'.

Next day Flora crossed the Chilkoot dressed, in the words of her biographer, 'as always, like an English gentlewoman'. Her hair was neatly coiled, her skirts were of ladylike length and she carried a bee-keeper's net to protect her against mosquitoes and leggings to save her limbs from bruises. Flora spent two wet, miserable days in her tent at Lake Bennett waiting for a boat down to Dawson, 'writing letters for *The Times* sitting on my bedding with rain dripping on my shoulders'.

Having been introduced to Sam Steele she had the further advantage, though she was unaware of it, of his instruction that she should be afforded police assistance at all times. So blithely she praised 'the good, orderly North West Mounted Police, near whose headquarters I intend always to pitch my tent', and at one stop on the way downriver Flora wrote, 'The nice, comfortable police are engaged in putting up my tent for me.'

Chapter 21

'THE PRIDE OF CANADA'

As the Yukon ice heaved and rumbled beneath an uncommonly warm spring sun, Dawson waited anxiously for supplies, news and newcomers from the outside. Word had filtered through from the occasional trapper or Mounted Policeman returning from Lake Bennett of the horde of stampeders poised to float down the Yukon, but before the tide of humanity hit the town Dawson underwent a more straightforward flood. On 8 May the river ice shattered, giant ice-cakes were hurled up on to the banks – and the citizens suddenly realised that the town's site was a flood hazard. (Dr J. W. Good, who became health officer of Dawson, described the place when he arrived at the end of 1897 as 'one vast swamp which was usually navigable in the early spring'.)

For the rest of the month the riverside section of Dawson lay under water, sometimes to a depth of five feet. Even the Mounted Police barracks did not escape. Two feet of water lapped around the orderly room, hospital, sergeants' quarters and store, and provisions had to be stacked on the roofs for safety. Inspector Frank Harper was forced to take to a canoe every time he wanted to enter or leave his quarters. Gradually the waters subsided, leaving a morass of mud. Before Dawson's population could begin to clear up they were swamped by the human tidal wave released from the bottleneck of Miles Canyon. Boats by the hundred swept onto Dawson's muddy waterfront, and their occupants squelched ashore carrying their goods, their news and their hopes

341

of making a fortune. Soon after, the first steamboats chugged in, tied up and discharged whiskey, wine, food and girls. By the end of August fifty-six steamboats had delivered their supplies. Never again would Dawson be short of food, liquor or diversions.

The newcomers' tents sprouted among the muck and filth of the recent flood. The canvas cities of Bennett, Lindemann and Tagish were re-erected in and around Dawson and the Klondike gold-fields, and the scenes of frenzied construction witnessed at the lakes the previous winter were enacted afresh. By the end of June Dawson had six churches (Roman Catholic, Church of England, Methodist, Presbyterian, Salvation Army and Greek Orthodox), two newspapers, two banks and saloons and bars by the score. It also had the biggest population west of Winnipeg. Between May and July it boomed from 5000 to 16,000.

Conditions were primitive in the extreme. Rubbish and filth of all kinds lay around, and the crude hospitals overflowed with typhoid and scurvy victims. The indefatigable Flora Shaw arrived late in July and found 'all the refuse of the town flung out of doors, no order of a sanitary kind, and the so-called main street, along which wooden warehouses and hotels are rapidly going up in a continuous row, a mere lane of mud holes and dust heaps'.

But Flora was undaunted. In pioneer fashion she pitched her tent on a hillside behind the town, near a spring of clear water. Seeking the equivalent of an English charwoman she found instead 'a handyman, a sort of knight errant' at a salary of four dollars a day. The money was well invested:

He brings all the resources of his knowledge to bear on my comfort. My tent is stretched as it has never been before, my bed arranged on a heap of brushwood, as springy as a good spring mattress. The floor of the tent, covered with fresh spruce boughs, smells delicious as I step on it. A little table and stool have been rigged up for me and a kitchen established outside, in which hot water is provided every morning for my bath.

Flora, who was also delighted with the variety of pies, curries, hashes and stews which this northern Jeeves managed to conjure out of bacon and tins of corned beef, might have been picnicking at Epsom or Windsor. Certainly, she was just as safe. An Englishman, Robert Kirk, wrote after visiting the Yukon, 'A man is infinitely safer walking at midnight along the streets of Dawson than he is on Victoria Embankment, London, or Broadway, New York.'

The police permitted no one to carry a firearm without a licence. Confiscated revolvers were auctioned for a dollar each as sideboard souvenirs, and rifles – selling by the gross – fetched the same price. Even the newly established, American-owned newspaper, the *Klondyke Nugget*, which wasn't renowned for friendliness towards the Canadian government or its local administrators of justice, commented on the 'astonishing state of order'.

Though the vast majority of offences were trivial – cutting wood without a permit, selling liquor out of hours, selling bad food, cruelty to animals – the police had to deal with occasional crimes of violence. In September 1897 a prospector named Edward Henderson had an argument with his partner Thomburg Petersen in their camp, clubbed him over the head with a revolver and then shot him. People nearby heard the firing, and police were called in so quickly that they were able to get a statement from Petersen before he died.

On 10 May 1898, another prospector, Charles Fox, staggered into a cabin near Tagish with a bullet hole through his body. He and his companion, William Meehan, had been fired on in their small boat by a group of Indians. Meehan fell dead into the water but Fox lay in the bottom of the boat until it had drifted out of sight of the Indians. Two days later a police party led by Corporal Herbert Rudd, an Irish vicar's son from County Meath, arrested an Indian called Jim, and within a fortnight three more – Joe, Dawson and Frank Nantuck – were brought in.

Henderson and the four Indians were sent to Dawson. Frank Nantuck, 'a mere lad', got life imprisonment but the others were sentenced to hang on 1 November by Mr Justice Dugas, who had arrived in the Yukon during the summer as replacement for the original appointee, Judge McGuire, who had never got over the stress of spending the previous winter frozen in at Big Salmon with Walsh, and had left as soon as he could get away.

Eight hours before they were due to be carried out, the executions were deferred since 1 November, All Saints Day, was a public holiday and apparently it was considered un-Christian to hang men on a holiday. This decision came as an acute embarrassment to an over-enterprising journalist, Faith Fenton of the Toronto *Globe*, who had penned a vivid 'eye-witness account' of the executions and had rushed it off to the outside world the previous day by the mail sleigh. When she heard of the stay of execution, Miss Fenton went in tears to see Sam Steele, imploring him to help. The gallant Steele saved the woman's job by sending a police dog-team after the mail and retrieving the article 'for future use, much to the relief of the distraught damsel'.

There were further petitions from the condemned men's counsel, and it was not until 4 August the following year that Henderson (who suffered from Bright's disease and was described as 'a quiet sort of chap, always cheerful') and the Indian Jim were hanged. The other two, Joe and Dawson, cheated the scaffold by dying in prison hospital from chest infections.

If there was a lack of serious crime in the Yukon in the summer of 1898 there was no lack of anger among the Klondike's population, particularly the miners. The imposition of a ten-per-cent royalty on all gold dug out of the Yukon led to a string of bitter protest meetings, and the fury of the prospectors – most of whom were Americans – at having to pay this tax was hardly soothed when Walsh announced that he would take back to Canada with him 'more gold and material to make wealth than Caesar brought to Rome on his return from Gaul'.

And in the Dawson claims office run by Gold Commissioner Thomas Fawcett, under-organisation and overwork led to heated accusations of graft. When Fawcett had arrived in Dawson in

June 1897 he found fewer than 800 claims on record. Fifteen months later there were more than 17,000, and many of these had been transferred up to forty times. The recording office ran so short of paper that some transactions were written on pieces of wood. People queued as long as three days to get into the claims office (though there were stories of the existence of a 'five-dollar door' at the side of the building which granted swift admission), and since women were allowed to the front of the line prostitutes and dance-hall girls were hired to register claims.

Poor Fawcett was hounded whenever he appeared on the streets, his only relief coming on Sundays when he led the choir of the Dawson Presbyterian church, and he was forced out of the Yukon towards the end of the year by the sheer volume of complaints about his office, which were widely publicised in American and Canadian newspapers.

James Walsh spent only two months in Dawson before his one-year appointment as Commissioner of the Yukon expired, and he left having done practically nothing to sort out the terrible mess in Dawson, though on his return to eastern Canada he vigorously refuted the stories of corruption and graft as 'utterly false', and reported to Clifford Sifton:

> During my stay in Dawson City I several times requested the public to send in any charges which they had against any of the officials in the employ of the government, and I also had the request made from the platform at a mass meeting but not one single charge was presented. . . . Officials of any government entering into a new and isolated district where the people are not closely restricted by law and are free of taxation have almost invariably met with just such an experience as we have had. The introduction and enforcement of law and taxation naturally made us unpopular. Added to this, some 20,000 people of all nationalities had flocked into the district in a few weeks. They did not find things as they were in their own country and, as might be expected, in a few weeks everyone was dissatisfied with everything around him.

Sifton attempted to defend his choice of Walsh. 'I thought Major

Walsh was the best man for the position ... and I have not changed my mind,' he said. 'In a district overrun with all classes of people it was almost impossible to maintain order and the very name of Walsh was as good as a thousand men in maintaining order.' But in the end Walsh paid heavily for his temerity in undertaking such a vast task, returning to private life with a tarnished reputation.

Walsh's successor was the fifty-two-year-old William Ogilvie, who had already spent more than twenty years in survey and exploratory work in the area and who, according to Sam Steele, was 'a delightful companion and a perfect mimic'. Ogilvie certainly needed his sense of humour when he got to Dawson:

> Immediately after my arrival I was beset by a great multitude, each individual of whom expected that he or she was going to secure everything that was just and right – and of course their own views were just and right. For weeks after my arrival, not one moment of the long day – generally from eight in the morning till well towards midnight – was I at peace. Someone was complaining to me or arguing with me about their rights or their claims or whatever their grievances or expectations were. It appears it was thought that I was armed with exceptional powers, such as only the most absolute autocrat on the face of the earth could have; it was expected I would reverse decisions without hearing anything but a simple statement made by one party, and because I could not do this great disappointment was expressed.

The thorough Ogilvie investigated every statement and complaint made to him about government corruption, eventually dismissing them as hearsay and rumours at the official inquiry in Dawson in May 1899. Of these rumours he said:

> It has not been necessary [in Dawson] to do more than insinuate that some official or officials have been guilty of corrupt acts to have it within a few hours generally so reported and, I regret to say, generally so believed, notwithstanding that there may not be a tittle of evidence in support of the charge. Transactions that have been actuated by the purest and highest motives have been attributed to the very worst. Of this I have personal

knowledge and experience. In concluding, I may say that with such a class there cannot exist, in their minds at least, any honest government at all.

On 24 June 1898, Charles Constantine, by now promoted to superintendent, left the Yukon after an exhausting four-year tour of duty. His departure was recorded by the Dawson correspondent of the Toronto *Star*, which headlined the story

YUKON PIONEER
CAPTAIN CONSTANTINE'S WORK
He It Was Who Secured Respect
For the Flag Among
the Lawless.

The article commented that 'the whole community bade him and his good wife a sorrowful goodbye, and it is safe to say that no man or woman ever left behind them more sincere friends and kindly well-wishers than they did'. As a farewell present the Constantines were handed a silver plate piled with $4000 worth of nuggets, which were eventually made up in their natural form into a loving-cup. It was the only gold Constantine took out of the Yukon. Though it was a sentimental occasion, Constantine's diary for that day leaves no doubt about his feelings. 'Thank God for the release,' he wrote.

At the beginning of September Constantine's job was taken over by Sam Steele, who had been appointed Officer Commanding the Mounted Police and a member of the territorial council when the Yukon was separated from the North West Territories and created a Territory in June 1898. Steele set about reorganising and improving in his usual brisk manner. Inspector Frank Harper was sent upstream by steamer with a party of police to establish a string of posts between Dawson and the Alaska ports. Then, with only fifty-one hopelessly overworked men of all ranks at his disposal, he obtained William Ogilvie's authority to 'borrow' three officers and fifty men from the Yukon Field Force, the

347

battalion of the Canadian Army quartered about 150 miles upstream from Dawson at Fort Selkirk.

With his force now doubled to the size of a full police division, Steele abandoned the police guard-room at Fort Constantine in Fortymile and began to build extra prison accommodation in Dawson, reasoning that it was just as easy to look after fifty prisoners as twenty-five in a place where there was nowhere to escape, and that prisoners were invaluable when it came to chopping wood and shovelling snow. 'At the present rate of wages these men are worth at least $5 a day each to the government,' he reported. Police and government officials in Dawson alone burned enough wood annually to make a pile two miles long and four feet square. 'Fires had to be kept up all night, except in my quarters', said Steele, 'and the absence of it was for self-preservation for, had my stove caught fire, I should not have been able to escape, as it was between me and the door. I preferred to have the water bucket frozen to the bottom every night. This was a regular occurrence, although my fire did not go out until about 3 a.m. and was replenished and lighted at six.'

When funds ran out for the administration of the hospitals, crowded with typhoid and scurvy victims (there were eighty-four deaths from typhoid in Dawson in 1898) Steele, who was chairman of the local board of health among his myriad other tasks, increased the severity of fines on offenders and also levied a heavy licence fee on dance halls and saloons. During the winter of 1898–9 more than $90,000 was collected from these two sources to pay for the maintenance of the Yukon hospitals. When one gambler, fined $50 by Steele, said contemptuously, 'Fifty dollars – is that all? I've got that in my vest pocket,' Steele added, 'And sixty days on the woodpile. Have you got that in your vest pocket?'

Steele's attitude of firm benevolence worked wonders. He issued liquor licences in what he termed 'numbers sufficient to meet the needs of the population with the result that "dives" and low drinking dens are a thing of the past'. Gambling-houses were left as he found them – wide open but closely watched: he realised that the life of Dawson City would be brief indeed and its like would never be seen again. He soon stamped out what he termed 'contempt for the authorities' and by the end of the year had these remarkable words to say about what should have been the wildest town in North America:

> Any person, man, woman or child, can go about from one end the place to the other at any hour of the day or night, without being in the slightest danger of insult, interruption or interference. . . . No drunken men are to be seen on the streets, no riot or noise can be heard at any time, in fact the place is all that can be desired; this is remarkable when one considers the fact that there are hundreds of people who have led wicked lives elsewhere . . . but no one could form any idea that they were other than law-abiding, respectable citizens.

By his own reckoning, Steele averaged no more than three hours of sleep a night. He rose every morning at six, left his quarters at seven for a five-mile walk up the Klondike River and back over the hills which stood behind Dawson. During the day he visited every institution for which he had responsibility, saw every police prisoner, sat on various boards and committees, and got to the town police station about midnight 'to see how things were going'. Every night after midnight his quarters were packed with people who had called in to see him 'until about 2 a.m. when they usually retired to rest, and in winter I was in my sleeping bag by 3 a.m.'

Yukon service was equally demanding of the constables under Steele. One of the most onerous duties was the carrying and sorting of mail which, like many other jobs for which they were untrained and unprepared, was cheerfully wished on them because they were the only representatives of government in the country. The carrying of letters was handled exclusively by police until July 1898, when a civil contract was drawn up for the service, but the police still found themselves acting as postmen for some time afterwards. The first heavy mail-consignment since the last of the steamers had gone downriver left Dawson by dog sleigh on 15 November 1897, bound for Skagway. It contained important government and police reports, documents and returns, and the two men in charge, Corporal Richardson and Constable Bell, had travelled 190 miles upstream when the river ice, although a foot thick, broke beneath their sleigh. The two policemen were swept downstream but saved themselves by hanging onto the low branch of a tree, though the mail was a total loss.

Soon a regular trail was blazed with frequent stopping-points for changes of dog teams, but because of the severe winter weather a mountain of Dawson-bound letters piled up at Big Salmon where James Walsh was stranded. Eventually Constable W. R. Newman set out on Christmas Eve 1897 in charge of ten dog teams, each loaded with 100 lb of mail. He and his companions, who included Mr Justice McGuire and Prosecuting Attorney F. C. Wade of Walsh's government party, carried into Dawson the first delivery to reach the town for seven months. Constable Newman recalled:

> Our arrival was greeted with wild enthusiasm. Before we reached the town a fresh dog team belonging to a miner passed us and spread the news that mail was coming in from the outside, and upon our entry into Dawson about two o'clock in the afternoon the well-beaten trail was lined on both sides for a distance of perhaps half a mile by the excited population and many a cheer and encouraging word was given as our party passed.

On his return trip to Skagway Newman was given a nugget, worth about $12, by a man in Dawson for promising to post a letter to his mother.

Dawson's first (unpaid) postmaster was Inspector Frank Harper, who had been sworn in for the job before leaving Victoria in August 1897 on his way to the Yukon. On arrival in Dawson, Harper found mail being distributed from a tent, but with the arrival of winter the post office was moved to a ten-foot-square lean-to alongside the guard-room at Fort Herchmer. When Newman mushed into Dawson with his 1000 lb of mail this office was swamped and Harper managed to obtain the loan of a temporarily disused saloon, the Palace. Huge queues formed outside as half a dozen policemen battled to sort the huge delivery, while civilian employees held back the crush from the doors.

The sorting system was primitive and totally unsatisfactory. There was only one pigeon hole for each letter of the alphabet, and some of them contained more than a thousand pieces of mail. People were admitted in groups of thirty at a time and some men, desperate for news from home, stood in line for three days before they could get into the post office. Abuses of this makeshift system were inevitable. Women were admitted by a side door without having to queue and prostitutes quickly discovered they could make good money collecting letters for prospectors who couldn't spare the time to leave their claims. The Yukon Commissioner, William Ogilvie, estimated that the post office entailed as much work as in a city of 150,000 since there was no delivery system. Inevitably, in a gossip-ridden community like Dawson, allegations of bribery were levelled against the harassed policemen-cum-postmen as the town's population mushroomed and thousands of bags of mail arrived in the summer of 1898.

One Ontario man wrote to his home-town newspaper, the Kingston *Star*, 'There was a side door through which you might enter the office. If you went in at that door the officers expected a tip, and they generally got it. [About a dozen of us] wanted our mail and were tired of waiting for it. We clubbed together, chipping in 50 cents apiece, and gave it to a Mounted Policeman and then got our mail.'

The chaotic condition of the post office was one of Sam Steele's priorities when he reached Dawson in September 1898. He investigated the complaints and reported that, though no money had been taken by policemen between the regular post-office hours of 8 a.m. to 5 p.m., some constables had accepted money to sort letters after hours. 'I removed all the police from the office and sent them to duty, and gave orders that on no account was any money to be taken at any time.' The police were delighted to be rid of the chore. Constable E. Harris, who worked in the post office for three months, called the work 'the most disagreeable it has ever been my duty to perform'.

An indigent Church of England clergyman, Frederick Goodman, who worked in the post office (and was himself accused of taking bribes) said of the police with whom he worked, 'I have never seen anything that would leave even a trace of suspicion in my mind of their dishonesty or corruption . . . they were unapproachable.'

Inspector D'Arcy Strickland received a salary of $20 a year – plus the grand title of Postmaster of Tagish – in exchange for handling a volume of mail which he termed 'simply astonishing'. Strickland reported in 1898, 'Nearly every one of the 28,000 people who passed here mailed letters.' At some of the smaller posts constables who undertook the postmaster's job were paid the absurd sum of three cents a day. The following year Postmaster Strickland got a 400-per-cent pay increase, to $100 a year, but his commanding officer, Superintendent Zachary Wood, felt this was still low because of the amount of work involved.

With nothing more rewarding than pride in their job at stake, the police started a competition among themselves to see who could break the 600-mile Dawson–Skagway mail-run record. The best time was ten days in January 1899. 'I cannot speak too highly of the interest taken by all ranks in the attempt to break the record,' said Superintendent Wood. 'N.C.O.s and men travelled day and night to accomplish it.' In 1899 the police covered more than 64,000 miles carrying the mails.

As on the prairies, the Mounties found that their efforts to help the public were not always received with gratitude. Destitute, ill and frostbitten people were carried to police posts (sometimes on the backs of constables) and cared for, causing a rumour to spread – as only rumours *could* spread in the Yukon – that anyone travelling into or out of the territory over the ice in winter would be furnished with free meals, accommodation, blankets and fresh dog-teams at police detachments *en route*. The story even appeared in Canadian and American newspapers, and at the end of 1898 Superintendent Wood reported to Ottawa, 'Many persons arriving in Skagway from the interior boasted that they had lived on the police on the way out, though they had lots of money.' As more roadhouses and stopping-places were built along the Dawson trail, Wood instructed his men, 'No provisions are to be given away unless a man is absolutely destitute or in such health that he cannot work. As long as he can perform any manual labour he must do enough work to earn his meals.' He gave an example of how five men had arrived at Tagish from Dawson, walked into the orderly room and demanded food, saying they had been told the police would provide anything they required.

> I told them to go to the stopping place and they said they had no money. Taking them to the woodpile, I told them that they could get food here for nothing. They could have an hour's work after dinner sawing wood. Not a bit of it, however. They were not going to work and demanded food. . . . They were so insolent that I ordered them out of the barracks. They went back to the stopping place, where they produced money and not only paid for their meal but expended $48 before they left.

There was an embarrassing mistake when A. M. Morrison, an M.P. from British Columbia, was refused shelter at the police post at Selwyn River by Constable John Connors. Morrison said he had a letter from Superintendent Steele authorising him to stay at police detachments, but when he could not produce it Connors directed him to a nearby roadhouse. The next morning, flourishing his letter from Steele, Morrison threatened he would report Connors and told him, 'I am a taxpayer of this country and help to support you lazy fellows loafing around.' In view of his importance, Morrison received an apology to which he certainly didn't seem entitled. Comptroller Frederick White wrote to him soothingly, 'As a rule the police have done their best to help travellers but unfortunately all men are not cast in the mould of civility and courtesy.' Not even Morrison, he might have added.

Those 'lazy fellows loafing around' were hardly a crippling burden on the Canadian taxpayer, however. Many constables had all their regular pay sent direct to their dependents, and had to exist on their fifty cents a day Yukon allowance. Even so there was a flood of letters from hard-up wives waiting for the cash to come through. Typical was the plea of Mrs Walter McDonald, who wrote to Frederick White from Picton, Ontario in July 1898, 'My husband said I would get 15 dollars every month. Please send it at once as I am so much in need of it. I am nearly helpless and my poor children are in want of wearing material. . . . How I wish my husband could come home, but I suppose I'll have to bear it. Please grant me this favour at once.'

Bank clerks in Dawson were allocated $800 a year, plus board and clothing, and even labourers continued to earn more in a day than the police collected in a week. Their poverty was so well recognised that it was customary to send them complimentary tickets for shows. Officers were little better off, despite their extra Yukon allowance of $1.25 daily. As D'Arcy Strickland pointed out from Tagish, 'An officer has, in this district where there are no hotels, to do a great deal of entertaining and not only to his friends but to a large number of people who arrive, as they did last summer, armed with letters of introduction from their influential friends in the east . . . a government official was quartered on me last July for nearly two weeks.' When they bought extra food to entertain these uninvited guests the cost was ruinous. Superintendent Wood and two other police officers ordered three 50 lb sacks of potatoes, which arrived with a bill for $45.

Astonishingly, there are no recorded cases of Mounted Police dishonesty during the Klondike rush, and one rich prospector named Pat Galvin gave every police officer a beautiful nugget in appreciation of their hard work. His high opinion of the police was shared by William Ogilvie: 'The police force has a large field to fill, numerous duties to perform and vast interests to protect, and when I say that the field is filled, the duties performed and these interests protected in the highest possible manner and with the greatest efficiency, I am simply stating what everyone in this territory knows.'

In September 1899 Sam Steele, whose reputation in the Yukon was 'as wide as the continent of America' according to Ogilvie, was ordered back to the North West Territories and replaced by Superintendent A. Bowen Perry as commanding officer in the north. A group of Dawson's leading citizens pleaded with Steele to stay on but he told them he had no intention of remaining in the Yukon any longer than he was forced. 'My time, almost two years, was the most trying that has ever fallen to the lot of a member of the NWMP,' he wrote. And he could be permitted the modest boast that 'at no time in its history did the police show to better advantage than during the trying years of 1898–9 when I commanded its fine officers and men on the Yukon'.

When Steele boarded his steamer at Dawson on 26 September, the farewell address was in the hands of a wealthy ex-miner, Big Alex McDonald, known as King of the Klondike, whose riches far outstripped his speechmaking abilities. With the whole town looking on eagerly, McDonald thrust a bag of gold dust into Steele's hands with the words, 'Here Sam – here y'are. Poke for you. Goodbye.' Steele recalled: 'I was suprised to find that many thousands of people had assembled from the creeks and every part of Dawson to give me a parting cheer. Every wharf, steamboat and point of vantage was packed with people. . . . When the boat threw off her lines and started up the river, steamers whistled, and the people cheered and waved hats and handkerchiefs until we passed out of sight.'

In the year he had been in command at Dawson, Steele and the other members of the Yukon Council had wrought a miraculous change in living conditions. Perry admitted, after arriving to take command, 'I was astonished to find so many substantial buildings and enormous warehouses. Some of the shops would be a credit to any city and the articles exposed for sale are of the costliest and handsomest description.' Pavements had been laid, streets graded and provided with drains, water piped in, electric lighting introduced and a telephone system installed. The Health Officer Dr J. W. Good was able to describe health conditions in Dawson as 'about as favourable as those to be found in any part of Canada'. Yet only a year earlier he had written that Dawson was 'practically one vast swamp, with cesspools and filth of all kinds'.

The police also enjoyed a sharp increase in their standard of living. Under Superintendent Perry the Yukon command was split into two divisions, H at Tagish (Superintendent Wood) and B at Dawson (Superintendent Primrose). In addition to the two headquarters posts, there were thirty detachments and a total police strength in the Yukon of 258, more than a third of all the Mounted Police. At Dawson part of the old barracks was torn down and new buildings erected, and canteens were established at both headquarters posts, selling 'luxury' items such as canned food at low prices. According to Wood, the Tagish barracks was 'beautifully situated on the slope of a hill, surrounded by fine pine trees. . . . In front run the pure waters, cool and clear as crystal, of the Tagish River.' The substantial buildings were warm and comfortable, and soon a flourishing vegetable garden was provid-ing the garrison with a summer crop of cabbages, radishes, lettuce, onions, carrots and potatoes. But when the White Pass Railway from Skagway was extended for a distance of 110 miles to White Horse Rapids H Division had to leave their snug set-up at Tagish and live in tents until they had built a new barracks at the railway terminus (now the capital of the Yukon, Whitehorse).

Though mining was still being carried on vigorously in the last years of the nineteenth century (ten per cent royalty was collected on more than $8 million worth of gold mined from the Klondike creeks), the introduction of sophisticated transportation facilities coincided with the decline of Dawson and the gold rush. In 1900 there were twenty steamboats plying the Yukon between Dawson and White Horse Rapids to connect with the railway which ran two trains daily in each direction. They took into Dawson 4064 people but brought out 5465. And the thirty-two steamers running downriver from Dawson to St Michael also took out more passengers than they brought in. Gradually, Dawson began to sub-side into a ghost town in the early 1900s as the creeks became played out and the miners drifted away.

But the old century went out in spectacular style with a triple murder case. And the way it was eventually solved typified the dedication which the North West Mounted Police had brought to their thankless job in the first twenty-five years of their existence.

Corporal Paddy Ryan, in charge of the police detachment at Hootchiku, south of Dawson on the river trail, was expecting as his Christmas Day dinner guest Lawrence Olsen, a Norwegian repairman for the government telegraph line. When Olsen had still not turned up two days later Ryan set off to look for him. At a nearby roadhouse he was told that Olsen had left there at eight on Christmas morning, bound for his dinner appointment, and accompanied by two Americans, Fred Clayson and Linn Relfe. Clayson, a prosperous Skagway merchant, had been to the Klon-dike to buy gold and Relfe, who had worked as a barman in a Dawson saloon, was on his way back to the United States to visit his family, carrying more than a thousand dollars in cash.

Checking the trail between the roadhouse and the Hootchiku police post, Ryan found a crude camping spot among the trees – a square of logs roofed over with canvas. Inside were a pair of linesmen's pliers, a rifle, a stove, some blankets and several tins of food which had been stolen from a food cache. Since a con-stable from the Fort Selkirk detachment, Alex Pennycuick, was working on the food theft, Ryan called him in. Pennycuick, thirty-two years old and a former British army officer, had been born in India and lived for some time in Brighton before moving to Canada and joining the Mounted Police.

Pennycuick identified the stove as the property of two English-men calling themselves Miller and Ross, whom he suspected of stealing and selling food. A description of the two men was wired to Tagish, the last police checkpoint before the Alaskan border, and two days later a man named George O'Brien, who had served a prison term in Dawson and answered one of the descriptions, was detained there. A police investigation team commanded by Inspector William Scarth set out to retrace O'Brien's movements since he and his companion, 'Little Tommy' Graves, had been released from Dawson jail a month previously. In February Scotland Yard wired the information that Graves had once been employed by the Chinese government to shoot army deserters and O'Brien had spent six years in Dartmoor for shooting a policeman who caught him robbing a shop.

Circumstantial evidence pointed to O'Brien's implication in the disappearance of Olsen, Clayson, Relfe – and of his partner, Graves. The industrious and patient Pennycuick, joined by an American private investigator named Philip McGuire, who had been hired by Clayson's brother, began systematically to search a stretch of wilderness sixteen miles long and two and a half miles wide in the depths of an Arctic winter for clues to the whereabouts of the missing men.

Eventually they discovered a spot where a clump of trees had been chopped down with a dull and nicked axe to give a better view of the junction of the Yukon River trail with what was known as the Pork Trail, the main supply route from Alaska to Dawson City. Their next clue was a lucky one. When a husky dog baulked at a shallow depression in the snow, Pennycuick and McGuire uncovered a patch of frozen blood. A yellow St Bernard which belonged to O'Brien was brought to the area and turned loose. It made straight for the canvas-covered log-shelter which Corporal Ryan had found.

Over the next six weeks, working in intense cold, the two men conducted one of the most thorough inch-by-inch searches in the history of crime detection. They dug and sifted three feet of snow from half an acre of forest and, in the words of one writer, 'rolled the winter back three months to Christmas'. They found three bullet-scarred trees, a piece of tooth embedded in a bullet, a slice of human skull, six cartridge cases and more patches of frozen blood. Near the canvas shelter they uncovered the axe with the nicked blade which had been used to chop down the trees, and in the ashes of the camp fire were some moccasin eyelets and charred fragments of clothing. When the Yukon River melted, it delivered up its grim hoard. The bodies of Olsen, Clayson and Relfe were recovered from a sandbar. All had been shot. Relfe's jawbone had a stump which fitted exactly the piece of tooth found embedded in a bullet. Later the body of Graves was recovered from the river, too.

Now the Mounties were able to piece together their case against O'Brien. He and Graves had laid an ambush at the fork of the two trails leading to Dawson. Olsen and his companions were their Christmas Day victims, held up and then gunned down as, suspecting they were about to be murdered, they made a break for it. The three bodies were pushed through a hole in the river ice, and – with O'Brien determined to leave no witnesses – Graves followed them soon after.

The robbery scheme had been concocted by O'Brien while in Dawson jail. Though Graves had agreed to join him, two others had turned down O'Brien's offer of a partnership. One, an American card sharp named George 'Kid' West, was located in Washington State Pentitentiary and escorted manacled from the United States to testify against O'Brien in Dawson. He was the most important of the eighty witnesses assembled by the Mounted Police for the biggest and most expensive murder-trial in the Yukon's history.

After eleven days of evidence and argument in court, the jury needed only two hours to find O'Brien guilty. Under sentence of death O'Brien first feigned insanity, pretending he was the Virgin Mary. Next he tried to commit suicide. Although a Catholic, he refused to see a priest or seek confession. He was hanged on 23 August 1901, cursing Constable Alex Pennycuick, the Sherlock Holmes of the North West Mounted Police.

The case drew warm tributes and praise for the police from Parliament, the Press and the trial judge, who in his summing-up called the Mounties 'the pride of Canada and the envy of the world'.

Chapter 22

HERCHMER'S FALL

WHEN the Boer War broke out in 1899 immediate plans were made for a contingent of Canadian volunteers to sail to South Africa and fight for the Queen. Lawrence Herchmer, celebrating his fourteenth year as Commissioner, was given permission to lead a police group, and when the specially formed 2nd Canadian Mounted Rifles left Halifax, Nova Scotia, for Cape Town in January 1900 it contained Herchmer, ten of his officers and 134 men of the Mounted Police. Among them were Superintendent Joseph Howe, Inspector John Moodie, of Yukon fame, Inspector Gilbert Sanders, Inspector Ross Cuthbert and that remarkable veteran Inspector John Allan, now sixty-two and fully recovered from the severe arm-wound inflicted by Almighty Voice.

The police also contributed seven officers and twenty-six men to a mounted corps known as Lord Strathcona's Horse, which left for South Africa two months later. In command of the corps was Sam Steele, with the rank of honorary lieutenant-colonel. With him were several officers who had served under him in the Yukon – Robert Belcher, Frank Harper and F. L. Cartwright.

Competition among the police for a place on the South Africa contingents was so keen that, when his application was turned down, Corporal Lindsay committed suicide at Regina out of disappointment. Of the 245 officers and men who served in the Boer War, many were decorated and one, Sergeant A. H. Richardson, won the Victoria Cross; four were killed and three others died of disease.

The South African campaign ruined Lawrence Herchmer's police career. By the time the 2nd Canadian Mounted Rifles arrived in South Africa, the commanding officer, Major-General Edward Hutton, was convinced that Herchmer was mentally and physically unfit to be in charge of the Mounted Police detachment, and that 'even if fit was too severe and harsh to command'. Trouble began when Herchmer attempted to return to duty after a bout of dysentery. Major-General Hutton notified him that he was 'not well enough' to resume command and reported to Canada that Herchmer's resumption of authority 'would have a most serious and detrimental effect on officers and men'. Unwisely but typically, Herchmer contested his commanding officer's orders. He tried to get doctors to produce fitness certificates, and persuaded some of his officers and men to sign declarations of support for him. When this failed he made matters worse by returning to Canada to plead his case, but the Prime Minster, Sir Wilfrid Laurier, accused him of insubordination and setting a bad example, and dismissed him from the Commissionership.

Herchmer was still fighting this sacking eleven years later. He wrote to Inspector Gilbert Sanders, 'You will be astonished to hear from me but I am starting up my case again *re* my summary retirement from the police in 1900. . . . I worry more and more every year over the stigma my character rests under of having used my position as Commanding Officer to bully you all in such a manner as to make me quite unfit to command, and am asking for an inquiry to clear off the stain.' But after eleven years no one was interested. Herchmer died in Vancouver on 17 February 1915, bitter and disillusioned – and still fighting to clear his name.

Herchmer was succeeded as Commissioner in August 1900 by Superintendent Aylesworth Bowen Perry, who was still under forty when he assumed command of a force he had already served for eighteen years. He kept his post for twenty-two years, and remains the longest-serving Commissioner in the history of the Mounted Police.

Of the other early stalwarts, Sam Steele became the most

famous. After the Boer War he stayed in South Africa until 1906 to organise the South African Constabulary on the lines of the Mounted Police, and on his return to Canada was appointed to the permanent staff of the Canadian Army. When the First World War began Steele was promoted to Major-General and led the Canadian Second Division to England. He was knighted in 1918 and retired that year after more than fifty years' distinguished police and military service. Sir Samuel Steele, one of Canada's foremost frontiersmen, died in Putney at the age of sixty-eight on 30 January 1919. His body was taken to Winnipeg and buried among other pioneers of Canada's west in St John's Cemetery.

That other Yukon hero, Charles Constantine, never rid himself of his deserved reputation as a northern expert. He returned to the Yukon on special duty in 1902, and in 1905 was put in charge of a small police-party which attempted to cut a graded road from Fort St John to the Yukon in the country travelled eight years earlier by Inspector John Moodie – which now approximates to the Alaska Highway. The work, which was abandoned after three years, wrecked his health and he died on 5 May 1912 at the age of sixty-three while on leave at Long Beach, California.

When Perry gave up his command in the Yukon to take over as Commissioner, he was replaced by the American President's descendant, Zachary Taylor Wood, who had left Calgary for the Yukon in 1897 with instructions to deliver his detachment of men and return immediately to the prairies. But it was thirteen years before he left the Yukon. In 1902 Wood succeeded John McIllree as Assistant Commissioner, a post he held for thirteen years until his death while on sick leave at Ashville, North Carolina on 15 January 1915.

In 1904, by command of King Edward VII, the prefix 'Royal' was added to the Force's title, but the segmentation of the prairies into the provinces of Alberta and Saskatchewan, and the consequent establishment of these provinces' own police forces, reduced the duties and the importance of the Mounted Police. With the disappearance of Canada's frontier days there seemed little need for a frontier law-enforcement group, and in 1916 Superintendent Richard Burton Deane wrote, 'Canadians as a whole are very proud of the world-wide reputation which the Force has made, but they may as well face the unquestionable fact that the Force is now on the down-grade and should be abolished before its reputation is quite gone.'

By 1918, with many of its members on active service, the strength of the Royal North West Mounted Police was down to 300 – the number with which it had started on its march west in 1874. Fortunately for Canada – and for romantics everywhere – the Force was not allowed to die.

In 1920 its future and enduring fame was assured when it was renamed the Royal Canadian Mounted Police, with Dominion-wide responsibilities and a strength of 1200. Now, with its headquarters in a five-storey former Catholic seminary in a quiet suburb of Ottawa, it has a police and civilian strength of about 12,000. Air and marine divisions have replaced horse and dog-sled patrols, the red coat is reserved for ceremonial occasions and the only Mounted Policemen who ride horses these days are the members of the drill formation team known as the Musical Ride, which performs around the world.

But, a hundred years later, their motto still stands: Maintain the Right.

ACKNOWLEDGEMENTS

In Canada: Commissioner W. L. Higgitt of the Royal Canadian Mounted Police, who kindly placed at my disposal study facilities at the Force's headquarters; S. W. Horrall, the RCMP Historian, who gave unstintingly of his time and advice; Miss Juliette Bourque, Chief Librarian at the Public Archives of Canada, Ottawa; Miss Sheilagh A. Jameson (Archivist) and Hugh A. Dempsey (Director of History) at the Glenbow-Alberta Institute; and Dr and Mrs C. D. Shepard of Ottawa.

In Britain: Mrs Joyce White of the London Office of the Public Archives of Canada; the staff of the Public Record Office, London; Frank Galipeau, U.K. manager of the Canadian Government Travel Bureau; Mike Hildred of Air Canada; and Jean Land and Ann Melsom, who read the manuscript.

R.A.

LIST OF FORTS AND BARRACKS BUILT BY, OR ON THE ORDERS OF, THE NORTH WEST MOUNTED POLICE

1874–1900

(not including detachments and outposts)

Swan River barracks	Fort Macleod
Fort Walsh	Fort Saskatchewan
Fort Calgary	Battleford
Fort Qu'Appelle	Regina
Prince Albert	Maple Creek
Lethbridge	Fort Steele
Fort Constantine (Yukon Territory)	Fort Herchmer (Yukon Territory)

Hudson's Bay Company forts and trading posts used by the NWMP

Lower Fort Garry (The Stone Fort)	Fort Edmonton
	Fort Carlton
Fort Ellice	Fort Pitt

CHRONOLOGY

1867 Confederation of provinces of British North America into Dominion of Canada

1869–70 Red River Rebellion led by Louis Riel; province of Manitoba created.

1870 Transfer of Rupert's Land to Canada by Hudson's Bay Company

1873 *May* Massacre of Assiniboine Indians by white trappers in Cypress Hills
  August Order-in-Council passed by Canadian Parliament forming the North West Mounted Police
  October The first 150 men recruited and sent west to winter at Lower Fort Garry, Manitoba; George Arthur French appointed the NWMP's first Commissioner

1874 *April* Size of Force increased to 300
  July Start of the Mounted Police's march west from Dufferin; Swan River chosen as first headquarters site
  December First police post, Fort Macleod, built.

1875 Fort Calgary built on present site of city of Calgary

1876 *June* Custer killed at the Little Big Horn; Sioux begin to move north into Canada
  September James Macleod appointed Commissioner in place of French; headquarters moved from Swan River to Fort Macleod

1877 Treaty No. 7 signed with the Blackfoot Confederacy

1878 Headquarters moved from Fort Macleod to Fort Walsh

1879 First Mounted Policeman (Marmaduke Graburn) murdered

1880 Acheson Gosford Irvine replaces Macleod as Commissioner

1881 Sitting Bull and the last of the Sioux refugees surrender to U.S. government

1882 New training depot and headquarters built at Regina; Fort Walsh demolished

1884 Louis Riel returns to Canada from American exile

1885 *March* North West Rebellion breaks out; Mounted Police column defeated in Duck Lake battle
  May Rebel headquarters of Batoche captured; Louis Riel surrenders

November Riel hanged for treason; Canadian Pacific Railway completed

1886   Lawrence W. Herchmer replaces Irvine as Commissioner

1890   Death of Crowfoot, the Blackfoot chief

1891   Death of Sir John Macdonald, 'Father of the Force'

1895   Inspector Charles Constantine leads first police detachment of twenty men to the Yukon; Fort Constantine built – the most northerly post in the British Empire

1896   Discovery of Klondike goldfields by George W. Carmack; Dawson City founded

1898   The height of the gold rush; Mounted Police seize summits of passes in border demarcation dispute with Alaska.

1900   Mounted Police volunteers under Commissioner Herchmer sail to South Africa to fight in the Boer War; Herchmer relieved of Commissionership, replaced by A. Bowen Perry

1904   The prefix 'Royal' added to the Force's name by command of King Edward VII.

1918   Strength of Force down to 300, its lowest since the march west in 1874

1920   The Force renamed Royal Canadian Mounted Police with Dominion-wide responsibilities

BIBLIOGRAPHY

PRIMARY SOURCES

PUBLIC RECORD OFFICE, LONDON

Sessional Papers of Canada (Colonial Office Records, Group 45/813)
Annual Reports, Commissioner of Mounted Police, 1874–1900
(Colonial Office Records, Group 45)

HUDSON'S BAY COMPANY, LONDON

Brass, John	'Narrative of John Brass' (MS. on North West Rebellion)
McLean, W. J.	'Reminiscences of the Tragic Events at Frog Lake and in Fort Pitt District'. MS.

PUBLIC ARCHIVES OF CANADA, OTTAWA

Record Group 10:	Department of Indian Affairs
Record Group 15:	Department of the Interior
Record Group 18:	RCMP Records
Manuscript Group 26:	Sir John A. Macdonald, Papers
Manuscript Group 27:	Marquis of Lansdowne, Papers
,, ,,	Marquis of Lorne, Papers
,, ,,	Alexander Morris, Papers
Manuscript Group 29:	(F. 53) Richard Burton Deane, Diary
,, ,,	(F. 44) James Finlayson, Diary
,, ,,	(F. 52) Robert N. Wilson, Diary
Manuscript Group 30:	Charles Constantine, Letters and diaries
,, ,,	James M. Walsh, Papers and correspondence
Manuscript Group 30:	(E. 14) Z. T. Wood, article
Gagnon, Insp. Sévère	'Diary Respecting a Journey', 1874 (Record Group 18, B–1, Vol. 1)
Rondeau, Fr. Clovis	'La Montagne de Bois' (MS.) (RG 18, B–10, Vol. 5)

RCMP HEADQUARTERS, OTTAWA

Dyre, Algernon R.	Letters (File 6516–73)
Braithwaite, E. A.	'Early Days of the NWMP' (MS.)
French, George A.	Letterbook
Smith, W. Osborne	Letterbook
Wilson, Robert N.	Diary (File G–516–256)

GLENBOW–ALBERTA INSTITUTE ARCHIVES, CALGARY

Bagley, Fred A.	'The 74 Mounties' (MS.) (A.B146)
Barnett, Edward	Reminiscences 1877–1885 (D.920)
Clarke, Simon J.	Biography (A.C611)
Connor, C. H.	Diary (A.S215)
Dewdney, Hon. Edgar	Papers 1861–1915 (A.D515)
Giveen, Robert H.	Notebooks of a NWM Policeman (A.G539)
Herchmer, William M.	Tributes, newspaper clippings (A.H539)
Hetherington, Sgt S.	NWMP diaries (A.H441)
Higinbotham, John D.	Correspondence and general papers (A.H634)
Hilliard, Staff Sgt C.	Diary 1892 (A.H654A)
Jukes, Dr Augustus	Personal Papers (A.J93)
Julien, Henri	Diary of an Artist with the NWMP (A.J94A)
Macleod, James F.	Papers 1856–1919 (A.M165A)
Maunsell, E. H.	Papers (A.M451)
Metzler, William H.	Diary (File 2740)
Parker, Capt. William	Thirty-Eight-and-a-Half Years' Service and Experience in the Mounties (MS.)
„ „ „	Letters
Patterson, Robert	Memoirs 1876–1879 (C364.971)
Primrose, P. H.	Biographical sketches (D.920)
Robertson-Ross, Lt-Col. P.	Diary of a Trip from Fort Edmonton to the Rockies 1872 (A.R651)
Sanders, Gilbert E.	Personal and general papers (A.S215)
Shaw, Frederick Davis	Papers (A.S534)
Steele, Supt S. B.	Letters and documents (A.S814)
Walsh, James M.	Letters (D364.971)

SECONDARY SOURCES

PART ONE: BOOKS

Adney, Tappan, *The Klondike Stampede* (New York, 1900).
Andrews, Ralph W., *Indians as the Westerners Saw Them* (Seattle, 1963).
d'Artigue, Jean, *Six Years in the Canadian North-West* (Toronto, 1882).
Barbeau, Marius, *Henri Julien* (Toronto, 1941).
Begg, Alexander, *History of the North-West*, 3 vols (Toronto, 1894).
Bell, E. Moberly, *Flora Shaw* (London, 1947).
Berry, Gerald L., *The Whoop-Up Trail: Early Days in Alberta-Montana* (Edmonton, 1953).
Berton, Laura B., *I Married the Klondike* (London, 1956).
Berton, Pierre (1), *Klondike: The Life and Death of the Last Great Gold Rush* (Toronto, 1958).
— (ed.) (2), *Historic Headlines: A Century of Canadian News Dramas* (Toronto, 1967).
Black, William, *Green Pastures and Piccadilly* (London, 1877).
Blue, John, *Alberta Past and Present* (Chicago, 1924).
Boulton, Major C. A., *Reminiscences of the North-West Rebellion* (Seattle, 1963).
Bowsfield, Hartwell, *Louis Riel: The Rebel and the Hero* (Toronto, 1971).
Brown, Dee, *Bury My Heart at Wounded Knee* (New York, 1971).
Buchan, John, *Lord Minto: A Memoir* (London, 1924).
Butler, William Francis, *The Great Lone Land* (Edmonton, 1968).
Cameron, William B., *The War Trail of Big Bear* (London, 1926).
Campbell, Marjorie W., *The Saskatchewan* (Toronto, 1965).
Campbell, Walter S., *Sitting Bull* (Boston, 1932).
Chambers, Ernest J., *The Royal North West Mounted Police* (Montreal, 1906).
Carnarvon, Earl of, *Speeches on Canadian Affairs* (London, 1902).
Collard, Edgar A., *Canadian Yesterdays* (Canada, 1963).
Cramer, James, *The World's Police* (London, 1964).
Creighton, Donald, *John A. Macdonald*, 2 vols (Toronto, 1952).
Dafoe, John W., *Clifford Sifton in Relation to His Times* (Toronto, 1931).
Davenport, Montague, *Under the Gridiron: A Summer in the United States and the Far West* (London, 1876).
Davidson, William M., *Louis Riel 1844-1885* (Calgary, 1955).
Deane, R. Burton, *Mounted Police Life in Canada* (London, 1916).

Denny, Cecil E. (1), *The Riders of the Plains* (Calgary, 1905).
— (2), *The Law Marches West* (London, 1939).
Donkin, John G., *Trooper and Redskin* (London, 1889).
Douthwaite, L. Charles, *The Royal Canadian Mounted Police* (London, 1939).
Drake, Earl F., *Regina : The Queen City* (Toronto, 1955).
Dufferin and Ava, Marchioness of, *My Canadian Journal 1872–1878* (London, 1891).
Dustin, Fred, *The Custer Tragedy* (Ann Arbor, 1939).
Dwight, Charles P., *Life in the North West Mounted Police and Other Sketches* (Toronto, 1892).
Fetherstonhaugh, R. C., *The Royal Canadian Mounted Police* (New York, 1938).
Finerty, John F., *Warpath and Bivouac* (Chicago, 1881).
Fitzpatrick, Frank J. E., *Sergeant 331* (New York, 1921).
Graham, Col. W. A., *The Custer Myth* (New York, 1953).
Graves, S. H., *On The White Pass Payroll* (Chicago, 1908).
Griesbach, W. A., *I Remember* (Toronto, 1946).
Hardy, W. G., *From Sea Unto Sea* (New York, 1960).
Haydon, A. L., *The Riders of the Plains* (London, 1910).
Hayne, Murray H. E., *The Pioneers of the Klondyke* (London, 1897).
Hill, Douglas, *The Opening of the Canadian West* (London, 1967).
Hill, Alexander Staveley, *From Home to Home : Autumn Wanderings in the Northwest in the Years 1881–1884* (London, 1885).
Higinbotham, John D., *When the West Was Young* (Toronto, 1933).
Horan, J. W., *West Nor' West, A History of Alberta* (Edmonton, 1945).
Howard, Joseph Kinsey, *Strange Empire : The Story of Louis Riel* (Toronto, 1965).
Jenness, Diamond, *The Indians of Canada* (Ottawa, 1932).
Johnson, W. Fletcher, *Life of Sitting Bull* (1891).
Kelly, Nora, *The Men of the Mounted* (Toronto, 1949).
Kemp, Vernon A. M., *Scarlet and Stetson* (Toronto, 1964).
Longstreth, T. Morris (1), *In Scarlet and Plain Clothes* (New York, 1946).
— (2), *The Silent Force* (New York, 1927).
Macbeth, R. G., *Policing the Plains* (Toronto, 1931).
MacGregor, J. G., *Edmonton : A History* (Edmonton, 1967).
MacInnes, C. M., *In the Shadow of the Rockies* (London, 1930).
Macoun, John, *Manitoba and the Great North-West* (Guelph, 1882).
McCourt, Edward (1), *Saskatchewan* (Toronto, 1968).
— (2), *The Yukon and Northwest Territories* (Toronto, 1969).

McDougall, John (1), *On Western Trails in the Early Seventies* (Toronto, 1911).

— (2), *Saddle, Sled and Snowshoe* (Toronto, 1896).

McPherson, Arlean, *The Battlefords: A History* (Saskatoon, 1967).

Middleton, Gen. Sir Frederick, *Suppression of the Rebellion in the North West Territories, 1885* (Toronto, 1948).

Miles, Nelson A., *Personal Recollections and Observations* (Chicago, 1896).

Milton, Viscount, and Cheadle, W. B., *The North-West Passage by Land* (London, 1865).

Morris, The Hon. Alexander, *The Treaties of Canada with the Indians* (Toronto, 1880).

Morton, Arthur S., *A History of the Canadian West* (London, 1939).

Mulvaney, Charles P., *The History of the North-West Rebellion* (Toronto, 1885).

Needler, George H., *Louis Riel: The Rebellion of 1885* (Toronto, 1957).

Newton, Rev. William, *Twenty Years on the Saskatchewan* (London, 1897).

Ogilvie, William, *Early Days on the Yukon* (London, 1914).

Osler, E. B., *The Man Who Had to Hang: Louis Riel* (Toronto, 1961).

Parkin, Sir George, *Sir John A. Macdonald* (Oxford Univ. Press, London, 1926).

Parsons, John E., *West on the 49th Parallel* (New York, 1963).

Phillips, Alan, *The Living Legend* (London, 1957).

Pope, Sir Joseph (1), *Memoirs of the Rt Hon. Sir John Alexander Macdonald*, 2 vols (London, 1894).

— (2), *Correspondence of Sir John Macdonald* (London, 1894).

Rodney, William, *Kootenai Brown, His Life and Times* (Sidney, B.C., 1969).

Roe, Frank G., *The North American Buffalo: A Critical Study of the Species in its Wild State* (Toronto, 1951).

Sharp, Paul F., *Whoop-Up Country* (University of Minnesota Press, 1955).

Shaw, Charles A. (ed. Raymond Hull), *Tales of a Pioneer Surveyor* (Toronto, 1971).

Shepherd, George, *West of Yesterday* (Toronto, 1965).

Shepherd, Major William, *Prairie Experiences in Handling Cattle and Sheep* (London, 1884).

Southesk, The Earl of, *Saskatchewan and the Rocky Mountains* (Edinburgh, 1875).

Spettigue, Douglas, *The Friendly Force* (Toronto, 1956).

Spry, Irene M., *The Palliser Expedition* (Toronto, 1963).

Stanley, George F. G. (1), *Louis Riel* (Toronto, 1963).
— (2), *The Birth of Western Canada* (London, 1936).
Steele, Harwood, *To Effect an Arrest* (Toronto, 1947).
Steele, Sir Samuel B., *Forty Years in Canada* (London, 1914).
Stegner, Wallace, *Wolf Willow* (Toronto, 1966).
Strange, Maj.-Gen. T. B., *Gunner Jingo's Jubilee* (London, 1893).
Symington, Fraser, *The Canadian Indian* (Toronto, 1969).
Thomas, Lewis Herbert, *The Struggle for Responsible Government in the North-West Territories: 1870–97* (Toronto, 1956).
Turner, John Peter, *The North West Mounted Police 1873–1893*, 2 vols (Ottawa, 1950).
Vestal, Stanley, *Sitting Bull, Champion of the Sioux* (Oklahoma, 1932).
Waite, Peter B., *Canada 1874–1896: Arduous Destiny* (Toronto, 1971).
Ward, R. D., *Climates of the United States* (Boston, 1925).
Webb, Walter P., *The Great Plains* (New York, 1931).
Wetton, Cecilia, *Historic Battleford* (1955).
Winslow, Kathryn, *Big Pan-Out: The Klondike Story* (London 1952).

PART TWO: NEWSPAPERS AND MAGAZINES

Calgary Herald
Canadian Pictorial and Illustrated War News
Edmonton Bulletin
Fort Benton Record
Fort Macleod Gazette
Helena Herald
Kingston Star
Klondyke Nugget
Manitoba Free Press
Medicine Hat Times
Moline Despatch
Montreal Star
National Republican, Washington
New York Herald
New York Tribune
New York World
Prince Albert Times
Qu'Appelle Progress
Regina Leader
Saskatchewan Herald
Saturday Citizen, Ottawa
Seattle Post-Intelligencer
The Times (London)
Toronto Globe
Toronto Mail
All The Year Round
Canadian Historical Review
Canadian Magazine
Chambers's Journal
Colorado Quarterly
Cornhill
Historical Society of Alberta
Maclean's
McClure's
Outing
Scribner's
The American West
Royal Canadian Mounted Police Quarterly, 1933–71
Scarlet and Gold (published by the RCMP Veterans' Assn, Vancouver)

PART THREE: PAMPHLETS AND THESES

Dempsey, Hugh A., 'Jerry Potts, Plainsman' (Glenbow Foundation, Calgary, 1966).

Jameson, Sheilagh A., 'The Inspector and the Fort' (Glenbow, a publication of the Glenbow–Alberta Institute, May 1970).

Lachance, Vernon, 'Diary of Francis Dickens' (Bulletin 59 of the Dept of History and Political and Economic Science, Queen's University, Kingston, May 1930).

Macleod, R. C., 'The North West Mounted Police and the Development of the Canadian West 1874–1883' (Paper delivered to Duke University, May 1968).

Morgan, Charles Edwin, 'The North West Mounted Police 1873–1883' (M.A. thesis, University of Saskatchewan, April 1970).

Steele, Harwood, *The R.C.M.P.*, Jackdaw Productions, C.12 London 1968.

Ward, William P., 'The Administration of Justice in the North West Territories 1870–1887' (M.A. thesis, University of Alberta, 1966).

REFERENCE SOURCES

The following notes list the principal source material utilised in each chapter. Works to be found in the bibliography bear the author's name only; where there are more than one by the same author, the appropriate number is given.

Abbreviations

CO	Colonial Office Files
CR	Commissioner's Annual Reports
GFA	Glenbow Foundation Archives, Calgary
PAC	Public Archives of Canada
PRO	Public Record Office, London

Chapter 1: The Great Lone Land
The March West, CR 1874, p. 10; 'Rough and ready', Chambers, p. 18; 'It was a splendid sight', d'Artigue, p. 40; 'Great Lone Land', Butler, Preface xv and p. 359; 'Hailstones, hostile Indians', Haydon, p. 6; 'A clean people', MacInnes, p. 32; Formation of the Hudson's Bay

Company, Douglas Hill, pp. 2–3, 8; Stanley (2), pp. 3–18; 'The knowledge of the country', Spry, p. 16; Southesk and quotes, Southesk, pp. 54, 66, 146, 235; Milton and Cheadle's pudding, McCourt (1), pp. 21–2; Milton and Cheadle, pp. 157–8; 'I would be quite willing', Sir John Macdonald quoted in Douglas Hill, p. 58; Hudson's Bay Company sell Rupert's Land, Douglas Hill, pp. 71–2; Stanley (2), pp. 35–42; 'You cannot force your way in', Macdonald to McDougall, 20 Nov. 1869, Pope (1) Vol. 2, pp. 52–3; 'Will have a good deal of trouble', Macdonald to George Brown, 14 Oct. 1869, Macdonald Papers Vol. 516, MG 26, PAC; Description of Louis Riels Butler, p. 133; Red River rebellion, Douglas Hill, pp. 78–87; Stanley (2), pp. 44–143; 'Very chop-fallen and sulky', Macdonald to Sir John Rose, Pope (2), p. 120; 'His habit is to retire', Sir Stafford Northcote to Disraeli, 28 April 1870, quoted in Creighton, Vol. 2, p. 67; 'A province named Manitoba erected', Turner, Vol. 1, p. 59.

Chapter 2: The Prairie Buccaneers
Smallpox outbreaks, Butler, pp. 367–9, MacInnes, pp. 76–7, Hill, pp. 128–9, Howard, pp. 219–23; 'Sagebrush Sodom', Howard, p. 299; 'A revelation!', *Scarlet and Gold*, Vol. 6, p. 58; 'Religion and education', MacInnes, p. 66; 'The American eagle', Davenport, p. 53; Whiskey traders, Berry, p. 42; Sharp, p. 40, Howard, pp. 223–9, Hill, p. 129; Whiskey forts, Sharp, pp. 46–9; MacInnes, p. 71; 'It is very humiliating', McDougall to Laird, 7 Jan. 1874, Laird Papers D.10 MG27, PAC; 'The red man was . . .', McDougall (1), p. 129; 'The region is without law', Butler, p. 367; Butler's recommendations, ibid., pp. 381–382; Robertson-Ross expedition, Chambers, pp. 11–16; 'A moderate grant', Debates of the House of Commons, 31 March 1873 (reported in the Toronto *Globe*); Cypress Hills massacre, Pierre Berton (2), pp. 21–30, McCourt (1), pp. 74–7, Stegner, pp. 74–80, Sharp, pp. 55–66; 'An unsavoury loafer', McCourt (1), p. 75; 'Whites on the War Path', *Helena Herald*, 11 June 1873.

Chapter 3: A Harsh Cradle
'Yankee ruffians', *The Times*, 1 July 1874; 'An upstanding young man', Reminiscences of Edward Barnett, File D920.B261, GFA; 'What have you done . . .', Morris to Macdonald, 20 Sept. 1873, Macdonald Papers Vol. 522 MG 26, PAC; 'It would not be well', Macdonald to Dufferin, 24 Sept. 1873, Macdonald Papers Vol. 523 MG 26, PAC; 'The first recruits', RCMP HQ file G-516-104; 'My friends who wanted me',

Scarlet and Gold Vol. 17, p. 17; 'Two men blind', RCMP HQ files, Comptroller's file, 115–75; Collingwood–Fort Garry trip, Douthwaite, pp. 18–19, Turner Vol. 1, pp. 96–7; 'Like half-drowned rats', *Scarlet and Gold*, Vol. 17, p. 17; 'We did have one good feed', ibid.; Accommodation at Lower Fort Garry, Record Group 18 A-1, Vol. 1, PAC; Griesbach descr., Griesbach, pp. 2–4; Steele descr., Berton, p. 272, Steele, pp. 1–52, Kelly, pp. 10–11; 'I shall not be at all sorry', Smith letterbook, RCMP files; 'I'd as soon be . . .', Toronto *Globe*, 2 Jan. 1874; 'Mornings we get bread', Longstreth (2), p. 11; 'Skating was our chief amusement', *Scarlet and Gold*, Vol. 17, p. 17; 'I took notes', Steele, p. 62; 'Hot work next summer', Commissioner's letterbook, RCMP HQ files; 'If the outlaws', ibid.; 'I am well aware', ibid.; 'It is the intention of my Government', William Parker joins the Force, Parker, unpub. manuscript, GFA; 'I am an apostle of temperance', d'Artigue, pp. 14–15; 'From the time I arise', French to Bernard, 8 May 1874, Commissioner's letterbook, RCMP HQ files; 'Very youthful but may develop', Bagley, unpub. manuscript, GFA; 'A famous country for weak lungs', CR 1875, Kittson Report, p. 23; 'Most of us had overrated', d'Artigue, pp. 16–17; 'I still like the life', Parker letters, 3 June 1874, GFA; Departure from Toronto, d'Artigue, pp. 19–20, Bagley, p. 11, Kelly, pp. 13–14; 'There are only two creatures, *New York Herald*, 10 May 1878; 'They must not forget', d'Artigue, pp. 24–5; Arrival at Fargo, CR 1874, p. 7; 'The greatest tumult', d'Artigue, p. 27; 'Tear a net to pieces', Longstreth (2), p. 22; 'The circus was on . . .', *Scarlet and Gold*, Vol. 1, p. 31; 'The reasons French had . . .', d'Artigue, p. 30; 'The country here', Parker letters, GFA; 'I must say I felt . . .', CR 1874, p. 7; Dufferin stampede, Bagley, pp. 17–18, Denny (2), pp. 28–9, d'Artigue, pp. 33–4, Steele, pp. 63–64, *Scarlet and Gold*, Vol. 1, pp. 31–5, CR 1874, p. 8; 'How often I toppled', *Scarlet and Gold*, Vol. 2, p. 52; 'Bad cooking made conditions worse', CR 1874, p. 8; 'One feels they acted properly', ibid., p. 9; 'All around here', Parker letters, 26 June 1874, GFA; 'The prairie was carpeted . . .'. Deane, p. 2; 'With a friendly eye', Sharp, p. 82; 'We may safely calculate', *The Times*, 1 July 1874; 'It is curious to remember', Denny (1), p. 23.

Chapter 4: The March West
'A thousand fingernails', Howard, p. 54; 'A wondrous, rheumatic vehicle', Donkin, p. 8; Richer arrested, d'Artigue, pp. 40–1; Gagnon descr., Griesbach, p. 47; 'Orangemen Day', Gagnon, p. 1, PAC; 'No water. No wood', Finlayson diary, MG 29, F.44, PAC; 'One flapjack for

breakfast', ibid.; 'What a day I had of it', Denny (1), p. 32; 'I do not believe his statement', CR 1874, App. A, p. 36; 'Simply dreadful', Julien diary, A.J94, GFA; Hailstones the size of walnuts, CR 1874, App. A, p. 35; 'This was the most severe jolt', Bagley, pp. 26, 31; d'Artigue and the oxen, d'Artigue, p. 44; Great rivalry, CR 1874, App. A, p. 37; 'The very place for a picnic', Gagnon diary, p. 4, PAC; 'What a change . . .', d'Artigue, pp. 50–1; Church service at Roche Percée, CR 1874, App. A, p. 37, d'Artigue, p. 54; 'Confound their politics', Turner, Vol. 1, p. 145; 'Our skin felt as if on fire', Julien diary, GFA; 'If you saw the delight', French to Richardson, quoted in Turner, Vol. 1, p. 139; The machine oil, Kelly, p. 29; 'Sooty Sons of the Plains', CR 1875, p. 29; 'No imagination could manufacture', *Scarlet and Gold*, Diamond Jubilee Ed., p. 12; 'They came marching in line', Julien diary GFA; 'Within a week', *Scarlet and Gold*, Diamond Jubilee Ed., p. 12; 'I grudged the loss of a day', CR 1874, p. 13; 'Here we got better water', *Scarlet and Gold*, Diamond Jubilee Ed., p. 12; 'Raining again this morning', Finlayson dairy, MG 29, F.44, PAC; Buffalo hunt, CR 1874, App. A., p. 44, Denny, pp. 30–1; 'For some weeks', *Scarlet and Gold*, Diamond Jubilee Ed., p. 12; 'When one is without', ibid.; 'The farther west we travelled', Denny, p. 31; 'Immense herds', Southesk, p. 92; 'We were now more than two miles', Spry, p. 122–3; 'They are now rapidly disappearing', Southesk, pp. 254–5; 'He is the greatest liar', CR 1874, App. A, p. 46; 'Last night it was very cold', Finlayson diary, MG 29 F.44, PAC; 'Bagley's boots', Bagley, p. 34; 'A glance around the camp', ibid., p. 35; 'If the people of Canada', Finlayson diary, MG 29, F.44, PAC; 'A capital fellow', letter from French to Richardson, 12 Aug. 1874, RCMP HQ files; John Glenn's wagon, Denny, p. 41; Jerry Potts, Dempsey; 'An unquenchable thirst', Cpl R. G. Mathews, in *Scarlet and Gold*, Vol. 3, p. 18; 'Dey damn glad', ibid.; 'The chief difficulty', Dempsey, p. 17; Building Fort Macleod, Denny (1), p. 51, Denny (2), pp. 47–8, Kelly, pp. 35–6; 'I have made up my mind', CR 1874, App. B, p. 58; Kamoose Taylor, MacInnes, p. 99; 'I am happy to be able to report', CR 1874, App. B, p. 62; 'They have taken all our best horses', Gagnon diary, PAC; 'Jarvis was as fond of short marches', d'Artigue, p. 60; 'By October . . .', ibid., p. 75; 'Our progress was slow', Steele, p. 73; 'I wonder how we ever . . .', CR 1874, p. 68; 'The men could not build . . .', ibid., p. 18; 'Why such a spot was chosen', Toronto *Globe*, 2 Sept. 1876; 'It don't strike a person', *Manitoba Free Press*, 18 Aug. 1874; 'A wonderful sight', Parker letters, 8 Nov. 1874, GFA; 'Tied down by no stringent rules', CR 1874, p. 27.

Chapter 5: Monotony and Mutiny
'Before you came', CR 1874, App. B, p. 64; Crowfoot's visit, Turner, Vol. 1, pp. 193, 195; 'These combined miseries', Denny (2), p. 59; Mutiny at Fort Macleod, RG 18, A-1, Vol. 8, File 480–75, PAC; Christmas dinner at Macleod, *RCMP Quarterly*, Vol. 1, No. 1, pp. 35–6, Berry, p. 66; 'The boys kept up', Parker letter, 27 Dec. 1874 GFA; Christmas at Edmonton, Steele, pp. 84–5; Two men frozen to death, Denny (2), pp. 54–6; Swan River winter, Kemp, p. 20; 'Life is fearfully monotonous', *Manitoba Free Press*, 16 Jan. 1875; Swan River mutiny, RG 18 A-1, Vol. 5, Files 206–75 and 487–75, PAC; Swan River uniforms, Bagley, p. 74; Insp. LeCain dismissed, Commissioner's letterbook, RCMP files, pp. 77–8; 'On parade, in our uncouth garments', Denny (2), p. 74; The trip to Helena, ibid., p. 67–70; Deserters re-engaged, RG 18 A-1, Vol. 18, File 19–76, PAC; Hewitt Bernard's telegram, Commissioner's letterbook, RCMP files, p. 66; 'It may possibly . . .', ibid.; 'The actions of Col. French', Longstreth (2), p. 55; 'We have had a great deal of trouble', Mackenzie to Alexander Morris, 6 Aug. 1874, Morris Papers, MG 27, PAC; 'In entire ignorance', French to Dorion, 15 Feb. 1875, RCMP Comptroller's file, 51–75; 'Full particulars . . .', Commissioner's letterbook, RCMP files; Swan River uniforms, Bagley, p. 74; French's complaints, RG 18 A-1, Vol. 8, File 454–75, PAC; Carvell resignation, RG 18 A-1, Vol. 9, File 30–76, PAC; Helena trial, Turner, Vol. 1, pp. 227–35, 251–2; 'Will do more to establish', *Manitoba Free Press* quoted in *The Times*, 12 Oct. 1875; 'If we had only been allowed', Alexander Hill, p. 160; Settlement around Fort Macleod, Denny (2), pp. 61, 88; Fort Walsh 'nicely situated', *RCMP Quarterly*, Vol. 8, No. 1, July 1940; 'The view amazed us', Denny (2), p. 83; Fort Calgary's name, MacInnes, p. 105; 'With blood in their eyes', Steele, p. 88; 'I have no doubt', ibid., p. 88; Building Fort Saskatchewan, RG 18 A-1, Vol. 5, File 225–75, PAC, d'Artigue, pp. 100–1; Selby Smyth's tour, Sessional Papers, CO45/461; Police band formed, RG 18 A-1, Vol. 7, file 482–75, PAC; French sacked, RG 18 A-1, Vol. 10, file 118–76; 'Col. French was a man . . .', *Scarlet and Gold*, Vol. 2, p. 57.

Chapter 6: 'The Good Indian Has nothing to Fear'
'Generally the severity . . .', Fitzpatrick, p. 3; 'As the evening wore on . . .', Deane, p. 68; Indian treaties, Morris, Stanley (2), pp. 207–12; Treaty No. 6, Stanley (2), pp. 212–13, Morris, pp. 168–245; Treaty No. 7, Morris, pp. 245–75; The Man Who Talks Straight, Macbeth, p. 65;

'I have proposed a triangular duel', Macleod to Capt. T. R. Jackson, 7 March 1877, quoted in *Scarlet and Gold*, Vol. 9, p. 60; 'There must have been a thousand lodges', Denny (2), p. 106; Laird's speech, Haydon, pp. 63–8; Button Chief's speech, Morris, p. 270; 'Like a dark Duke of Wellington', Gen. T. B. Strange, p. 386; Crowfoot's speech, Morris, p. 272; 'Sent the bullets whistling', Denny (2), p. 116; 'They were only half in fun', ibid., p. 117; 'Given the labels off fruit jars', ibid., p. 118.

Chapter 7: 'The Warriors Were Silent and Solemn'

Legaré and the Sioux, Rondeau, unpub. MS., pp. 12–13, RG 18 B-10, Vol. 5, PAC; 'Long Life to our Inspector', *Manitoba Free Press*, 3 October 1876; 'The Mounted Police don't scare . . .', *Fort Benton Record*, 13 Oct. 1876; 'Fetched their man every time', ibid., 13 April 1877; Sioux arrive at Wood Mountain, CR 1877, pp. 28–30, Walsh to Irvine, 15 March 1877, RG 21, No. 2001, Vol. 3, PAC; 'The warriors were silent', Turner, Vol. 1, pp. 313–14; 'As we rode up', ibid., p. 327; Sitting Bull description, CR 1877, p. 35; Irvine–Sitting Bull meeting, ibid., pp. 35–7; RG 21, No. 2001, Vol. 3, 'Verbatim report of council with Sitting Bull on 2 June 1877', PAC; 'He sat on my bed', CR 1877, p. 37; Blackfoot mercenaries suggested, Irvine to Macleod, 14 April 1879, RG 10 (Records of Dept of Indian Affairs), Black Series, 13893, PAC; 'A matter of very grave importance', CR 1877, p. 30; International discussions on Sioux, RG 21, 2001, Vol. 3, PAC; Foreign Office Series 5, Vol. 1758, PRO; 'A diplomatic scalp dance', Sharp, p. 266; 'Sitting Bull is not a denizen', *National Republican*, 15 Aug. 1877; 'Perfectly satisfied with their new quarters', *Manitoba Free Press*, 28 Nov. 1878; 'In an extremely short time', CR 1881, p. 3; Sitting Bull–Gen. Terry conference, Vestal, pp. 214–23; Denny (2), pp. 125–126; CR 1877, p. 37; Sharp, pp. 271–2, Turner, Vol. 1, pp. 357–73; 'Their red uniforms', *New York Herald*, 22 Oct. 1877; 'Suddenly Fort Walsh came into view', ibid.; 'We wish the Great Mother joy', ibid., 23 Oct. 1877; 'We need deal no more', *New York World*, 14 Dec. 1877.

Chapter 8: The Prairie Life

Recruiting figures, CR 1877, p. 22; 800 applicants, House of Commons Debates 1879, Vol. 5, p. 127; Patterson's medical, *RCMP Quarterly*, Vol. 6 No. 2, Oct. 1938, p. 115; Kennedy and the asthmatic, CR 1879, pp. 33–4; 'Man, talk about the burning sands', Clarke diary, A.C611B, GFA; 'In every sense of the word', *The Times*, 22 Aug. 1879; Inferior uniforms, RG 18 A-1, Vol. 8, File 456–75 PAC; 'I regret very much', Macleod letter, File D364.971 R.888 GFA; 'If anything is required', Supt John Cotton, CR 1882, pp. 29–30; 'A cross between . . .', *Manitoba Free Press*, 21 May 1875; 'Only three horses fit', CR 1879, p. 7; Water frozen on Walker's stove, ibid., p. 22; 'A few coloured prints', Griesbach, p. 39; Flour sack suits, ibid., p. 54; Weather at Fort Macleod, Parker diary; Sanders Papers, File 7 A.S215; Patterson reminiscences; all GFA; Christmas at Macleod, Parker diary; Fort Walsh celebrations, *Manitoba Free Press*, 11 Nov. 1876; Fort Calgary ball, ibid., 20 March 1876; Fort Saskatchewan ball, Griesbach, pp. 89–91; 'No white woman was in the country', Fitzpatrick, p. 24; 'Very, very good looking', Denny (2), p. 89; Denny court case, Simon Clarke diary, A.C611B, GFA; Denny tombstone inscription, *Scarlet and Gold*, Vol. 24, p. 33; 'Reports are brought to me', Morgan, The North West Mounted Police, M.A. thesis; 'Some of the men', Fitzpatrick, p. 75; *Montreal Star* advertisement, quoted in *Manitoba Free Press*, 11 May 1881; 'At Wood Mountain they drink . . .', ibid., 25 May 1880; 'By dint of continued experiments', *Fort Benton Record*, quoted in *Manitoba Free Press*, 19 Feb. 1880; Crozier's whiskey, Sharp, p. 129; 'I can assure you', *Manitoba Free Press*, 31 July 1876; 'We heated rocks', William Parker MS., p. 66; Snow-blindness cure, Steele, pp. 158–9; Fever at Fort Walsh, CR 1879, pp. 20–32; CR 1880, pp. 13, 44–8; Carrying the guard, Kelly, p. 61; The pet goose, ibid., p. 62; 'I scribble to you', *RCMP Quarterly*, Vol. 8, No. 2, Oct. 1940; 'I don't see much of the noble savage', ibid., vol. 8, No. 1, July 1940; Reduction in pay, Steele, pp. 143–4.

Chapter 9: 'Sitting Bull's Boss'
'I regret to have to write', Butler, p. 267; Horse stealing, Stegner, pp. 73, 98; 'When the Indians are made to understand', CR 1880, p. 33; 'I gave them a good lecture', Begg, Vol. 3, p. 409; Crow's Dance incident, CR 1877, pp. 53–4; 'Custer's charge was not a braver deed', quoted in Phillips, *The Living Legend*, p. 212; 'The day is coming . . .', Denny to Irvine, 18 July 1876, CO 42/744; Buffalo robe figures, Begg, Vol. 2, p. 253; 'Almost as good as a candle', Longstreth (2), p. 102; 'No man can starve better', Butler, p. 310; 'If you will drive away the Sioux', Dewdney to Supt. Gen. of Indian Affairs, 2 Jan. 1880, Sessional Papers 1880, Vol. 3, No. 4; 'Not only have the Sioux killed off . . .', CR 1878, p. 21; Buffalo ordinance, Begg, Vol. 2, pp. 247–9, Stanley (2), pp. 222–3; 'Week followed week', CR 1878, p. 20; 'Not even a rabbit track', Stanley (2), p. 224; 'During the spring', CR 1879,

p. 3; 'It was a pitiable sight', Denny (1), p. 127; 'Large bands were continually . . .', CR 1879, p. 23; 'To all of them provisions had to be given', ibid., p. 18; Scraping and licking the dishes, d'Artigue, p. 106; 'Their appearance was . . .', Fitzpatrick, pp. 72–3; Swift Runner, d'Artigue, pp. 129–31; *RCMP Quarterly*, Vol. 10, No. 1, July 1942, pp. 56–9; Little Man case, CR 1879, p. 8; 'Hungry men are dangerous', CR 1878, p. 21; 'The conduct of those starving . . .', CR 1880, pp. 26–27; Graburn's murder, Fetherstonhaugh, pp. 42–5; CR 1881, p. 25; Steele, pp. 151–2; 'I do not think that one ounce of food was wasted', CR 1880, p. 27; 'Intense humanity of Walsh,' Finerty; Walsh's bizarre uniform, *Scarlet and Gold*, Vol. 16, p. 23; 'Little Ass', *Fort Benton Record*, 22 Aug. 1879; 'In my opinion', Walsh to Min. of Interior, 11 Sept. 1880, RG 10 Black Series, Vol. 13893, PAC; 'He would be joined . . .' ibid.; 'Check the flight of locusts', Macdonald to Lord Lorne, 15 May 1880, Lorne Papers, MG 27, PAC; 'I read the message three times', RG 10, Black Series, File 8589, Vol. 1, PAC; 'Besides being covered with Sioux', Report of W. L. Lincoln, 3 June 1879, ibid.; Miles attacks Sioux, Miles, p. 62; 'The Dominion suffers . . .', RG 10, Black Series, File 8589, Vol. 1, PAC; Prince Albert incidents, CR 1879, p. 25; Wood Mountain incidents, ibid., p. 12; CR 1880, p. 27; 'Their fear of being sent back', CR 1879, p. 16; 'The most suspicious Indian', Allen to Supt Gen. of Indian Affairs, 11 Dec. 1880, RG 10 Black Series, File 8589, PAC; Father Hugonard, Fr. Rondeau, p. 16, RG 18 B-10, Vol. 5, PAC; Walsh transferred, CR 1880, p. 27; 'I explained to him', ibid.; 'I believe if he were assured', Walsh to Min. of Interior, 11 Sept. 1880, RG 10 Black Series, File 13893, PAC; Walsh's offer rejected, Macdonald to Dewdney, 1 Nov. 1880, Dewdney Papers, Vol. 3, p. 382, GFA; Crozier takes over, CR 1880, pp. 31–3; 'I gave Walsh my fine clothing', RG 10 Black Series, File 8589, Vol. 1, PAC; Sioux trade souvenirs, McCourt (2), p. 107; 'I feel certain that their surrender', RG 10 Black Series, File 8589, Vol .1, PAC; 'Leave hunger to do its work', ibid.; 'We received orders . . .', Fitzpatrick, pp. 66–7; 'I am cast away', Steele, p. 160; Legaré takes back the Sioux, Reference file 1541, PAC; Rondeau, pp. 21–2, RG 18 B-10, Vol. 5, PAC; 'The Americans swung in . . .', Reminiscences of Edward Barnett, File D290.B261, GFA; Sitting Bull's surrender, Vestal, pp. 231–2, Turner, Vol. 1, p. 584; Sitting Bull's death, Brown, pp. 426–8, RG 10 Black Series, File 13893, PAC; 'I regard him as incompetent', RG 18 A-1, Vol. 12, File 460–1880, PAC; Walsh retires, RG 18 B-1, Vol. 4, File 367, PAC; 'Would not stand investigation', Macdonald Papers, MG 26, Vol. 21, Part 2, p. 293, PAC.

Chapter 10: Railway Days
Irvine description and background, Chambers, pp. 58–9, Donkin, p. 24; 'Almost too good-natured', RG 18 A-1, Vol. 9, File 41–76, PAC; Bigger force recommended, CR 1880, p. 4, CR 1881, p. 11; 'An odd, unsightly jumble', *The Times*, 7 Sept. 1881; 'A striking likeness of Mr Gladstone', ibid., 5 Oct. 1881; 'It is certainly disenchanting', ibid., 21 Oct. 1881; Poundmaker description, ibid., 1 Nov. 1881; The buffalo hunt, ibid., 9 Nov. 1881; 'He wants grub', Fitzpatrick, p. 81; Fort Shaw reception, *Scarlet and Gold*, Vol. 10, pp. 17–21, Sharp, pp. 30–1; 'Always cheery, most willing', *The Times*, 2 Nov. 1881; Fort Benton's decline, Sharp, pp. 5, 183, 213–15; 'What a name', Dewdney Papers, p. 737, GFA; 'No city, with the possible . . .', McCourt (2), p. 83; 'An Australian bush township', Bell, p. 137; 'I wish to goodness . . .', Irvine to Dewdney, 24 June 1882, Dewdney Papers, GFA; CPR's troubles with Indians, CR 1883, pp. 7–8; Piapot and CPR, Turner, Vol. 1, p. 672; Vol. 2, pp. 5–7; Peach Davis and the Assiniboine, ibid., Vol. 1, pp. 645–50, *RCMP Quarterly*, Vol. 14, No. 2, p. 96; Starvation rations, Stanley (2), p. 234; 'These Indians have always . . .', CR 1882, p. 3.

Chapter 11 : 'Off to Charm Almighty God'
'Each succeeding Springtime', *Fort Macleod Gazette*, 14 Nov. 1882; The new Fort Macleod, CR 1884, p. 35; 'Decidedly ramshackle', Higinbotham, p. 77; 'A wide, muddy lane', Hill, p. 214; Kamoose Taylor's hotel, Fort Macleod Historical Association: 'Fort Macleod', pp. 100–2; 'A number of the very young lads', Toronto *Globe*, 13 May 1882; The recruits' journey, CR 1882 (Surgeon's Annual Report); 'A very fine old gentleman', Deane, p. 11; 'Everything as far as I am concerned', Augustus Jukes Papers, A.J93, GFA; 'I had three pairs of blankets', ibid.; The invalid's story, *Manitoba Free Press*, 20 July 1881; Regina barrack buildings, CR 1883, pp. 23–4; 'Any homesick youth', Donkin, p. 19; 'At the sound of a bugle call', Dwight, p. 23; Regina riding drill, ibid., pp. 41–6; 'An armed mob', Deane, p. 2; 'One of the officers . . .', ibid., p. 5; 'The children of Israel', Kemp, p. 26; Regina guard duties, Donkin, p. 33; 'Off to charm Almighty God', Longstreth (2), p. 181; 'From our boots . . .', Dwight, p. 50; 'There are no recruits . . .', RG 18 B-1, Vol. 7, File 662 PAC; Const. Garratt invalided, RG 18 B-1, Vol. 6, File 635 PAC; Const. James discharged, RG 18 B-1, Vol. 5 PAC; Desertions from Macleod, RG 18 B-1, Vol. 9, File 880 PAC; Mutiny at Macleod, Diary of Robert Wilson, MG 29, F.52

PAC; 'The boys found a cache of whiskey', Metzler diary, File 2740, GFA; 'We are living very well here', Parker letters, 20 Feb. 1880, GFA; Life at East End, Fitzpatrick, pp. 46–9; Souris River patrol, Donkin, pp. 262–79; 'Even if it is only . . .', Dyre letters, 6 Oct. 1882, RCMP HQ file 6516–73; 'We had the barrack rooms decorated', ibid., 8 Nov. 1882; 'I *do* like Calgary', ibid.; 'There was a flash bar', Donkin, p. 39; 'My comrades were more like . . .', ibid., pp. 37–8, 84; 'In my time', Roger Pocock, *Chambers's Journal*, Vol. 75, 1898; Sam Taylor and William Maitland, Griesbach, pp. 50–1; Jakey Temple, RCMP HQ personnel files.

Chapter 12: Strikers and Smugglers
Stuttaford incident, CR 1880, p. 6; 'If we are obliged to fight', *Fort Macleod Gazette*, 14 July 1883; 'We finally got the best of the fire', Fitzpatrick, pp. 117–18; 'What an advantage Rome has', Southesk, p. 167; 'Large numbers of gamblers', Steele, pp. 180–1; 'The greatest obstacle', ibid., pp. 186–7; 'We had a great deal of trouble', ibid., p. 194; 'No people in the world', ibid., p. 195; Beaver River strike, ibid., pp. 196–200, CR 1885, pp. 16–17; 'Without the assistance . . .', Van Horne to Irvine, 1 Jan. 1883, quoted in Turner, Vol. 2, p. 2; 'We acted as magistrates', Fitzpatrick, pp. 22, 111; Parker's chase, Parker MS., pp. 98–101; Cpl Hogg incident, Douthwaite, p. 92; 'A permit was known', Fitzpatrick, pp. 29–30; 'Never intended for civilisation', *Regina Leader*, 21 Feb. 1884; 'Against the will of the majority', Steele, pp. 176–7; 'The law is daily broken', *Fort Macleod Gazette*, 4 Oct. 1887; 'Men who were law-abiding', CR 1885, p. 14; Davin's accusation, Morgan thesis, pp. 165–6; 'The suppression of this traffic', CR 1884, p. 20; 'Whiskey hunting is not popular', Donkin, p. 90; Edmonton arrests, Griesbach, p. 112; Liquor smuggling, Chambers, p. 111, Donkin, pp. 90–1, RG 18 B-3 ,Vol. 15, File 566, PAC; 'For every gallon . . .', *Fort Macleod Gazette*, 4 Oct. 1887; 'Would reverently gather up', Donkin, p. 92; 'The boys soon gathered it up', Metzler diary, File 2740, GFA; Arresting smugglers, Wilson diary, MG 29 F. 52, PAC; Hop beer, CR 1888, p. 67; 'Low, mean and infamous', *Medicine Hat Times*, 10 Sept. 1887; Indignation meeting, RG 18 B-1, Vol. 195, PAC; 'I live well', Dyre letters, 14 Nov. 1884, RCMP HQ file 6516–73; 'It became incumbent', Pocock, *Chambers's Journal*, Vol. 75, 1898; 'We were as God made us', Longstreth (2), p. 108; Police bring in liquor, Donkin, pp. 14–15; 'It was no crime to steal . . .', Braithwaite MS., p. 15, RCMP HQ files; Const. Alexander and the tinctures, RG 18 B-1, Vol. 6, File 577 PAC; 'There is not the slightest

doubt', Irvine to Frederick White, 20 Feb. 1882, RG 18 B-3, Vol. 3 (Letterbooks), PAC; 'The amount of drinking', *Manitoba Free Press*, 20 July 1881; Fort Walsh liquor theft, RG 18 B-1, Vol. 1, File 52, PAC; The Battleford punch, RG 18 B-1, Vol. 1, File 5, PAC; Toby O'Brien, *Scarlet and Gold*, Vol. 3, p. 18; 'Got a bottle of whiskey', Metzler diary, File 2740, GFA.

Chapter 13: Sliding to Disaster
Francis Dickens's background, Manning, *Colorado Quarterly*, Vol. 8 No. 1, Summer 1959; 'A very poor officer', RG 18 A-1, Vol. 9, File 41-76, PAC; 'I consider this officer', RG 18 A-1, Vol. 12, File 460-80, PAC; Bull Elk incident, CR 1881, pp. 50-5; 'We are the wild animals', Stanley (2), p. 238; Stealing their own turnips, ibid., p. 241; 'Why should not these poor people', Buchan, pp. 176-7; Sun Dance description, Dyre letter, 6 Oct. 1882, RCMP HQ file 6516-73; Deane and Steele on the Sun Dance, CR 1889, pp. 42, 64-5; 'The contingency by bullet', CR 1884, p. 16; Sleeping with horses, CR 1885, p. 11; Baker Co.'s horses, CR 1883, p. 18; 'Taking care that no expense', ibid., p. 16; Healy's letter, CR 1881, pp. 15-16; Horse thieves released, ibid.; Dried String Meat, Strange, pp. 388-9; 'With all savages', ibid., p. 401; 'The presence of the Mounted Police', ibid., p. 391; 'Piapot's Indians stole ...', CR 1884, p. 16; Dickens and the Bloods, CR 1881, p. 16; Parker arrests two Indians, Parker MS., pp. 74-7, GFA; Parker's party, Parker letters, 2 Jan. 1880, GFA; 'I could have killed them all', Wilson diary, MG 29 F52, PAC; 'You ought to be capable of performing ...', Denny (2), pp. 175-6; 'Considering all that is at stake', Crozier to Frederick White, 25 June 1884, Dept of Indian Affairs, RG 10 File 13990, PAC; Crooked Lakes incident, Deane, pp. 140-53, CR 1884, pp. 6-7, Stanley (2), pp. 278-80; Little Pine incident, CR 1884, pp. 10-11, Stanley (2), pp. 286-8, *RCMP Quarterly*, Vol. 26 No. 4, April 1961; 'Another of those many instances', Bagley diary, p. 99, GFA; 'Gay, idle, dissipated', Butler, p. 363; 'In all respects they are like ...', Southesk, p. 360; 'As a whole law-abiding', Denny (2), p. 212.

Chapter 14: The '85 Follies
Riel in exile, Bowsfield, pp. 68-93, Stanley (2), pp. 295-7, Howard, pp. 274-305; 'He wore a lofty cap', Donkin, pp. 103-4; 'I think it is really the duty', Stanley (2), p. 310; 'We have no money to give Riel', Macdonald to Dewdney, 20 Feb. 1885, Dewdney Papers, p. 545, GFA; Donkin's winter journey, Donkin, pp. 43, 67; Riel and the eclipse, ibid.,

pp. 104–5; 'Wiped out of existence', Deane, p. 201; 'Very uneasy and saucy', CR 1885, p. 74; Irvine's column leaves Regina, Braithwaite MS., pp. 2–5, CR 1885, pp. 22–23, Deane, p. 21; Pocock frostbitten, *RCMP Quarterly*, Vol. 9 No. 3, Jan. 1942, *Chambers's Journal*, Vol. 75, 1898; Riel's letter to Crozier, Turner, Vol. 2, pp. 102–3; Battle of Duck Lake, ibid., pp. 105–10, Stanley (2), pp. 325–8, CR 1885, pp. 25–37; Griesbach, pp. 59–66, *Scarlet and Gold*, Vol. 12, p. 72, ibid., Vol. 7, pp. 15–32, Donkin, pp. 116–20; Retreat from Fort Carlton, CR 1885, pp. 26, 36, 40, Braithwaite MS., pp. 5–6; 'Like a disjointed snake', Donkin, p. 86; 'Murmur, growl and threaten', Bowsfield, pp. 123–4; Big Bear, Stanley (2), pp. 280–81, 293; 'We are agreed and determined', Dewdney to Macdonald, 12 April 1885, RG 10, File 19550, PAC; Moosomin and the Union Jack, Antrobus, *The Canadian Magazine*, Vol. 8 No. 1, Nov. 1896; 'The principal recipient', Donkin, p. 107; Battleford besieged, Haydon, pp. 141–2, Stanley (2), pp. 335–6, Howard, pp. 345–6; Fort Saskatchewan, Edmonton defences, Griesbach, pp. 68–70, CR 1885, pp. 74–5; Fort Pitt description, LaChance, The Diary of Francis Dickens, pp. 1–3; 'They might kill me', Cameron, p. 56; Frog Lake massacre, ibid., pp. 66–76, Stanley (2), pp. 336–40; 'Everyone in the fort', McLean, unpub. MS., Hudson's Bay Company archives, London; Big Bear and Fort Pitt, ibid., CR 1885, pp. 78–9; Loasby and Lone Man, *Scarlet and Gold*, Vol. 14, p. 21; Fort Pitt evacuated, Cameron, p. 116, CR 1885, p. 79; Henry Quinn captured, Turner, Vol. 2, pp. 142–3, RG 18 A-1, Vol. 20, PAC; 'Suffering two severe flesh wounds', CR 1885, p. 93; Dickens's death, *Moline Despatch*, 16 March 1934, 17 May 1949, 3 May 1960, 29 Aug. 1970.

Chapter 15: A Curious Little War
Middleton descr. and background, Longstreth (2), p. 154, Middleton (introductory notes); Middleton's campaign plan, ibid.; Moving the troops, Berton (2), pp. 32–42, Howard, pp. 336–8; Battleford relieved, Stanley (2), p. 360; Middleton's march, Middleton, p. 19; 'Why we did not march out . . .', Donkin, p. 134; 'A cross between', ibid., p. 136; Fish Creek, Middleton, pp. 34–5; 'We had a very sharp brush', Middleton to Dewdney, 3 May 1885, Dewdney Papers, p. 1412, GFA; The *Northcote*, Begg, Vol. 3, pp. 226–30; 'O my God, do not permit England', *Saturday Citizen*, Ottawa, 5 June 1971; Batoche battle, Stanley (2), pp. 368–71, Howard, pp. 392–406, Begg, Vol. 3, pp. 218–225; Riel captured, *Scarlet and Gold*, Vol. 7, p. 27, Braithwaite, MS., p. 8; 'I found him a mild-spoken . . .', Middleton, pp. 56–7; 'Look at my men, sir', Donkin, p. 148; 'Why you abandoned Carlton', CR 1885,

p. 42; Irvine defends himself, ibid.; 'He has always been deemed', *Illustrated War News* 1885, p. 19; 'Circumstances have been unfavourable', ibid., p. 119; Garrison sports at Prince Albert, Sgt C. H. Connor diary, Sanders Papers, Vol. 2, A.S215, File 6, GFA; 'Everything quiet around here', Metzler diary, File 2740, GFA; Cut Knife Hill battle, McCourt, pp. 152–3, Stanley (2), pp. 366–8, Turner, Vol. 2, pp. 175–179; 'Several tepees filled with bodies', CR 1885, p. 54; 'You can picture my amazement', ibid., p. 31; *The Girl I Left Behind Me*, Donkin, p. 151; Poundmaker, Middleton letters, Begg, Vol. 3, p. 233; Middleton and the squaw, Middleton, p. 61; Gen. Strange description, Griesbach, pp. 70–1, Strange, pp. 380–3; 'Indians on the warpath', Strange, p. 410; Steele's Scouts, Steele, p. 219; 'A splendid-looking fellow', Strange, p. 426; The Edmonton guns, Griesbach, pp. 78–9; Cowan's body, Steele, p. 219; 'You don't need a pistol', Strange, p. 468; 'You were in a hurry . . .', McLean MS.; Battle of Frenchman's Butte, Strange, pp. 481–93, Cameron, pp. 182–93, Steele, pp. 222–3; 'I did not tell them at home', Dyre letters, 3 Sept. 1885, RCMP HQ file 6516–73; 'General Strange had won this battle', McLean MS.; 'From this time . . .', ibid.; 'Taking a piece of white cotton', ibid.; 'All who wish to look on me', Cameron, p. 211; Big Bear's surrender, Chambers, p. 93; Big Bear description, Donkin, pp. 155–6, 211; 'Hang me now . . .', *Scarlet and Gold*, Vol. 14, p. 93; 'Thank you, Captain', Deane, p. 213; Medical reports on Riel, Begg, Vol. 3, pp. 263–4; 'He shall hang', Parkin, p. 244; 'Everyone expected that Riel . . .', Donkin, p. 182; 'He occupied the cell', ibid., p. 185; Execution day weather, *Regina Leader*, 17 Nov. 1885; '*Deliver us from evil*', Creighton, Vol. 2, pp. 438–9; 'A few locks of hair had been taken', Deane, p. 232; 'Simply an egotistical', Dyre letters, 3 Sept. 1885, RCMP HQ files 6516–73; Police medals, Macbeth, p. 204; 'An unfortunate prank', Rondeau MS., RG 18 B-10, Vol. 5, PAC; 'Get rid of Irvine', Macdonald to Dewdney, Nov. 1885, Dewdney Papers, p. 587, GFA.

Chapter 16: Cracking the Whip

Lord Melgund offered Commissionership, Buchan, pp. 82–3; Lawrence Herchmer background, *RCMP Quarterly*, April 1935; Size of police force increased, CR 1886, pp. 10–11; The Edmonton mutiny, Longstreth (2), pp. 161–5, Griesbach, pp. 85–6; Const. Hutchinson and the pigs, Longstreth (2), p. 169; 'I had dry-nursed Herchmer . . .', Deane, pp. 36–7; Deane's 'insubordinate reports', RG 18 B-10, Vol. 3, PAC; 'Your division affords me more anxiety', ibid.; Bagley demoted, RG 18 B-3, Vol. 99, p. 188, PAC; 'It is to be distinctly understood',

RG 18 B-3, Vol. 3, PAC; The drunken bugler, ibid.; 'Making a beast of himself', RG 18 B-3, Vol. 99, p. 813, PAC; Cellars nailed down, RG 18 C-4, Vol. 5, PAC; 'I regret to hear', RG 18 B-3, Vol. 100, p. 740, PAC; Calgary whiskey theft, RG 18 A-1, Vol. 16, File 143–88, PAC; Three officers leave, Herchmer letterbooks: RG 18 B-3, Vol. 99, pp. 203, 210, 222, 489, PAC; *Scots wha hae*, ibid., pp. 552–3, PAC; 'I think it would be advisable', ibid., p. 114, PAC; Herchmer's liquor supply, RG 18 A-1, Vol. 22, File 516–88, PAC; 'Endless succession of drills', Mathews: *Scarlet and Gold*, Vol. 16, p. 31; 'Drilled us morning, noon and night', *Scarlet and Gold*, Vol. 3, p. 20; 'It was quite usual', ibid.; 'He was quite unfitted for the Force', CR 1893, p. 26; Probationary period for recruits, CR 1898, p. 19; 'Those who are not satisfactory', ibid., p. 28; 'There was no great danger', *Scarlet and Gold*, Vol. 3, p. 12; 'The officers mess consists of . . .', CR 1888, p. 62; 'The most uninviting couch', Dwight, p. 27; 'The finest body of men', CR 1888, p. 25; 'With pipes lighted', Dwight, p. 67; 'A bastard beverage', *Qu'Appelle Progress*, 2 Aug. 1888; Regina canteen profits, CR 1890, p. 11; 'We are in a position to pay', CR 1900, p. 26; 'To put it mildly, out of date', CR 1898, p. 81; Faulty Winchesters, CR 1892, pp. 6, 42, 54; Useless cartridges, CR 1894, p. 148, CR 1895, p. 37; 'It would be criminal', CR 1894, p. 7; 'Helmets are too conspicuous', CR 1886, p. 29; Maple Creek hospital conditions, CR 1888, CR 1889, p. 128; 'Made it almost impossible', Herchmer to White, 28 July 1891, RG 18 B-3, Vol. 100, p. 425, PAC; 'Impudent malingerers', CR 1892, pp. 86–7; 'I am deluged with applications', CR 1888, p. 15; 'A very high state of efficiency', Steele, p. 257; Herchmer–Cotton row, RG 18 A-1, Vol. 79, File 241, PAC; Herchmer and Cuthbert, RG 18 B-10, Vol. 3, PAC; 'If the wife of the Commanding Officer, RG 18 B-3, Vol. 100, pp. 317–320, PAC; 'My life is hardly safe', ibid., p. 353; 'The most disgraceful . . .', ibid., p. 321; Herchmer and Rolph, RG 18 A-1, Commissioner's letterbook, PAC; Davin's accusations, RG 18 B-3, Vol. 99, p. 814, PAC; The Herchmer inquiry, RG 18 A-1, Vol. 79, File 241, PAC.

Chapter 17 : 'The Law Is a Disgrace'
'The most disagreeable', CR 1886, p. 11; 'It has outlived its usefulness', *Prince Albert Times*, 9 Dec. 1887; 'Why any Mounted Police officer', *Fort Macleod Gazette*, 21 Feb. 1887; Judge Rouleau's rulings, RG 18 A-1, Vol. 17, File 204–88; RG 18 B-1, Vol. 147, PAC; 'The town abounds . . .', RG 18 B-1, Vol. 189, File 297, PAC; 'If you find that you cannot . . .', Herchmer's confidential letterbook, RG 18 B-3, Vol. 99,

PAC; Const. Leslie arrested, RG 18 A-1, Vol. 17, PAC; 'It is the common practice', RG 18 A-1, Vol. 13 ,File 2–1888, PAC; 'It was a tough game all right', Parker MS., p. 78, GFA; Regina tug-of-war, Deane, pp. 26–8; Gus Brede's death, CR 1891, p. 33; 'There is much less liquor sold now', CR 1893, p. 29; 'A most remarkable absence of crime', CR 1888, p. 7; Dave Akers murder, CR 1894, p. 93; Knife-grinder murdered, CR 1893, p. 42, CR 1894, p. 49; Hector McLeish murder, RG 18 A-1, Vol. 15, File 42–1888, PAC; 'You must shoot them at once', Herchmer to Sanders, 5 Nov. 1887; Sanders Papers, File No. 10 A.S215, GFA; The Forward brothers, CR 1895, p. 70; Stagecoach robberies, Turner, Vol. 2, pp. 296, 300; Lethbridge 'lynch law', CR 1895, pp. 91–2; Deane, pp. 266–76; Peg-Leg Brown, CR 1898, p. 3; 'Too busy to get into trouble', G. J. Duncan to S. W. Horrall, RCMP Historian, interview 17 Jan. 1969; Police ordered off land, Neale to Herchmer, 30 Aug. 1887, RG 18 D-1, File 313, PAC; Patrol mileage, CR 1895, p. 44; William Herchmer's mileage, CR 1887, p. 18; Const. Herron frozen to death, Turner, Vol. 2, p. 499; 'The icicles on my moustache', Parker letters, 21 Feb. 1882, GFA; Cpl Mathews's winter trip, Scarlet and Gold Vol. 3, p. 17; Foxes and skunks, CR 1889, p. 44; 'A day and night have scarcely passed,' CR 1889, p. 119; 'There was scarcely a day', CR 1893, p. 46; 'I personally saw six fires', ibid., p. 62; 'Unless a fire is actually ...', CR 1894, p. 12; 'After fighting fires day and night', CR 1895, p. 74; 'A party left Fort Macleod', CR 1894, p. 37; Police and Mormons, RG 18 A-1, 1890, File 250, PAC; Police and Chinese, CR 1892, p. 128;'It does seem that at times', CR 1887, Supt Perry's report.

Chapter 18: The Almighty Voice Affair
'Horse stealing, even among Indians', CR 1889, p. 2; The Kootenay Indians, Spry, pp. 256–7, 271; William Herchmer visits Kootenays, CR 1887, p. 18; RG 18 A-1, Vol. 13, File 16–1888; 'The effect on the minds of Indians', ibid., Steele–Isadore negotiations, RG 18 A-1, Vol. 15, File 60–1888, Steele, p. 250; Fort Steele sports day, CR 1888, pp. 91–2, Steele, pp. 253–4; Crowfoot's death, Turner, Vol. 2, pp. 483–5, Scarlet and Gold, Vol. 20, pp. 19–20; 'A growing inclination to make money', CR 1898, pp. 3–4; 'While a few Indians have been arrested', CR 1895, p. 2; Red Crow's house, CR 1895, pp. 5, 45; 'The Indians have made great advances', Buchan, p. 176; 'I have no difficulty in making arrests', CR 1888, p. 59; 'Excitement or the natural cussedness', CR 1895, p. 6; Scraping High shot, ibid., p. 6, 126, 129; Bad Dried Meat, RG 18 A-1, Vol. 19, File 249–88, PAC; 'A brave

Mountie', Parker MS., p. 103, GFA; Almight Voice reward notice, Harwood Steele, *The RCMP*, Jackdaw C12; 'If the Australian police', CR 1895, p. 4; Charcoal kills Wilde, CR 1896, pp. 2, 16, 22–31, 44–58, RCMP headquarters file 223; Charcoal's execution, CR 1897, pp. 38, 211; *Scarlet and Gold*, Vol. 3, p. 21; Napoleon Venne wounded, Parker MS., p. 103, GFA; 'For the space of a minute or two', *Scarlet and Gold*, Vol. 6, p. 34; 'I held the Captain's arm', Parker MS., p. 103, GFA; The Almighty Voice fight, *RCMP Quarterly*, Vol. 23, No. 1, July 1957; Haydon, pp. 174–81.

Chapter 19: Gold! Gold! Gold!
Gathering gold with a spoon, Ogilvie: p. 86, 'Hootch' description, Hayne: p. 91; Bishop Bompas, Berton (1), pp. 19, 27; 'Already one nearly fatal brawl', Bombas to Minister of Interior 9 Dec. 1893, Constantine Papers MG30 E.2, Vol. 1, PAC; John J. Healy, Ogilvie, p. 68, Berton (1), pp. 25–7; Charles Constantine, RG 18 A-1, Vol. 22 File 383–8, PAC; 'The most colourful character', Kemp, p. 149; Constantine's trip to Yukon, CR 1894, pp. 70–85, Constantine Papers MG 30 E. 2, Vol. 1, PAC; Police group of 20 leaves, Hayne, pp. 3–34; Arrival at Fortymile, building a fort, ibid., pp. 41–65, Macbeth, p. 158; The first Yukon prisoner, Hayne, pp. 71–3; 'As entirely shut off . . .', ibid., p. 74; Monotonous food, ibid., pp. 87–8; Mrs Constantine's leg fracture, Constantine Papers MG 30 E. 2, Vol. 4, p. 124, PAC; 'He has a taste for low company', ibid., Vol. 4; 'His motto seems to be . . .', ibid., Vol. 4, p. 148; Miners' meeting clash, ibid., Vol. 4, pp. 126–9; Hayne, pp. 121–4; 'I took a photogreph', Hayne, p. 128; Carmack and the Klondike, Adney, pp. 275–87, Winslow, pp. 20–1; Berton (1), pp. 40–3, Ogilvie, p. 125; 'Like cheese in a sandwich', Berton (1), p. 47; Mounted Police stake claims, Hayne, pp. 143–5, 169–70; Dawson City founded, Winslow, pp. 139–41, Berton (1), pp. 73–6; 'Battle of Waterloo fought', Constantine Diary 18 June 1896, MG 30 E.2, Vol. 1, PAC; Constantine letters to Herchmer, RG 18 A-1, Vol. 140, File 525, PAC; CR 1896, 232–9; 'Been a hard year', Constantine Diary, MG 30 E. 2, Vol. 1, PAC; Ogilvie and the claims, Ogilvie, pp. 188–92; How the world heard, Hayne, pp. 169–70; Berton (1), pp. 96–109, Winslow, pp. 26–32; Scarth's trip to Yukon, CR 1897, Appendix K; Walsh appointed, Sessional Papers CO 45/813 (Walsh Report) 1897, PRO; Walsh departs, ibid., John Dafoe, p. 156; 'Just for a jolly good time', Adney, p. 15; 'I saw a horse . . .', S. H. Graves, pp. 36–7; 'Such a scene of havoc', Sessional Papers 38B (Walsh Report) 1898, PRO; 'All mad with a common madness', Ogilvie, p. 278; The

suicidal horses, Berton, p. 155; Walsh frozen in for winter, Sessional Papers 38B 1898, PRO; 'When I want the place', Constantine to Herchmer 6 Dec. 1896, RG 18 A-1, Vol. 140, File 525, PAC; Building Fort Herchmer, ibid., 26 July 1897; 'Money, whiskey, whores and gamblers', ibid., 11 Aug. 1897; 'The whole country . . .', Constantine Papers MG 30 E. 2 ,Vol. 1, p. 399, PAC; The starvation notice, Adney, p. 187; Dawson's winter, CR 1897 Appendix LL.

Chapter 20: A Short Walk to the Yukon
The all-Canadian route, Dafoe, pp. 162–3; 'The money which has already been lost', *Edmonton Bulletin*, 27 Sept. 1897; 'Off for the Yukon!', ibid., 2 Sept. 1897; 'Hell can't be worse than this', Berton (1), p. 233; Moodie's expedition, CR 1898, Part 2, pp. 3–82; Steele goes to the Yukon, Steele, pp. 291–2; CR 1898, Part 3, p. 4; Skagway description, Steele, pp. 295–7; CR 1898, Part 3, p. 4; Soapy Smith, McCourt (2), p. 45; Winslow, pp. 104–8; Berton (1), p. 112; Police seize the summits, RG 18 A-1, Vol. 145, File 69, PAC; The Customs posts, Steele, pp. 297–9, 306, 308; CR 1898 Appendix F, Appendix G; CR 1898 Part 3, pp. 3–56; The drunk and the Union Jack, RG 18 A-1, Vol. 162, File 127, PAC; Police accused of dishonesty, RG 18 A-1, Vol. 153, File 358, PAC; The lakeside scenes, CR 1898 Appendix F, Appendix G; CR 1898, Part 3, pp. 21–2; Berton (1), pp. 268–75; Winslow, pp. 129–32; Steele, pp. 300–8; Z. T. Wood and Soapy Smith, Steele, p. 313; Berton (1), pp. 275–6; Walsh tries to resign, Sessional Papers CO 45/813, pp. 321–4; Dafoe, pp. 177–80; The Yukon boat rush, CR 1898, Part 3, pp. 22, 30; Steele, pp. 302–3; 310–12, Berton (1), pp. 274–86; Chilkoot aerial tramway, Berton (1), pp. 254–5; White Pass railway, Graves, pp. 58–9; Flora Shaw in the Yukon, Bell, pp. 204–7, 212–13, Steele, p. 315.

Chapter 21: 'The Pride of Canada'
Dawson in the summer of 1898, CR 1898 Part 3, p. 73, Adney, p. 368, Berton (1), pp. 288–306, Bell, pp. 207–9, McCourt (2) pp. 96–7; 'A man is infinitely safer', McCourt (2), pp. 96–7; Petersen, Meehan murders, CR 1898 Part 3; The murder 'scoop', Steele, p. 327, Berton, p. 332; 'More gold and material', Dafoe, p. 180; Graft accusations and royalty, Sessional Papers CO 45/813 (Walsh Report) 1898, pp. 330–1, Dafoe, pp. 175–81, Steele, pp. 318–19, 327, 333; 'During my stay in Dawson City', Walsh Report 1898, pp. 330–1, PRO; 'I thought Major Walsh . . .', Dafoe, p. 178; 'A delightful companion', Steele, p. 319; 'Immediately after my arrival', Sessional Papers CO 45/813 (Ogilvie

Report) 1898, pp. 2–3, PRO; 'It has not been necessary', ibid.; Constantine leaves, Toronto *Star*, 13 Aug. 1898; Constantine Diary MG 30 E.2, Vol. 1, PAC; Steele takes over in Dawson, Steele, pp. 321–322; 'At the present rate of wages', RG 18 A-1, Vol. 156, File 555, PAC; 'Fires had to be kept up', Steele, p. 328; 'Fifty dollars – is that all?', Berton (1), p. 321; 'Any person, man, woman or child', RG 18 A-1, Vol. 162, File 127, PAC; Steele's hours of work, Steele, pp. 324, 331; Mail lost in river, CR 1898 Steele Report, p. 11; Const. Newman brings in the mail, *Scarlet and Gold* Vol. 1, pp. 27, 29; Dawson post office chaos and criticisms, Sessional Papers CO 45/813 (Ogilvie Report) 1898; RG 18 A-1, Vol. 162, Files 117–18, PAC, CR 1898 Part 3, pp. 67–8; 'There was a side door', *Kingston Star*, 12 Oct. 1898; Strickland's salary, CR 1898, Part 3, pp. 51–2; 'I cannot speak too highly', CR 1899, pp. 28–9; 'Many persons arriving in Skagway boasted . . .', CR 1898, Part 3; 'I told them to go', ibid.; MP refused shelter, RG 18 A-1, Vol. 162, File 109, PAC; 'My husband said', RG 18 A-1, Vol. 142, File 4, PAC; Officers' allowance, CR 1898, Part 3, pp. 85–6; 'The police force has a large field', Sessional Papers CO 45/813 (Ogilvie Report) 1898, pp. 11–12, PRO; Steele leaves, Steele, pp. 334–335, Berton, p. 420; 'I was astonished to find', CR 1899, Part 2, p. 3; Tagish barracks, CR 1899, p. 23; The O'Brien murders, *RCMP Quarterly*, Vol. 35 No. 3, Jan. 1970, Phillips, pp. 83–95, Fetherston-haugh, pp. 81–4; Douthwaite, pp. 153–65; 'The pride of Canada', Longstreth (2), p. 215.

Chapter 22: Herchmer's Fall
Boer War contingents, CR 1900, p. 76; Fetherstonhaugh, pp. 100–2; Herchmer's fall, Sanders Papers A.S215, File 17, GFA; Kelly, p. 87; 'Canadians as a whole', Deane, p. 9.

INDEX

Abbot, Sir John, 273
Aberdeen, Earl of, 199, 316
Akers, Dave, 76, 279
Alexander, Cons. W. W., 194, 291
Allan, John Beresford, 295–6, 360
Almighty Voice, 292–7, 360
André, Fr Alexis, 213, 251
Antrobus, Cons. William, 95, 111, 260, 270
Archibald, Adams G., 35, 41
d'Artigue, Jean, 49, 50, 51, 52, 54, 62, 64–5, 66, 80, 81, 144
Austin, Charles, 160–3, 181

Bagley, Fred, 50, 56, 64, 67, 73, 74, 89, 90, 209, 260
Bainbridge, Cons., 263
Baker, Col. James, 287, 288, 308–9
Baker & Company, I. G., 75, 78, 87, 97, 98, 112, 201
Barnett, Cons. Edward, 154
Batoche, 214, 215, 217, 233, 234, 235, 236, 237, 238, 240, 242
Battle Creek, 97, 134
Battle River, 124
Baxter, Cons. Frank, 87, 88, 93, 281
Bear That Scatters, 121, 122
Beaver River, 184
Belcher, Insp. Robert, 330, 332, 333, 360
Bell, G. M., 96
Bennett, Lake, 301, 302, 315–16, 318, 319, 330, 334, 335, 336, 338, 339, 341, 342
Bernard, Hewitt, 41, 44, 48, 89, 92, 93, 95
Big Bear, 209, 210, 215, 223, 225, 226, 227, 229, 231, 233, 241, 244, 245, 246, 247, 249
Big Salmon River, 319, 330, 336, 344, 350
Blackfoot Crossing, 107, 108, 109, 112, 162, 197, 198, 208

Bompas, Bishop William, 300–1, 320
Bonanza Creek, 309–10, 313, 314, 323
Bond, William, 78, 79, 86
Boundary Commission, 55, 58, 67, 69, 82, 115, 258
Bourget, Bishop Ignace, 212, 213
Bow River, 72, 73, 76, 107, 108, 164
Bow Valley, 289
Braithwaite, E. A., 194, 215, 216, 220
Brisebois, Ephraim A., 41, 60, 61, 98–9, 160
Brockville, 151, 317, 320
Brooks, Insp. William, 261
Brown, Staff-Sgt Charles, 301, 302, 304, 308
buffalo, 22, 26, 34, 35, 70, 71–2, 74, 91, 113, 118, 123, 134, 137, 140–1, 148, 210, 283
Bull Elk, 197–9, 208
Bull Head, Henry Tatankan, 155
Butler, Capt. William Francis, 21, 32, 35, 36, 37, 137, 140, 210
Button Chief, 110

Cameron, William B., 226
Canada: climate, 21, 45, 86, 88, 178; confederation, 26, 28; Militia, 28, 36, 100, 105, 232, 252; House of Commons, 30, 37, 125, 223, 312; Army, 46, 348, 360; Department of Public Works, 82, 95; Conservative Party, 93, 100, 135, 156; Department of Justice, 119, 174; Liberal Party, 135, 212; Department of Indian Affairs, 174, 197, 205, 216; Department of Railways and Canals, 174; Department of State, 174; Department of the Interior, 174; Customs, 303, 304, 307, 318, 330, 331, 332, 333, 337, 338
Cardston, 284, 293

393

National Half-Breed Committee of Red River, 26, 27
National Republican, 119
Neale, Supt Percy, 46, 264, 281, 290
Nelson, 186, 187
Nevitt, Richard B., 60–1, 66
New Fort, 50
New York Herald, 52, 120–1, 123
New York World, 123
Norman, Cons. Frank, 66, 95, 167, 271
North Portal, 187
North Saskatchewan River, 22, 107, 124, 210, 214, 215, 217, 220, 222, 225, 227, 229, 244, 246
Northcote, Sir Stafford, 28
North West Field Force, 236, 252
North West Mounted Police: formation, 19, 25, 29, 37, 39, 40; march west, 19, 20, 49, 60–84, 101, 107; uniform, 19, 40, 126–7; horses, 20, 127, 363; recruiting, 29, 42, 45; medical examinations, 42, 125; pay, 50, 86, 91, 92, 136, 321–2; desertion, 57, 91, 92, 95, 262; weapons, 58, 266–7; troubled by mosquitoes, 63–4; motto, 85, 363; food, 86–7, 90, 172–3, 177; mutinies, 88; band formed, 101; shortage of women, 131–2; liquor problem, 132–3, 260–2; struck by mountain fever, 133–4; ranks, 135–6; increased in size, 160, 163, 169–70; Standing Orders, 174; fight prairie fires, 282–3; collect Customs duties, 303, 304, 307, 318, 330, 331, 332, 333, 337, 338; distribute mail, 349–52; become Royal North West Mounted Police, 362–3; become Royal Canadian Mounted Police, 363
North West Rebellion (1885), 212–31, 233–53, 257, 258, 261, 267, 279, 280, 286, 301

O'Brien, George, 357–8, 359
Ogilvie, William, 300, 310, 311, 313, 318, 319, 346, 347, 351, 354, 355
Old Man's (Oldman) River, 77, 168
Old Wives Lake, 68, 69, 82
Olsen, Lawrence, 357–8, 359
Ottawa, 28, 37, 46, 48, 58, 59, 62, 67, 74, 79, 83, 91, 92, 93, 94, 101, 119, 139, 144, 151, 153, 160, 178, 184, 189, 190, 194, 230, 232, 239, 242, 259, 301, 304, 312, 324, 330, 336, 353
Otter, William Dillon, 233, 234, 240, 241

Palliser, John, 23, 71, 286
Parker, William, 49, 51, 52, 54, 57, 83, 87, 128, 133, 177, 186, 187, 204–5, 277, 282, 296
Patterson, Robert, 130, 146
Peace River, 324, 326
Pelly, River, 327
Pembina, 26, 27, 54
Pembina Hills, 62
Pennycuick, Alex, 357–8, 359
Perry, Supt A. Bowen, 267, 276–7, 283, 285, 286, 330, 355, 356, 361, 362
Piapot, 166, 167, 203, 294
Picton, 354
Pincher Creek, 240, 271, 293, 294
Pine Coulee, 78
Pitts, F. A., 269, 272
Pocock, Roger, 180, 193, 216
Poett, John L., 61, 73
Porcupine Hills, 76
Pork Trail, 358
Portage La Prairie, 160
Potts, Jerry, 75, 76, 77, 91, 97, 145, 146, 162, 191
Poundmaker, 161–2, 208, 209, 210, 223, 233, 240, 241, 242, 243, 249, 250
Powers & Company, T. C., 97, 98
Primrose, Insp. Philip, 339, 356
Prince Albert Times, 274
Prince Albert Volunteers, 217, 218, 219

Qu'Appelle Progress, 265
Qu'Appelle Valley, 124, 151, 152, 153, 165
Quebec City, 211, 253
Quinn, Henry, 226, 227, 228, 229
Quinn, Thomas Trueman, 225–6

Radisson, Pierre, 22
railways, 25, 44, 164, 165–6, 172, 181–95, 210, 338; Canadian Pacific, 23, 83, 153, 160, 163, 164, 177, 185, 233, 262, 275, 280–1, 283, 294; White Pass, 356
Rainy Lake, 43
Red Crow, 110, 111, 286, 290, 293
Red River, 21, 23, 25, 26, 27, 28, 29, 35, 42, 43, 44, 45, 46, 53, 54, 55, 61, 105,